UNDERSTANDING THE AMERICAN REVOLUTION

Issues and Actors

UNDERSTANDING THE AMERICAN REVOLUTION

Issues and Actors

Jack P. Greene

UNIVERSITY PRESS OF VIRGINIA
Charlottesville and London

THE UNIVERSITY PRESS OF VIRGINIA

Copyright © 1995 by the Rector and Visitors
of the University of Virginia

First published 1995

Library of Congress Cataloging-in-Publication Data
Greene, Jack P.
    Understanding the American Revolution : issues and actors / Jack
P. Greene.
        p.   cm.
    Includes index.
    ISBN 0-8139-1608-9 (alk. paper).—ISBN 0-8139-1609-7 (pbk.:
alk. paper)
    1. United States—History—Revolution, 1775–1783.   2. United
States—Politics and government—1775–1783.   I. Title.
E208.G815   1995   95-8292
973.3—dc20   CIP

Printed in the United States of America

Contents

Preface

A S A GRADUATE STUDENT, I would never have predicted that the American Revolution would become an area of serious intellectual interest for me. I had taken advanced courses on the Revolution as an undergraduate with Hugh T. Lefler at the University of North Carolina in 1950 and as a graduate student with Lynn Turner at Indiana University in 1951, and my doctoral mentor John R. Alden was of course principally interested in the Revolution, writing more books on that subject than any other professional historian of his generation. I was by no means immune to Alden's contagious enthusiasm for the military history of the Revolution, especially for military biography. Indeed, my admiration for him was such that I assumed that in order to establish my credentials as an early American historian I too would eventually have to write on some similar topic, and, with his encouragement, I very briefly considered undertaking as a postdoctoral project a biography of Banastre Tarleton. During my years as both a graduate student and a young historian, however, I always thought of myself as a student not of the Revolution but of the colonial era, and as I got a bit older, began to teach graduate students myself, and began to understand how important it was for each of them to have an independent identity, I also came to realize that my choice of research interests had been powerfully shaped by an urge to define myself as a person who had interests different from and was intellectually independent of his mentor.

My interest in the Revolution was largely a function of my growing engagement with the exciting new work being done on that subject during the late 1950s and early 1960s. In graduate school I had of course read some of the earlier examples of that work, including Oliver M. Dickerson's *The Navigation Acts and the American Revolution*[1] and Edmund S. and Helen M. Morgan's *The Stamp Act Crisis: Prologue to Revolution*.[2] But I had not thought very seriously about how those works were reopening the interpretation of the Revolution until I heard Edmund Morgan deliver his important paper on that subject, "The American Revolution: Revisions in Need of Revising,"[3] at the Mississippi Valley Historical Association meeting in Pittsburgh in the spring of 1956. If Morgan's paper awakened my interest in this subject, my first advanced course on the American Revolution at Michigan State University in the fall of 1956 greatly expanded it, and my research began to focus more and more on the Revolutionary era. For one thing, my decision to expand my book on the southern colonial legislatures to cover the years from 1763 to 1776 required me to do considerable additional research on those years and to assess how colonial legislative development affected colonial responses to post-1763 metropolitan initiatives. For another, by far the greater part of the Landon Carter diary, which I was editing for publication, dated from the 1760s and 1770s and required me to come to terms with Carter's response to the deepening crisis between Britain and the colonies. Finally, Keith Berwick and I undertook a book on Revolutionary Virginia for which I agreed to write the four chapters on the period from 1750 to 1776.

Even more than this research, however, my teaching during the 1960s and early 1970s at Western Reserve University, the University of Michigan, and The Johns Hopkins University focused my attention on the many problematic features of the era of the Revolution. My endeavors to make sense of the proliferating literature on this subject so I could introduce advanced undergraduate and graduate students to it resulted in two historiographical essays which my former teacher William B. Hamilton published in the *South Atlantic Quarterly*.[4] With these essays, I acquired a new role as commentator on changing interpretations of the

---

[1] Philadelphia, 1951.

[2] Chapel Hill, N.C., 1951.

[3] *William and Mary Quarterly*, 3d ser., 14 (1957): 3–15.

[4] "The Flight from Determinism: A Review of Recent Literature on the Coming of the American Revolution," *South Atlantic Quarterly* 61 (1962): 235–59; "The Plunge of Lemmings: A Consideration of Recent Writings on British Politics and the American Revolution," ibid., 67 (1968): 141–75.

American Revolution, and during the late 1960s I published a booklet,[5] two anthologies,[6] and several additional essays and reviews on that subject.[7] By the early 1970s I had begun to move beyond historiography and to produce some substantive pieces on aspects of the Revolution. Although my interest in the Revolution waned following the bicentennial of 1976, I have since occasionally—in response to an invitation or as a by-product of other work—written another essay that touches on the Revolutionary era.

Written one at a time over two decades and widely scattered in many publications, the sixteen essays published in this volume include a substantial proportion of this work. All have been previously published, seven as chapters in books, six as journal articles, one as a review essay, and one as the introduction to a book. Ten were written between 1972 and 1976, one in 1981, three in the mid-1980s, and two in the early 1990s. All are informed by my perspective as a colonial historian who looks at the Revolution not as the first step in the creation of an American nation but as an episode in British imperial history.

Although the essays range over many different subjects, they principally address four general themes. First is the question of why the Revolution occurred and how contemporaries explained it (chapters one, two, three, four, five, six, seven, eight, and ten). Second is the question of how developments in the colonial era and the nature of colonial political societies affected the shape and character of the Revolution (chapters two, six, seven, eight, nine, twelve, thirteen, fourteen, fifteen, and sixteen). Third is the impact of the Revolution upon existing political cultures, particularly in Virginia (chapters nine, ten, and fourteen). Fourth is how the experiences of important individual actors, especially various cultural brokers, can be used to illuminate aspects of the origin, nature, and impact of the Revolutionary experience (chapters ten, eleven, twelve, and thirteen).

The first eight chapters deal with the origins of the Revolution. Chapter one, "Explaining the American Revolution: Questions Resolved and

---

[5] *The Reappraisal of the American Revolution in Recent Historical Literature* (Washington, D.C., 1967).

[6] *The Ambiguity of the American Revolution* (New York, 1968); *The Reinterpretation of the American Revolution, 1763–1789* (New York, 1968).

[7] For instance, "Ideas and the American Revolution," *American Quarterly* 17 (1965): 592–95; and "The Relevance of the American Revolution," *Virginia Quarterly Review* 43 (1967): 524–28.

Unresolved," attempts to define in brief compass the central questions relating to why the Revolution occurred. Chapter two, "The Deeper Roots of Colonial Discontent: William Knox's Structural Explanation for the American Revolution," and chapter three, "Pride, Prejudice, and Jealousy: Benjamin Franklin's Explanation for the American Revolution," examine how two perceptive and well-placed contemporary observers explained the Revolution and evaluate their explanations. Chapter four, "The American Revolution: An Explanation," and chapter five, "Origins of the American Revolution: A Constitutional Interpretation," present aspects of my own explanation for the Revolution, chapter four emphasizing the importance of certain powerful deterrents to revolt during the years following the Stamp Act crisis and chapter five reexamining and reassessing the significance of the constitutional issues involved. Chapter six, "The Social Origins of the American Revolution: An Evaluation and an Interpretation," considers the various social explanations that have been advanced to explain the Revolution and evaluates the causal role of the several factors stressed by those explanations, while chapter seven, "Social Structure and Political Behavior in Revolutionary America: An Analysis of John Day's *Remarks on American Affairs*," calls attention to the social categories one contemporary commentator used in his endeavor to make sense of the divisions within the several colonial political communities. Chapter eight, "The Problematic Character of American Union: The Background of the Articles of Confederaion," looks at the conditions that determined why in the first formal attempt at American union the balance of power would tilt so powerfully in favor of the states.

Chapters nine and ten look at aspects of Virginia political behavior during the Revolutionary era. Chapter nine, "'Virtus et Libertas': Political Culture, Social Change, and the Origins of the American Revolution in Virginia, 1763–76," analyzes how their response to various internal social and political problems in the mid-1760s enabled elite Virginians to overcome any challenges to their political authority during the Revolution. Chapter ten, "Character, Persona, and Authority: A Study in Alternative Styles of Political Leadership in Revolutionary Virginia," analyzes the political self-fashioning of three prominent political leaders— Richard Henry Lee, Edmund Pendleton, and George Mason—as a vehicle for examining the cultural determinants of political leadership in Revolutionary Virginia.

Chapters eleven through thirteen look at the role of three cultural brokers at critical junctures during the Revolution. Chapter eleven, "The Alienation of Benjamin Franklin, British American," shows how the explicit rejection of Franklin's insistent endeavors to mollify metropolitan hostility toward the colonies led to his humiliation and alienation from Britain. Chapter twelve, "Paine, America, and the 'Modernization' of Political Consciousness," reexamines Paine's role as a cultural broker first in the colonies and then in the Old World and argues that he drew his radical message less from inherited ideologies than from contemporary American political society. Chapter thirteen, "Philip Mazzei: Cultural Broker in America and Europe in the Age of Enlightenment and Revolution," similarly reassesses Mazzei's role and shows how, like Paine, he used his knowledge of the Old World to demystify it for Americans, and his knowledge of the New World to construct a vision of a new social and political order for Europeans.

Chapter fourteen, "The Intellectual Construction of Virginia in the Age of Jefferson," examines the impact of the Revolution and other contemporary developments upon the corporate identity of Virginia during the years from 1780 to 1810. It shows how Virginia interpreters, including Thomas Jefferson, St. George Tucker, Edmund Randolph, and John Daly Burk, used Virginia's contributions to the Revolution as a device to construct and maintain a positive sense of collective self in an era when the state was exhibiting many signs of economic and political decline.

The last two chapters address the character of the Revolution. Chapter fifteen, "The Limits of the American Revolution," endeavors to define the cultural and social imperatives and behaviors that informed the Revolution and confined the impulse toward reform and the expansion of the public realm. Chapter sixteen, "The American Revolution and Modern Revolutions," is a general essay that asks why the American Revolution had such a short half-life as model for large-scale revolutions. Exploring the relationship between the American Revolution and the later revolutionary tradition, it argues that the modernity and relatively high levels of economic, political, and cultural development of colonial societies made the Americans' revolutionary experience irrelevant to all but a few revolutionary political societies during the next two centuries.

In preparing this volume for publication, I have been careful to make no substantive changes in the chapters. For that reason, the volume contains some minor repetitions of general themes. I have, however, made a few minor editorial changes; standardized form, spelling, and citations; and added at the end of each chapter a short paragraph recounting its history and giving the details of original publication.

Several people helped to put this volume together. Peter S. Onuf pro-

vided superb advice on selection and arrangement. Amy Turner Bush-
nell gave me excellent editorial help. Sarah Springer retyped some of the
older essays that were not already on computer disks and started the
process of standardizing citations. Nuran Çinlar and Kim Klein read
proofs and Nuran did the index. The Johns Hopkins University provided financial support.

UNDERSTANDING THE AMERICAN REVOLUTION

Issues and Actors

—ONE—

Explaining the American Revolution: *Questions Resolved and Unresolved*

Over the past quarter century (from 1950 to 1975), there has been a massive and wholly unprecedented outpouring—almost a deluge—of detailed studies on most aspects of the origins of the American Revolution in both Britain and America. Eight major questions have been identified, and it may be useful to take stock of present scholarly opinion upon them. Despite many disagreements about emphases and points of detail, a rough consensus has emerged over the past two decades on two points. First, Americans were not, before the 1760s, sufficiently dissatisfied with either the economic or political relationship with Britain to think in terms of separation. Membership in the empire worked to the colonists' advantage down to 1763. They had long since found ways to live with (when they could not evade entirely) aspects of the imperial system they found objectionable, and they were, in any case, tightly bound to Britain through close ties of interest, habit, affection, and patriotism. A second point on which a general agreement has emerged is that what did create widespread American discontent, resistance, and eventually a movement for separation were the many efforts by metropolitan authorities, beginning in the early 1760s, to tighten control over colonial economic and political life through parliamentary taxation and a variety of other legislative and administrative restrictions.

Much more controversial are six additional questions: first, why the Bute and Grenville governments undertook the new restrictive measures in the first place; second, why the colonists resisted them so vigorously from so very early on; third, why successive British governments persisted in such measures in the face of such animated and widespread resistance; fourth, why no British government could see that there might be some middle ground between total subordination and complete independence; fifth, why, given the depth and extent of their opposition, the colonists waited so long to opt for independence; and, sixth, what bearing social and political tensions within the colonies had upon the colonial response.

The first of these six questions has received little systematic attention. Yet it is in many ways the salient question about the Revolution. If the colonists were in fact acclimated to the imperial system by the 1760s, and if it was only the new British measures thereafter that drove them to resistance and revolution, then the question why the metropolitan government chose to tamper with a system that had yielded Britain such extraordinary economic and strategic returns at so little cost—before 1756 Britain had kept no effective military force in the continental colonies—is one that demands careful scrutiny.

The conventional answer has been that the Seven Years' War and its successful outcome either revealed or created a whole series of problems that required more active and qualitatively different metropolitan involvement in colonial affairs: the vast new territories acquired from the French and Spanish by the peace of 1763 had to be organized and administered, trade regulations in the colonies had to be enforced, the army in America had to be provided for, British merchants had to be protected against the inflation of colonial paper currencies, and, most important of all, the vast debt incurred as a result of the war had to be paid.

While not underestimating the importance of such considerations, several scholars, in a commendable effort to go beyond the traditional explanation, have recently traced the new policies to a deep-seated and broadly shared suspicion "that the colonies were thrusting towards independence"[1] and a corresponding fear that colonial independence would inevitably affect national security adversely: that, as Colonial Secretary Lord Dartmouth put it in 1774, national "destruction must follow disunion." America was thought to have provided Britain "with the balance of strength which gave her the edge over her formidable French rival," and it followed that without America "the country would no longer have the power to keep itself safe in the jungle of international politics."[2]

But it is possible to go even further in the search for an answer to this

---

[1] Ian R. Christie and Benjamin W. Labaree, *Empire or Independence, 1760—1776* (London, 1976), 24.

[2] Ibid., 192–93.

question. Quite as much as strategic considerations, economic calculations, specifically the growing awareness within Britain of the enormous and seemingly ever-increasing economic worth of the colonies, particularly as markets for British exports, would seem to have animated the fears of independence. Increasingly reiterated through the middle decades of the eighteenth century, such fears, long in evidence but previously largely latent, appear to have been activated as early as the late 1740s by the simultaneous eruption of severe political disturbances in several colonies and mounting evidence of metropolitan weakness in many others.[3]

Despite the expenditure of much time and effort, metropolitan authorities were unable to deal with these problems through existing mechanisms of colonial administration, and this ineffectiveness further intensified fears of loss of the colonies and led, well before the Seven Years' War had further underscored the weakness of metropolitan control, to a widespread conviction among people in power in Britain that Parliament itself would have to intervene before metropolitan authority could be securely established.[4] By making it less necessary to court colonial cooperation for purposes of imperial defense, the removal of the French and Spanish from eastern North America as a result of the war gave later British governments a much freer hand to undertake a broad program of colonial reform, while the presence of 7,500 royal troops in the colonies seemed for the first time to give them the might necessary to suppress any colonial opposition.

Why American resistance was so vigorous and so immediate is a second and an equally complex unresolved question. Current scholarly orthodoxy attributes it largely to the traditional British suspicion of unlimited power.[5] But it is important to add that that suspicion derived not merely from the colonists' experience with politics inside the colonies but also, as an older generation would have appreciated, from the ambiguous constitutional arrangements that obtained within the empire. Having repeatedly tried and failed before 1730 to obtain explicit constitutional guarantees that would put them on a comparable footing with people in the home islands and secure their liberties and property from any pos-

---

[3] See Jack P. Greene, "'A Posture of Hostility': A Reconsideration of Some Aspects of the Origins of the American Revolution," American Antiquarian Society, *Proceedings* 87 (1977): 27–68.

[4] Ibid.

[5] Bernard Bailyn, *The Ideological Origins of the American Revolution* (Cambridge, Mass., 1968).

sible misuse of the new unlimited might of the metropolis, the colonists had been left with no stronger defenses than local custom (in no case of more than 150 years' standing) or their uncertain claim to the traditional rights of Englishmen, however those rights might or might not be applicable to distant colonies. Anxieties arising from this constitutional insecurity were largely dormant after 1725 as a consequence of the relaxed colonial administration under Walpole and his immediate successors. But they remained close to the surface and were easily activated when imperial reorganization after 1763 "inevitably involved the use of power in ways which had not hitherto been customary."[6]

The apparent significance of this reorganization was also important to most politically informed Americans. It seemed to be an arbitrary and dangerous breach of the traditional relationship between them and the metropolis; it threatened both to deprive them of effective control over the internal affairs of their own political societies and to reduce them to a status within the empire that was equivalent to that of the politically excluded classes in the home islands. Such a status might be fitting for servants and slaves, women and children, the propertyless and the incompetent. But it was scarcely suitable for independent adult male Britons. In colonial British America, quite as much as in early modern Britain, civil emasculation was a familiar condition. With the vivid and omnipresent example of the unrepresented African slaves (who were not yet confined to the southern portion of the continent) and other dependent groups in their own societies constantly before them, the colonists' complaint that taxation by, without representation in, Parliament would reduce them to slavery came directly from the heart. Far from being empty rhetoric or mere cultural mimicry, this complaint was expressive of the most profound fears and anxieties. Not just their liberties and property but their identity as freeborn Britons, their manhood itself, seemed to be threatened by the metropolitan posture toward the colonies.[7]

The timing of the new measures, moreover, further stimulated colonial opposition—and not just for the familiar reason that the recent removal of the French and Spanish from the eastern half of North America made the colonists less dependent upon Britain for protection.[8] For the colonists, the Seven Years' War had been a psychologically liberating

---

[6] Christie and Labaree, *Empire or Independence*, 52.

[7] See Jack P. Greene, *All Men Are Created Equal: Some Reflections on the Character of the American Revolution* (Oxford, 1976).

[8] Most fully in Lawrence Henry Gipson, "The American Revolution as an Aftermath of the Great War for Empire, 1754–1763," *Political Science Quarterly* 65 (1950): 86–104.

and reinforcing experience. That so much of the war had been fought on American soil and that the British government had made such an enormous effort to defend the colonies gave rise to an expanded sense of colonial self-importance. In addition, no matter how it appeared in London, many of the colonies had contributed a substantial amount of money and a significant number of men to the war effort. Virginia and Massachusetts, the two colonies that, in all probability not accidentally, subsequently took the lead in the resistance, had, in terms of liquid economic resources, virtually bankrupted themselves in voting men and money for the war. For the colonists, the knowledge that they had made such an important contribution to so great a national cause increased the immediacy and the strength of their ties with Britain and created heightened expectations for a larger role and a higher status within the empire.[9] The new measures after 1763 thus tended to create a classic situation of frustrated expectations and to heighten the intensity of the colonial response.

The third and fourth unresolved questions about the origins of the Revolution—why various governments persisted in restrictive measures in the face of such intense colonial opposition, and why none of them were able to find a peaceful solution to the controversy that would satisfy the protesting colonists—are closely related. What historians have described is a situation in which an underlying resentment against what seemed in Britain to be the more favored fiscal position of the colonies interacted with increasing outrage at American resistance to metropolitan authority, misconceptions about the character and thrust of that resistance, and an almost xenophobic contempt for the colonists' capacity to offer effective opposition to British arms. Successive British governments moved progressively further from the conciliatory posture that had traditionally characterized metropolitan behavior toward the colonies (and was still manifest in the repeal of the Stamp Act in 1766 and of most of the Townshend duties in 1770) toward a growing feeling in 1774–76 that firmness and coercion were the only effective instruments to secure colonial obedience to metropolitan authority.

The almost univeral commitment within the British political nation—

[9] See Jack P. Greene, "The Seven Years' War and the American Revolution: The Causal Relationship Reconsidered," *Journal of Imperial and Commonwealth History* 7 (1980): 85–105; "Social Context and the Causal Pattern of the American Revolution: A Preliminary Consideration of New-York, Virginia, and Massachusetts," in *Le Revolution Americaine et l'Europe: Colloques internationaux du Centre National de la Recherche Scientifique*, no. 577 (Paris, 1979), 24–63.

a commitment that extended even to advocates of conciliation such as Chatham and Burke—to the beliefs that sovereignty was indivisible, that, as the embodiment of that sovereignty, the king-in-Parliament was supreme throughout the whole of the British Empire, and that economic control over distant colonies could not be maintained without political hegemony, meant that colonial resistance would be widely interpreted in Britain as a fundamental and dangerous challenge both to the existing constitutional system (the universally praised Revolutionary Settlement of 1688–1715) and to the prosperity and security of the nation. So deep and widespread was this commitment that no political group following the Stamp Act crisis could risk giving "the impression that it might be lax towards America";[10] and no significant element within the political nation could perceive that colonial demands for exemption from parliamentary taxation and, after 1774, for autonomy over their internal affairs could lead anywhere except to the nullification of the navigation system, colonial independence, and, for the metropolis, a rapid slide to the bottom of the international status hierarchy.

Most recent analysts have taken pains to insist that the "events of 1775 and 1776 were not inevitable."[11] Yet the failure of anyone in or close to power in Britain to come up with a solution that might have been acceptable to the colonists strongly suggests that the chances against finding such a solution were so low as to be practically nonexistent. A few people in opposition—Isaac Barré, Edmund Burke, Lord George Cavendish, William Pitt, earl of Chatham—understood the fundamental political truth that, in Cavendish's words, "that country which is kept by power is in danger of being lost every day." Recognizing that "a great Empire" could only be governed "by consent," they advocated, as Barré put it, bringing over "the affections of all of our colonies by lenient measures."[12] But not one of the conciliatory schemes they produced came close to meeting the American demands, made in response to the Coercive Acts of 1774, for a constitutional settlement that would provide Americans with strict guarantees of their liberties and property and complete autonomy over their internal affairs. And even these limited schemes went vastly too far for the overwhelming majority of the metropolitan political nation, who agreed with George III that there could be no halfway between submission and independence. In rejecting concilia-

---

[10] Christie and Labaree, *Empire or Independence*, 119.

[11] Ibid., 278.

[12] Ibid., 187, 191, 233.

tion in favor of force, the government "was carrying out Parliament's—indeed, the Country's—will."[13]

The inability of anyone—either in office or in opposition—to perceive the viability of the American proposal for an empire of coordinate polities united through a common monarch, a proposal that was essentially similar to the commonwealth system worked out less than a century later, strongly suggests that the political failures of the mid-1770s are attributable less to the political myopia of most of the men involved, as has so often been asserted, than to the political culture that permitted, even demanded, that myopia; a political culture that was so widely celebrated and so successfully repressive as to preclude any possibility of the sort of flexibility required by conditions in 1774–76. The kinds of innovations demanded by the Americans could not be seriously entertained until mercantilism had given way to free trade and the power of the monarchy had so far declined as to allay the residual fears of prerogative that underlay the widely expressed anxiety that the crown might deploy its colonial resources in such a way as to render monarchy independent of Parliament and Parliament unnecessary to the monarchy.

But such changes lay far into the future. During the late eighteenth century, the extreme structural or systemic rigidity of British political culture meant that, once the Americans had determined to accept nothing less than explicit metropolitan renunciation of the doctrine of parliamentary sovereignty over the colonies, the British decision to use force, the political revolution that followed that decision, and the eventual demise of the First British Empire were, as Sir Lewis Namier suggested almost fifty years ago, virtually as certain as "the revolution of planets . . . the migration of birds, and . . . the plunging of hordes of lemmings into the sea."[14]

On the American side, the Stamp Act crisis made the colonists profoundly suspicious of metropolitan intentions, but it did not inaugurate a movement for colonial independence. "Should [the British] government be so temperate and just as to place us on the old ground on which we stood before the Stamp Act," Samuel Cooper wrote to Benjamin Franklin from Boston as late as 1771, "there is no danger of our rising in our demands."[15] Resistance did not become revolution until the outbreak

---

[13] Ibid., 234.

[14] Jack P. Greene, "The Plunge of Lemmings: A Consideration of Recent Writings on British Politics and the American Revolution," *South Atlantic Quarterly* 67 (1968): 141–75.

[15] Christie and Labaree, *Empire or Independence*, 150.

of hostilities at Lexington Green on April 19, 1775. Why it took so long for a revolutionary movement to develop, the fifth unresolved question listed at the beginning of this chapter, is to be explained primarily by the presence of several powerful deterrents.

Some of the best known of these include the fear of British power, the persistent parochialism of the individual colonies, the lack of political institutions capable of coordinating a central resistance movement, the continuing willingness of the metropolitan government to eschew the final solution to the knotty problem of Parliament's authority over the colonies, the illusion among the colonists that they had a large reservoir of political support in Britain, and most important of all, the great residue of affection felt by so many colonists for Britain. Another deterrent was the fear among traditional leaders in the colonies that the removal or attenuation of British authority might mean loss of political control by local elites, domination by the French or the Spanish, or a republican form of government—any or all of which might lead to political chaos or to a tyranny far worse than any they might, on the basis of their experience before the mid-1770s, expect to suffer at the hands of the metropolis.[16]

The rapid spread within the colonies of a generalized belief in the evil intentions of men in power in Britain and in the corruption of the central governing institutions of the empire contributed to the gradual alienation of colonial affections for Britain betwen 1766 and 1774, while other important developments helped to weaken the force of still other deterrents over the same period. The inability of the metropolitan government to enforce its will in the colonies at any point in the long controversy led to a gradual weakening of respect for British power among the colonists. The increasing politicization of the colonies around a central focus of opposition to British policy effectively mobilized large groups of previously politically inert people without resulting in political or social chaos. The alienation of the overseas trading merchants in Britain, the colonists' main allies in the metropolis, by the adoption of economic boycotts during the late 1760s and again in 1774, removed the one most effective voice for moderation in metropolitan circles. The Continental Congress, the Revolutionary conventions at the state level, and the committees of safety in the localities provided the colonists with the necessary organization for a unified resistance movement and, through their successful functioning, helped to allay fears that separation from Britain

---

[16]This theme is developed more fully in Jack P. Greene, "The American Revolution: An Explanation," in George C. Suggs, ed., *Perspectives on the American Revolution: A Bicentennial Contribution* (Carbondale, Ill., 1977), 51–73 [chap. 4 below].

and republican political institutions would result in political collapse. Finally, the course of the war during the first year and the increasing prospect of French aid encouraged the colonists in the belief that they might successfully oppose British military might.[17]

The sixth and final question, the relationship between social and political tensions within the colonies and colonial resistance to Britain, is in many ways the most complex. Considerable research and even more theorizing has been done on this question over the past decade (between 1965 and 1975). Although no one has yet been able to show that the social situation in any colony was sufficiently brittle as to make internal revolution very probable without the altercation with Britain, historians have demonstrated clearly that the peculiar socioeconomic character of each colony affected both its response to the controversy with Britain and its behavior following Independence; the many variations in the "face" of the Revolution from one colony to the next can only be explained in terms of the widely differing character of political society in each.[18]

The view that better communications might have produced a clearer understanding on both sides of the Atlantic of the intentions of the protagonists, an understanding which presumably might have averted the dismemberment of the empire, has gained much currency over the past few years.[19] But is it really very plausible? To be sure, each side misunderstood the motives of the other. But the role that the British actually envisioned for the colonies, which was not so widely misunderstood in the colonies as has recently been contended, was no more acceptable to the colonists than American demands for a more equivalent and autonomous role within the empire were acceptable to the British political nation. It can be argued at least as plausibly that better communications would have hastened rather than prevented revolution.

This essay is adapted and reprinted with permission and the addition of footnotes from "From Resistance to Revolution," *Times Literary Supplement*, no. 3882 (Aug. 6, 1976), 971–72. It used as a point of departure Ian R. Christie and Benjamin W. Labaree, *Empire or Independence: A British-American Dialogue on the Coming of the American Revolution* (Oxford, 1976). It has been previously reprinted in Richard M. Fulton, ed., *The Revolution that Wasn't: A Contemporary Assessment of 1776* (Port Washington, N.Y., 1981), 169–76.

---

[17] Ibid.

[18] See Jack P. Greene, "The Social Origins of the American Revolution: An Evaluation and Interpretation," *Political Science Quarterly* 88 (1973): 1–22 [chap. 6 below].

[19] See, for instance, Michael G. Kammen, *A Rope of Sand: The Colonial Agents, British Politics, and the American Revolution* (Ithaca, N.Y., 1968).

—Two—

The Deeper Roots of Colonial Discontent:
William Knox's Structural Explanation for the American Revolution

T HE DEFEAT of Burgoyne at Saratoga in the fall of 1777, the Franco-American alliance of February 1778, and the limited military achievements of the British army in the colonies throughout 1778 forced many people in and out of government in Britain to reconsider the underlying assumptions that had guided British behavior toward the colonies since the Stamp Act crisis.[1] Among these was William Knox, then one of two undersecretaries of state for the colonies and a close confidant of American secretary Lord George Germain. Born in Ireland in 1732, Knox had had firsthand experience in the colonies as provost marshal of the infant colony of Georgia from 1756 to 1762, had acted as agent for Georgia in London from 1762 to 1766, and was one of the chief penmen for the Grenville faction before his appointment to the American Department in 1770. An undersecretary for twelve years during the successive administrations of Hillsborough, Dartmouth, and Germain, Knox played a significant role as an architect of American policy.[2] With sizable property holdings in Georgia, he had a vested interest in retaining the American colonies under British dominion, and, as his pamphlets and numerous unpublished official memoranda attest, few people in power in

---

[1] For an assessment of the impact of these events upon Britain's posture toward its former colonies, see Piers Mackesy, *The War for America, 1775–1783* (Cambridge, Mass., 1964), 147–61.

[2] See Franklin B. Wickwire, *British Subministers and Colonial America, 1763–1783* (Princeton, N.J., 1966), esp. 42–44.

Britain thought more seriously or more deeply about the quarrel with the colonies at any stage of its development.[3]

The quality of his thought is readily apparent in his "Considerations on the Great Question, What Is to Be Done with America?" Written no later than mid-1779 and probably about the time of the appointment of the Carlisle Peace Commission in the spring of 1778[4] and subsequently submitted to several members of the ministry,[5] this document was primarily concerned with presenting Knox's "idea of the Constitution to be offered to the Colonies by the Supreme Legislature" as a basis for quieting fears of British intentions among the colonists and thereby "attaching" them to Britain and "continuing them under her Dominion."[6] "Part Second" of the document is an elaboration of the details of this idea, while the somewhat shorter "Part First" consists largely of Knox's penetrating explanation for the American Revolution, the subject of this chapter.[7]

In its focus, Knox's analysis is strikingly modern. He organized his discussion around the same central question that fascinated historians between 1960 and 1976: how to explain the colonists' passionate suspicion or, in Knox's terminology, "jealousy of the Intentions of [the metropoli-

---

[3] Many of Knox's unpublished writings may be found among his papers in the William L. Clements Library, Ann Arbor, Michigan. These papers are calendared in Historical Manuscripts Commission, *Report on Manuscripts in Various Collections* (Dublin, 1909), 6. Knox's most important published pamphlet on the American question was perhaps *The Controversy between Great Britain and Her Colonies Reviewed* (London, 1769). A full bibliography is listed in Wickwire, *British Subministers*, 203–4.

[4] None of the copies of the manuscript known to me bears any date. The content strongly suggests that it was written after Saratoga, and it was certainly written before October 1779, when Earl Gower, who received a copy of "Part First," resigned from the ministry.

[5] Knox may have sent copies to all members of the ministry. At the very least, he submitted copies of the entire document to Dartmouth, Germain, and North, and of the first part to Gower. The Dartmouth copy, along with a covering note indicating that North had also been sent a copy, is in the Dartmouth Papers in the William L. Salt Library, Stafford, Eng., while the Germain copy is among Germain's papers in the Clements Library.

[6] Jack P. Greene, ed., "William Knox's Explanation for the American Revolution," *William and Mary Quarterly*, 3d ser., 30 (1973), 298.

[7] The precise citation is PRO 30/29/3/6, ff. 556–73, Public Record Office, London.

tan] Government."[8] His explanation for that jealousy is, however, much closer to that of Charles M. Andrews than to those of more recent students. Arguing that revolutions are invariably the product of complex long-range developments, Andrews saw the Revolution as the result of a steady divergence between metropolis and colonies from 1607 to 1776. Expansive conditions in the colonies, according to Andrews, stimulated the emergence of a new kind of dynamic society which in turn gave rise to a new mentality and a new form of participatory polity that differed profoundly from and coexisted uneasily with those found in contemporary Britain. This growing social, political, and intellectual divergence, Andrews thought, made a collision between metropolis and colonies almost unavoidable.[9]

Like Andrews, Knox argued that colonial opposition to Britain derived from two main sources. The first was to be found in the social circumstances of colonial life. To begin with, the widespread availability of land produced a system of land ownership that, in its social dimensions, differed dramatically from that in England. To promote "the speedy settlement and culture of the soil," Knox explained, was the "first" object of the founders of the colonies. To that end, they granted land "in small tracts to each Individual in perpetuity, with the reservation of a small Quit Rent payable to the Crown." The wide diffusion of property that resulted from this arrangement had several important consequences. First, it effectively made "every Male Inhabitant . . . a Freeholder, and by consequence entitled to a share in the Government." This broad empowerment of the male population in turn led unavoidably to a democratization of authority. The "poverty and mean condition of the first settlers," Knox noted, meant that offices and legislative seats were often filled by men whose characters were often "far from spotless," so that "men who had hardly escaped hanging in England, became vested with authority to make" or enforce "Laws for hanging others." "By being filled in this manner," the "functions . . . which were meant to establish subordination and distinction," Knox observed, entirely "failed of that effect."[10]

---

[8] "William Knox's Explanation," 297. An extended discussion of the literature on the origins of the Revolution is in Jack P. Greene, *The Reinterpretation of the American Revolution, 1763–1789* (New York, 1968), 7–50.

[9] Andrews's principal writings on the origins of the Revolution are *The Colonial Background of the American Revolution* (New Haven, 1924), 121–218, and "The American Revolution: An Interpretation," *American Historical Review* 31 (1926): 219–32.

[10] "William Knox's Explanation," 299–300.

Widespread property ownership, according to Knox, wholly prevented the replication in America of traditional English patterns of
property relationships. "Where every Man held by the same tenure and
all derived immediately from the Crown," the "relation between Land-
lord and Tenant," with the social and political subordination that such a
relationship implied in England, "could have no existence." Nor did the
subsequent social differentiation that took place in all the colonies
change this situation. While the "superior industry or better fortune of
some" men "enabled them to extend their possessions by purchase," and
"others became wealthy thro' successful trade," their "riches brought
them little Influence for if they parcelled out their Lands it was upon the
same tenure as they held it, only requiring a stated rent in addition to
The King's Quit rent, or they sold the fees for a sum paid down."[11]

Under these conditions, Knox complained, "Influence with the people
was . . . only to be obtained by following the humor or disposition of the
People. To be the greatest was to be the servant of all. Withholding
Grants or opposing Taxes in the Assembly was the ready road to their
favor." Because "it flattered the People's pride by reducing those who
assumed a higher rank than they, to become their dependants and suppli-
ants," Knox added, "the oppression of The King's Officers, by curtailing
their Fees, and lessening the profits of their Offices . . . never failed to
attract their regard and confidence."[12]

Religious arrangements in the colonies, in Knox's view, contributed to
the same effect. The neglect by early colony organizers "to interweave a
religious Establishment with the Civil Polity" had left the inhabitants
"at liberty in each Colony to adopt such mode of religious Worship as
they liked best." "So great a latitude in the choice of a religious system,"
Knox observed, "naturally begets republican and independent ideas in
politics": "Every Man being thus allowed to be his own Pope, he becomes
disposed to wish to be his own King." Nor did metropolitan authorities
subsequently make much effort to remedy this situation. They provided
"no Hierarchy or degrees of Eminence among the Clergy, no distinction
of Bishops, Priests and Deacons, no Rule or Order, no Deans Chapters
or Archdeacons," with the result that all clerics were merely "Priests and
nothing more." By thus keeping the Church of England largely "out of
sight" in the colonies, these arrangements, Knox thought, "totally dissolved" the church's "alliance with Monarchy" and meant that, in con-

[11] Ibid.

[12] Ibid., 300.

trast to the situation in England, religion in the colonies would prove no help in reconciling "the People to other Gradations."[13]

As Knox explained, these several characteristics of colonial societies meant that they operated on entirely different principles than did the traditional society of old England. Combined with the absence of any legally sanctioned distinctions of rank and degree, the relatively undifferentiated social systems of the colonies, he lamented, proved to be entirely uncongenial to the development of those feelings "of subordination that property, ancestry or dignity of station . . . naturally excited" among Britons in the home islands. They not only "excluded all ideas of . . . dependence" but also everywhere—in royal as well as in proprietary and charter colonies—contributed to the emergence of polities that were deeply "tinctured with republicanism."[14]

The second main source of the colonists' jealousy of the home government lay in the deficiencies in the political arrangements that had gradually taken shape within the empire. Again like Andrews, Knox thought that these deficiencies were ultimately much more important in explaining why the Revolution had occurred than were the many social divergencies between Britain and the colonies. Indeed, several of the deficiencies Knox cited are precisely the same as those Andrews emphasized. First was the ascendancy of the colonial legislatures not only in the charter colonies of New England, which were nothing other than "simple republics," but also even in the proprietary and royal colonies, where the elected lower houses had obtained excessive influence and virtually "unlimited" powers through their control of the purse and the crown's failure to stand behind its governors. Those bodies had early "assumed the authority of deciding" which English laws were in force in the colonies, declaring "by an Act of their own . . . Acts of Parliament binding or useless as they judged proper." Moreover, they had "assumed the power of appointing the provincial Officers" to perform all sorts of services for which "the Crown would not be at the expence" and the inhabitants had to pay.[15]

Knox and Andrews also agreed on two further reasons why even in royal colonies the "Democracy" had "the leading influence, and the general tendency" was "to Republicanism": the inattention and incapacity of those charged with colonial administration in the home government

[13] Ibid., 303–4.

[14] Ibid., 299–300.

[15] Ibid., 298, 300–301, 303.

and, even more importantly, the failure of the metropolitan administration to provide suitable constitutions that would have guaranteed the colonists a degree of security in their rights and property comparable to that the British constitution provided for Britons at home.[16]

In his handling of this last point, Knox went considerably beyond Andrews in explaining precisely how this failure contributed to imbue the colonists with an ingrained "Jealousy and Distrust" of "the Royal Authority." By insisting both that the royal colonies "had no Constitution but the King's Commission" and instructions and that each of those documents was "revocable at pleasure," crown officials, in effect, Knox argued, declared the royal colonies "without any Constitution at all," called into doubt the very permanency of their existing "form of Government," fostered the suspicion that they might someday be subjected to a new one "secretly modelled by the King's Ministers and privately introduced, without their ever being able to know what it was," and made the very colonies that should have been most supportive of the crown envious of the seemingly more secure status of the charter colonies.[17]

Knox did not explicitly address the question of why metropolitan authorities pursued such a disastrous policy. He did not consider the extent to which their "zeal for making the Crown absolute in America" and the lack of trust that zeal implied may have been a response to the distinctive social and political conditions that had emerged in the colonies. Because that policy had raised such deep suspicions and had thereby "been so destructive of all Good Will to the Royal Authority," however, Knox had absolutely no doubt that it was the single most "important and . . . fatal cause of the predominancy of the Democratic power" and the weakness of royal power in America.[18]

As a result of that predominancy, colonists in the royal provinces had little difficulty in thwarting "the feeble attempts of the Royal Power," but their uncertain situation, Knox was persuaded, made them profoundly anxious. "However inefficiently those Claims had been supported," the crown's continuing assertion of "high Claims of Prerogative," its frequent reiterations of the doctrine that the colonies "were the mere Creatures of the Prerogative, belonged to the Crown, and were the King's Domain" under the absolute control of the "King's Ministers," greatly "excited" the colonists' "jealousy," and their suspicions increased

---

[16] Ibid., 299.

[17] Ibid., 301–2.

[18] Ibid.

exponentially after "they saw those Claims suddenly transferred to Parliament, as more able to carry them into effect."[19]

"Was it to be expected," Knox asked, that polities with such powerful tendencies "to Republicanism," tendencies that had long been increasing "with their Wealth, and in a little time, if their prosperity had continued, must have swallowed up the Monarchic powers," would "readily acquiesce in the claim of absolute uncontrolable Jurisdiction all at once set up by Parliament, and that, not for the benefit of the Colonies, but for burthening them?" Once Parliament had announced in the Declaratory Act of 1766 that "it had full power to bind them in all Cases whatsoever," the colonists' eventual embrace of "the alternative of renouncing all Connection with Great Britain in preference to a submission which left them neither Rights nor Property" seemed, to Knox, to be entirely predictable.[20]

What Knox's explanation suggests and what Andrews also would have seconded is, of course, that the colonists' extreme "jealousy of the Intentions of Government" during the 1760s and 1770s, their ardent opposition to British policy, and their fervent rhetoric sprang from a source far deeper than those many recent commentators have emphasized.[21] His analysis implies that that jealousy derived, not only from the persuasive power of a specific body of ready-made ideas that seemed to be explanatory of the situation in which the colonists found themselves,[22] not out of the intense social strains that were present in many colonies in the decades before Independence,[23] and certainly not out of some broadly diffused colonial paranoia.

Rather, Knox's explanation traced the origins of that jealousy to two interrelated sources. First were the long-standing structural defects within the metropolitan-colonial relationship, defects that arose directly out of the very conditions of colonial social and political experience and

---

[19] Ibid., 302, 305.

[20] Ibid., 299, 305.

[21] Ibid., 297.

[22] The case for this argument is presented in Bernard Bailyn, *The Ideological Origins of the American Revolution* (Cambridge, Mass., 1967), 1–159, and *The Origins of American Politics* (New York, 1968), 3–58.

[23] For a brief statement of this argument, see Gordon S. Wood, "Rhetoric and Reality in the American Revolution," *William and Mary Quarterly*, 3d ser., 33 (1966): 19–32.

the many "instances of neglect[,] Ignorance, bad Law, and worse Policy, so conspicuous in the formation and conduct of the Colonies." Second were the profound—and by no means unfounded or paranoid—apprehensions that those defects had spawned. From this perspective, Knox suggested, events after 1764 gave greater substance and more emotional charge to fears and anxieties that were already deeply rooted in the American experience.[24]

This is an explanation that Andrews would have appreciated. It is also one to which future historians must give greater emphasis as they sort through the many causal strands of the American Revolution and seek to bring that complex event into clearer focus.

This chapter is an expanded version of the introduction to a documentary article prepared for the journal in which Knox's document appeared. It is here reprinted with permission from *William and Mary Quarterly*, 3d ser., 30 (1973): 293–97.

[24] "William Knox's Explanation," 305.

Three

Pride, Prejudice, and Jealousy: *Benjamin Franklin's Explanation for the American Revolution*

For the better part of a century following the development of professional historical studies in the United States in the decades after the Civil War, the origins of the American Revolution was one of the central concerns of historians of early America. As topics involving intellectual and social history became more popular during the last quarter century, however, scholars displayed considerably less interest in political history. To the extent that the Revolutionary era continued to be a source of concern, attention tended to focus on questions involving the social impact of the War for Independence and the ideological foundations of political and constitutional developments. Not even the Bicentennial generated much new scholarship on the old problem of why the Revolution occurred. Yet another widely heralded effort to find the roots of the Revolution in internal American social divisions yielded many hypotheses but little conclusive evidence that American society was ripe for revolution in the mid-eighteenth century or that social antagonisms or strains can explain much more than the differing faces of the Revolution from one colonial polity to another.[1] A thoughtful and commendably

---

[1] See Kenneth A. Lockridge, "Social Change and the Meaning of the American Revolution," *Journal of Social History* 6 (1973): 403–39; Alfred F. Young, ed., *The American Revolution: Explorations in the History of American Radicalism* (De Kalb, Ill., 1976); Jack P. Greene, "The Social Origins of the American Revolution: An Evaluation and an Interpretation," *Political Science Quarterly* 88 (1973): 1–22 [chap. 6 below]; and "Social Context and the Causal Pattern of the American Revolution: A Preliminary Consideration of New-York, Virginia, and Massachusetts," in *Le Revolution Americaine et l'Europe:*

analytical attempt to explain the Revolution as the product of surging *American* nationalism elicited few resonances.[2]

As a result, we have advanced little beyond where Bernard Bailyn brought us in the late 1960s. Bailyn explained the Revolution largely in terms of the cultural mind-set of the Revolutionaries, particularly their allegedly unfounded belief, derived from radical Whig or country ideology in Britain, in a metropolitan conspiracy to crush British liberty by beginning first with the colonies.[3] Astonishingly, no scholar seems to have sought to test this explanation through an examination of the large body of contemporary testimony produced by Benjamin Franklin. Yet no American was more closely involved with events in Britain during the critical years between 1764 and 1775. A symposium dedicated to rethinking Franklin is an appropriate forum for examining how this involvement may help us reconsider the question of the origins of the Revolution.

Franklin scholarship, like this symposium, has tended to concentrate upon Franklin's wide-ranging activities as a cultural figure and upon his undeniable contributions to science and literature. Those who have interested themselves in his political activities have probably paid more attention to his later diplomatic efforts in France than to his earlier role in Britain. Yet few happenings in Franklin's life caused him any more anguish or occupied more of his time than the deepening dispute between Britain and the colonies after 1764. Even before the controversy began, Franklin saw himself as what modern scholars would recognize as a cultural broker, a person with responsibility for diffusing knowledge about the culture from which he came in the colonies within his host culture in metropolitan Britain.[4] "I think it of Importance to" the "General Welfare" of the British Empire, he told the philosopher David Hume in September 1760, "that the People of this Nation should have right Notions of" the colonies.[5]

Colloques internationaux du Centre National de la Recherche Scientifique, no. 577 (Paris, 1979), 24–63.

[2] Robert W. Tucker and David C. Hendrickson, *The Fall of the First British Empire: Origins of the War of American Independence* (Baltimore, 1982).

[3] Bernard Bailyn, *The Ideological Origins of the American Revolution* (Cambridge, Mass., 1967); *The Origins of American Politics* (New York, 1968); and "Central Themes of the American Revolution: An Interpretation," in Stephen G. Kurtz and James H. Hutson, eds., *Essays on the American Revolution* (Chapel Hill, N.C., 1973), 3–31.

[4] An excellent discussion of the role of the cultural broker is Greg Dening, *Islands and Beaches, Discourses on a Silent Land: Marquesas, 1774—1880* (Melbourne, 1980).

[5] Franklin to David Hume, Sept. 27, 1760, in *The Papers of Benjamin Franklin,* ed. Leonard W. Labaree, et al., 28 vols. to date (New Haven, 1959–), 9:229.

In his endeavors to allay misconceptions about the colonies in Britain, Franklin, as Verner W. Crane has shown in rich detail,[6] was indefatigable in writing newspaper essays and pamphlets for a London audience. In the interest of imperial harmony, Franklin, in these writings, frequently softened his own private views. In his private letters and in his running commentaries in the marginalia with which he filled contemporary British pamphlets,[7] however, Franklin left behind a large amount of material from which the modern scholar can reconstruct his explanation for the American Revolution.

From the beginning of the contest between metropolis and colonies, Franklin saw it as a conflict over the problem of the true nature of British imperial governance, and he brought to that problem a perspective that was shared by relatively few people on either side of the Atlantic. At least from the time of his magazine project in 1740, he exhibited an enlarged view of the Anglophone world that, powerfully nurtured by his involvement in colonial defense in the 1740s and 1750s and especially by his participation in the Albany Congress of 1754, was subsequently enhanced by his long residences in Britain beginning in July 1757.[8] Certainly by the early 1760s he was what might best be called a greater British Empire man. Moved by a vision of a Great*er* Britain in which the rapidly expanding colonies would play an increasingly significant role in Britain's rising international power, he was deeply committed to the perpetuation of a political union within the empire and endeavored to be a friend to both the colonies and Britain. Far from being appreciated by either side, however, his peacemaking efforts, as he lamented to an anonymous correspondent in November 1768, often served merely to

[6] *Benjamin Franklin's Letters to the Press,* ed. Verner W. Crane (Chapel Hill, N.C., 1950). See also Crane, *Benjamin Franklin, Englishman and American* (Baltimore, 1936), and *Benjamin Franklin and a Rising People* (Boston, 1954).

[7] See Verner W. Crane, "Franklin's Marginalia and the Lost 'Treatise' on Empire," Michigan Academy of Science, Arts, and Letters, *Papers* 42 (1957): 163–76.

[8] See, for instance, "Advertisement of the General Magazine," Nov. 13, 1740, in *Franklin Papers* 2:264. For an elaboration of these remarks on Franklin's conflicted loyalties and his perspective on public life, see Jack P. Greene, "The Alienation of Benjamin Franklin—British American," *Journal of the Royal Society of Arts* 124 (1976): 52–73 [chap. 11 below].

render him suspect, "in England of being too much an American, and in America of being too much an Englishman."[9]

Rooted in his attachment to the active intellectual and cultural life of London, his position as a metropolitan placeman, his eagerness to play the role of imperial statesman and to have access to other metropolitan resources, including grants to western lands, and his implicit confidence in the collective wisdom and superiority of British political institutions, Franklin's deep veneration for Britain invariably during the 1760s and early 1770s made him put the most charitable possible construction on metropolitan behavior. Nevertheless, as he wrote to his son William in 1768, he was ever "too much an American"[10] to achieve a genuinely impartial Atlantic perspective on the issues in contention. If, as he told Lord Kames in early 1760, he was "a Briton,"[11] he was, ultimately and aggressively, an *American* Briton.

Though he was defensive about the prevalence of slavery in the colonies,[12] his intense colonial patriotism was abundantly revealed by his pride in the colonists' achievements, in just "a few Years," in making "a Garden of a Wilderness."[13] He repeatedly celebrated their high standard of living, vigorous demographic growth, increasing wealth, and gradual development from rusticity to cultural respectability. In comparison with the free inhabitants of British North America, "the depressing Multitudes" of Ireland, Scotland, and even "many parts of England," he reported following a trip through the western and northern extremities of the British Isles in 1772, lived "below the Savage State." In "no Country of Europe," he wrote, was "there . . . so much general Comfort and Happiness as in America, Holland perhaps excepted."[14] If, moreover, British-American colonists already lived much better than all but a few Europeans, their wealth, as measured by their "abundant property," was increasing "every year,"[15] while their earlier preoccupation with the

---

[9] Franklin to ——, Nov. 28, 1768, in *Franklin Papers* 15:273.

[10] Franklin to William Franklin, Jan. 9, 1768, ibid., 16.

[11] Franklin to Lord Kames, Jan. 3, 1760, ibid., 9:6–7.

[12] Franklin, "Observations concerning the Increase of Mankind," 1751, "A Conversation on Slavery," Jan. 30, 1770, ibid., 4:230–31, 17:37–42.

[13] "An Account of the Export of Provisions from Philadelphia," Feb. 16, 1741, ibid., 2:303.

[14] Franklin to Joshua Babcock, Jan. 13, 1772, to Thomas Cushing, Jan. 13, 1772, to Joseph Galloway, Feb. 6, 1772, ibid., 19:7, 22–23, 71–72.

[15] Gottfried Achenwall, "Some Observations on North America from Oral Information by Dr. Franklin," 1766, ibid., 13:366.

"Drudgery" of settlement was giving way to a situation in which many people had "Leisure to cultivate the finer Arts, and improve the common Stock of Knowledge."[16] And he delighted to contrast the corruption of British public life with the "publick Spirit" of "a new virtuous People" in America.[17]

His devotion to the colonies translated into an acute, perhaps even exaggerated, sense of their value to Britain. The colonies, he believed, ought to be viewed "as so many Counties gained to Great Britain," the different climates and products of which made them even "more advantageous to it than if they had been gained out of the sea around its coasts."[18] Already high by the mid-eighteenth century, "the value of North America[n trade]," he argued during the debate over whether Canada or Guadaloupe should be retained at the conclusion of the Seven Years' War, was "capable of an immense increase," which, he predicted a few years later, could be expected to increase from an annual sum of two million to as much as four or five million within the foreseeable future.[19] Pointing out that the "trade of the nation" had "hitherto increased with the growth of the colonies," he argued in 1765 that as the colonies flourished, "the trade, the riches, and [the] strength of the Nation" would increase "in the same proportion."[20] Indeed, as he informed Lord Kames in 1760 in a much quoted passage, he had "long been of Opinion, that the Foundations of the future Grandeur and Stability of the British Empire" lay "in America." As the enormous region east of the Mississippi "fill'd with British People" over the next century, he predicted, "Britain itself" would "become vastly more populous by the immense Increase of its Commerce; the Atlantic Sea will be cover'd with your trading Ships; and[,] your naval Power thence continually increasing, will extend your influence round the whole Globe, and awe the World."[21]

To explain what bound these enormously valuable colonies to the parent state, Franklin, like many other early modern Britons, employed a voluntary or consensual model of political relations. According to this

---

[16] Franklin, "A Proposal for Promoting Useful Knowledge among the British Plantations in America," May 14, 1743, ibid., 2:380.

[17] Franklin to Jonathan Shipley, July 7, 1775, ibid., 22:94.

[18] Franklin to William Shirley, Dec. 22, 1754, ibid., 5:450.

[19] Franklin, *The Interest of Great Britain with Regard to Her Colonies* (London, 1760), ibid., 9:98; Franklin to *London Chronicle*, Aug. 16–18, 1768, ibid., 15:188.

[20] Franklin to *Lloyd's Evening Post*, Sept. 5, 1765, ibid., 12:254–55.

[21] Franklin to Kames, Jan. 3, 1760, ibid., 9:7.

model, "Dominion," especially in a "Free government," did not depend on coercion, "on the brutal Force of a Standing Army." Rather, said Franklin, in echoing David Hume and many other early modern political writers, it was "founded in Opinion."[22] "Government," wrote Franklin to his political associate Joseph Galloway in early 1769, "is not establish'd merely by *Power;* there must be maintain'd a general Opinion of its *Wisdom* and *Justice,* to make it firm and durable."[23] Any government that had "not with it the Opinion of the People," he told the same correspondent a little over two years later, was invariably a weak government.[24]

With specific regard to the British Empire, Franklin used a family relations model to explain the basis for its success. The strength of the empire, as he saw it, lay precisely in the fact that the overwhelming majority of residents in its most distant parts in the American colonies had a favorable opinion of their connection with Britain. From the late 1750s on, however, he took every occasion to disabuse metropolitan people of the notion that that good opinion derived from colonial gratitude for the nurturance and protection Britain had provided the colonies. With many other colonists, he correctly denied that Britain had much of a role in either settling or, before the midcentury wars, defending the colonies. "The Colonies [were] not *created* by Britain," he wrote, "but by the Colonists themselves."[25]

"Excepting the yet infant colonies of Georgia and Nova Scotia" after 1730, he often pointed out to metropolitan readers, "*none of them* were settled at the expence of *any money* granted by parliament." Rather, they had been "purchased or conquered" by the colonists themselves "at the expense of their own private treasure and blood."[26] Franklin did not deny that Britain had spent large sums in imperial defense during the Seven Years' War. But he pointed out that even in that war, which, he rarely missed an opportunity to emphasize, had been undertaken as much to protect metropolitan economic interests and territorial claims as to defend the colonies, the colonists had "made *more extraordinary* Efforts in proportion to their Abilities than Britain did," having "rais'd, paid and

---

[22] Franklin to Richard Jackson, Mar. 14, 1764, to *Public Advertiser,* Feb. 1, 1770, ibid., 11:106, 17:53.

[23] Franklin to Galloway, Jan. 9, 1769, ibid., 16:12.

[24] Franklin to Galloway, Apr. 20, 1771, ibid., 18:78.

[25] Franklin, marginalia in [Matthew Wheelock], *Reflections Moral and Political on Great Britain and Her Colonies* (London, 1770), ibid., 17:385.

[26] Franklin to *Gazeteer and New Daily Advertiser,* Jan. 6, 1766, ibid., 13:22.

cloath'd for 5 or 6 Years near 25,000 Men besides providing for other Services as building Forts, equipping Guard Ships, paying Transports, &c."[27]

Rather than deriving from their dependence on the metropolis for either money or protection, neither of which they needed, the colonists'
good opinion of their relationship with Britain was traceable, Franklin
thought, to two other closely related sources. First was the colonists' faith
in the essential justice and equity of the British political system and its basic goodwill toward the colonies. Second was their delight in being associated with a great nation, renowned for its dedication to liberty.

Thoroughly conventional from a colonial perspective, Franklin's pre-
1765 view of the political status of the colonies within the empire was
rooted in a theory that had been worked out by leading colonists during
the earliest decades of colonization. According to this theory, some "British Subjects," in Franklin's words, exercised their natural right to migrate
to new countries in America, where, "at the Hazard of their own Lives
and Fortunes," they turned a wilderness into a cultivated landscape. By
these actions, the colonists both extended "the Dominion, and" increased "the Wealth, Commerce and Power of their Mother Country."
At the same time, as acknowledged by the crown in charters and practice, the emigrants took with them "their native Rights" as English
people.[28] Although he admitted that the full dimensions of these rights
had never been precisely defined, Franklin, like most other colonial leaders, had no doubt that they included, as he scribbled in the margins of a
pamphlet in 1769, "a Right to *such Parts* of the *Laws of the Land,* as" the
colonists "should judge advantageous or usefull to them; a Right to be
Free from those they thought hurtfull: And a Right to make such others,
as they should think necessary, not infringing the general Rights of Englishmen . . . And . . . as agreeable as might be to the Laws of England."[29]

For a century and a half, in Franklin's view, this arrangement had
worked extremely well. Throughout this long period, the metropolitan
government had left the colonists in largely undisputed possession of the
English rights they had brought with them. These included especially
the right to representative government, of taxing and "making laws

[27] Franklin to ——, Jan. 6, 1766, ibid., 24. See also Franklin, *Interest of Great Britain,*
1760, Franklin to *Gazeteer and New Daily Advertiser,* Dec. 23, 1765, Franklin, "Examination by the House Commons," 1766, Franklin to Kames, Feb. 25, 1767, ibid., 9:72,
12:411–12, 13:149, 151, 14:64–65.

[28] Franklin to *Pennsylvania Gazette,* Dec. 18, 1755, ibid., 6:299.

[29] Franklin, marginalia in [Israel Mauduit], *A Short View of the History of the Colony of
Massachusetts Bay* (London, 1769), ibid., 16:299.

among themselves" through their provincial assemblies,[30] a right that Englishmen had traditionally relied on to protect their most basic "natural right"[31] to be "Masters of the Fruits of their own Industry."[32] Because the colonists had enjoyed these rights without interruption for so long, they were thus established not simply through formal contracts between the crown and the initial settlers of the several colonies but also through "long establish'd Custom."[33]

While they thus enjoyed "the most substantial rights of English freemen,"[34] the colonists retained enormous "Respect for their Mother Country." They submitted quietly to a variety of patently unfair restraints on their trade and manufacturing as well as to other disadvantageous measures[35] and exhibited a heartfelt attachment to the parent state and the royal family. "True British Subjects," the colonists, Franklin noted in 1754 in first articulating a theme to which he often returned during the next two decades, were "as loyal and as firmly attach'd to the present Constitution and reigning Family as any Subjects in the King's Dominions."[36]

In stressing the colonists' attachment to Britain, Franklin never suggested that there was no colonial discontent with the metropolis. His own pointed resentment against the policy of transporting criminals to the colonies[37] and the several economic restrictions that, in Franklin's view, seemed to regard "the private interests" of petty lobbies in Britain more highly than the welfare of all the colonies[38] was presumably widely shared. Similarly, long-standing metropolitan efforts to govern the "Col-

---

[30] Franklin, "Reasons and Motives for the Albany Plan of Union," [July 1754], to Shirley, Dec. 4, 1754, to *Lloyd's Evening Post*, Sept. 5, 1765, ibid., 5:403–4, 443–45, 12:255.

[31] Franklin to *London Chronicle*, Jan. 5–7, 1768, ibid., 15:10.

[32] Franklin to *Public Advertiser*, Jan. 4, 1770, ibid., 17:7. Earlier in 1768, Franklin had elaborated upon this point, central to the emerging Anglo-American system of values, more fully. "There cannot be a stronger natural right," he told London readers "than that of a man's making the best profit he can of the natural produce of his lands, provided he does not thereby hurt the state in general" (Franklin to *London Chronicle*, Jan. 5–7, 1768, ibid., 15:10).

[33] Franklin to ——, [Jan. 6, 1766], ibid., 13:23.

[34] Philadelphia Merchant [Charles Thomson] to Franklin, June 19, 1765, ibid., 12:184.

[35] Franklin, "Fragments of a Pamphlet on the Stamp Act," Jan. 1766, ibid., 13:78–79. See also Franklin to Shirley, Dec. 4, 22, 1754, ibid., 5:446, 451.

[36] Franklin to Shirley, Dec. 4, 1754, ibid., 5:444–45.

[37] Franklin to *Pennsylvania Gazette*, May 9, 1751, Franklin, "Fragments of a Pamphlet on the Stamp Act," Jan. 1766, Franklin to *London Chronicle*, Jan. 5–7, 1768, to *Public Advertiser*, Jan. 26, 1770, ibid., 4:131–33, 13:78–79, 15:11, 17:42.

[38] Franklin to Shirley, Dec. 22, 1754, ibid., 5:449.

onies by Instructions"[39] and rumors that some leaders wanted to reduce colonial privileges by "Clipping the Wings of Assemblies"[40] elicited widespread fears that, instead of trying "to secure freedom to her children," Britain, in Franklin's words as early as 1753, might "seek to oppress us"[41] by employing "the *Weight of Prerogative*" to reduce colonial liberties.[42] In such an event, however, as Franklin told the House of Commons during his testimony on the repeal of the Stamp Act early in 1766, the colonists counted on successfully seeking redress from Parliament, that "great bulwark and security of their liberties and privileges."[43]

According to Franklin, however, these discontents and fears in no way undermined colonial affections for the parent state. Before the Stamp Act, Franklin told the House of Commons, the "temper of America towards Great Britain" was the "best in the world. They submitted willingly to the government of the Crown, and paid, in all their courts, obedience to acts of parliament. Numerous as the people" were "in the several old provinces, they cost" Britain "nothing in forts, citadels, garrisons or armies, to keep them in subjection. They were governed by this country, at the expence only of a little pen, ink and paper. They were led by a thread. They had not only a respect but an affection, for Great-Britain, for its laws, its customs and manners, and even a fondness for its fashions, that greatly increased its commerce. Natives of Britain were always treated with a particular regard; to be an Old England-man was, of itself, a character of some respect, and gave a kind of rank among us."[44]

That the colonists thus "love[d] and honour[ed] the name of Englishman"[45] chiefly depended, in Franklin's view, on the proud boast "that they could claim their Original from the Kingdom of Great Britain"[46] and enjoyed "those distinguishing and invaluable rights of Britons, of being governed by laws of their own making."[47] Drawing the attention of metropolitan readers to the events and conditions that pro-

---

[39] Franklin to James Bowdoin, Jan. 13, 1772, ibid., 19:19.

[40] Franklin to Isaac Norris, Mar. 19, 1759, ibid., 8:293–95.

[41] Franklin to Peter Collinson, May 9, 1753, ibid., 4:486.

[42] Franklin to Norris, Mar. 19, 1759, ibid., 8:296.

[43] Franklin, "Examination," 1766, ibid., 13:136. See also Pennsylvania Assembly to Governor, Sept. 5, 1753, and Franklin to *Pennsylvania Gazette*, Dec. 18, 1755, ibid., 5:32, 6:300.

[44] Franklin, "Examination," 1766, ibid., 13:135.

[45] Franklin to *London Chronicle*, Nov. 6–8, 1770, ibid., 17:268.

[46] Franklin to *Public Advertiser*, Sept. 8, 1773, ibid., 20:389.

[47] Philadelphia Merchant [Charles Thomson] to Franklin, June 19, 1765, ibid., 12:184.

duced and sustained the long and successful revolt of the Netherlands against Spain almost two centuries earlier, Franklin suggested as early as 1760 that only "the most grievous tyranny and oppression,"[48] "some violent measure . . . such as the abolition of the assemblies,"[49] could destroy the colonists' passionate attachment to Britain. "People who have property in a country which they may lose, and privileges which they may endanger," he wrote, "are generally disposed to be quiet; and even to bear much, rather than hazard all. While the government is mild and just, while important civil and religious rights are secure," he emphasized, "such subjects will be dutiful and obedient. The waves do not rise, but when the wind blows."[50] "No people under easy circumstances ever desire a change of Government," Franklin later wrote in an unacknowledged paraphrase of a point made by John Locke in his *Second Treatise:* "It is not a thing ever wantonly undertaken; and even if some ambitious men, from selfish views, should desire it; unless there be some great grievance, they can have no handle to make use of for the purpose."[51]

For Franklin, then, the central question in explaining why the colonists revolted, why the American Revolution occurred, was what made the waves rise. During the course of his long engagement with this question, he broke it down into two subordinate questions: first, why metropolitan leaders risked alienating the affections of the colonies by adopting that "unhappy new system of politics"[52] in 1764–65 and, even more bewildering to him, why over the following decade, successive administrations persisted in trying to implement that system in the face of such determined and widespread resistance in the colonies.

Franklin never wavered in his belief that American discontent was wholly a function of these actions. As he pointed out during the Stamp Act crisis and repeatedly thereafter, by explicitly depriving the colonists of "the same protection of property and domestic security which prevails in England"[53] and otherwise seeming to put "their Liberties and Privi-

[48] Franklin, *Interest of Great Britain*, 1760, ibid., 9:90.

[49] Franklin to *Lloyd's Evening Post*, Sept. 5, 1765, ibid., 12:254–55.

[50] Franklin, *Interest of Great Britain*, 1760, ibid., 9:90–91.

[51] Franklin to *Lloyd's Evening Post*, Sept. 5, 1765, ibid., 12:254.

[52] Franklin to *London Chronicle*, Jan. 5–7, 1768, ibid., 15:12–13.

[53] Franklin to *Gazeteer and New Daily Advertiser*, May 2, 1765, ibid., 12:120.

leges, as English men . . . in great Danger,"[54] the new system of colonial governance rendered the colonists' claims to "the [very] name of Englishman" highly problematic.[55] By thus threatening their most basic identity as Englishmen, that system, as Franklin predicted, quickly begat "resentment, and provoke[d the colonists] to [commit] acts never dreamt of."[56] For, as the colonists immediately sensed, only by "shewing the Spirit of Men, of free-born British Subjects," could they demonstrate to themselves as well as to those in the metropolis that they were deserving of the name of Englishmen, that, as Franklin once put it, they were the sons and not the "Bastards" of Britain.[57]

As Franklin early foresaw, however, merely by expressing their resentment through an active display of their "British Spirit of Liberty,"[58] the colonists only succeeded in goading the metropolitan government into treating them with even "more severity."[59] In turn, these actions invariably tended "to alienate still more the affections"[60] the colonists felt for Britain, eventually so exasperating them as to drive them "to despair."[61] As this escalating dialectic produced ever-greater "Violences, Excesses and Severities,"[62] the "cordial Amity" that had so long "subsisted between the two Countries" rapidly degenerated "into the most implacable mutual Hatred."[63] Such "a deep-rooted Aversion," Franklin repeatedly warned, could only lay "the Foundations for a future total Separation,"[64] make "an open Rupture unavoidable,"[65] and deprive Britain of "all the Commercial and Political Advantages that might have attended the Continuance of that Regard and Affection" traditionally extended by the colonists to the parent state.[66]

Throughout the decade beginning with the Stamp Act crisis, Franklin

---

[54] David Hall to Franklin, Sept. 6, 1765, ibid., 12:257.

[55] Franklin to *London Chronicle*, Nov. 6–8, 1770, ibid., 17:268.

[56] Charles Thomson to Franklin, [Sept. 24, 1765], ibid., 12:280.

[57] Franklin to *Public Advertiser*, Feb. 5, 1770, ibid., 17:59.

[58] Franklin to *Public Advertiser*, Aug. 31, 1768, ibid., 15:191.

[59] Franklin to *Public Advertiser*, Jan. 17, 1769, ibid., 16:23.

[60] Franklin to *Pennsylvania Gazette*, Mar. 8, 1768, ibid., 15:67.

[61] Franklin to *Public Advertiser*, Jan. 17, 1769, ibid., 16:23.

[62] Franklin to William Franklin, Nov. 9, 1765, ibid., 12:363.

[63] Franklin to *Public Advertiser*, Jan. 17, 1769, ibid., 16:23.

[64] Franklin to William Franklin, Nov. 9, 1765, ibid., 12:363.

[65] Franklin to *Public Advertiser*, Jan. 17, 1769, ibid., 16:23.

[66] Franklin to ——, [Jan. 6, 1766], ibid., 13:25.

engaged in an ongoing quest to explain why Britain thus put itself in what he referred to as "a Posture of Hostility against America,"[67] why, through its continuing pursuit of its "new-fashioned vigorous measures," it effectively risked, as he put it in 1768, "kill[ing] the goose which lays the golden egg."[68] Franklin traced the answer to this question to a series of metropolitan misconceptions about the colonies and their inhabitants.

As Franklin identified them over time, these misconceptions seemed to fall into two distinct categories. First were those that surfaced or resurfaced long before the Stamp Act crisis, mostly during and immediately after the Seven Years' War. These included the mistaken, in Franklin's opinion, impressions that colonial loyalty to Britain was weak,[69] that the colonists had demonstrated their lack of imperial patriotism by making little contribution to the war,[70] that the colonists were ungrateful for the enormous effort made by the metropolis in a war that had been fought *"for their advantage only,"*[71] that the colonies had far "too many and too great Privileges," which it was "not only the Interest of the Crown but of the Nation to reduce,"[72] and that the colonists were only biding their time until they could declare their independence.[73]

A second cluster of misconceptions grew out of the Stamp Act crisis and the later debate over the nature of the imperial constitution. Among these were the notions that the colonies were conquered countries without claim to British rights,[74] that they had been settled at metropolitan expense,[75] that the constitution of the British Empire was firmly fixed

---

[67] Franklin, marginalia in *Good Humour* (London, 1766), ibid., 16:283.

[68] Franklin to *London Chronicle*, Aug. 16–18, 1768, ibid., 15:188.

[69] See Franklin to Shirley, Dec. 4, 1754, ibid., 5:444.

[70] See Franklin to *London Chronicle*, May 9, 1759, Franklin to ——, [Jan. 6, 1766], Franklin, "Examination," 1766, ibid., 8:344, 356, 13:24, 149, 151.

[71] See Franklin, *Interest of Great Britain*, 1760, Franklin to *Lloyd's Evening Post*, Aug. 23, Sept. 5, 1765, to *Gazeteer and New Daily Advertiser*, Dec. 27, 1765, to Kames, Feb. 25, 1767, ibid., 9:72, 12:245, 253, 411–12, 14:64–65.

[72] See Franklin to Norris, Mar. 19, 1757, ibid., 8:293–95.

[73] See Franklin to *London Chronicle*, [Dec. 27, 1759], Franklin, *Interest of Great Britain*, 1760, ibid., 8:450, 9:75–78, 93.

[74] See Franklin to *Gazeteer and New Daily Advertiser*, Jan. 15, 1766, Franklin, marginalia in [Allan Ramsay], *Thoughts on the Origin and Nature of Government* (London, 1769), ibid., 13:47–48, 16:323–24.

[75] See Franklin to *Gazeteer and New Daily Advertiser*, Jan. 6, 1766, to Kames, Feb. 25, 1767, Franklin, marginalia in [Wheelock], *Reflections Moral and Political*, ibid., 13:22, 14:68, 17:385.

and clearly understood and that it could be conflated with the constitution of Britain itself,[76] that Parliament had always exercised jurisdiction over the colonies[77] or that the Glorious Revolution had endowed it with such jurisdiction,[78] that the colonies were part of the realm and therefore under the sovereignty of Parliament or even the British people,[79] that the metropolis could change the imperial constitution without the consent of the colonists,[80] that petitions disputing Parliament's authority in the colonies constituted rebellion,[81] that colonial opposition came primarily from New England,[82] that unpopular metropolitan laws might be enforced by coercion,[83] and that metropolitan honor was best preserved by enforcing disputed measures.[84]

Regarding all these impressions as not only wrong or at the very least highly disputable but also poisonous to the welfare of the empire, Franklin spent much time and energy in endeavoring both to "disabuse the

---

[76] See Franklin to *Gazeteer and New Daily Advertiser,* Jan. 6, 1766, Franklin, Preface to *Votes and Proceedings of the Freeholders and Other Inhabitants of the Town of Boston* (London, 1773), ibid., 13:22, 20:85.

[77] See Franklin to *Gazeteer and New Daily Advertiser,* Jan. 6, 1766, to *London Chronicle,* Apr. 11, 1767, to William Strahan, Nov. 29, 1769, Franklin, marginalia in [Josiah Tucker], *A Letter from a Merchant in London to His Nephew in North America* (London, 1766), ibid., 13:22, 14:111, 16:244, 17:354.

[78] See Franklin to *London Chronicle,* Oct. 18–20, 1768, ibid., 15:234–35.

[79] See Franklin, marginalia in *Protest against the Bill to Repeal the American Stamp Act* (Paris, 1766), Franklin to Kames, Feb. 25, 1767, Franklin, marginalia in [Ramsay], *Thoughts on the Origin and Nature of Government,* Franklin to *Public Advertiser,* Jan. 8, 1770, Franklin, marginalia in [Tucker], *Letter from a Merchant in London,* Franklin, marginalia in [Wheelock], *Reflections Moral and Political,* ibid., 13:221, 231, 14:68–69, 16:316, 325, 17:15, 350–51, 385, 388, 396, 398.

[80] See Franklin, marginalia in *Protest against the Bill,* 1766, Franklin, "Observations upon [Thomas Pownall], *State of the Constitution of the Colonies* [London, 1769?]," Franklin to *Gazeteer and New Daily Advertiser,* Feb. 7, 1770, Franklin, marginalia in *An Inquiry into the Nature and Causes of the Present Disputes* (London, 1769), Franklin to William Franklin, Sept. 1, 1773, ibid., 13:226, 232, 16:301, 17:64, 335, 20:386.

[81] See Franklin to *London Chronicle,* Apr. 9, 1767, ibid., 14:106–7.

[82] See Franklin to *Lloyd's Evening Post,* Sept. 5, 1765, to *Public Advertiser,* Jan. 2, 1766, Franklin, marginalia, in [Mauduit], *Short View,* ibid., 12:253–54, 13:5, 16:296–97.

[83] See Franklin to *Gazeteer and New Daily Advertiser,* Dec. 27, 1765; to ——, [Jan. 6, 1766], Franklin, marginalia in *Protest against the Bill,* 1766, Franklin to Kames, Feb. 25, 1767, Franklin, marginalia in *Inquiry into the Nature and Causes,* Franklin to ——, [Aug. 1772], Franklin to *Public Advertiser,* Apr. 2, 1774, ibid., 12:413, 13:26, 223, 14:67, 17:341, 19:224, 21:180.

[84] See Franklin to ——, [Jan. 6, 1766], ibid., 13:26.

[British] Public"[85] and government about them and to explain why they carried any credibility within the British political nation. From his first engagement with this problem, Franklin recognized that some of the explanation could be traced to the structure of the empire, specifically to the "great distance"[86] separating Britain and the colonies. Distance inevitably contributed to the "Ignorance"[87] and inattention of which he often complained. "A want of Attention to what passes in such remote Countries as America; an Unwillingness even to read any thing about them," he lamented after a decade of frustration in trying to correct metropolitan assumptions about the colonies, was a "great Defect . . . in all sorts of People" in the metropolis.[88]

Distance also lent credence to misrepresentation by interested metropolitan officials in the colonies. "Not always Men of the best Abilities and Integrity," rarely having any estates or "natural Connections" with the colonies, and "frequently" willing to use power "merely to make Fortunes"[89] in the colonies, too many "Governors and other Officers of the Crown, even the little Officers of the Revenue," Franklin charged in frustration during the Stamp Act crisis, systematically misrepresented the colonists in an effort to place their own conduct "in a more advantageous Light" and thereby contributed to "the most unfavourable idea [possible] of Americans" as "refractory, and disaffected; . . . turbulent, disloyal, impatient of Government, . . . inclin'd to *Smuggling*," and "overwhelmed with vice, irreligion, ignorance and error!"[90] Thus had the government's own servants often "exasperated" it against the colonies "by their false insinuations against the *absent* and the *distant*" in America.[91]

Combined with a lamentable, if, to Franklin, understandable, tendency for metropolitan leaders to think of the welfare of the empire as a whole in terms of "the partial Advantage of Britain,"[92] such misrepresentations and inattention, as Franklin noted as early as 1759, had com-

[85] Franklin to *London Chronicle*, May 9, 1759, ibid., 8:340.

[86] Franklin to William Franklin, Mar. 13, 1768, ibid., 15:75–76.

[87] See Franklin to *Public Advertiser*, Mar. 4, 1774, ibid., 21:132.

[88] Franklin to Samuel Cooper, July 7, 1773, ibid., 20:271.

[89] Franklin, extract from *Pennsylvania Gazette*, July 30, 1741, Franklin to Shirley, Dec. 4, 1754, ibid., 2:327, 5:444.

[90] Franklin, "Fragments of a Pamphlet on the Stamp Act," Jan. 1766, ibid., 13:80–81.

[91] Franklin to *London Chronicle*, Apr. 11, 1767, ibid., 14:116.

[92] Franklin to Strahan, Nov. 29, 1769, ibid., 16:244. See also Franklin to Shirley, Dec. 22, 1754, ibid., 5:451.

bined over the decades to produce "a good deal of Prejudice . . . against the Colonies" as insufficiently respectful of metropolitan authority and perhaps even "unworthy [of] the name of Englishmen," and that prejudice, Franklin believed, was nourished by jealousy born of the fear that the colonies would eventually become independent and rival the metropolis economically. With the rapid growth of the colonies, Franklin wrote Isaac Norris in Pennsylvania, every major segment of the British establishment—the trading, manufacturing, and landed interests—had begun "to be jealous of us."[93]

Evidence of such fears and jealousies already was abundant in the 1750s. So deeply implanted were they in metropolitan consciousness that Franklin eventually began to suspect that metropolitan leaders had not sanctioned the Albany Plan of Union in 1754 out of "a Jealousy that such an Union might make the Colonies in some degree formidable to the Mother Country as well as to the Enemy."[94] Similarly, in 1759–60, he felt compelled explicitly to refute the argument that Canada should be restored to the French in order to "check the growth of" the colonies and thereby prevent them from becoming "*dangerous* to Britain" by developing into "a numerous, hardy, *independent* people."[95] After Canada had been retained and Britain's "western World" had been thereby "left almost independent," this new situation, a Scottish correspondent wrote Franklin in December 1764, left Britain "more afraid of your shaking us off, than of any other object what ever," a fear that, this correspondent continued, was the true reason behind the decision to tax the colonies in order to pay for an army to "preserve a Military Awe over you."[96] In 1764–65, moreover, the colonial response to the proposed Stamp Act exacerbated this fear. As Franklin reported to his friend Charles Thomson in July 1765, the "Nation was [so] provok'd by [what it took to be] American Claims of [legislative] Independence" that "all Parties join'd in resolveing by this Act to Settle the Point."[97]

That what appeared to Franklin to be nothing more than a "ground-

---

[93] Franklin to Norris, Mar. 19, 1759, ibid., 8:295; Franklin, "Fragments of a Pamphlet on the Stamp Act," Jan. 1766, ibid., 13:81. See also Achenwall, "Some Observations," 1766, ibid., 13:366–67.

[94] Franklin, "Fragments of a Pamphlet on the Stamp Act," Jan. 1766, ibid., 13:76.

[95] Franklin, *Interest of Great Britain,* 1760, ibid., 9:77. See also Franklin to *London Chronicle,* Dec. 27, 1759, ibid., 8:450.

[96] Alexander Small to Franklin, Dec. 1, 1764, ibid., 11:482.

[97] Franklin to Charles Thomson, July 11, 1765, ibid., 12:207.

less jealousy"[98] had eventuated in such undesirable measures in 1764–65 could be chalked up partly to irresponsible or ignorant ministers, but Franklin also knew that those measures would never have been undertaken had the metropolitan political nation not already held such deeprooted prejudices against, and such profound misconceptions about, the colonies. Thus, turning on its head the traditional interpretation about the effects of the removal of the French from North America on the controversies between Britain and the colonies, Franklin eventually became persuaded that, far from freeing the Americans to oppose Britain, the elimination of the French had been the signal for metropolitan officials to act on their prejudices and fears by introducing their "unhappy new system" of colonial governance.[99] "Had the French Power . . . continu'd at our Backs, ready to support and assist us whenever we might think proper to resist your Oppression," Franklin wrote in the margins of an anonymous British pamphlet in 1769, "you would never have thought of a Stamp Act for us; you would not have dared to use us as you have done."[100]

If a combination of misconceptions, misrepresentations, prejudice, and, perhaps most important, fear of losing the colonies was thus, in Franklin's view, responsible for the Stamp Act and other Grenville measures of 1764–65, he found the resumption of similar measures following the compromise represented by repeal of the Stamp Act in 1766 more difficult to explain. Probably no other contemporary had a keener appreciation of the underlying centripetal forces that had long helped to hold the empire together and to contribute to its success. As Franklin thought about these forces, they included mutual interests, goodwill, habits of political moderation, and a structure of governance that permitted residents of distant colonies to enjoy traditional metropolitan rights.

Franklin regarded both interest and sentiment as powerful adhesives. So closely intertwined were the interests of metropolis and colonies, Franklin pointed out in 1764, that there was "scarce anything" Britain could do to injure the colonies that would not "be as much or more so to"

---

[98] Franklin to *Lloyd's Evening Post*, Sept. 5, 1765, ibid., 12:255.

[99] See Franklin to *London Chronicle*, Jan. 5–7, 1768, ibid., 14:12–13.

[100] Franklin, marginalia in *Inquiry into the Nature and Causes*, and in [Tucker], *Letter from a Merchant*, 1766, ibid., 17:343–44, 372.

Britain itself.[101] Sentiment strongly reinforced interest. Notwithstanding either the evident "Malice against us in some powerful People"[102] or all the "invective and abuse" that had been "so lavishly bestowed on the Americans" in the press,[103] Franklin continued as late as 1773 to believe that much of the British public harbored no ill will toward the colonists. "The Majority of the Nation," he wrote Samuel Cooper in July, "wish us well, and have no Desire to infringe our Liberties."[104] Nor, despite their resentments against the treatment they had received from the metropolitan government, had the colonists ever lost their enormous "Respect, Veneration and Affection for Britain."[105] Calling for a return to the "Considerateness, Moderation and Justice" that Britain had formerly exhibited "towards its remote Subjects" in America,[106] Franklin insisted throughout the controversy that, "with kind Usage and tenderness for their Privileges," the colonies "might be easily govern'd still for Ages, without Force or any considerable Expence."[107] Nothing more than metropolitan recognition of their right "to all the Privileges of Englishmen," he wrote in the London press in September 1773, was required to produce such joy among the colonists that it would "operate as a new Cement" that would "for ever ensure their future Loyalty and Obedience."[108]

Not just interest and sentiment but the framework of governance that had emerged out of a century and a half of experience also helped to hold Britain's extended empire together. "The Excellency of the Invention of Colony Government, by separate independent Legislatures," Franklin noted in 1770, was that it permitted "the remotest Parts of a great Empire" to "be as well governed as the Center." At once, such a contrivance facilitated the extension of metropolitan authority "without Inconvenience over territories of any Dimension how great soever," prevented "Misrule, Oppressions of Proconsuls, and Discontents and Rebellions" in the peripheries,[109] and allowed people in every segment of the empire

---

[101] Franklin to Collinson, Apr. 30, 1764, ibid., 11:181.

[102] Franklin to Galloway, June 11, 1770, ibid., 17:170.

[103] Franklin to *Pennsylvania Chronicle*, Mar. 8, 1768, to *Gazeteer and New Daily Advertiser*, Sept. 28, 1768, ibid., 15:64, 221.

[104] Franklin to Cooper, July 7, 1773, ibid., 20:271.

[105] Franklin to Kames, Feb. 25, 1767, ibid., 14:70.

[106] Franklin to William Franklin, Nov. 9, 1765, ibid., 12:364.

[107] Franklin to Kames, Feb. 25, 1767, ibid., 14:70.

[108] Franklin to *Public Advertiser*, Sept. 11, 1773, ibid., 20:389.

[109] Franklin, marginalia in *Inquiry into the Nature and Causes*, ibid., 17:322.

to "enjoy their own opinions, without disturbing them when they do not interfere with the common Good."[110]

Once there had been so much "Agitation" over "Question[s] of Right"[111] during the Stamp Act crisis, Franklin thought it desirable to codify these arrangements in a formal constitution, and by 1770 he was despairing that "the old Harmony" could ever "be restor'd . . . till some [formal] Constitution is agreed upon and establish'd ascertaining the relative Rights and Duties" of metropolis and colonies.[112] In the immediate wake of the Stamp Act crisis, however, he was persuaded that if the London government would treat the colonists with regard to taxation as it did the Irish and refrain from violating their rights,[113] relations could "remain upon their old footing." Britain could continue to exert political control through the crown's power to review colonial laws and, at little cost, to reap the many valuable economic and strategic benefits supplied by the colonies, while the colonists could enjoy their rights as Englishmen through their local governing institutions.[114] "The true Art of governing the Colonies lies in a Nut-Shell," he declared in 1770: "It is only letting them alone."[115]

Regarding the Stamp Act as the product of a temporary sacrifice of reason to passion, Franklin hoped that the Stamp Act crisis would bring metropolitan leaders to their senses by recalling them to the moderation and wisdom that had traditionally characterized British colonial governance. For any government trying to exercise authority "over different kinds of people," he wrote, "it has been thought wisdom . . . to have some regard to prevailing and established opinions among the people to be governed," especially "wherever such opinions might in their effects obstruct or promote publick measures."[116] Never wavering in his own belief that such "Wisdom would do more towards reducing Things to order, than all [the] . . . Force" at metropolitan command,[117] he was quick to interpret the repeal of the Stamp Act as an expression of metro-

---

[110] Franklin to Strahan, Nov. 29, 1769, ibid., 16:246.

[111] Franklin, marginalia in *Protest against the Bill*, ibid., 13:224.

[112] Franklin to Galloway, Jan. 11, 1770, ibid., 17:24.

[113] Franklin, "Examination," 1766, Franklin to Joseph Fox, Mar. 1, 1766, ibid., 13:141, 187.

[114] Franklin to *Lloyd's Evening Post*, Sept. 5, 1765, ibid., 12:254–55.

[115] Franklin to *Public Advertiser*, Feb. 5, 1770, ibid., 17:60.

[116] Franklin to *London Chronicle*, Jan. 5–7, 1768, ibid., 15:4.

[117] Franklin to William Franklin, Nov. 9, 1765, ibid., 12:363.

politan political wisdom and a foundation for the restoration of imperial harmony.

But Franklin soon came to understand that he had seriously underes-
timated the residue of anger and suspicion that the Stamp Act crisis had
generated in Britain. Many metropolitans thought that the colonists'
defiance of the Stamp Act fell little short of rebellion and seemed, as
some members of the House of Lords announced in protest against the
repeal of the act, to imply that a large number of colonists not only subscribed to the subversive opinion that the colonies were outside the jurisdiction of Parliament but also to that "most *dangerous doctrine, destructive to all Government*, . . . that the obedience of *the subject*" was "not due
to the Laws and Legislature of *the Realm*, farther than he in his *private
judgment* shall think it conformable to the ideas he has formed of a free
constitution." [118]

Stimulated by subsequent colonial resistance to other components of
the new system, such suspicions lay behind the metropolitan government's decision in 1767 to revive its efforts to tax the colonies and even
to threaten to take away "all the powers of legislation" from New York
unless it complied with a parliamentary statute concerning the terms of
quartering metropolitan troops in the colonies.[119] When these measures
yielded still further resistance from the colonies, London leaders re-
sponded with a series of hostile measures. "Suspending their Legislative
Powers, for not making Laws by *Direction* from hence"; rewarding the
colonists' "Adversaries by . . . Pensions paid out of the Revenues ex-
torted from them by Laws to which they have not given their Assent;
. . . sending over a set of rash, indiscreet Commissioners to collect that
Revenue, who by insolence of Behaviour, harrassing Commerce, and per-
petually accusing the good People (out of whose Substance they are
supported) to Government here, as Rebels and Traitors, have made
themselves universally odious there"; the "arbitrary Dissolution of Assemblies, and the Quartering Troops among the People, to menace and
insult them"—"Every Step taken for some time past" with regard to the
colonies, Franklin declared in 1772, seemed to have been designed to
"provoke them to rebellion [so] that" Britain might then have justification for taking "their lives" and confiscating "their Estates." [120]

As far as the colonists were concerned, the Stamp Act crisis, as Frank-

---

[118] *Protest against the Bill*, 1766, ibid., 13:221.

[119] Franklin to *London Chronicle*, Jan. 5–7, 1768, ibid., 15:7.

[120] Franklin to ——, Aug. 1772, ibid., 19:225–26.

lin repeatedly informed his London readers, had forced them to examine a series of points about the nature of the imperial constitution that, as he said, had never before even been "agitated," much less "thoroughly considered and settled."[121] Once the struggle had been renewed in 1767, this "awakened . . . spirit of enquiry" quickly led the colonists into "a fuller knowledge of their rights" and made them at once "more attentive and watchful against the encroachments of power" and "more sensible of the resources they" had "among themselves for" sustaining their resistance.[122]

Thus did the "severe partial" measures visited upon them by the metropolitan government teach the colonists to consider themselves "distinct from the inhabitants of Great Britain."[123] Eventually learning to view the colonies as "so many separate little States"[124] outside the realm of Great Britain and attached to the parent state only through a common king, they came to see that there was no constitutional basis for the "implicit Obedience" they had formerly shown to many "Acts of the British Parliament"[125] and that their relation to Britain involved "no . . . *Dependence*," but "only a Connection, of which the King" was "the common link."[126] Having come to these conclusions, they could only regard Parliament's efforts to bind them by statute as "unconstitutional" and disobedience to those efforts "as Patriotism."[127]

In trying to understand why British leaders would be so heedless as to dissipate all of the traditional centrifugal forces of empire and permit things to come to this pass, which for him was the central question in the controversy, Franklin put some emphasis on almost every factor emphasized by later historians. Like Edmund S. Morgan, among others,[128] he placed some weight on the ineptness of most British leaders after 1766 and their absorption in factional struggles for power. He would not have disputed the truth of Charles Thomson's remark to him in November 1769 that the ministry, caught up in the "madness of politics," had,

---

[121] Franklin to *Gazeteer and New Daily Advertiser*, Jan. 11, 1766, ibid., 13:22.

[122] Charles Thomson to Franklin, Nov. 26, 1769, ibid., 16:239.

[123] Franklin to *London Chronicle*, June 19, 1765, ibid., 12:184.

[124] Franklin to Kames, Feb. 25, 1767, ibid., 14:68–69.

[125] Franklin, Preface to *Votes and Proceedings of Boston*, Feb. 1773, ibid., 20:85.

[126] Franklin, marginalia in [Wheelock], *Reflections Moral and Political*, ibid., 17:393.

[127] Franklin, Preface to *Votes and Proceedings of Boston*, Feb. 1773, ibid., 20:86.

[128] See Edmund S. Morgan, "The American Revolution: Revisions in Need of Revising," *William and Mary Quarterly*, 3d ser., 14 (1957): 12–13.

through their own "weak[ness and] short-sighted[ness,] been [inadvertently] ruining their country, and hastening a period they seemed to dread, by the very means which they intended to prevent it." [129]

Like a still older generation of modern historians,[130] Franklin also assigned some importance to the related theme of corruption. That Parliament permitted itself to be imposed upon by feckless ministers could be partly attributed to the dependence of so many of its members upon pensions and places. By the late 1760s, however, Franklin was beginning to think that corruption had reached deep into British society, too many members of which, he remarked in 1768 in condemning the riots over Wilkes and a host of other issues in London, seemed to be guilty of "ungratefully abusing the best Constitution . . . any Nation was ever blest with" in the blind pursuit of "Luxury, Licentiousness, Power, Places, Pensions and Plunder." [131]

Similarly to a long tradition of Whig and neo-Whig historians of the Revolution, Franklin also gave some weight to the ostensible determination among some powerful people in London to oppress the colonies by depriving them of some of their liberty. Thus, he interpreted as proof "of the old British Intention to enslave America" Attorney General Edward Thurlow's remark in Parliament during the debate over the Quebec Act in 1774 that the unrepresentative constitution proposed for the non-English inhabitants of conquered Quebec was precisely the kind of "Constitution that ought to have been given originally to all the Colonies; and which it would be right now to reduce them to." [132]

Unlike the American pamphleteers emphasized by Bailyn, however, Franklin did not attribute such attitudes to a conspiracy of evil men or to the corrosive effects of power. Rather, he explained them as a combination of other factors. Long frustrated by their powerlessness to exert tighter controls over the colonies, many metropolitan leaders, Franklin had long recognized, had become convinced that the colonists were "not sufficiently obedient," [133] and this conviction was in turn reinforced by what Franklin came to regard as a prevailing "Spirit of Toryism" [134]

---

[129] Charles Thomson to Franklin, Nov. 26, 1768, in *Franklin Papers* 16:239.

[130] Among many others, see George Otto Trevelyan, *The American Revolution,* 4 vols. (London, 1899–1913).

[131] See Franklin to John Ross, May 14, 1768, to Cooper, June 8, 1770, in *Franklin Papers* 15:129, 17:163–64.

[132] Franklin, "Notes on Britain's Intention to Enslave America," [1774–75?], ibid., 21:608.

[133] Franklin to Norris, Mar. 19, 1759, ibid., 8:295.

[134] Franklin to Cooper, June 8, 1770, ibid., 17:164.

among people in power. At the same time that many metropolitan leaders were concluding that the colonies were far too "refractory,"[135] the
colonists had "the Misfortune to be *Whigs* in a Reign when *Whiggism*"
was "out of Fashion."[136] Indeed, far from giving any credence to the belief
among some colonial supporters in a conspiracy against liberty, Franklin
ridiculed similar notions held by people in Britain about the colonists.
That metropolitans were "Apprehensive of chimerical dangers" and "suspect[ed] plots and deep designs where none exist[ed]" struck him as
"symptoms" of not "a malignity of *heart*" but "an insanity of *head*."[137]

But such suspiciousness, Franklin thought, was primarily attributable
to three other attitudes that determined metropolitan behavior toward
the colonies: jealousy, prejudice, and pride. In his view, the same
"groundless jealousy" that had been such a strong component of the decision to pass the Stamp Act[138] continued to operate during the following
decade. Even more inclined following the widespread colonial resistance
to the measures of Grenville and later ministers to regard the colonists
"with a jealous Eye," "some of the Great," Franklin knew, continued to
think that Britain, as he once bitterly remarked, had "an Interest in
keeping us down and fleecing us."[139] Moreover, once the colonists had
articulated the theory that their connection to Britain was only through
the king, some metropolitans began to be jealous lest the colonies, as
Franklin wrote in 1768, "'being the child of prerogative, and consisting
of some millions of commercial subjects daily encreasing in riches and
power, ranged under its banner, and bound to it by the strongest ties of
interest,'" might, "in some imagined future contest between the crown
and parliament, strengthen the hands of the former against the latter,
to the utter 'ruin of parliamentary authority.'"[140]

Franklin endeavored to show the folly of these fears and jealousies in
a satirical piece published in the London press in the spring of 1768. For
Britons to charge Americans "with *dreaming* that" they had it in their
"power to make" Britain "a bankrupt nation . . . by engaging us in new
wars; with *dreaming* that" they might "thereby encrease" their "own
strength and prosperity; with *dreaming* that the seat of government will

[135] Franklin to Jackson, Sept. 1, 1764, ibid., 11:328.

[136] Franklin to *Publick Ledger*, after Mar. 9, 1774, ibid., 21:134.

[137] Franklin to *Gazeteer and New Daily Advertiser*, Jan. 13, 1768, ibid., 15:19.

[138] Franklin to *Lloyd's Evening Post*, Sept. 5, 1765, ibid., 12:255.

[139] Franklin to Cooper, July 7, 1773, June 8, 1770, ibid., 20:271, 17:163–64.

[140] Franklin to *Gazeteer and New Daily Advertiser*, Jan. 21, 1768, ibid., 15:19.

then be transported to America, and Britain dwindle to one of its provinces," Franklin suggested, was absurd. For "Joseph's brethren" to hate "him for a dream he *really* dreamed" was at least comprehensible. But for Britons "to hate" the colonists "for a dream" they "never *dreamed,* and which" Britons "only *dream[ed]*" they had "*dreamed,*" seemed to Franklin even more ridiculous."[141]

The depth of such fears, Franklin thought, was dramatically revealed in a manifest proliferation and intensification of the long-standing prejudices displayed toward the colonies in the metropolis. Fueled by their growing anger and resentment at what they regarded as the colonists' impudent denials of parliamentary jurisdiction, these prejudices seemed to harden into a "settled Malice against the Colonies."[142] Among the powerful, Franklin wrote Joseph Galloway in June 1770, that malice discovered "itself in all their Expressions when they speak of us."[143] Among the broader populace, it was evident in many "rancorous Libels with which the papers" were "daily fill'd against them, exciting this Country to embrue its Hands with their Blood."[144]

Nothing made Franklin angrier than the "virulence," the "harsh and contemptuous treatment" visited upon "Americans in the public papers."[145] Among "the sweet flowers of English rhetorick, with which our colonists have of late been regaled," Franklin complained in a newspaper essay during the Stamp Act crisis, the "gentle terms of *republican race, mixed rabble of Scotch, Irish and foreign vagabonds, descendents of convicts, ungrateful rebels &c.*" conveyed only the most violent "contempt and abuse."[146] By "lumping all the Americans under the general Character of 'House-breakers and Felons'";[147] by "raving" against them "as 'diggers of pits for this country,' 'lunaticks,' 'sworn enemies,' 'false,' 'ungrateful' . . . 'cut-throats'";[148] by "treating them as Miscreants, Rogues, Dastards, [and] Rebels";[149] by reviling them "as Cheats, Hypocrites, Scoundrels,

[141] Franklin to *Gazeteer and New Daily Advertiser,* Apr. 18, 1767, ibid., 14:131.

[142] Franklin to Cushing, June 10, 1771, ibid., 18:122.

[143] Franklin to Galloway, June 11, 1770, ibid., 17:170.

[144] Franklin, "Fragments of a Pamphlet on the Stamp Act," Jan. 1766, ibid., 13:77.

[145] Franklin to *Gazeteer and New Daily Advertiser,* Jan. 6, 14, 1766, ibid., 13:20, 38.

[146] Franklin to *Gazeteer and New Daily Advertiser,* Dec. 28, 1765, ibid., 12:414.

[147] Franklin to *Public Advertiser,* Jan. 2, 1766, ibid., 13:5.

[148] Franklin to *Gazeteer and New Daily Advertiser,* Jan. 6, 1768, ibid., 15:13.

[149] Franklin to Strahan, Nov. 29, 1769, ibid., 16:248–49.

Cowards, [and] Tyrants"[150] who, "though . . . descended from British Ancestors," had "degenerated to such a Degree, that one born in Britain" was "equal to twenty Americans"[151]—by all this abusive language, Franklin objected over and over during the decade after 1765, the many "Enemies [of] the Colonies"[152] had repeatedly and effectively branded the colonists "as foreigners,"[153] who were "unworthy the name of Englishmen, and fit only to be snubb'd, curb'd, shackled and plundered."[154] Nor was it only in newspapers and pamphlets that Americans were treated with such "invective and abuse."[155] In Parliament as well, speakers loaded "many base Reflections on American Courage, Religion, Understandings, &c.," treating them "with the utmost Contempt, as the lowest of Mankind, and almost of a different Species from the English of Britain."[156]

Ultimately, Franklin concluded that, even more than contempt, fear of loss, jealousy, ideology, or corruption, pride was the principal animating force behind this deep-rooted and widespread prejudice against the colonies and the posture of hostility it expressed. A healthy amount of pride he recognized was "natural to so great a Nation."[157] But the English, he became persuaded during the American controversy, had carried pride to an excess. "Mixed with your many virtues," he told the readers of one metropolitan paper during the Stamp Act crisis, was "a pride, a haughtiness, and an insolent contempt" that expressed itself both "in rudeness to foreigners" and scorn "even to your own family," including the Welsh, Scotch, Irish, and American colonists.[158]

Franklin purported to witness the adverse operation of this excessive pride at every stage of the American controversy. The ability to consider "himself as King of America, and peculiarly interested in our Subjection," so gratified the pride of ordinary Englishmen,[159] Franklin believed,

---

[150] Franklin to *Public Ledger*, [after Mar. 9, 1774], ibid., 21:138.

[151] Franklin to *Public Advertiser*, Apr. 5, 1774, ibid., 21:185.

[152] Franklin, "Fragments of a Pamphlet on the Stamp Act," Jan. 1766, ibid., 13:77.

[153] Franklin, "Examination," 1766, ibid., 13:150.

[154] Franklin, "Fragments of a Pamphlet on the Stamp Act," Jan. 1766, ibid., 13:81.

[155] Franklin to *Pennsylvania Chronicle*, Mar. 8, 1768, ibid., 15:64.

[156] Franklin to William Franklin, Mar. 22, 1775, ibid., 21:598.

[157] Franklin to Noble Wimberly Jones, June 7, 1769, ibid., 16:152.

[158] Franklin to *Gazeteer and New Daily Advertiser*, Jan. 15, 1766, ibid., 13:47–48.

[159] Franklin to *Pennsylvania Gazette*, Sept. 6, 1770, ibid., 17:214.

that they found it extremely difficult to conceive of the colonists as genuine Englishmen. By thinking of themselves as having "a Piece of a Sovereign over America" and talking "of OUR *Subjects in the Colonies,*" Franklin observed in 1767, "Every Man in England" seemed "to jostle himself into the Throne with the King." [160] "This People," he had decided as early as 1766, was "too proud, and too much despises the Americans, [ever] to bear the Thought of admitting" their representatives into Parliament and thereby recognizing their right to "an equitable Participation in the Government of the whole" empire.[161] "The *Pride of this People,*" he wrote his friend Lord Kames in February 1767, simply could not "bear the Thoughts of it." [162]

In Franklin's view, the overweening pride of "this haughty insolent Nation" [163] and the prejudice and jealousy with which it was associated largely explained why its leaders treated the colonists' "Pretentions to English Liberty with the utmost Contempt" [164] and why the American challenge to Parliament's jurisdiction over the colonies so offended "the dignity and honor of Parliament, and of the Nation" [165] that political leaders were susceptible to arguments by George Grenville and other hard-liners that appeasing the colonies represented a sacrifice of "the Honour, Dignity, and Power of this Nation" to America.[166] Even those who "acknowledge[d] that" the measures the colonists found objectionable "ought not to have been made," Franklin believed, were so fearful of "being despis'd by all the Nations round if they repeal[ed] them" that they did not dispute the argument that "the National Honour [was] concerned in supporting them." [167] Rather than risk suffering the "contempt of all Europe, as being compelled into measures by the refractoriness of the colonies," [168] he wrote, they were determined that it was "of [the] great[est] Importance to this Nation that the World should see [that] it is Master of its Colonies," lest "its Enemies on a Conceit of its Weakness, might be encourag'd to insult it." [169]

---

[160] Franklin to Kames, Feb. 25, 1767, ibid., 14:65.

[161] Franklin to ———, [Jan. 6, 1766], ibid., 13:23.

[162] Franklin to Kames, Feb. 25, 1767, ibid., 14:65.

[163] Franklin to James Bowdoin, Feb. 25, 1775, ibid., 21:507.

[164] Franklin, "Fragments of a Pamphlet on the Stamp Act," Jan. 1766, ibid., 13:79.

[165] Franklin to Cushing, Feb. 5, 1771, ibid., 18:26.

[166] Franklin to William Franklin, Nov. 9, 1765, ibid., 12:364–65.

[167] Franklin to Galloway, Jan. 9, 1769, ibid., 16:11.

[168] Franklin to Cushing, Feb. 5, 1771, ibid., 18:26.

[169] Franklin to Galloway, Jan. 9, 1769, ibid., 16:11.

Thus by simple pride, in Franklin's view, had metropolitan leaders been seduced into the mistaken opinion "that the Honour and Dignity" of Britain would be "better supported by persisting in" what he thought were so obviously "wrong measure[s] . . . than by rectifying an Error as soon as it" was "discover'd."[170] Thus were metropolitan leaders wantonly sacrificing the welfare of the empire to the "Vanity and Pride of Power."[171] Thus was the nation "so blinded by its pride and other passions as not to see its dangers."[172]

If, in Franklin's view, pride was the main root of the hostility Britain displayed toward the colonies after 1764, the prejudice and jealousy which that pride represented were, insofar as Franklin was representative of American opinion, at least as important as the measures through which it was expressed in alienating colonial affections from Britain. Repeatedly stung by metropolitan *"Arrogance"*[173] toward the colonists, Franklin often discovered himself on the defensive during his long residences in London. With increasing bitterness, he found it necessary to protest that, in terms both "of expression and accent," the colonists spoke English with more "exactness" than the "natives of several of the counties of England";[174] that the colonists had "as high a sense" of "civil and religious liberty . . . as any Briton whatsoever" and that they possessed "as much virtue, humanity, civility, . . . and *loyalty to their Prince,* as" was "to be found among the like number of people in any part of the world";[175] that they were "as learned and polite, and more so, than any part of Britain, for their Numbers";[176] and that, if only because they lived in a new country, Americans were "much purer, much less corrupt" in their morals than the English.[177] Far from being cowardly, as metropolitans charged, colonial behavior in the Seven Years' War had made it clear that, as Franklin first remarked in 1759, "the *Children* of Britain [had] retain[ed] their native intrepidity to the third and fourth generation in the regions of America,"[178] while colonial resistance to oppressive

---

[170] Franklin to ——, [Jan. 6, 1766], ibid., 13:26.

[171] Franklin to *Public Advertiser,* Sept. 11, 1773, ibid., 20:389.

[172] Franklin to ——, Nov. 28, 1768, ibid., 15:272.

[173] Franklin to *Public Advertiser,* Mar. 16, 1773, ibid., 20:118.

[174] Franklin to *London Chronicle,* May 9, 1759, ibid., 8:342.

[175] Franklin to *Gazeteer and New Daily Advertiser,* Dec. 28, 1765, ibid., 12:413–14.

[176] Franklin, marginalia in [Wheelock], *Reflections Moral and Political,* ibid., 17:389.

[177] Franklin to *Gazeteer and New Daily Advertiser,* Jan. 29, 1766, ibid., 13:64.

[178] Franklin to *London Chronicle,* May 9, 1759, ibid., 8:356.

British measures after 1764 showed once again that they had been "nursed up in the same Old English Principles"[179] and had as "brave Spirits"[180] and as "strong [a] sense of liberty"[181] as the original English immigrants to the colonies.

Over and over, Franklin warned metropolitans of the necessity to change their behavior. He urged them to listen to American opinion.[182] He pressed them to acquiesce in a constitutional arrangement that would put the colonists "on an exact level . . . with their fellow subjects in the old [British] provinces" on the eastern side of the Atlantic.[183] Citing Thucydides' report of the Corcyreans' complaint to their mother city of Corinth that colonists were "not sent out to be slaves, but as lawful equals to those who remain[ed] at home,"[184] he pleaded with his London readers to stop regarding the colonists "as foreigners"[185] and to recognize that their claims to the rights and privileges of Englishmen rested on exactly the same basis as those of the British themselves. "If the British Subjects, residing in this Island, claim Liberty, and the Disposal of their Property, on the Score of that unalienable Right that all Men, except those who have justly forfeited those Advantages[,] have to them," he wrote in January 1770, "the British People, residing in America, challenge the same on the same Principle. If the former alledge, that they have a Right to tax themselves, from Prescription, and Time immemorial, so may the latter. There is no one Species of Claim, natural or artificial," Franklin contended, "on which the former can found their Right to the Disposal of their own Property, to which the latter is not equally intitled."[186]

Only pride, and the prejudice, jealousy, and fear it both fed upon and nourished, Franklin ultimately concluded, could explain why metropolitan leaders ignored his objections and advice. He had long and frequently argued that Britain could retain the friendship and loyalty of the colonies only by "using them kindly."[187] "Military arguments, used

---

[179] Franklin to *Public Advertiser*, Jan. 23, 1766, ibid., 13:56.

[180] Franklin to Cooper, July 7, 1773, ibid., 20:273.

[181] Franklin to *Gazeteer and New Daily Advertiser*, Dec. 28, 1765, ibid., 12:413.

[182] Franklin to *London Chronicle*, Jan. 5–7, 1768, ibid., 15:4.

[183] Franklin to *Gentlemen's Magazine*, Jan. 1768, ibid., 37.

[184] Achenwall, "Observations on North America," 1766, ibid., 13:377.

[185] Franklin, "Examination," 1766, ibid., 13:150.

[186] Franklin to *Public Advertiser*, Jan. 4, 1770, ibid., 17:7.

[187] Franklin, marginalia in *Inquiry into the Nature and Causes*, ibid., 341.

in a political controversy," he remarked during the Stamp Act crisis, might *"silence"* but were "extremely improper to *convince.*"[188] "Instead of terrifying [the colonists] into a Compliance," force could only be expected "to exasperate and sour the Minds of the People,"[189] as had indeed been the case in Boston after 1768. "If the People hate you," he warned, sovereignty would be illusory and obedience too costly to maintain.[190] Only pride could explain why British leaders thought they could bring so vast and populous a country into subjection. Unlike his adversaries in the British political establishment, Franklin was virtually certain that "a great Country of hardy Peasants" like America was "not to be subdued."[191]

To explain the American Revolution, to account for both the success and the breakup of the early modern British Empire, Franklin employed a domestic relations model that put major stress upon the emotional dimensions of the metropolitan-colonial relationship. In Franklin's view, the empire was not a coercive but a voluntary political association in which colonies and metropolis were bound together by powerful ties of interest and, far more importantly, affection. Notwithstanding some occasional and quite specific lapses, the metropolis benignly presided over this association, prudently cultivating the colonists' affections by devising and subscribing to a set of constitutional arrangements which ensured that the colonists could enjoy their traditional rights as English people and the English identity that those rights conferred upon them, while at the same time they expanded the territory, wealth, and power of Britain.

To understand how this happy arrangement came apart, how his vision of a Great*er* Britain was shattered in little more than a decade after 1764, Franklin, in contrast to many modern scholars, focused primarily on developments not in America but in Britain. Specifically, he emphasized the emergence among a large segment of the metropolitan political nation of a posture of hostility toward the colonies. By revealing that the metropolis had little respect for their rights and no intention of treat-

---

[188] Franklin to *Gazeteer and New Daily Advertiser,* Dec. 27, 1765, ibid., 12:413.

[189] Franklin to ——, [Aug. 1772], ibid., 19:224.

[190] Franklin, marginalia in *Inquiry into the Nature and Causes,* 1770, ibid., 17:341.

[191] Franklin to *Public Advertiser,* Apr. 2, 1774, ibid., 21:180.

ing them as equals, that posture, Franklin believed, slowly alienated the colonists' affections and persuaded them that they could only achieve their aspirations for equality through separation, only become fully English by becoming independent Americans.

To account for this change in posture in 1764–65, Franklin cited a variety of factors. These included a few structural preconditions, including the misconceptions and misrepresentations that inevitably derived out of the distances in an extended polity such as the British Empire and the elimination of any need to cultivate the colonies for strategic purposes following the removal of the French from Canada as a result of the Seven Years' War. Other causes he cited included ignorance about and inattention to the colonies, a preoccupation with domestic politics, and a partiality for metropolitan interests. But he placed most emphasis upon what he interpreted as a growing prejudice against and jealousy of the colonies, associated with the fear that Britain might lose them. Such attitudes and fears, he thought, lay behind the emerging convictions among people in power that the colonies had too many privileges, that they were not sufficiently respectful of metropolitan authority, and that they secretly lusted after independence.

To explain the resumption of this posture after it had evidently been abandoned with the repeal of the Stamp Act, Franklin again pointed to a variety of factors. Among these were the weakness and shortsightedness of British political leaders, a rising spirit of Toryism that was unfriendly to the Whiggish devotion to liberty manifest in the colonial resistance to metropolitan measures, and a misreading by metropolitan officials of the thrust of that resistance. As with the initial change in posture in 1764–65, however, he also explained the persistence of that posture largely in terms of the deepening jealousy of and prejudice against the colonies in the metropolis. Although he knew that these emotions had been powerfully reinforced by the extent and depth of colonial opposition to metropolitan measures, he ultimately came to think that they could be traced directly to the excessive pride of the British, a pride that first prevented them from considering the colonists worthy of an equality of status in the empire and that then supported the foolish illusion that they were incapable of defending themselves against superior metropolitan power.

In Franklin's view, then, the British Empire was a victim of metropolitan pride and of the prejudice and jealousy that it sustained. By stressing the primacy of such emotional forces in explaining the American Revolution, Franklin, a perceptive and highly informed, if partial, observer of the events that brought it about, presents a formidable challenge to those scholars whose interpretations have posited the preeminence of either economic or ideological determinants. His analysis strongly suggests the need for a fuller and broader exploration of the emotional dimensions within the causal pattern of the Revolution.

This chapter was written for and presented in an abbreviated version on April 17, 1990, at a conference on "Reappraising Franklin: A Bicentennial Perspective," held in Philadelphia. It is here reprinted with permission from J. A. Leo Lemay, ed., *Reappraising Franklin: A Bicentennial Perspective* (Newark: University of Delaware Press, 1992), 119–42.

—Four—

The American Revolution:
An Explanation

Two hundred years after the event, historians still do not have a clear answer to the great question of why the American Revolution occurred, why, after a decade of relatively tempered and largely peaceful, if also firm, protest against certain specific measures and policies of the parent state, the American colonists suddenly took up arms, rose in rebellion, and rejected any further political association with that state? To put the question more specifically, what transformed that cautious and studied defiance still exhibited by the First Continental Congress in 1774 into the intense militancy of mid-1775 and the bitter revulsion against Britain during the first half of 1776?

There is, of course, a simple and obvious answer: the determination of the British government to use force to secure colonial obedience to its authority and the consequent outbreak of hostilities at Lexington and Concord on April 19, 1775. But such an answer only raises larger questions. Why did the British reach a determination to use force? Why did the Americans resist it? What gave the Americans any hope that their resistance, against the strongest power in the Western world at that moment, might actually meet with success? These questions, in turn, raise still others. After they have happened, great events such as the American Revolution tend to take on an aura of inevitability. The "logic" of the event becomes so clear that it is difficult to entertain the possibility that it might not have happened at all. But only by understanding under what conditions the Revolution might not have occurred or the related question of why it did not occur earlier can we ever hope to understand the larger problem of how political protest escalated into armed rebellion and political revolution.

Any satisfactory examination of this problem must go back at least two decades to consider the nature of the bond that had held Britain and the colonies together for more than 150 years after the founding of the colonies.[1] The character of that bond is clearly revealed in the following four quotations.

The first dates from 1757 and is from Governor Thomas Pownall of Massachusetts Bay. Mocking the charge, made increasingly by people in Britain during the middle decades of the eighteenth century, that "in some future time the [American] Provinces should become Independent of the Mother Country," Pownall observed: "if by becoming Independent is meant a Revolt, nothing is further from their Nature, their Interest, their Thoughts; their Liberty & Religion is incompatible with French Government, and the only thing that the French could throw as a temptation in their way namely a *Free Port* is no more than they do enjoy now as their Trade is at present Circumstanced. They could hope for no Protection under a Dutch Government, and a Spanish cou'd give them neither the one nor the Other." "If," on the other hand, Pownall continued, "a Defection from the Alliance of the Mother Country be suggested, That their Spirit abhors, Their Attachment to the Alliance of the Mother Country is inviolable, Their Attachment to the Protestant Succession in the house of Hanover will ever Stand unshaken, Nothing can eradicate these attachments from their Hearts."[2]

The second is from Thomas Barnard, pastor of the First Congregational Church in Salem, Massachusetts. In a sermon celebrating the conclusion of the Seven Years' War in 1763, Barnard declared:

Now commences the Area of our quiet Enjoyment of those Liberties, which our Fathers purchased with the Toil of their whole Lives, their Treasure, their Blood. Safe from the Enemy of the Wilderness [the Indians], safe from the griping Hand of arbitrary Sway and cruel Superstition [the French]; Here shall be the late founded Seat of Peace

---

[1] Portions of this chapter are adapted from Jack P. Greene, "An Uneasy Connection: An Analysis of the Preconditions of the American Revolution," in Stephen C. Kurtz and James H. Hutson, eds., *Essays on the American Revolution* (Chapel Hill, N.C., 1973), 32–80.

[2] Thomas Pownall, "The State of the Government of Massachusetts Bay As It Stood in ye Year 1757," Colonial Office Papers, 325/2, Public Record Office, London.

and Freedom. Here shall our indulgent Mother, who has most gener-
ously rescued and protected us, be served and honoured by growing
Numbers, with all Duty, Love and Gratitude, till Time shall be no
more.[3]

The third quotation is from Daniel Leonard, the articulate Massachusetts loyalist and lawyer. Writing on the very eve of the outbreak of war
in the colonies in 1775, Leonard surveyed the crisis that then beset the
British Empire with amazement:

When we reflect upon the constitutional connection between Great-
Britain and the colonies, view the reciprocation of interest, consider
that the welfare of Britain in some measure, and the prosperity of
America wholly depends upon that connection, it is astonishing, indeed almost incredible, that one person should be found on either side
of the Atlantic, so base and destitute of every sentiment of justice, as
to attempt to destroy or weaken it. If there are none such, in the name
of Almighty God, let me ask, wherefore is rebellion, that implacable
fiend to society, suffered to rear its ghastly front among us, blasting
with haggard look, each social joy, and embittering every hour?[4]

The fourth and last quotation is from the patron philosopher of so
many of the men of the Revolution, John Locke. In commenting in his
Second Treatise of Government on the supposed susceptibility of governments founded on the will of the people to revolt and tumult, Locke
made the sage observation that

People are not so easily got out of their old Forms, as some are apt to
suggest. They are hardly to be prevailed with to amend the ac-
knowledg'd Faults, in the Frame they have been accustom'd to. And
if there be any Original defects, or adventitious ones introduced by
time, or corruption; 'tis not an easie thing to get them changed, even
when all the World sees there is an opportunity for it. This slowness
and aversion in the People to quit their old Constitutions, has, in the
many Revolutions which have been seen in this Kingdom, in this and
former Ages, still kept us to, or, after some interval of fruitless at-

---

[3] Thomas Barnard, *A Sermon Preached before His Excellency Francis Bernard, Esq.,* . . .
May 25th, 1763 (Boston, 1763), 44.

[4] [Daniel Leonard], *To the Inhabitants of the Province of Massachusetts Bay,* Feb. 6, 1775,
in Barnard Mason, ed., *The American Colonial Crisis* (New York, 1972), 56.

tempts, still brought us back again to our old Legislative of King, Lords and Commons.[5]

Together, these four quotations can help us to delineate the ingredients of British imperial success during Britain's first century and a half of empire. Locke's penetrating remarks remind us how very addicted people in traditional societies become to what Thomas Jefferson, paraphrasing Locke, referred to in the Declaration of Independence as "the forms to which they are accustomed,"[6] and how extraordinarily wary under any circumstances they are of any fundamental political change. As Leonard's remarks underline, this deep aversion to change was reinforced by the reciprocal economic—not to mention the political—benefits of empire. Britain had certainly profited from the colonies, but as Leonard emphasizes, the colonists had also derived great economic benefits from the connection with Britain. Students of the Navigation Acts have traditionally asked how much those economic restrictions cost the colonies. Far more deserving of emphasis perhaps is the extraordinary extent to which the colonies had been able to prosper under that system and by the middle of the eighteenth century had actually developed a strong vested interest in maintaining their economic ties with it. As Barnard's and Pownall's words particularly point up, however, the colonists were tied to Britain not only by interest and habit but also by deep affection and attachment. To overemphasize the strength of these bonds of allegiance and affection that tied the colonies to Britain is almost impossible.

These bonds had powerful symbolic and psychological roots. For the colonists, Britain was the source of political, cultural, and moral authority: it was at once the repository of the sacred "order of symbols, of values and beliefs" thought to give structure and legitimation to the lives of all Englishmen, whether in Britain or the colonies, and the site of those institutions—the crown, Parliament, and the courts—charged with the exemplification and protection of that order.[7] Equally important, the connection with Britain also served the colonies as a source

---

[5] John Locke, *Two Treatises of Government,* ed. Peter Laslett (Cambridge, Eng., 1960), 462–63.

[6] The Declaration of Independence, July 4, 1776, reprinted in Jack P. Greene, ed., *Colonies to Nation, 1763–1789: A Documentary History of the American Revolution* (New York, 1975), 298–301.

[7] Edward Shils, "Centre and Periphery," in *The Logic of Personal Knowledge: Essays Presented to Michael Polanyi* (Glencoe, Ill., 1961), 117–24.

of pride and self-esteem, as Barnard's exclamations so clearly under-
score. To have even a small share in the achievements of Britain during
the eighteenth century—in the internal civil achievements exemplified
by the establishment of an orderly government that permitted extensive
individual liberty following the Glorious Revolution and in the external
achievements represented by the enormous expansion of foreign trade
and the victory over the French and Spanish in the Seven Years' War—
was an exhilarating experience that heightened British patriotism in the
colonies and strengthened still further the psychological bonds between
the colonists and Britain. Unlike most modern empires, then, the British
Empire, at least as it existed before 1760, was held together not by force
or by overwhelming coercive powers—indeed, Britain's coercive powers
in the colonies before the Seven Years' War were notoriously weak—but
by the voluntary attachment of the colonists, an attachment rooted in
strong ties of habit, interest, and, more importantly, affection.

Of course, this voluntary attachment of the colonists to Britain depended to a large extent, we can now see, upon a set of implicit expectations about metropolitan behavior toward the colonies. These expectations proceeded from the assumption that it was the moral obligation of
the mother country to provide nurturance and protection for the colonies. What nurturance and protection had come to mean to the colonists
can be briefly summarized: first, that the metropolitan government
would interfere as little as possible with their ability to pursue whatever
purposeful economic activities seemed to them to be in their best interest; second, that it would respect the sanctity of the local self-governing
institutions on which the colonists depended for the immediate protection of the property they had acquired as a result of those activities; and,
third, that in its dealings with the colonies it would continue to manifest
respect for all of those central imperatives of Anglo-American political
culture that were thought by Englishmen everywhere to be essential for
the preservation of liberty and property.[8]

Once we understand the nature and power of the bonds that tied the
colonies to Britain, we can see more clearly why it took so long for those
bonds to become sufficiently weak to permit the colonists to seek to sever
them altogether. In most explanations of the American Revolution, two
events—the Seven Years' War and the Stamp Act crisis—are justifiably
accorded a position of prominence. For eight years before the war—from
the end of the previous war in 1748, to be precise—metropolitan officials

---

[8] For an elaboration of these points, see Greene, "An Uneasy Connection," 53–62.

had been systematically trying to reinforce British political authority in the colonies. The simultaneous eruption of severe political disturbances in several colonies during the late 1740s and early 1750s activated deep-seated—and during these years often reiterated—fears in Britain that the colonies might, if not immediately restrained, eventually become independent.

The response of the British government was to seek to tighten metropolitan controls at every possible point. Operating primarily through executive orders, British officials moved to place colonial governors under very close restraints, subjected colonial legislation to a more thorough scrutiny than they had for many decades, and, through a variety of expedients, sought to achieve some balance of political power in the colonies by curtailing the authority of the colonial lower houses of assembly, the elected bodies which had been nibbling away at the prerogatives of royal and proprietary governors for over a century. By the mid-1750s, it had become clear that these efforts were only minimally effective, and an increasing number of British officials had become persuaded that Parliament itself would have to intervene before British authority in the colonies could be adequately restored.

But the need for colonial support against the French and Spanish during the Seven Years' War forced British officials to abandon this tougher policy beginning in 1755–56, and colonial behavior during the war only increased the conviction in London that British authority in the colonies was dangerously weak and in need of considerable augmentation. Throughout the war, aggressive lower houses openly used Britain's need for defense funds to pry still more power away from governors; many colonial traders flagrantly violated British trade laws by carrying on direct commerce with the enemy and avoiding the payment of duties, in many cases with the implicit connivance of the colonial governments and even of metropolitan customs officials; and many of the colonial legislatures failed to comply with metropolitan requisitions for men and money for the war effort, even with the promise of partial reimbursement of their expenses by Parliament.

The war experience thus reinforced London's preexisting fears of loss of control over the colonies. It deepened suspicions that the colonists harbored secret desires for independence and intensified the determination among people in power in Britain to overhaul the imperial system. As soon as the British and colonial armies had defeated the French in Canada in 1759–60 and colonial support for the war effort was no longer vital, London authorities undertook a variety of new restrictive measures to bolster metropolitan authority over the colonies.[9] The impulse behind these measures was not new. The shift from a permissive to a restrictive policy, from the traditional reliance upon the colonists' affections and allegiance to Britain to a dependence upon the threat of coercion to keep the colonies bound closely to Britain, had already occurred during the critical years from 1748 to 1756. The new measures of 1759 to 1764 were merely a renewal and an extension of that earlier reform program.

But—and this is the importance of the Seven Years' War for the origins of the American Revolution—they were an extension within a significantly different—and far more fragile—context. The war had been a psychologically liberating and reinforcing experience for the colonists. That so much of the war was fought on American soil and that the British government made such an enormous effort to defend the colonies gave rise to an expanded sense of colonial self-importance. Moreover, the colonists had contributed a substantial amount of money and a significant number of men to the war effort. Virginia and Massachusetts, the two colonies that subsequently took the lead in the resistance, in particular had, in terms of liquid resources, virtually bankrupted themselves in voting men and money for the war. As the Massachusetts pamphleteer Oxenbridge Thacher later protested, the colonies had "been guilty of no undutiful behavior towards" Britain "but on the contrary have greatly increased her wealth and grandeur and in the . . . [Seven Years'] war" had "impoverished themselves in fighting her battles."[10]

For the colonists, the knowledge that they had made such an important contribution to so great a national cause increased the immediacy and the strength of their ties with Britain. The war thus produced a surge of British patriotism among the colonists and created among them heightened expectations for a larger role within the empire, a role that would raise the status of the colonies from dependence upon to at least a nearer equivalence with the mother country.[11] By contrast, the war left British officials with feelings of bitterness and resentment toward the colonists and a determination to put them in a proper state of dependence. Having incurred an enormous debt and a heavy tax burden in

[9] See, especially, Bernhard Knollenberg, *Origin of the American Revolution, 1759–1766* (New York, 1960).

[10] [Oxenbridge Thacher], *Sentiments of a British American* (Boston, 1764), as quoted by Edwin G. Burrows and Michael Wallace, "The American Revolution: The Ideology and Psychology of National Liberation," *Perspectives in American History* 66 (1971): 191–92.

[11] See Richard Koebner, *Empire* (Cambridge, Eng., 1961), 105–65.

defense of the colonies and having had exaggerated reports of American opulence and low taxes, they regarded colonial smuggling, failures to comply with royal requests for defense funds, and other examples of non-compliance with metropolitan regulations during the war as evidence of extreme ingratitude that verged on disloyalty. Such recalcitrant behavior, London officials feared, might eventually rob Britain of the large investment it had made in protecting and securing the colonies during the war.

If the experience of the war caused the postwar expectations of people on opposite sides of the Atlantic to veer off in such sharply different directions, the war itself altered the very structure of the relationship between Britain and the colonies. The expulsion of the French and Spanish from eastern North America removed the need for the last essential material benefit the British had to offer the mainland colonies—protection against the French and Spanish—and thereby presumably eliminated a major, if by no means the most powerful, block that had helped to keep whatever fantasies the colonists may have had about equivalence and independence unarticulated.[12] Far more importantly, by destroying French power in North America and thus making it less necessary to pacify the colonists, the British victory left subsequent British governments with a much freer hand to go ahead with their program of colonial reform. Moreover, for the first time, during and after the war, the British had a large number of royal troops in the colonies, 7,500 men in all.[13] By giving them an excessive confidence in their ability to suppress potential colonial opposition, the presence of these troops seems to have made British ministers less cautious and less conciliatory in dealing with the colonies than they had been a decade earlier.

In combination, these psychological consequences and structural changes produced by the war made the relationship between Britain and the colonies much more volatile than it had been earlier. The colonists now had heightened expectations about their position in the empire and less need for Britain's protection, while British officials were bitter about colonial behavior during the war, more determined than ever to bring the colonies under closer control, persuaded that they would have to use the authority of Parliament to do so, and possessed of an army to back them up if it should be needed. Given this set of converging conditions, it was highly predictable that British officials in the 1760s would take

---

[12] See Lawrence Henry Gipson, "The American Revolution as an Aftermath of the Great War for Empire, 1754–1763," *Political Science Quarterly* 65 (1950): 86–104.

[13] Knollenberg, *Origin of the American Revolution*, 87.

some action, probably even by bringing parliamentary authority to bear upon the colonies in new, unaccustomed, and hence, for the colonists, illegitimate ways that the colonists would interpret as a fundamental violation of the existing relationship between themselves and Great Britain.

The colonial program of George Grenville did precisely that, and therein lies its principal importance for any understanding of the causes of the American Revolution. In 1763 and 1764, the American Revenue Act and various associated reforms sought to tighten British control over colonial shipping, curtail colonial smuggling, raise a revenue from American trade, and restrict colonial control over internal fiscal policy and western lands. In 1765, the Stamp Act threatened the colonies with still additional taxation. Direct parliamentary taxation of the colonies was unprecedented, and this quick succession of measures seemed to the colonists to be an intolerable breach of traditional relationships within the empire. Along with the severe political crisis produced in the colonies by the Stamp Act, the Grenville measures did in fact profoundly alter the quality and character of metropolitan-colonial relations.

The first of the metropolitan reform measures to affect equally all of the colonies at once, the Stamp Act forced the colonists to identify more fully than ever before some of the major ambiguities and sources of strain within the metropolitan-colonial relationship as it had existed in the past. From the new perspective supplied by the Grenville program, they began to redefine their situation in a way that permitted them to interpret as grievances things that had previously gone unremarked and to perceive components of the earlier ad hoc metropolitan reform programs between 1748 and 1756 and between 1759 and 1764 as parts of a comprehensive assault upon the existing order that had been in progress for some time. This new perspective made the colonists hypersensitive to any subsequent violations or seeming violations of the existing order as they understood it.[14] The Stamp Act thus mobilized significant opposition in the colonies to Britain for the first time, and, even more important, opposition on the basis of a new definition of the colonial situation vis-à-vis recent British behavior. Morever, because the Stamp Act could be interpreted as at least a partial withdrawal of affection by the parent state, it permitted the colonists to articulate whatever preexisting hostile feelings they may have had toward Britain and thereby to legitimate aggressive actions against the metropolitan government. By

---

[14] On this point, see Bernard Bailyn, *The Ideological Origins of the American Revolution* (Cambridge, Mass., 1967), 60–85.

thus weakening the ties of affection and allegiance the colonists had traditionally felt for Britain, the crisis over the Stamp Act began a process
of erosion, or what some political scientists have referred to as desacralization, of the traditional moral order within the old British Empire.[15]

For British political leaders, on the other hand, the intensity of colonial opposition to the Stamp Act only confirmed their long-standing suspicions that the colonists wanted nothing more than "to throw off all
dependance and subjection."[16] The Stamp Act, declared Lord Sandwich,
was "not the Object of their Sedition but to try their ground whether by
Resistance they can get themselves loose from other Acts more disagreeable and detrimental to them." "The Americans," it appeared clearly,
wanted "to get loose from the Act of Navigation" and all metropolitan
political restraint.[17] How else could a community that was committed to
the beliefs that Parliament was omnipotent and sovereignty indivisible
interpret such an outrageous challenge to parliamentary authority? The
consequences of such a development were almost too abhorrent to con-
template. Separation of the colonies would inevitably mean, many
people thought, that Britain would "dwindle and decline every day in
our trade, whilst . . . [the colonists] thrive and prosper exceedingly," so
that Britons would "run away as fast as they can from this country to
that, and Old England" would "become a poor, deserted, deplorable
kingdom."[18] Thus reduced to impotence and robbed of its power by its
own children, Britain would ultimately "be Conquered in America & become a Province to her own Colonies."[19] Clearly, metropolitan authorities
had been right in the impulse that had animated them since 1748: the
colonies had to be brought under tighter control, metropolitan political
authority had to be firmly and fully established.

The Grenville program and the Stamp Act crisis thus put a further
strain upon a relationship already rendered fragile by the experience of

---

[15] The impact of the Stamp Act crisis is examined in Edmund S. Morgan and Helen M.
Morgan, *The Stamp Act Crisis: Prologue to Revolution* (Chapel Hill, N.C., 1953).

[16] "Anti-Sejanus" to *London Chronicle*, Nov. 28–30, 1765, in Edmund S. Morgan, ed.,
Prologue to Revolution: Sources and Documents on the Stamp Act Crisis, 1764–1766
(Chapel Hill, N.C., 1959), 100.

[17] Quoted by Bernhard Knollenberg, *The Growth of the American Revolution, 1766–1775*
(New York, 1975), 24.

[18] "John Plowshare" to *London Chronicle*, Feb. 20, 1766, and "Anti-Sejanus" to *London
Chronicle*, Jan. 23, 1766, in Morgan, *Prologue to Revolution*, 103, 131.

[19] Lord Northington's statement in the House of Lords, Dec. 17, 1765, as quoted by Knollenberg, *Growth of the American Revolution*, 17.

the Seven Years' War and the metropolitan reform programs of 1748–56 and 1759–63. They combined to push the colonies into what modern systems theorists would call a *dysfunctional situation*, that is, one highly susceptible to disruption, breakdown, and malfunction. But a dysfunctional situation, however fragile, is not yet a *revolutionary situation*. The important analytical, and substantive, difference between a dysfunctional and a revolutionary situation—and the reason why the situation in the colonies did not become a revolutionary one for another nine years—was the presence of certain important deterrents, deterrents with sufficient power to forestall the complete breakdown of the imperial system, the emergence of a massive armed resistance, or even the development of a revolutionary movement bent upon changing the existing political order. Over the whole period from the repeal of the Stamp Act in 1766 until the outbreak of war at Lexington and Concord in April 1775, there were at least seven such deterrents.

First, and least important, was fear among colonial political leaders of loss of internal political control should British authority be removed. "We think ourselves happier . . . in being dependent on Great Britain, than in a state of independence," said an anonymous writer in the *New York Mercury* in 1764, "for then the disputes amongst ourselves would throw us into all the confusion, and bring on us all the calamities usually attendant on civil wars."[20] And, as Oliver Delancy of New York wrote his sister in England during the Stamp Act crisis, "should such unhappy Times come," the colonial elite would be extremely vulnerable to "the Ravages of the Populace" and "all [social] Distinction" would "then be lost . . . in such a scene of Confusion and Distress."[21]

How many people held such fears is not clear. Certainly, the willingness of many traditional political leaders to bring seamen, tradesmen, and laborers into their protest against the Stamp Act and later measures suggests not a fear of the populace but an extraordinary—if, as we now know, somewhat misplaced—confidence in their ability to manipulate and control it. Yet the intensity of the Stamp Act riots—especially the sacking of Lieutenant Governor Thomas Hutchinson's house in Massachusetts and similar actions in some other colonies—did give the colonial political elite concrete reasons to fear the uncontrolled wrath of an

---

[20] *New York Mercury*, Aug. 27, 1764, as quoted by Burrows and Wallace, "American Revolution," 191.

[21] Oliver Delancy to Lady Susannah Warren, Jan. 10, 1766, Peter Warren Papers, G/Am/ 84, East Sussex Record Office, Lewes, Eng.

aroused mob, reasons which were reinforced by some incidents between 1767 and 1770 during the crisis over the Townshend Acts.[22]

A corollary of this fear of loss of internal political control and a second deterrent was a manifest lack of confidence in the colonists' ability to fend for themselves in a hostile world. "Exposed by our situation, by a rivalship and competition of Interests, and yet in a state of infancy," said Joseph Reed in 1766, "it would be extremely difficult, if not impossible, to form any Union among ourselves that would be sufficient to repel the attacks of a formidable invader." Thus "to throw off all dependence on the mother country" would only be to "put themselves in the situation of a silly girl, who leaves the guidance and protection of a wise and affectionate parent, and wandering away exposes herself to ruin by the artful insinuations of every wicked and designing stranger."[23]

As the remarks of Governor Pownall quoted earlier illustrate, it was a widespread belief that the colonies were too disunited and too immature to make it on their own and that independence from Britain would necessarily mean something far worse: domination by France, Spain, or the Netherlands, all of which had established records of permitting their colonies vastly less freedom—in both the political and economic spheres—than that allowed to the colonies by the British. And, given the vaunted disunion of the colonies, the best that could be hoped for, as John Dickinson, the famous Pennsylvania farmer, wrote to William Pitt, was "a multitude of Commonwealths, Crimes and Calamities—centuries of mutual Jealousies, Hatreds, Wars and Devastations, till at last the exhausted Provinces shall sink into Slavery under the yoke of some fortunate conqueror."[24]

A third and related deterrent was a deeply rooted fear of—and aversion to—republicanism as a form of government. The colonists, like Britons generally, had unhappy memories of the chaotic republican experiments in England during the English Revolution of 1640–60, and, as both Thomas Pownall's and Thomas Barnard's remarks indicated, they were deeply attached to the British variant of monarchical government. Moreover, eighteenth-century political theorists believed almost universally that re-

---

[22] See also Merrill Jensen, "The American People and the American Revolution," *Journal of American History* 57 (1970): 5–35.

[23] Joseph Reed, *Four Dissertations on the Reciprocal Advantages of Perpetual Union between Great Britain and Her American Colonies* (Philadelphia, 1766), 108.

[24] John Dickinson to William Pitt, Dec. 21, 1765, Chatham Papers, PRO 30/8/97, Public Record Office, London.

publicanism was suitable only for very small political units like Geneva or Venice or the United Provinces of the Netherlands. However republican American societies might appear to contemporary Englishmen,[25] republicanism, the only possible form of government for the colonies should they become independent, was, if not a frightening prospect, certainly by no means an attractive one for virtually any colonial political leaders.[26] "A republican form of government," as one American loyalist categorically declared, "would neither suit the genius of the people, nor the extent of America."[27]

The fourth deterrent was fear of British coercive power. The colonists had always had a healthy respect for British power, but such respect could only have been increased by the new military and naval presence in the colonies after 1756, a presence that for the first time in the continental colonies gave the British government significant coercive powers. How could the colonies, weak in liquid economic resources, the very sinews of war, have any chance at all against such a mighty power? Clearly, for them to enter into martial combat with Britain would only be to court "Devastation and ruin."[28]

A fifth deterrent was the lack of political institutions capable of mounting and sustaining any generalized resistance movement. The disunion of the British continental colonies was notorious. In most cases, the connection of individual colonies with Britain was far more direct than it was with any other colony. The local lower houses of assembly in each colony could— and did—supply some leadership in any protest movement, but they could be—and were—frequently dissolved or not summoned at all because they depended for their legal authority upon some metropolitan charter or upon the governor's royal commissions. More importantly, perhaps, there was no central governing institution capable of providing the leadership necessary for a successful general opposition movement.

---

[25] See, for instance, the remarks of William Knox in Jack P. Greene, ed., "William Knox's Explanation for the American Revolution," *William and Mary Quarterly*, 3d ser., 30 (1973): 293–306.

[26] See W. Paul Adams, "Republicanism in Political Rhetoric before 1776," *Political Science Quarterly* 85 (1970): 397–421; and Jack P. Greene, "The Preconditions for American Republicanism: A Comment," in Library of Congress, First Symposium on the American Revolution, *The Development of a Revolutionary Mentality: Papers* (Washington, D.C., 1972), 119–24.

[27] Charles Inglis, *An American: The True Interest of America Impartially Stated* (Philadelphia, 1776), reprinted in Leslie F. S. Upton, ed., *Revolutionary versus Loyalist: The First American Civil War, 1774–1784* (Waltham, Mass., 1968), 76.

[28] Ibid., 75.

A sixth deterrent was what might best be called the British penchant for compromise, for finding a political solution to fundamental issues of conflict in the public sphere. The repeal of the Stamp Act in 1766 and the removal of all the Townshend duties except for a token tax on tea in 1770 were classic examples of the operation of this penchant. Both of these actions removed the major sources of immediate contention and ignored the basic issues in dispute. In their relations with the colonies over the previous century, metropolitan authorities had repeatedly adopted this mode to the immediate mutual satisfaction and advantage of the parties concerned. The continued willingness of British officials to eschew the search for a final solution about such questions as Parliament's authority over the colonies in return for the immediate advantage of political tranquillity and the continuing economic benefits derived from the colonies was always, as colonial behavior during the quiet period that obtained between repeal of the Townshend duties in 1770 and the renewal of contention in 1773 so powerfully attests, a strong deterrent to revolution and a necessary precondition for the continued viability of the empire.

The seventh, last, and by far most important deterrent was the continuing power of the habitual ties of allegiance and affection felt for Britain by the colonists and the colonists' deep psychological dependence upon Britain. Sustained by the widespread illusion that the colonies had a large reservoir of political support in Britain, an illusion rooted in a fundamental misreading of both the motives behind ministerial and parliamentary support for yielding to American demands during the Stamp Act and Townshend Acts crises and the influence of Wilkeite radicals and other pro-American groups in British political life,[29] those ties and that dependence were so strong—the residue of affection was so large— as to prevent most colonists, even in the face of a long chain of what they interpreted as serious violations of the traditional relationship between 1764 and 1774, from permitting any unconscious fantasies they may have had about equivalence and independence to become conscious wishes or goals and from allowing their resentment of British official behavior to become so great as to cause them to reject their connection with Britain.

The continuing force of these deterrents explains why the Revolution

---

[29] See Pauline Maier, *From Resistance to Revolution: Colonial Radicals and the Development of American Opposition to Britain, 1765–1775* (New York, 1972); and Jack P. Greene, "The Alienation of Benjamin Franklin—British American," *Journal of the Royal Society of Arts* 124 (1976): 52–73 [chap. 11 below].

did not occur earlier; to explain why the Revolution occurred when it did requires an examination of how these extraordinarily powerful deterrents were sufficiently weakened as to give so many colonists the heart and the nerve to rebel. A number of interrelated developments, first in the period between the repeal of the Stamp Act in 1766 and the passage of the Coercive Acts in early 1774 and then in the crucial period between the end of the First Continental Congress in the fall of 1774 and the Declaration of Independence in July 1776, are relevant to a consideration of this question.

A development of major importance in the earlier period was the gradual deflation of British power in the colonies as illustrated by the successful colonial defiance of, first, the Townshend measures, then, the Tea Act and, finally, the Coercive Acts themselves. The ability of the colonies to defy these measures and, what is more important, the inability of British officials in the colonies to enforce them helped to weaken colonial respect for British coercive power and to encourage the suspicion that it might be successfully defied. On the other side, successful colonial defiance of parliamentary measures left the British government with three clear choices. First, it might in the traditional manner seek to allay colonial opposition by making minor policy concessions. This is the course it followed to put an end both to the Stamp Act and to the Townshend Acts crises. Second, and this choice was the one colonial leaders were demanding, it might undertake some structural rearrangements in the direction of increased colonial autonomy specifically designed to remove all long-term causes of colonial discontent. Third, it could remain essentially intransigent and seek to enforce its will by force.

Assuming that it could be successfully implemented, either the second or the third choice had the attraction of promising to put an end to the now seemingly perpetual discord between Britain and the colonies. But the second choice was never a legitimate option for the British political nation. It would have required not merely some conservative changes in institutional structure; it would also have required the acceptance of some form of multisovereignty within the empire, an arrangement that was unacceptable to the British government and had no support whatever within the British political nation, being at direct variance with the basic British beliefs that sovereignty was indivisible and the authority of Parliament absolute.[30]

---

[30] The crucially limiting importance of these beliefs is considered in Jack P. Greene, "The Plunge of Lemmings: A Consideration of Recent Writings on British Politics and the American Revolution," *South Atlantic Quarterly* 67 (1968): 141–75.

The more Americans seemed to challenge these two beliefs—and they did so explicitly throughout the last half of 1774—the more tightly the British clung to them; the more fearful the British became of colonial independence, of the loss of control over the colonies, and of the economic benefits they derived from the colonies, the less viable the first choice—that of making further political concessions—seemed to be, and the more the British were pulled toward the third alternative of seeking a resolution to the controversy by enforcing British authority in the colonies at whatever cost. This was the course they adopted in rejecting Congress's appeals to remove the Coercive Acts. They were the more easily pulled in this direction by the general belief that the colonists could neither sustain a unified resistance—had not the nonimportation movements of 1768–70 collapsed as public spirit had yielded to private interests?—nor put up an effective defense, a belief that was rooted in and reinforced by a deep, almost xenophobic contempt for the colonists' martial capabilities.

A second development of importance in weakening the many deterrents to revolution in the colonies was the increasing politicization of the colonies around a central focus of opposition to British policy. The controversy with Britain tended to draw an increasing number of people into political activity. The traditional elite was at the forefront, as the most anglicized sector of the colonial population and presumably the most sensitive to metropolitan violations of traditional British values. But most other segments of the population were recruited relatively easily, partly because British moral authority had presumably lost strength in the colonies over time and partly because—for reasons of ideology, habit, and, in some cases, interest—they were accustomed to following the lead of the elite.[31]

Corollaries of this process of political mobilization were, first, the opening up of new career opportunities in politics and the attachment of higher status to political activity (in the great crisis after 1765 the road to fame was in the political arena rather than in religion or economic life);[32] second, heightened political sensibilities throughout the politically

---

[31] This is not however to imply that the aims and motives of all opposition elements were the same.

[32] In this connection, see Edmund S. Morgan, "The American Revolution Considered as an Intellectual Movement," in Arthur M. Schlesinger, Jr., and Morton White, eds., *Paths of American Thought* (Boston, 1963), 11–33; and Douglass Adair, "Fame and the Founding Fathers," in Edmund P. Willis, ed., *Fame and the Founding Fathers: Papers and Comments* (Bethlehem, Pa., 1967), 27–52.

relevant segments of society; and third, the fixing of the attention of a broad spectrum of colonial society firmly upon political questions involving the relationship between Britain and the colonies.[33] A final aspect of this increased politicization of colonial society was the routinization of collective violence to achieve political objectives. Each new crisis produced a greater recourse to extralegal force, the burning of the British revenue cutter *Gaspee* in Rhode Island in 1772 and the Boston Tea Party in 1773 being only the most dramatic examples.[34] Very importantly, however, these extralegal and crowd actions were sufficiently controlled as to give the colonists increasing confidence in their capacity to govern themselves and to help persuade many colonial leaders that the removal of British authority would not necessarily lead to anarchy.

A third and related development—one that was critical in driving British authorities toward a less moderate stand—was the alienation of the overseas trading merchants, the colonists' main allies in Britain, by the adoption of agreements not to import goods from or export products to Britain, first at the time of the Townshend Acts and again in response to the Coercive Acts. "The Americans have by this Measure lost many valuable Friends," wrote the Bristol merchant Richard Champion to a South Carolina correspondent in 1770. America, he said, "should have levelled her Resentment upon Administration, who really oppressed her, and not upon the Commercial and Manufacturing part of the Kingdom, who were always her best Friends."[35]

But by far the most important development was what might be called the gradual desacralization of the customary moral order, always the primary binding force between Britain and the colonies. This process was especially evident in the rapid spread and intensification of a generalized belief in the evil intentions of men in power in Britain and in the corruption of the central governing institutions of the empire. Such "a series of

---

[33] On this process of political mobilization, see R. A. Ryerson, "Political Mobilization and the American Revolution: The Resistance Movement in Philadelphia, 1765–1775," *William and Mary Quarterly*, 3d ser., 31 (1974): 565–88; Pauline Maier, "The Charleston Mob and the Evolution of Popular Politics in Revolutionary South Carolina, 1765–1784," *Perspectives in American History* 4 (1970): 173–96; and Jesse Lemisch, "Jack Tar in the Streets: Merchant Seamen in the Politics of Revolutionary America," *William and Mary Quarterly*, 3d ser., 25 (1968): 371–407.

[34] See Richard Maxwell Brown, "Violence and the American Revolution," in Kurtz and Hutson, *Essays on the American Revolution*, 81–120.

[35] Richard Champion to Caleb Lloyd, Nov. 1770, in *The American Correspondence of a Bristol Merchant, 1766–1776: Letters of Richard Champion*, ed. G. H. Guttridge (Berkeley, Calif., 1934), 22.

oppressions" as the British government had since the early 1760s "pursued unalterably through every change of ministers," declared Jefferson in the summer of 1774, "too plainly proved a deliberate and systematical plan of reducing us to slavery."[36] Through the end of 1774, however, the process was still incomplete. The colonists had moved from a belief in ministerial conspiracy to a conviction that Parliament was also corrupt. But they retained a great amount of respect for the king and for the essential justice and virtue of the British people.

The growing belief in ministerial and parliamentary corruption had, however, permitted a gradual lapse of the repressions that had previously prevented the articulation and internalization of aggressive feelings toward Britain. Moreover, during the crisis over the Townshend Acts and after, colonial leaders came to see resistance to British corruption as the best way to purge colonial society of its own inner stains as they were becoming disturbingly manifest in excessive consumerism and self-oriented behavior. They envisioned self-denial—through the non-consumption of British goods—as the best possible way of recalling the colonists to the industrious, frugal, and virtuous ways of their ancestors. They thus explicitly coupled opposition to Britain and the purification of colonial society.[37]

Each of these developments—the deflation of British power with a growing predisposition to use force to seek a final resolution of the colonial problem, the increasing politicization of the colonies, the alienation of the colonists' primary friends in Britain, and the gradual desacralization of the customary and binding moral order—helped to undermine the main deterrents to revolution between 1766 and 1774. But it was only as a result of the crisis engendered by the Tea Act of 1773, the colonial response to it, and the Coercive Acts of 1774 that those deterrents were sufficiently weakened to convert the highly fragile or dysfunctional situation into a potentially revolutionary one. There were several critical developments in this process.

First, from the colonial point of view, the Coercive Acts themselves

---

[36] Thomas Jefferson, "A Summary View of the Rights of British America," Aug. 1774, in Greene, *Colonies to Nation*, 231.

[37] This theme is developed in Jack P. Greene, "Search for Identity: An Interpretation of the Meaning of Selected Patterns of Social Reponse in Eighteenth-Century America," *Journal of Social History* 3 (1970): 189–220; Edmund S. Morgan, "The Puritan Ethic and the American Revolution," *William and Mary Quarterly*, 3d ser., 24 (1967): 3–41; Perry Miller, "From the Covenant to the Revival," in James Ward Smith and A. Leland Jamison, eds., *The Shaping of American Religion*, 3 vols. (Princeton, N. J., 1961), 1:322–50.

and the chain of events that followed could be—and were—interpreted as new and fundamental violations of the customary moral order that bound the colonies to Britain. Such blatant violations were those measures that they seemed to leave no doubt, as Ebenezer Baldwin, Congregational pastor at Danbury, Connecticut, declared, that the British ministry was indeed pursuing that "settled fixed plan . . . for *inslaving* the colonies" that many colonists had come more and more to suspect over the previous decade had been at the root of their difficulties with the metropolitan government. This growing conviction that submission would lead to "a state of abject slavery"[38] gave rise not only to a broadly diffused determination to resist the Coercive Acts even if it meant taking up arms—a completely new level of militancy that was signified and given semiofficial sanction with the adoption in September 1774 by the First Continental Congress of the Suffolk Resolutions advising the inhabitants of beleaguered Massachusetts to arm themselves.

This conviction also resulted in a sharply articulated and widely generalized belief among a large segment of the colonial political community that fundamental changes in the traditional structure of the empire were absolutely necessary if the colonists were ever to be secure in their liberty, property, and fundamental life goals. As North Carolina instructed its delegates to the First Continental Congress, the colonists required not only the removal of existing grievances but a clear statement "*with certainty*" of "the rights of Americans"[39] and, said the Rhode Island instructions, "proper measures . . . to establish" those "rights and liberties of the Colonies, upon a just and solid foundation."[40] For only when that was done, experience from the perspective of the many "assaults upon American liberty" over the last decade seemed to indicate, would the colonists have that security of liberty and property that was the indispensable precondition for the restoration, in the words of the New Hampshire credentials, of "that peace, harmony, [and] mutual confi-

[38] Ebenezer Baldwin, "An Appendix Stating the Heavy Grievances the Colonies Labor Under . . . ," Aug. 31, 1774, in Greene, *Colonies to Nation*, 213, 217.

[39] See David Ammerman, *In the Common Cause: American Response to the Coercive Acts of 1774* (Charlottesville, Va., 1974). The quotation is from the North Carolina Instructions, Aug. 25, 1774, in Jack P. Greene, ed., "The First Continental Congress: A Documentary History," in U.S. Congress, House, *Commemoration Ceremony in Honor of the Two Hundredth Anniversary of the First Continental Congress,* 93d Cong., 2d sess., H. Doc. 93-413 (Washington, D. C., 1975), 86.

[40] Rhode Island Instructions, Aug. 14, 1774, in Greene, "The First Continental Congress," 80.

dence which once happily subsisted between the parent country and her Colonies."[41]

Nor was this a parochial matter. At issue, said Eliphalet Dyer, a Connecticut delegate to the Congress, was nothing less than "the liberties of the West Indies and of the people of Great Britain, as well as our own, and perhaps of Europe."[42] The stakes could scarcely have been higher, nor the determination not to give in until proper safeguards had been achieved, greater.

Escalating militancy in the colonies was met by mounting intransigence in Britain, where the extremity of the colonial position cost the colonists most of their remaining friends in British political life. Temporizing in the face of such a blatant challenge to British authority, British leaders believed, would only mean the certain loss of the colonies—the very outcome that so many Britons had all along feared and, in their effort to avoid, set in motion the long chain of actions so objectionable to Americans; and the loss of the colonies, most British writers thought despite demurs from economists like Adam Smith and Josiah Tucker, could only mean that Britain would "sink for want of trade" as "a new empire America controuls all Europe."[43] Such fears were behind the fateful decision by metropolitan authorities in late 1774 and early 1775 to use force if necessary to secure colonial obedience to parliamentary authority.

More than anything else, however, the actual use of force beginning at Lexington and Concord and the subsequent clash of arms completed the destruction of British moral authority in the colonies. It encouraged the expression of previously repressed and unacceptable militant feelings toward Britain—so evident in the bitter outpourings against Britain and in the hostile treatment of those colonists who could not or did not oppose Britain—as well as thitherto unarticulated fantasies about independence, which were brought into the open following publication of Thomas Paine's *Common Sense* in early 1776.[44] Once expressed, these aggressions and fantasies formed a new basis for the evaluation of the traditional metropolitan-colonial relationship, an evaluation that permitted

---

[41] New Hampshire Instructions, July 21, 1774, ibid., 79.

[42] John Adams, Notes on Debates, Sept. 26–27, 1774, ibid., 101.

[43] Thomas Falconer to Charles Gray, May 17, 1766, Gray-Round Archives, D/DRg 4/14, Essex Record Office, Chelmsford, Eng.

[44] See Winthrop D. Jordan, "Familial Politics: Thomas Paine and the Killing of the King, 1776," *Journal of American History* 60 (1973): 294–308; Burrows and Wallace, "American Revolution," 268–94.

the consideration of what had previously been impossible to consider: the desirability of monarchy and of the connection with Britain. Once these previously illegitimate ideas had been rendered legitimate by the collapse of British moral authority in the colonies and the conversion of colonial affection for Britain into total dislike during the summer and fall of 1775, the colonists found themselves, for the first time, in a genuinely revolutionary situation.

If the collapse of British moral authority and the consequent alienation of colonial affections removed the inhibitors that had kept the controversy from advancing into a revolutionary state, other developments during 1774 and 1775 removed still other deterrents. To begin with, the course of the war during its first year helped to encourage the colonists in the belief that they might successfully oppose the coercive might of Great Britain as long as they held together, a belief reinforced by the vastness of their combined territory, the consequent difficulties of conquest, and the ever-increasing likelihood of assistance from France.

In addition, Congress supplied the colonies for the first time with an agency capable of directing and sustaining unified political resistance, while the provincial congresses at the colony level and the committees of safety at the local level provided them with local governing institutions not dependent for their legal authority upon Britain. These protorepublican institutions provided reasonably coordinated leadership of the resistance; more importantly, their successful functioning helped both to allay fears that the removal of British authority would lead to political collapse in the colonies and to demonstrate the viability of republican government.[45] In fact, the prospect of creating successful republican governments for the colonies came increasingly to be seen as a great and formidable challenge, a once-in-history opportunity that might serve as an example for the rest of mankind—who, said the British radical philosopher Dr. Richard Price, mostly still lived in "ignominious slavery"[46]— at the same time that it managed to restrain power and luxury and promote liberty and virtue in the colonies.

For a significant and respectable segment of Americans, of course, Britain continued to retain much of its old moral authority, British military and naval power its old awe, and the prospect of life without the

---

[45] Pauline Maier, "The Beginnings of American Republicanism, 1765–1775," in Library of Congress, First Symposium on the American Revolution, *Development of a Revolutionary Mentality: Papers*, 99–117.

[46] Dr. Richard Price, "Observations on the Importance of the American Revolution," Mar. 1784, in Greene, *Colonies to Nation*, 423.

superintending power of Britain its old fears. These were the antirevolutionaries or the nonrevolutionaries who found the prospect of independence, republicanism, and government under the leaders of colonial resistance far more frightening than the continuation of the traditional connection with Britain, albeit most of them believed with the First Continental Congress that that connection ought to be based on strict guarantees of American liberty and property.[47] For the leaders of the resistance, however, nothing could be more frightening than the prospect of a continued connection with a degenerate Britain unable to resist the tyrannical schemes of a power-hungry king and his minions in administration and Parliament.

The colonists had not come to this conclusion lightly or quickly. On the contrary, their course of behavior had been accurately predicted by John Locke in a paragraph following the one quoted earlier. "*Revolutions,*" said Locke,

> *happen* not upon every little mismanagement in publick affairs. *Great mistakes* in the ruling part, many wrong and inconvenient Laws, and all the *slips* of humane frailty will be *born by the People*, without mutiny or murmur. But if a long train of Abuses, Prevarications, and Artifices, all tending the same way, make the design visible to the People, and they cannot but feel, what they lie under, and see, whither they are going; 'tis not to be wonder'd, that they should rouze themselves, and endeavour to put the rule into such hands, which may secure to them the ends for which Government was at first erected; and without which, ancient Names, and specious Forms, are so far from being better, that they are much worse, than the state of Nature, or pure Anarchy; the inconveniences being all as great and as near, but the remedy farther off and more difficult.[48]

Just such a long train of apparent abuses primarily explained to colonial leaders of the resistance why they were justified, nay, compelled, to reject the old order and why they could take solace in their belief that the governments they would create would be the only remaining legitimate embodiments of what—and it was much—was worth preserving in that order.

---

[47] The most comprehensive treatment of these loyalists will be found in Robert McCluer Calhoon, *The Loyalists in Revolutionary America, 1760–1781* (New York, 1973), but see also Burrows and Wallace, "American Revolution," 295–99.

[48] Locke, *Two Treatises of Government,* 463–64.

Insofar as it is desirable or permissible to talk about the sufficient cause of any event so complex as the American Revolution, one would thus have to turn to the British effort at colonial reform beginning in 1748 and the long series of abuses that it represented to so many colonists. These "abuses" resulted in the slow erosion of British moral authority in the colonies, the gradual loss of confidence in Britain's capacity to provide satisfactory government for the colonies, and the tortured alienation of the strong affections the colonists had originally held for Britain—an alienation that itself ran so deep as to persuade the leaders of colonial resistance that not even the awesome power of Britain, the unhappy history of republican governments, their own notorious disunion, or the few remaining friends they had in Britain could deter them from seeking to break off all further connections.

Under the title "United Colonies and the Silent War: Americans Grow Militant," the first draft of this chapter was written for presentation on October 30, 1974, as a lecture at "Perspectives on the First Continental Congress: Forum Series," organized by Philadelphia '76, Inc., and held at Congress Hall, Philadelphia. In subsequent forms it was offered as a lecture many times during 1975 and 1976: at Old Dominion University, Norfolk, Virginia, February 3, 1975; as the Callahan Lecture at the University of West Virginia at the Jackson Mill Conference Center, Jackson Mill, March 21, 1975; at the State University of New York at Geneseo, September 23, 1975; at Connecticut College, New London, September 24, 1975; at Southeast Missouri State University, Cape Girardeau, October 1, 1975; at Oregon State University, Corvallis, October 2, 1975; at the University of Copenhagen, Denmark, November 28, 1975; at the Institute of General History, Soviet Academy of Social Science, Moscow, USSR, January 12, 1976; at the History Department, Moscow State University, USSR, January 14, 1976; at the American Library, Bucharest, Romania, January 16, 1976; at the University of Warwick, Coventry, England, January 22, 1976; at Southampton University, England, January 30, 1976; at the University of Nottingham, England, February 12, 1976; at the University of Sussex, Brighton, England, February 26, 1976; at the University of Newcastle-upon-Tyne, England, March 8, 1976; at Durham University, England, March 9, 1976; at the American Studies Weekend Conference sponsored by the University of Wales at Gregynog, March 13, 1976; at East Carolina University, Greenville, North Carolina, March 30, 1976; at Holy Names College, Oakland, California, April 2, 1976; at the University of Edinburgh, Scotland, April 22, 1976; at the University of Paris I, France, April 26, 1976; at Queen's University, Belfast, Northern Ireland, May 3, 1976; at University College, Galway, Eire, May 5, 1976; at the Department of American Studies, Manchester University, England, May 13, 1976; at the University of York, England, May 20, 1976; at a Colloquium on the American Revolution, Institute for United States Studies, University of London, May 29, 1976; at a session on "Reinterpreting the Revolution," at the 7th Biennial Conference of the Australia and New Zealand American Studies Association, Monash University, Melbourne, Australia, August 18, 1976; at the Australian National University, Canberra, August 23, 1976; as the Carl L. Becker Memorial Lecture at the University of Northern Iowa, Cedar Falls, September 28, 1976; at the English Institute, University of Bergen, Norway, October 6, 1976; at the Historical Institute, University of Oslo, Norway, October 8, 1976; at the English Institute, University of Paris-Sorbonne, France, March 12, 1977; at the English Institute, University of Montpelier, France, March 17, 1977; and at the University of Lille, France, March 24, 1977. It is here reprinted with minor corrections and permission from George G. Suggs, Jr., ed., *Perspectives on the American Revolution: A Bicentennial Contribution* (Carbondale: Southern Illinois University Press, 1977), 51–73, 122–25.

—FIVE—

Origins of the
American Revolution:
A Constitutional Interpretation

FUNDAMENTALLY, the American Revolution was the unforeseen consequence of the inability of the disputants to agree upon the nature of the constitution of the British Empire. As the controversy over this question became more intense during the thirteen years between 1763 and 1776, many other issues came to the surface. But the constitutional question always remained at the core of the controversy. So significant was it that, if it could have been resolved, no revolution would have occurred in the mid-1770s. The debate over this question proceeded in three sequential phases in association with three distinct crises: the Stamp Act crisis in 1764–65, the long controversy initiated by the Townshend measures in 1767–72, and the final crisis of imperial authority and independence in 1773–76. How this debate unfolded and the divergent conceptions of the imperial constitution it produced are the primary subject of this chapter.

When the Seven Years' War ended in 1763, the only certainty about constitutional arrangements within the large extended polity that comprised the early modern British Empire was their ambiguity. There simply was no explicit definition of the balance of authority between the metropolis at the center and the colonies in the peripheries of the empire. Recurrent disputes over the extent of the crown's colonial authority throughout the previous century and a half had left that issue unresolved, while the nature of Parliament's relation to the colonies had never been explicitly examined. Parliament's efforts to impose revenue taxes on the colonies in the mid-1760s precipitated the first intensive and systematic exploration of this problem on either side of the Atlantic.

Ostensibly, the issue raised by these efforts, especially by the Stamp Act of 1765, was no more than whether, in the succinct words of Massachusetts governor Francis Bernard, "America shall or shall not be Subject to the Legislature of Great Britain." But the controversy rapidly moved on to a more general level. In the process, it provoked a broad-ranging consideration of fundamental issues involving the nature of the constitutional relationship between Britain and the colonies and the distribution of power within the empire. Far from producing either a theoretical or a practical resolution of these issues, however, the Stamp Act crisis of 1764–66 revealed a deep rift in understanding between metropolis and colonies, a rift that would never be bridged within the structure of the empire.[1]

Some metropolitan supporters later admitted that the Stamp Act was an innovation. For at least three decades, however, metropolitan officials had casually assumed that Parliament's colonial authority was unlimited. For over a century, moreover, Parliament had routinely laid duties upon colonial exports and imports for the purposes of regulating trade. But parliamentary legislation for the colonies had been confined almost entirely to commercial and other economic regulations of general scope. The only precedent for any other sort of tax was the Post Office Act of 1710, and revenue was not its primary objective. If, before the Stamp Act, there were no precedents for Parliament's taxing the colonies for revenue, neither had anyone explicitly articulated a theoretical justification for the exertion of parliamentary authority in that area.

The traditional link between taxation and representation in British constitutional thought and practice made this problem potentially troublesome—for metropolitans and colonials. Indeed, metropolitan disquiet over the problem was clearly revealed during the Stamp Act crisis by proposals from several writers for colonial representation in Parliament. More important, the Grenville administration itself implicitly acknowledged its importance in the months just before final passage of the Stamp Act, when, to justify taxing the colonists, it invented the doctrine that,

---

[1] Francis Bernard to Lord Barrington, Nov. 23, 1765, in *The Barrington-Bernard Correspondence*, ed. Edward Channing and Archibald Cary Coolidge (Cambridge, Mass., 1912), 96.

like the many residents of Britain who had no voice in elections, they were virtually represented in Parliament.

As soon as it was raised, the specter of parliamentary taxation produced enormous unease in the colonies. Arguing that it was unprecedented, colonial spokesmen insisted that no community of Englishmen and their descendants could be taxed without their consent, an exemption they claimed "as their Right" and not "as a *Privilege*." They dismissed the idea of virtual representation out of hand and argued that no legislature had any right to legislate for any people with whom it did not have a common interest and a direct connection. For people in the peripheries of an extended polity like that of the early modern British Empire, this emphasis upon the local foundations of legislative authority made sense. Whatever Parliament might declare, few colonists had any doubt that their rights as Englishmen demanded both that they be exempt from taxes levied in a distant metropolis without their consent and that their own local assemblies have an exclusive power to tax them.[2]

In analyzing the colonial response to the Stamp Act crisis, most scholars have tended to treat the colonists' claims as demands for their individual rights as Englishmen, as indeed they were. But this emphasis has tended to obscure the very important extent to which, especially during the Stamp Act crisis, the colonists seem to have believed that security of individual rights depended upon security of corporate rights, which they thought of as virtually synonymous with the rights of the provincial assemblies. Throughout the colonial period, the status and authority of the assemblies had been a prime subject of dispute between metropolitans and colonials. Whereas earlier the conflict had been between the assemblies and the crown, after 1765 it was between the assemblies and Parliament.

During the Stamp Act crisis, colonial spokesmen put enormous stress upon the traditional conception of their assemblies as the primary guardians of both the individual liberties of their constituents and the corporate rights of the colonies. Noting that it was precisely because their great distance from the metropolis had prevented them from being either fully incorporated into the British nation or represented in the metropolitan Parliament that their assemblies had been initally established, they insisted that each of their own local legislatures enjoyed full legislative

---

[2] New York Petititon to the House of Commons, Oct. 18, 1764, in Edmund S. Morgan, ed., *Prologue to Revolution: Sources and Documents on the Stamp Act Crisis, 1764–1766* (Chapel Hill, N. C., 1959), 9–10.

authority and exclusive power to tax within its respective jurisdiction. This identification of individual rights with the corporate rights of the assemblies ran through the entire colonial argument.

The colonists based their claims for exclusive taxing authority and exemption from parliamentary taxation on their rights as Englishmen, their royal charters, and, especially, long-standing custom. For over a century, they argued, they had "uniformly exercised and enjoyed the privileges of imposing and raising their own taxes, in their provincial assemblies," and such "constant and uninterrupted usage and custom," it seemed to them, was, in the best traditions of English constitutional development, "sufficient of itself to make a constitution." With these arguments, colonial spokesmen merely turned against Parliament defenses that they and their ancestors had developed over the previous century to protect colonial rights against abuses of prerogative.[3]

Whatever the sources of the legislative authority of the assemblies, the most significant questions posed by the new intrusion of Parliament into the domestic affairs of the colonies, the most vital issues raised by the Stamp Act crisis vis-à-vis the constitutional organization of the early modern British Empire, were how extensive that authority was and how it related to the authority of the British Parliament. Linking authority to consent, few colonists could accept the metropolitan position that there were no limits to Parliament's colonial authority.

Although some argued that Parliament's authority was purely local and did not extend beyond the bounds of Britain, most colonists in 1764–66 took a far more cautious approach, admitting, as the Virginia lawyer Richard Bland put it, that the colonies were "subordinate to the Authority of Parliament" but denying that they were "absolutely so."

---

[3] [Tobias Fitch], *Reasons Why the British Colonies, in America, Should Not Be Charged with Internal Taxes* (New Haven, 1764), in Bernard Bailyn, ed., *Pamphlets of the American Revolution, 1750—1776* (Cambridge, Mass., 1965), 392; [Kenneth Morrison], *An Essay towards the Vindication of the Committee of Correspondence in Barbados* (Barbados, 1766), 10–11; Barbados Committee of Correspondence to London Agent, [1765], in John Dickinson, *An Address to the Committee of Correspondence in Barbados* (Philadelphia, 1766), in *The Writings of John Dickinson*, ed. Paul Leicester Ford, 2 vols. (Philadelphia, 1895), 1:255–56; *Letter to G. G.* (London, 1767), 35–36; Aequus, letter from the *Massachusetts Gazette*, Mar. 6, 1766, in Charles S. Hyneman and Donald S. Lutz, eds., *American Political Writing during the Founding Era, 1760—1805*, 2 vols. (Indianapolis, 1983), 1: 63, 65; Richard Bland, *The Colonel Dismounted: or The Rector Vindicated* (Williamsburg, 1764), in Bailyn, *Pamphlets*, 323; John Gay Alleyne, *A Letter to the North American, on Occasion of His Address to the Committee of Correspondence in Barbados* (Barbados, 1766), 4.

But what was the nature of that subordination? Where should the line be drawn between the authority of Parliament at the center and that of the colonial legislatures in the peripheries?[4]

The traditional view has been that during the Stamp Act crisis the colonists drew that line between taxation and legislation, that they denied Parliament's authority to tax the colonies for revenue but not its authority to legislate for the colonies. This argument is based on the fact that neither the Stamp Act Congress nor many of the assemblies explicitly commented on Parliament's authority outside the realm of taxation. But the failure of most of these bodies to challenge Parliament's legislative authority outside the area of taxation by no means constituted an admission of that authority, especially in view of the fact that there were several official bodies which explicitly denied that authority.

Indeed, considerable evidence suggests that the colonists' strong initial impulse was to exclude Parliament from all jurisdiction over the domestic affairs of the colonies. Denying Parliament's right to pass laws respecting either taxation or their internal polities, early protests from the Connecticut and Virginia legislatures and later declarations from the Virginia, Rhode Island, Maryland, Connecticut, and Massachusetts assemblies claimed for their constituents a right not merely to no taxation without representation but to no legislation without representation, and several writers, including Bland, Governor Stephen Hopkins of Rhode Island, and Samuel Adams, wrote elaborate statements in defense of this position. An analysis of the works of these writers suggests that, as Bernard Bailyn has emphasized, the supposed colonial distinction between taxation and legislation was less important to the colonial attempt to demarcate the jurisdictional boundaries between Parliament and the colonial assemblies than a distinction between "'internal' and 'external' spheres of government."[5]

Richard Bland provided the most extensive and systematic exploration of this distinction. Claiming for the colonists the authority "of directing their *internal* Government by Laws made with their Consent," he argued that each colony was "a distinct State, independent, as to their *internal* Government, of the original Kingdom, but united with her, as to their *external* Polity, in the closest and most intimate LEAGUE AND

---

[4] Richard Bland, *An Inquiry into the Rights of the British Colonies* (Williamsburg, Va., 1766), in William J. Van Schreeven, comp., and Robert L. Scribner, ed., *Revolutionary Virginia: The Road to Independence* I (Charlottesville, Va., 1973): 41, 43.

[5] Bernard Bailyn, *The Ideological Origins of the American Revolution* (Cambridge, Mass., 1967), 213 n. 55.

AMITY, under the same Allegiance, and enjoying the Benefits of a reciprocal Intercourse." Though Bland did not specify precisely what matters
were subsumed under the respective categories *internal* and *external*, he
implied that Parliament's authority—to legislate as well as to tax—
stopped short of the Atlantic coast of the colonies and did not extend
over any affairs relating exclusively to the domestic life of the colonies.
Such matters, according to Bland's formulation, were the exclusive preserve of the several colonial assemblies.[6]

This distinction between external and internal spheres effectively described the pragmatic and customary distribution of authority within
the empire as it had developed over the past century and a half. Notwithstanding metropolitan efforts to limit the extent of local self-
government in the peripheries of the empire, the colonists had continued
to enjoy considerable local authority. In the exercise of metropolitan authority, crown and Parliament had, in fact, as Bailyn has noted, usually
"touched only the outer fringes of colonial life" and dealt only "with matters obviously beyond the competence of any lesser authority" and with
"the final review of actions initiated and sustained by colonial authorities." All other powers—the vast area of "residual authority" that both
constituted "the 'internal police' of the community" and "included most
of the substance of everyday life"—"were enjoyed . . . by local . . . or-
gans of government." In view of this situation, it was only natural for
the colonists to conclude that, insofar as their respective internal affairs
were concerned', no part of the empire could be constitutionally subordinated to any other part.[7]

If, at the beginning of the Stamp Act crisis, the questions, in Franklin's words, of "how far, and in what particulars" the colonies were "*subordinate* and *subject* to the British parliament" were "points newly agitated
[and] never yet . . . thoroughly considered," that was no longer the case
by the time of the repeal of the Stamp Act in the late winter of 1766.
Over the preceding two years, the colonists had slowly begun to construct what John Adams called "a formal, logical, and technical definition" of the imperial constitution under which they lived. As a result of
this "great inquiry," they had learned that, as Richard Bland put it, it
was "in vain to search into the civil Constitution of *England* for Directions in fixing the proper Connexion between the Colonies and the
Mother Kingdom." The main underlying principles of that constitution
were certainly relevant to their inquiry, but the British constitution was

---

[6] Bland, *Inquiry*, in Van Schreeven and Scribner, *Revolutionary Virginia* 38–39.

[7] Bailyn, *Ideological Origins*, 203.

not, in and of itself, suitable as the constitution for an "extended and diversified" empire.[8]

Instead, in their efforts to understand the nature of the relationship between Britain and the colonies, the colonists turned for guidance to the traditional rights of Englishmen and to their own experience with the actual pattern of customary relations within the empire as they had developed over the previous century and a half. One of the central conclusions of their inquiry—and one of the arguments they pressed most vigorously in their claims against the intrusion of parliamentary authority in the colonies—was that, like Britain itself, both the individual colonies and the empire as a whole had long-standing constitutional traditions that, at least from the point of view of the colonies, seemed to supply legitimacy to their determined efforts to resist what Bland referred to as this "new System of Placing *Great Britain* as the Centre of Attraction to the Colonies."[9]

In 1764–66, only the most advanced thinkers among the colonists were willing to argue that Parliament had no role in either the imperial or the several colonial constitutions or to suggest that there was "no *dependence* or relation" between Britain and the colonies except "only that we are all the common subjects of the same King." What all colonial protests did have in common, however, was a clear concern to fix the boundaries between the authority of the metropolis and that of the colonies, between the power of Parliament and that of the colonial assemblies. If Parliament had a constitutional role in the empire, they were persuaded, that role had to be a limited one. They were virtually unanimous in agreeing that that role did not include authority to tax the colonies for revenue, and a substantial body of sentiment also held that it did not include authority to legislate for the internal affairs of the colonies.[10]

The colonial case against the Stamp Act got a generally hostile reception in Britain. Few seemed to understand that the colonists' challenge to parliamentary authority went beyond the realm of taxation, and even

---

[8] Benjamin Franklin, "On the Tenure of the Manor of East Greenwich," Jan. 11, 1766, in *Benjamin Franklin's Letters to the Press*, ed. Verner W. Crane (Chapel Hill, N.C., 1950), 48; Earl of Clarendon [John Adams] to William Pym, Jan. 27, 1766, in *The Works of John Adams*, ed. Charles F. Adams, 10 vols. (Boston, 1856), 3:477; Bland, *Inquiry*, in Van Schreeven and Scribner, *Revolutionary Virginia* 34; J. M., *The Legislative Authority of the British Parliament* (London, 1766), 11.

[9] Bland, *Inquiry*, in Van Schreeven and Scribner, *Revolutionary Virginia* 43; Thomas Rutherforth, *Institutes of Natural Law*, 2d American ed. (Baltimore, 1832), 296.

[10] Letter from a Plain Yeoman, *Providence Gazette*, May 11, 1765, in Morgan, *Prologue to Revolution*, 73.

with regard to this more restricted conception of the colonial position, only a few men in Parliament agreed with the colonists that there were limits upon Parliament's colonial authority. Most both rejected the colonists' contention that they were not represented in Parliament and dismissed the argument that inheritance, charters, and custom exempted the colonies from parliamentary taxation. Lord Mansfield sounded the predominant argument when he flatly declared that, "as to the power of making laws," Parliament represented "the whole British empire" and had "authority to bind every part and every subject without the least distinction."[11]

From this point of view, colonial claims for exemption from parliamentary taxation seemed, as Grenville had defined them when he first proposed to levy stamp duties on the colonies, to be nothing less than a challenge to British sovereignty. As it had gradually developed over the previous century and a half, the conventional conception of sovereignty was that in all polities, including "an Empire, extended and diversified, like that of *Great-Britain*," there had to be, as Blackstone wrote, "a supreme, irresistible, absolute uncontrolled authority, in which the *jura summi imperii*, or the rights of sovereignty reside[d]." Because, most contemporaries seem to have believed, the king-in-Parliament was sovereign in the British polity, it could accept no restrictions upon its authority without relinquishing the sovereignty of the nation over the colonies. By definition, there could be no limitation upon a supreme authority. It was either complete or nonexistent. For that reason, it seemed obvious that the king-in-Parliament had full authority over all matters relating to all Britons everywhere. For the same reason, it also seemed evident that no clear line could be drawn between Parliament's power to legislate for the colonies and its power to tax them.[12]

In the metropolitan view, there was thus no distribution but a concentration of authority within the empire: "as the sovereign of the whole," the king-in-Parliament had "control over the whole British empire." To most metropolitans, in fact, the colonial position appeared incomprehensible because it seemed to imply the existence of more than one sovereign authority within a single state, and sovereignty, according to conventional theory, could not be divided. An *imperium in imperio*—a sovereign

---

[11] Mansfield's speech, Feb. 3, 1766, in R. C. Simmons and P. D. G. Thomas, eds., *Proceedings and Debates of the British Parliament respecting North America, 1754–1783,* 6 vols. to date (New York, 1982–   ), 2:128–30.

[12] J. M., *Legislative Authority of the British Parliament,* 11; Sir William Blackstone, *Commentaries on the Laws of England,* 4 vols. (London, 1832), 1:50–51, 178–80.

authority within a sovereign authority—was a contradiction in terms. As Lord Lyttelton put it, the colonies were either "part of the dominions of the Crown of Great Britain" and therefore "proper objects of our legislature," or they were "small independent communities," each operating under its own sovereign authority. There was, according to metropolitan theory, no middle ground between these two extremes.[13]

The intensity of colonial opposition to the Stamp Act forced Parliament to repeal that measure, but it accompanied repeal with passage of the Declaratory Act, modeled on the Irish Declaratory Act of 1720 and asserting Parliament's authority "to bind the colonies and people of America . . . in all cases whatsoever." But this fiat from the center by no means resolved the question of the distribution of authority within the empire. As Colonel Isaac Barré announced in the House of Commons early in 1766, the Stamp Act crisis had provoked "the people of America to reason . . . closely upon the relative rights of this country and that" and the undefined and "loose texture" of Britain's "extended and diversified" empire had fostered the development of two widely divergent interpretations of how authority was distributed between metropolis and colonies. Whereas most people in the metropolis thought the empire a unitary state, most people in the colonies thought of it as a federal polity in which the authority of the center was limited by the authority exercised by the peripheries.[14]

If the Stamp Act crisis "first led the colonists into [systematic] Enquiries concerning the nature of their political situation," its resolution in early 1766 by no means put an end to those inquiries. Indeed, Parliament's renewed efforts early in 1767 to tax the colonies through the Townshend Acts quickly reopened the question. For the next six years, people on both sides of the Atlantic further explored the difficult problem of the constitutional organization of the empire.[15]

---

[13] *Letter to G. G.*, 74; Lyttelton's speech, Feb. 3, 1766, in Simmons and Thomas, *Proceedings and Debates* 2:126–27.

[14] Barré's speech, Feb. 24, 1766, in Simmons and Thomas, *Proceedings and Debates* 2:296; *The Political Balance, in Which the Principles and Conduct of the Two Parties Are Weighed* (London, 1765), 45; J. M., *Legislative Authority of the British Parliament*, 11.

[15] William Hicks, *The Nature and Extent of Parliamentary Power Considered* (New York, 1768), in Merrill Jensen, ed., *Tracts of the American Revolution, 1763–1776* (Indianapolis, 1967), 177.

The vast majority of people in the metropolitan establishment, in both Britain and the colonies, adhered strictly to the position articulated by Grenville and his supporters during the Stamp Act crisis. Interpreting all suggestions for any limitations upon Parliament's colonial authority as a challenge to the British constitution of parliamentary supremacy and to metropolitan sovereignty over the colonies, they continued to insist, as they had throughout the Stamp Act crisis, that sovereignty was indivisible and to view the maintenance of "the supremacy and legislative authority of Parliament" in its fullest extent over the colonies as "essential to the existence of the empire."[16]

Notwithstanding the tenacity with which they held to this point of view, metropolitan authorities resisted the impulse to take sweeping coercive measures against the colonies during the late 1760s. Sensing the expediency of Thomas Pownall's declaration that "*You may exert power over, but you can never govern an unwilling people,*" they instead wound up in 1770 taking what they regarded as a conciliatory approach. At the same time that they indicated that they would seek no new parliamentary taxes and guided through Parliament a repeal of most of the Townshend duties, they retained the tax on tea to stand as a symbol of Parliament's colonial authority.[17]

If anything, the urge toward conciliation during the crisis over the Townshend Acts was even more powerful in the colonies. On both sides of the Atlantic, John Dickinson's *Letters from a Farmer in Pennsylvania,* published in 1767, was certainly the most widely circulated expression of colonial opinion. Obviously intending to confine the controversy within the narrowest possible bounds, Dickinson addressed his pamphlet exclusively to the issue of the moment—Parliament's right to tax the colonies for revenue—and did not consider the wider problems of the relationship between metropolis and colonies, the extent and nature of metropolitan sovereignty over the colonies, or the distribution of authority within the empire.

By focusing debate so closely upon the narrow question of taxation, Dickinson helped to de-escalate the controversy. The widespread acceptance of his definition of the situation seems both to have inhibited the sort of wide-ranging discussion of the nature of the metropolitan-colonial relationship that had occurred during the Stamp Act crisis and to have been in no small part responsible for the fact that all but a few official

---

[16] Hillsborough's speeches, Dec. 15, 1768, May 18, 1770, in Simmons and Thomas, *Proceedings and Debates* 3:48, 334.

[17] Pownall's speech, Apr. 19, 1769, ibid., 3:156.

colonial challenges to parliamentary authority during the late 1760s and very early 1770s were confined to the single issue of taxation for revenue.

If, during the crisis over the Townshend Acts, most colonial assemblies, as the Massachusetts legislator Thomas Cushing later observed, "Acquiesced in the distinction between Taxation and Legislation and were disposed to Confine the dispute to that of Taxation only and entirely to waive the other as a subject of too delicate a Nature," a number of thinkers in both the colonies and Britain took a much deeper look at the controversy. As Benjamin Franklin wrote his son in March 1768, they concluded that, while "Something might be made of either of the extremes; that Parliament has a power to make *all laws* for us, or that it has a power to make *no laws* for us," "no middle doctrine" of the kind proposed by Dickinson could successfully be maintained. Although these thinkers regarded their conclusions as no more than an articulation and rationalization of long-standing constitutional practice within the empire, they in fact represented a radical challenge to the metropolitan belief in Parliament's supremacy over the whole empire.[18]

This radical interpetation proceeded from three underlying assumptions. The first was that Parliament's claims to colonial jurisdiction had to be proved and could "not [simply be] take[n] . . . for granted" or permitted to rest on "the monstrous idea of a *Virtual Representation*." The second was that the "civil constitution" of Britain "by no means" determined "the connection which ought to be established between the parent country and her colonies, nor the duties reciprocally incumbent on each other." The third was that the history of the colonies and of their relationship to the metropolis was the most authoritative guide to the exact nature of that connection.[19]

They put particular emphasis upon the history of the colonies, which seemed to them to make clear that the colonies had never been "incorporated with Great Britain in a legislative capacity." This being the case, it seemed equally obvious that Great Britain and the British Empire were distinct political entities. As the Georgia minister Johan Joachim Zubly explained, the British Empire was a far "more extensive word, and

---

[18] Thomas Cushing to Franklin, May 6, 1773, Franklin to William Franklin, Mar. 13, 1768, in *The Papers of Benjamin Franklin*, ed. Leonard W. Labaree et al., 28 vols. to date (New Haven, 1955–   ), 20:204, 15:75–76.

[19] [Gervase Parker Bushe], *The Case of Great Britain and America* (London, 1768), 27; [George Canning], *A Letter to the Right Honourable Wills Earl of Hillsborough, on the Connection between Great Britain and Her American Colonies* (London, 1768), 9–10; *A Letter to the Right Honourable the Earl of H—b——h* (London, 1769), 2–3.

should not be confounded with the kingdom of Great Britain." Rather, it was a "confederal" polity that consisted of both the home islands and a number of "extrinsic Dominions," including "several islands and other distant countries, asunder in different parts of the globe." As the "head of this great body," England was "called the mother country" and "all the settled inhabitants of this vast empire" were "called Englishmen." But those phrases by no means implied that the empire was "a single state." On the contrary, each of its many separate entities had a "legislative power . . . within itself," and "the several legislative bodies of Great-Britain, Ireland and the British Colonies" were "perfectly distinct, and entirely independent upon each other."[20]

In the view of its proponents, the real virtue of this emerging conception lay not in its foundations in past practice but in its appropriateness for the governance of an extended polity. The "Excellency of the Invention of Colony Government, by separate independent Legislatures," Franklin wrote in 1769, was that it permitted "the remotest Parts of a great Empire" to be "as well governed as the Center." By guaranteeing maximum autonomy to peripheral states and thereby helping to prevent wholesale "Misrule, Oppressions of Proconsuls, and Discontents and Rebellions" in those areas, the authority of the British monarch seemed to be infinitely expandable, capable, in Franklin's words, of being "extended without Inconvenience over Territories of any Dimensions how great soever."[21]

This conception of the British Empire as consisting, in Benjamin Prescott's words, "of a great and glorious King, with a Number of distinct Governments, alike subjected to his royal Scepter, and each governed by its own Laws" also seemed to its proponents to offer a solution to the problem of the indivisibility of sovereignty. Posed by metropolitan protagonists during the earliest days of the Stamp Act controversy, the logical dilemma of "an *imperium in imperio*" had remained at the heart of metropolitan resistance to colonial claims for exemption from parliamen-

---

[20] *Letter to H—b——h*, 109; "Matius Scavola" to *Boston Gazette and Country Journal*, Mar. 4, 1771; Johan Joachim Zubly, *An Humble Enquiry into the Nature of the Dependency of the American Colonies upon the Parliament of Great-Britain* (Charleston, S.C., 1769), in *"A Warm & Zealous Spirit": John J. Zubly and the American Revolution, a Selection of His Writings,* ed. Randall M. Miller (Macon, Ga., 1982), 57; Franklin, "Subject of Subjects," Jan. 1768, Franklin to Jacques Barbeu-Duborg, Oct. 2, 1770, Franklin, marginalia to *An Inquiry into the Nature and Causes of the Present Disputes* (London, 1769), in *Franklin Papers* 15:36–37, 17:233, 320.

[21] Franklin to William Strahan, Nov. 29, 1769, Franklin, marginalia to *An Inquiry into the Nature and Causes,* 1770, in *Franklin Papers* 16:246, 17:322.

tary authority. According to the emerging conception of empire among the most advanced defenders of the colonies, however, sovereignty within the extended polity of the British Empire resided not in Britain and not in the king-in-Parliament but in the institution of the monarchy alone. In the imperial realm, according to these writers, the theory of coordination, of the legal sovereignty of the king-in-Parliament, did not apply.[22]

To its proponents, this view of the empire as "many states under one Sovereign" seemed thoroughly defensible on the basis of both the terms of the colonial charters and the customary constitutional arrangements that had grown up since the establishment of the colonies. For over a century and a half the colonists, without interruption, had "been trusted in a good measure with the entire management of their affairs." Of course, as they recognized, the doctrine of usage on which their developing conception of the empire rested so heavily cut two ways. If Parliament had had no role whatever in their early history, and if, subsequently, Parliament had not customarily interfered in their internal affairs, they could not deny that, from the mid-seventeenth century on, Parliament had "exercised its Authority in the Colonies, for regulating their Trade, and afterwards for directing their exterior Policy." Furthermore, they had to admit that, even though Parliament's authority had "in some Instances been executed with great Partiality to Britain and Prejudice to the Colonies," they had "nevertheless always submitted to it" and thereby "consented to consider themselves as united to Great Britain in a commercial capacity, and to have their trade governed by its parliament."[23]

Deriving out of a century and a half of experience, custom thus seemed to prescribe a clear allocation of authority within the broad extended polity of the early modern British Empire, an allocation precisely along the lines identified by Bland and other colonial writers during the Stamp Act crisis. The many provincial governments—Ireland in the near-periphery and the several colonies in the distant American periph-

---

[22] Benjamin Prescott, *A Free and Calm Consideration of the Unhappy Misunderstandings and Debates* (Salem, Mass., 1774), 30; Franklin to *London Chronicle*, Oct. 18–20, 1768, in *Franklin Papers* 15:233. Though not published until 1774, the Prescott pamphlet was written in 1768.

[23] Franklin, marginalia to [Wheelock], *Reflections Moral and Political*, 1770, in *Franklin Papers* 17:385; Jonathan Shipley, *A Sermon Preached before the Incorporated Society for the Propagation of the Gospel in Foreign Parts* (London, 1773), in Paul H. Smith, comp., *English Defenders of American Freedoms, 1774–1778* (Washington, D.C., 1972), 22; Franklin to William Strahan, Nov. 29, 1769, in *Franklin Papers* 16:244; Edward Ban-

ery—had full jurisdiction over their own particular local and internal affairs, while the metropolitan government at the center had authority over all general matters, including the external relations of the several provincial governments.

In the absence of any impartial tribunal to settle constitutional disputes between the center and the peripheries, there was, as Pownall lamented in 1768, "no means of deciding the controversy" by law. Unwilling to give in, metropolitan leaders were, as yet, also unwilling to resort to force. They still understood that, in the words of Edmund Burke, there was "no such thing as governing the whole body of the people contrary to their inclinations," and such considerations were behind Parliament's decision in the spring of 1770 to repeal all of the Townshend duties except the tax on tea. This essentially political resolution of the crisis in effect went back to the settlement adopted in 1766; that is, it left the issue of the extent of Parliament's colonial authority to rest on the Declaratory Act and token taxes on sugar products and tea, with an implicit understanding that, as in the case of Ireland, Parliament would not thenceforth levy any further taxes on the colonies.[24]

Like the Stamp Act crisis, the controversy over the Townshend Acts had helped to illuminate still further the ancient question of how, within the extended polity of the British Empire, authority was distributed between metropolis and colonies. To be sure, it produced little change in the metropolitan position as it had been articulated in 1764–66, while the conciliatory thrust of both Dickinson's *Letters from a Pennsylvania Farmer* and most of the official colonial protests helped to obscure the radical drift of sentiment among spokesmen for the colonial side in both America and Britain. For, pursuing the logic of the customary constitutional arrangements that had obtained in the empire over the previous century, a great many writers between 1767 and 1770 had worked out detailed arguments to prove what a few colonial thinkers had already implied in 1764–66: that the British Empire was a loose association of distinct political entities under a common king, each of which had its own legislature with exclusive jurisdiction over its own internal affairs. As in 1764–66, a major constitutional crisis had thus functioned to intensify, rather than to resolve, differences in interpretations of the constitutional organization of the empire.

croft, *Remarks on the Review of the Controversy between Great Britain and Her Colonies* (London, 1769), 76; *Letter to H—b——h*, 29, 104.

[24] Pownall's speech, Apr. 19, 1769, in Simmons and Thomas, *Proceedings and Debates* 3:154.

Nevertheless, repeal of the Townshend Acts brought a temporary re-
spite from the turmoil that had beset metropolitan-colonial relations
over the previous six years. For the next three and a half years, debate
over the respective jurisdictions of Parliament and the several peripheral
legislatures in Ireland and the American colonies fell into temporary
abeyance. Yet throughout the early 1770s, constitutional relations
within the empire remained troubled. Coincident with the repeal of most
of the Townshend duties there was a new series of quarrels over the scope
of the crown's colonial authority, quarrels in several colonies that punctu-
ated the so-called period of quiet during the early 1770s and revealed
that the debate over the extent of the crown's prerogative in the colonies
was still hotly contested.

From the perspective of the crises over the Stamp and Townshend
Acts and the debate over Parliament's new pretensions to authority over
the internal affairs of the colonies, however, these old questions about
the crown's relationship acquired a heightened urgency in the colonies.
If, as an impressive number of colonial spokesmen had begun to argue
during the late 1760s, sovereignty within the empire rested not in the
crown-in-Parliament but in the crown alone, then it became especially
important for the colonists to establish the boundaries not just of parliamentary but also of royal authority in the colonies. For that reason, colonial defenders in all of the battles of the early 1770s revealed a pronounced tendency to build upon their own particular local constitutional
heritages to argue, as their predecessors in earlier generations had often
done, that, no less than in Britain itself, the crown's authority—the freedom of its "will"—in the colonies had been effectively limited over the
previous century by specific idiosyncratic constitutional developments in
each of the colonies. Again, just as in Britain, these developments had
led, colonial leaders believed, irreversibly in the direction of increasing
authority in the hands of the local legislatures and greater restrictions
on the prerogatives of the crown. By this process, they argued, the rights
of the inhabitants in the peripheries had gradually been secured against
the power of the center.

As refined and elaborated during the contests of the early 1770s, this
view of colonial constitutional history powerfully reinforced traditional
views of the colonial legislatures as both the primary guardians of the
local rights of the corporate entities over which they presided and, like
Parliament itself in Britain, as the dynamic forces in shaping the colonial
constitutions. Insofar as the constitution of the empire was concerned,
this emphasis upon the peculiarity and integrity of the several colonial
constitutions certainly constituted, as Peter S. Onuf has noted, a vigor-

ous "defense of constitutional multiplicity" that had profound implications for the ongoing debate over the nature of sovereignty within the empire. For, together with the emerging conviction that Parliament had no authority over the colonies, the renewed contention that the crown's authority in the peripheries was also limited by local constitutions as they had emerged out of not just the colonists' inherited rights as Englishmen and their charters but also local usage and custom pushed the colonists still further in the direction of a wholly new conception of sovereignty in an extended polity like the early modern British Empire. That conception implied that ultimate constitutional authority—sovereignty—lay not in any institution or collection of institutions at the center of the empire but in the separate constitutions of each of the many separate political entities of which the empire was composed.[25]

When Parliament's passage of the Tea Act in May 1773 revived the dispute over its colonial authority, colonial resistance to that measure provoked the crisis that would, in a mere two and a half years, lead to the dismemberment of the early modern British Empire. At no time during this crisis did either side show much disposition to compromise. As each quickly took a determined stance upon the position marked out by its most extreme proponents during the previous crises, the spirit of conciliation that had marked the crisis over the Townshend Acts rapidly gave way to complete intransigence.

In both Britain and the colonies, supporters of Parliament's right to legislate for the colonies insisted, as they had ever since the beginning of the controversy during the Stamp Act crisis, that the British Empire, consisting of Great Britain and all its territories, was a single state composed of "ONE people, ruled by ONE constitution, and governed by ONE King." Reiterating the same central contentions that had underlain their argument from the beginning, they continued to interpret the controversy as a dispute over sovereignty. They dismissed the doctrine of no legislation without representation as "an obsolete maxim" that had no applicability to the distant parts of an extended polity like the British Empire and persisted in asserting that "No maxim of policy" was "more universally admitted, than that a supreme and uncontroulable power must exist somewhere in every state." In the British Empire, they in-

---

[25] Peter S. Onuf, ed., *Maryland and the Empire, 1773: The Antilon-First Citizen Letters* (Baltimore, 1974), 29.

sisted, that power was vested "in King, Lords, and Commons, under the collective appellation of the Legislature," which as James Macpherson phrased it, was merely "another name for the Constitution of State," was, "in fact, the State itself."[26]

Thus, if the colonists refused obedience to Parliament, they were "no longer Subjects, but rebels" who, by arrogating "to themselves all the functions of Sovereignty," were obviously endeavoring to put themselves "on the footing of a Sovereign State." "The question between them and Great Britain," then, as Macpherson gravely noted in summarizing the dominant position within the metropolitan political nation, was nothing less than "dependence or independence, connection or no connection." With "no common Principle to rest upon, no common Medium to appeal to," wrote Josiah Tucker, the dispute seemed to have no middle ground. To admit any qualification in "the controuling right of the British legislature over the colonies," its proponents devoutly believed, would mean nothing less than the abandonment of "the whole of our authority over the Americans."[27]

While the metropolitan political nation refused to back down from its insistence that the king-in-Parliament was the supreme sovereign of the empire, the colonial assemblies and the First and Second Continental Congresses, composed of delegates from the thirteen colonies from New Hampshire south to Georgia, gave official sanction to radical views that had previously been held only by private individuals, views that had been developed by Franklin and others during the late 1760s and early 1770s and that called for complete colonial autonomy over the internal affairs of the colonies.

The colonial position, as it was enunciated in mid-1774 and elaborated over the next two years, was founded on a complete rejection of the prevailing metropolitan theory of an omnipotent Parliament. By ignoring the vital and traditional British constitutional principle of consent, of no legislation without representation, this "dreadful novelty," supporters

---

[26] *Colonising, or Plain Investigation of That Subject* (London, 1774), 8; [James Macpherson], *The Rights of Great Britain Asserted against the Claims of America* (London, 1776), 3–5, 11.

[27] [Macpherson], *Rights of Great Britain*, 3, 11; Nathaniel George Rice's speech, Mar. 7, 1774, and Charles Cornwall's speech, Apr. 19, 1774, in William Cobbett and T. C. Hansard, eds., *The Parliamentary History of England from the Earliest Period to 1803*, 36 vols. (London, 1806–20), 17:1149, 1214; Josiah Tucker, Tract 5, *The Respective Pleas and Arguments of the Mother Country, and of the Colonies, Distinctly Set Forth* (Gloucester, Eng., 1775), 38.

of the colonial position declared, was at total variance with both "the ancient rights of the people" and "the settled, notorious, invariable practice of" imperial governance within the empire over the previous century and a half.[28]

No less importantly, when applied to distant and unrepresented colonies, this "modern doctrine," it seemed to the colonists, obviously also represented "a total contradiction to every principle laid down at the time of the [Glorious] Revolution, as the rules by which the rights and privileges of every branch of our legislature were to be governed for ever." Indeed, by its insistence upon exerting a "*supreme* jurisdiction" over the colonies, Parliament seemed not merely to be violating the most essential principles of the Revolution but actually to have assumed and to be acting upon precisely the same "high prerogative doctrine[s]" against which that Revolution had been undertaken. Thus, the colonists believed, if by resisting Parliament they had become rebels, they were "rebels in the same way, and for the same reasons that the people of Britain were rebels, for supporting the Revolution."[29]

By 1774, few people in America any longer had any doubt that, over the previous decade, it had "been clearly and fully proved that the Assemblies or Parliaments of the *British* Colonies in *America*" had "an exclusive right, not only of taxation, but of legislation also; and that the *British* Parliament, so far from having a right to make laws binding upon those Colonies in all cases whatsover," had "really no just right to make any laws at all binding upon the Colonies." Far from being subject to the "supreme" authority of Parliament, most American leaders now believed, the colonies had "always enjoyed a supreme Legislature of their own, and . . . always claimed an exemption from the jurisdiction of a *British* Parliament." Not the king-in-Parliament, wrote the Virginian Thomson Mason, but the "King, at the head of his respective *Ameri-*

[28] *An Answer to a Pamphlet, Entitled Taxation No Tyranny* (London, 1775), 6; John Dickinson, *An Essay on the Constitutional Power of Great Britain over the Colonies in America* (Philadelphia, 1774), in Samuel Hazard et al., eds., *Pennsylvania Archives*, 138 vols., 2d ser. (Philadelphia and Harrisburg, 1852–), 3:601; *An Argument in Defence of the Exclusive Right Claimed by the Colonies to Tax Themselves* (London, 1774), 104; [Arthur Lee], *An Appeal to the Justice and Interests of the People of Great Britain* (London, 1774), 20–21.

[29] Dickinson, *Essay on the Constitutional Power*, in *Pennsylvania Archives*, 2d ser., 3:565; *An Argument in Defence*, 104; "An Apology for the Late Conduct of America," *London Gazetteer*, Apr. 7, 1774, in Peter Force, comp., *American Archives*, 4th ser. (Washington, D.C., 1837–53), 1:242; "To the Freemen of America," May 18, 1774, ibid., 336; [Hugh Baillie], *Some Observations on a Pamphlet Lately Published* (London, 1776), 2–3.

can Assemblies," constituted "the Supreme Legislature of the Colonies."[30]

Whether Parliament had any authority even over the external affairs of the colonies now became a point of contention. Already during the Townshend Act crisis, some colonial supporters were beginning to suggest that Parliament had no authority whatever over the colonies. By 1774, many of the most influential tracts, including those written by James Wilson of Pennsylvania and Thomas Jefferson of Virginia, took this unequivocable position. The legislative authority of each of the many independent legislatures within the empire, including Parliament, wrote Wilson, was necessarily "confined within . . . local bounds" and could not be imposed upon any of the other areas of the empire without their consent.[31]

During the early stages of the crisis of independence, however, most American leaders seemed still to believe that Parliament did have authority over external affairs. As both Alexander Hamilton and John Adams pointed out, they thought that that authority derived from the "long usage and uninterrupted acquiescence" by which the colonists, since the middle of the seventeenth century, had given their "implied consent" to the Navigation Acts and other trade regulations.[32]

But if few of their protagonists yet claimed for the colonists "external as well as internal sovereign jurisdiction" as "independent nations," virtually everyone now agreed with those people who had begun to argue during the late 1760s that "all the different members of the British Empire" were "distinct states, independent of each other, but connected together under the same sovereign." Upon close examination, they had discovered that, as an entity "composed of extensive and dispersed Dominions," the empire was "in some degree a new case" in political history that had to "be governed . . . more by its own circumstances, and by the genius of our peculiar Constitution, than by abstract notions of

---

[30] [Thomson Mason], "The British American," nos. 6–7, July 7, 14, 1774, "A Brief Examination of American Grievances," July 28, 1774, "To the Inhabitants of New-York," Oct. 6, 1774, in Force, *American Archives*, 4th ser., 1:522, 541, 658, 821.

[31] James Wilson, *Considerations on the Nature and Extent of the Legislative Authority of the British Parliament* (Philadelphia, 1774), in *The Works of James Wilson*, ed. Robert Green McCloskey, 2 vols. (Cambridge, Mass., 1967), 2:741, 745–46; Thomas Jefferson, *A Summary View of the Rights of British-America* (Williamsburg, Va., 1774), in *The Papers of Thomas Jefferson*, ed. Julian P. Boyd et al., 21 vols. to date (Princeton, 1950–), 1:125.

[32] Alexander Hamilton, *The Farmer Refuted* (New York, 1775), in *The Papers of Alexander Hamilton*, ed. Harold C. Syrett and Jacob E. Cooke, 26 vols. (New York, 1961–79), 1:122; John Adams, "Novanglus," 1775, in *Works of John Adams* 4:113–14.

government." Separated by vast distances, "inhabited by different people, [living] under distinct constitutions of government, with different customs, laws and interests," its several constituent elements could not possibly comprise a single civil state. Rather, each part had to be "considered as a [distinct] people, not a set of individuals." Presided over by its own legislature, each of these corporate entities was a separate realm that was entirely independent of all the others. According to this line of thought, no part of the empire was subordinate to any other part. As Franklin had remarked in 1770, there was no dependence among the several parts of the empire, "only a *Connection*, of which the King is the common Link."[33]

In view of the economic success of the empire, both Americans and their supporters in Britain regarded it as absurd for the metropolis to risk so many palpable advantages in pursuit of what increasingly appeared to them to be nothing more than an academic and irrelevant political abstraction. Sovereignty might appear to be the grand question in dispute to the vast majority in the metropolitan political nation. Throughout the pre-Revolutionary debates, however, most colonial leaders had resisted such reductionism and had endeavored, unsuccessfully, to focus debate upon the seemingly more tractable and certainly less abstract problem of how power was or should be allocated in a polity composed of several related but nonetheless distinct corporate entities. For the colonists, resolution of their dispute with the metropolis had never seemed to require much more than the rationalization of existing political arrangements within the empire.

For them, the "great solecism of an *imperium in imperio*" seemed, as James Iredell declared, to be little more than "a narrow and pedantic . . . point of speculation," a "scholastic and trifling refinement" that had no relevance to the situation at hand. "Custom and continual usage" seemed to be "of a much more unequivocal nature than speculation and refined principles." Notwithstanding the fact that it had been "so vainly and confidently relied on" by their antagonists, that "beautiful theory in

---

[33] Thomas Pownall, *The Administration of the British Colonies*, 2 vols., 5th ed. (London, 1774), 2:100; John Cartwright, *American Independence, the Interest and Glory of Great Britain* (Philadelphia, 1776), in Smith, *English Defenders of Freedom*, 138; Wilson, *Considerations*, in *Works of Wilson* 2:745; *An Answer to a Pamphlet, Entitled Taxation No Tyranny*, 8; Moses Mather, *America's Appeal to the Impartial World* (Hartford, Conn., 1774), 47; James Iredell, "To the Inhabitants of Great Britain," Sept. 1774, in *The Papers of James Iredell*, ed. Don Higginbotham 1 (Raleigh, 1976): 264; John Adams, "Novanglus," in *Works of John Adams* 4:123; Franklin, marginalia to [Wheelock], *Reflections Moral and Political*, 1770, in *Franklin Papers* 17:393.

political discourses—the necessity of an absolute power residing somewhere in every state"—seemed, as Iredell wrote, to be wholly inapplica-
ble to a situation involving "several distinct and independent legislatures, each engaged in a separate scale, and employed about different
objects."[34]

Colonial protagonists thus called upon the metropolitan government
to abandon its pursuit of the "vain phantom of unlimited sovereignty,
which was not made for man," and content itself with "the solid advantages of a moderate, useful and intelligible authority." As long as all
members of the empire adhered to the customary arrangements that had
developed over the previous century and a half, as long as the king was
the "supreme head of every legislature in the British dominions," he
would always have it in his power to "guide the vast and complicated
machine of government, to the reciprocal advantage of all his dominions" and, by his authority to veto laws, would on any occasion be able
to "prevent the actual injury to the whole of any positive law in any part
of the empire."[35]

In their efforts to explain—and to rationalize—existing constitutional
relationships within the empire, colonial protagonists, between 1764 and
1776, had discovered that the locus of authority necessarily had to reside
in each of the separate corporate entities that composed the empire.
Contrary to metropolitan theory as it had developed following the Glorious Revolution and more especially after 1740, authority, they now
clearly understood, had never been concentrated in a sovereign institution at the center. Rather, it had always been dispersed among the several parliaments that routinely had been established to preside over—
and express the collective will of—each new polity within the empire.
Indeed, this proliferation of legislatures was the only way that those
traditional English rights that had been confirmed to the inhabitants of
the metropolis by the Revolutionary Settlement—especially that most
fundamental right of no legislation without representation—could be extended to people in the peripheries of a large extended polity like the
early modern British Empire. For the inhabitants of those—by then—
quite ancient corporate entities, English liberty and their specific local

---

[34] Iredell, "To the Inhabitants of Great Britain," Sept. 1774, and "The Principles of an
American Whig," [1775–76], in *Papers of Iredell* 1:254, 264–67, 332; *Gov. Johnston's
Speech on American Affairs* (Edinburgh, 1776), 5–7.

[35] Jonathan Shipley, *Speech Intended to Have Been Spoken*, in Smith, *English Defenders
of Freedom*, 38; Hamilton, *Farmer Refuted*, in *Hamilton Papers* 1:99; Iredell, "To the
Inhabitants of Great Britain," Sept. 1774, in *Papers of Iredell* 1:266.

corporate rights were identical. Just as it had been throughout the colonial era, the integrity of those rights and of the constitutions and assemblies that embodied and protected them was thus, not surprisingly, the central theme of colonial constitutional protest during the 1760s and 1770s.

If, as Onuf has pointed out, this insistence upon the "autonomy and integrity" of the several colonial constitutions was indeed a "defense of constitutional multiplicity" within the empire, the ancient and continuing association of its several separate polities clearly implied the existence of a larger imperial constitution, a constitution of the empire. Though this constitution was obviously based upon and expressed the same fundamental constitutional principles, it was emphatically not identical to the British constitution. If by the 1760s the British constitution had become the constitution of parliamentary supremacy, the emerging imperial constitution, like the separate constitutions of Britain's many overseas dominions, remained a customary constitution in which, according to the colonial point of view, sovereignty resided not in an all-powerful Parliament but in the crown, the power of which had been considerably reduced over the previous century by the specific "gains made over the years in the direction of self-determination" by each representative body within the empire.[36]

Regarding any diminution of parliamentary sovereignty as a prelude to the eventual loss of control of the colonies that seemed to be so intimately associated with Britain's rise to world power, the vast majority of the metropolitan political nation found it impossible to accept such arguments. Besides, from the perspective of Britain's own internal constitutional development during the previous century, colonial theories about the organization of the empire seemed dangerously retrograde. By placing the resources of Ireland and the colonies directly in the hands of the crown and beyond the reach of Parliament, those theories appeared to strike directly at the root of the legislative supremacy that, for them, was the primary legacy of the Glorious Revolution.

By 1776, what had begun as yet another crisis over Parliament's right to tax the colonies had become a crisis over whether the colonies would become independent. The empire foundered over the inability of the center and the peripheries to agree on a formula for governance that would give the peripheries of that extended polity the same rights and control over their domestic affairs that the center enjoyed. Whether indepen-

---

[36] Onuf, *Maryland and the Empire,* 29; Barbara A. Black, "The Constitution of the Empire: The Case for the Colonists," *University of Pennsylvania Law Review* 124 (1976): 1203.

dence would be the first step toward the establishment of a viable union that would enable them to resolve the problem that had brought the British Empire to grief, the problem of how in an extended polity authority should be distributed between center and peripheries, was still an open question when they opted for independence in July 1776.

Driven by the specter of parliamentary taxation to investigate the constitutional organization of the empire, American colonials quickly decided in the 1760s that they were governed by a customary imperial constitution based upon the ideas of principled limitation and government by consent. As several legal historians have recently emphasized, the fact that metropolitan officials would not take the colonial case seriously does not mean that they were "right about the law." Constitutional arrangements within the British Empire were far from precise, and in the debates of the 1760s and 1770s each side could marshall effective legal arguments in behalf of its position. In this unsettled situation, constitutional questions were by no means so clear as they were said to be in London and has been assumed by so many later historians.[37]

The early modern British Empire was by no means yet a modern unitary state. Imperial institutions in the colonies had little coercive power and depended for their effectiveness upon the consent of local populations. Authority within the empire had long been dispersed into the hands of authoritative, powerful, and "largely autonomous local institutions." Not dependent for their effectiveness "on the support or the acquiescence of a central authority" and highly "resistant to centralized control," these institutions were regarded, both by those who composed them and those whom they served, as largely "independent recipients of constitutional power and authority." In this "diffuse and decentralized" political entity, local institutions invariably determined the nature of the constitution as much as did authorities at the center.[38]

---

[37] John Phillip Reid, "In a Defensive Rage: The Uses of the Mob, the Justification in Law, and the Coming of the American Revolution," *New York University Law Review* 49 (1974): 1063.

[38] John Phillip Reid, *In a Defiant Stance: The Conditions of Law in Massachusetts Bay, the Irish Comparison, and the Coming of the American Revolution* (University Park, Pa., 1977), 2, 161; Reid, "In a Defensive Rage," 1091; Hendrik B. Hartog, "Losing the World of the Massachusetts Whig," in Hartog, ed., *Law in the American Revolution and the Revolution in the Law* (New York, 1981), 146–47, 152–53, 160.

The argument of this chapter has been that with regard to extended polities in the era before the development of the modern consolidated state in the wake of the French Revolution, it should not automatically be assumed that the perspective of the center is the correct or even the dominant one. In any polity like the early modern British Empire in whose peripheries the authority and ideology of the center were weak while local power and traditions were strong, local institutions and customs were at least as important as those of the center in determining existing constitutional arrangements. In such an entity, the center perspective will almost automatically be a partisan one. In the particular case of the British Empire at the time of the American Revolution, the antiquity of the notion of a customary imperial constitution of principled limitation and the strength of local institutions combined with the comparative recentness of the doctrine of parliamentary supremacy and the weakness of metropolitan authority in the colonies to make the perspective of the center a "Tory perspective." Perhaps even more importantly, the failure of the center to establish the legitimacy of its perspective in the peripheries rendered it an anachronistic perspective when applied to legal and constitutional arrangements within the empire as a whole.[39]

This chapter was written for the volume in which it appeared. Before its publication, it was presented as a lecture to the German-American Lawyers Association, University of Mainz, Germany, January 7, 1987; at the John F. Kennedy Institute for North American Studies of the Free University of Berlin, Germany, January 8, 1987; at the Seminar on the History of North America at the University of Paris I, France, January 12, 1987; at the American Studies Institute, University of Cologne, Germany, January 15, 1987; at the Faculty of History, Ruhr University, Bochum, Germany, January 16, 1987; and at a seminar in the Department of American Studies, University of Tokyo, Komaba, July 1, 1987. It is here reprinted with permission and minor verbal changes from Leonard W. Levy and Dennis J. Mahoney, eds., *The Constitution: A History of Its Framing and Ratification* (New York: Copyright © 1987 by Macmillan Publishing Company, a Division of Macmillan, Inc.), 36–53, 355–56.

---

[39] Reid, *In a Defiant Stance*, 162.

Six

The Social Origins of
the American Revolution:
An Evaluation and an
Interpretation

GIVEN THE RICH theoretical literature on revolution that has been published mostly in the 1960s with its heavy emphasis on the relationship between revolutions and the social systems in which they occur,[1] it is hardly surprising that historians of modern political revolutions have increasingly turned their attention to the wider social context in their search for an explanation for those events or that their discussions of the causal patterns of revolutions now give as much attention to social strain as to political and ideological conflict; to social dysfunction, frustration, anomie, and their indices as to weaknesses and tensions within the political system.[2] This enlarged frame of inquiry has yielded a much more comprehensive understanding of several specific revolutions.[3] Several efforts to apply it to the American Revolution raise the question of whether it will prove equally fruitful for all varieties of great modern political revolutions.

---

[1] Especially Chalmers Johnson, *Revolutionary Change* (Boston, 1966). But see also Neil J. Smelser, *Theory of Collective Behavior* (New York, 1962); James C. Davies, "Toward a Theory of Revolution," *American Sociological Review* 27 (1962): 5–19; Barrington Moore, Jr., *Social Origins of Dictatorship and Democracy: Lord and Peasant in the Making of the Modern World* (Boston, 1966); Henry Bienen, *Violence and Social Change* (Chicago, 1968); and Ted Robert Gurr, *Why Men Rebel* (Princeton, N.J., 1970).

[2] See, for instance, Lawrence Stone's influential translation of this theoretical literature for historians: "Theories of Revolution," *World Politics* 18 (1966): 159–76.

[3] Two splendid examples are the chapters by J. W. Smit and Lawrence Stone, respectively on "The Netherlands Revolution" and "The English Revolution," in Robert For-

The idea that the American Revolution may have had a social content—that is, social origins and social consequences—is hardly a new one. It has existed in a crude form ever since the Revolution, and between 1900 and 1930 a number of individual scholars—especially Charles H. Lincoln, Carl L. Becker, Arthur M. Schlesinger, Sr., Charles A. Beard, and J. Franklin Jameson—formulated an elaborate social interpretation of the Revolution.[4] Investigating various aspects of the internal political life of the American colonies between 1760 and 1790, they discovered what they took to be serious economic and social antagonisms underlying the major events of the American Revolution at virtually every stage of its development. Far from being simply a war for independence from Great Britain, the American Revolution—in the view of these men—also came to be seen as a social struggle by underprivileged groups against the special privileges and political dominance of an old colonial aristocracy.

The details of this interpretation are too well known to require a lengthy discussion here. Colonial society by the middle decades of the eighteenth century was everywhere fraught with severe class conflict arising out of an ever-greater concentration of wealth into the hands of the privileged few and an ever more rigid social structure, an increasingly aristocratic political system, and severe resentment among the masses who were increasingly being deprived of any opportunity to realize their own economic and political ambitions. Not surprisingly, the resulting tensions among these antagonistic social groups came surging to the surface during the Revolutionary controversy between 1765 and 1776 and, as Merrill Jensen later argued, converted the Revolution from a simple movement for independence from Great Britain into a "war against the colonial aristocracy."[5] Assessing the results of this "internal revolution," J. Franklin Jameson explicitly argued that the American

---

ster and Jack P. Greene, eds., *Preconditions of Revolution in Early Modern Europe* (Baltimore, 1970), 19–108.

[4] Charles H. Lincoln, *The Revolutionary Movement in Pennsylvania, 1760–1776* (Philadelphia, 1901); Carl Becker, *History of Political Parties in the Province of New York, 1760–1776* (Madison, Wis., 1909); Arthur M. Schlesinger, Sr., *The Colonial Merchants and the American Revolution, 1763–1776* (New York, 1918); Charles A. Beard, *An Economic Interpretation of the Constitution of the United States* (New York, 1913); J. Franklin Jameson, *The American Revolution as a Social Movement* (Princeton, N.J., 1926).

[5] Merrill Jensen, *The Articles of Confederation: An Interpretation of the Social-Constitutional History of the American Revolution, 1774–1781* (Madison, Wis., 1940), 11.

Revolution profoundly altered many features of colonial social and economic life and represented a significant advance toward a "levelling democracy" in the Revolutionary era.[6]

In origins as well as in results, the American Revolution thus came to
be thought of as the product not merely of a quarrel between Britain and
the colonies but also of deep fissures within colonial society and as a
social upheaval equal to the French, if not the Russian, Revolution. Because of its clear indebtedness to the liberal concept of American public
life during the era from which it emerged, this view of the Revolution
has subsequently been labeled the Progressive interpretation.[7] But it was
elaborated by still other scholars during the 1930s and 1940s. So widespread was its acceptance that it continued well into the 1950s to be the
orthodox interpretation of the Revolution.[8]

As is well known, this whole interpretation was discredited by the research of a wide range of scholars between 1945 and 1965. A number of
detailed studies of segments and aspects of political life in virtually every
colony as well as many of the concrete social changes emphasized by
Jameson seemed to indicate that, far from being similar to the French
Revolution, the American Revolution was a peculiarly American event
in which there was remarkably little social discontent expressed, only
minor social upheaval, and relatively few changes in the existing American social structure. In the decades after the Second World War, the
American Revolution thus came to be interpreted as an event that was
almost entirely political with little specific social content, one that could
be understood almost exclusively in political terms. Where the Progressive historians had gone wrong was, first, in reading the fundamental
social conflicts of their own day back into the Revolution and, second,
in using a conceptual framework derived from the French and later European revolutions to identify the questions they brought to the American Revolution, questions, the data seemed to indicate, that were irrelevant to the American Revolutionary experience.[9]

---

[6] Jameson, *American Revolution as a Social Movement*, 18.

[7] A penetrating general discussion of the three leading Progressive historians is Richard
Hofstadter, *The Progressive Historians: Turner, Beard, Parrington* (New York, 1968). For
a more detailed analysis of the Progressive interpretation of the Revolution, see Jack P.
Greene, *Reappraisal of the American Revolution in Recent Historical Literature* (Washington, D.C., 1967), 7–17.

[8] Greene, *Reappraisal*, 13–17.

[9] Ibid., 17–79, discusses in detail the thrust of post-World War II scholarship on the
Revolution. A representative collection of this scholarship will be found in Jack P.

No sooner had we begun to feel comfortable with this new view of the origins and nature of the American Revolution than the new analysis itself came under assault. The most compelling call for a revival of interest in the social content of the Revolution came from Gordon S. Wood in 1966 in an extended analysis of Bernard Bailyn's book-length introduction to *Pamphlets of the American Revolution, 1750—1776.*[10] Commenting on Bailyn's heavy emphasis upon the role of ideas in the coming of the Revolution, Wood argued that it was "precisely the remarkable revolutionary character of the Americans' ideas now being revealed by historians [such as Bailyn] that best indicates that something profoundly unsettling was going on in society." The "very nature" of the colonists' rhetoric, "its obsession with corruption and disorder, its hostile and conspiratorial outlook, and its millennial vision of a regenerated society," Wood argued, revealed "as nothing else apparently can the American Revolution as a true revolution with its sources lying deep within the social structure." "For this kind of frenzied rhetoric," he contended, "could spring only from the most severe sorts of social strain."[11]

As yet, Wood's call for "a new look at the social sources of the Revolution"[12] has not been answered systematically or comprehensively. Most of the wide assortment of specialized studies of various aspects of American social life between 1725 and 1775 have been, at the most, only implicitly concerned with explaining the American Revolution. But the data and conclusions they have provided may be used to construct and to evaluate some hypotheses about the possible relationship between social strain and the origins of the Revolution. The findings of these studies seem to lend themselves to one or the other of two central hypotheses. The first, which has never been explicitly formulated but has been gradually taking shape over the past fifteen years, is that colonial society underwent a dramatic erosion of internal social cohesion over the period from 1690 to 1760. The second, an updated and more sophisticated variant of the old Progressive thesis, is that over the same period the social structure of the colonies was becoming increasingly rigid and social strain correspondingly more intense.

Greene, ed., *The Reinterpretation of the American Revolution, 1763—1789* (New York, 1968).

[10] Bernard Bailyn, Introduction to *Pamphlets of the American Revolution* (Cambridge, Mass., 1965–   ), vol. 1.

[11] Gordon S. Wood, "Rhetoric and Reality in the American Revolution," *William and Mary Quarterly,* 3d ser., 23 (1966): 3–32, quotations from pp. 26, 31.

[12] Ibid., 24.

The most extensive and systematic presentation of evidence for the first of these hypotheses will be found in Richard L. Bushman's *From Puritan to Yankee: Character and the Social Order in Connecticut, 1690—1765,*[13] a case study of the various strains created by the rapid economic and demographic growth of that colony. But many other studies can also be used for its elaboration. According to this hypothesis, a great variety of developments combined to keep colonial society in a state of perpetual and disorienting ferment, a state that was both rapidly accelerating and increasing in intensity and extensity in the decades just before the Revolution. Chief among these developments were, first, the rapid territorial and demographic expansion, including the influx of many previously unrepresented religious and ethnic groups, and, second, the extraordinary acceleration of the economy with an attendant increase in commercialization, economic opportunity, and abundance. But there were many other developments that contributed to the ferment: the shattering of religious uniformity by that great spiritual upheaval known as the Great Awakening;[14] the rise of towns and small cities with lifestyles and social dynamics that pointedly distinguished them from the traditional rural communities of colonial America;[15] a quickening of the pace of social

---

[13] Richard L. Bushman, *From Puritan to Yankee: Character and the Social Order in Connecticut, 1690—1765* (Cambridge, Mass., 1967).

[14] See especially Alan Heimert, *Religion and the American Mind: From the Great Awakening to the Revolution* (Cambridge, Mass., 1966); C. C. Goen, *Revivalism and Separatism in New England, 1740—1800: Strict Congregationalists and Separate Baptists in the Great Awakening* (New Haven, 1962); Edwin Scott Gaustad, *The Great Awakening in New England* (New York, 1957); William G. McLoughlin, *Isaac Backus and the American Pietistic Tradition* (Boston, 1967), 1–109; and Bushman, *Puritan to Yankee,* 147–232. All of these works concentrate on New England. For the impact of the Great Awakening elsewhere, see Rhys Isaac, "Religion and Authority: Problems of the Anglican Establishment in Virginia in the Era of the Great Awakening and the Parsons' Cause," *William and Mary Quarterly,* 3d ser., 30 (1973): 3–36, and "Evangelical Revolt: The Nature of the Baptists' Challenge to the Traditional Order in Virginia, 1765 to 1775," ibid., 31 (1974): 345–68, as well as two older works: Wesley M. Gewehr, *The Great Awakening in Virginia, 1740—1790* (Durham, N.C., 1930), and Charles Hartshorn Maxson, *The Great Awakening in the Middle Colonies* (Chicago, 1920).

[15] The social impact of urbanization has not been systematically analyzed, but see the older study by Carl Bridenbaugh, *Cities in Revolt: Urban Life in America, 1743—1776* (New York, 1955), and three recent studies of individual towns: Sam Bass Warner, Jr., *The Private City: Philadelphia in Three Periods of Its Growth* (Philadelphia, 1968), 3–45;

differentiation, marked by the appearance of an increasingly more complex institutional and social structure and greater extremes in wealth;[16] and the intensification of the seemingly endemic factionalism of colonial politics, as men competed vigorously and ruthlessly with one another in their quest for land, wealth, status, and supremacy.[17]

Some of the potentially corrosive effects of this ferment have been noted by a number of scholars. The movement of people from older communities into newly opened regions greatly weakened the ties of authority and community.[18] Extremely high rates of upward social mobility threatened the standing of traditional elites by devaluing their status and confronting them with a seemingly endless series of challenges to their social and political power. At the same time, their reluctance to share authority with new men created severe status inconsistencies in which the new men had wealth—the main attribute of elite status in the colonies—without the political power and social position to go with it. To the traditional elite, the movement toward a more inclusive leadership structure appeared too rapid, while to the new men it seemed too slow. Moreover, as new men challenged traditional leaders or as elites splintered in their bitter contests for political supremacy, the political

George C. Rogers, Jr., *Charleston in the Age of the Pinckneys* (Norman, Okla., 1969), 3–115; and G. B. Warden, *Boston, 1689–1776* (Boston, 1970).

[16] On the process of social differentiation, see, among other studies, Lawrence A. Cremin, *American Education: The Colonial Experience, 1607–1783* (New York, 1970), 271–571; James A. Henretta, "Economic Development and Social Structure in Colonial Boston," *William and Mary Quarterly*, 3d ser., 32 (1965): 75–92; Kenneth A. Lockridge, "Land, Population, and the Evolution of New England Society, 1630–1790," *Past and Present*, no. 39 (1968): 62–80, and "Social Change and the Meaning of the American Revolution," *Journal of Social History* 6 (1973): 403–39; James T. Lemon and Gary B. Nash, "The Distribution of Wealth in Eighteenth-Century America: A Century of Change in Chester County, Pennsylvania, 1693–1802," *Journal of Social History* 2 (1968): 1–24; and Jackson Turner Main, *The Social Structure of Revolutionary America* (Princeton, N.J., 1965).

[17] Bernard Bailyn, *The Origins of American Politics* (New York, 1968), 55–161.

[18] On this point, see Bushman, *Puritan to Yankee*, 41–82; Lockridge, "Social Change and the Meaning of the American Revolution," 403–39; and Philip J. Greven, Jr., *Four Generations: Population, Land, and Family in Colonial Andover, Massachusetts* (Ithaca, N.Y., 1970), 175–258. The character of life in newer communities may be surmised from Charles E. Clark, *The Eastern Frontier: The Settlement of Northern New England, 1610–1763* (New York, 1970), 111–267; Charles S. Grant, *Democracy in the Connecticut Frontier Town of Kent* (New York, 1961); and, for a very different area, Robert W. Ramsey, *Carolina Cradle: Settlement of the Northwest Carolina Frontier, 1747–1762* (Chapel Hill, N.C., 1964).

and social standing of the elite as a whole as well as its internal cohesion was seriously undermined.[19] Additionally, the settlement of new areas put severe strains upon existing political structures at both the local and provincial levels, as older centers of power sought to extend their authority over distant areas whose economic interests, social and political orientations, and ethnic and religious compositions diverged sharply from their own, and those strains sometimes—in North Carolina, New Hampshire, and New Jersey in the late 1740s and early 1750s, in Pennsylvania in the mid-1760s, and in both Carolinas in the late 1760s and early 1770s—resulted in open sectional conflict and in a few cases even in the breakdown of government.[20]

Nor are these by any means all of the examples of the severe destabilizing effects of the rapid changes taking place in the colonies during the middle of the eighteenth century. The Great Awakening unleashed and mobilized widespread discontent with existing religious establishments from New England south to Virginia. From this discontent emerged a militant evangelicalism that rejected many aspects of the traditional social as well as religious order of the colonies and demanded sweeping changes in the relationship between church and state.[21] Rapid urbaniza-

---

[19] See Bushman, *From Puritan to Yankee*, 41–134; Edward Marks Cook, Jr., "Social Behavior and Changing Values in Dedham, Massachusetts, 1700 to 1775," *William and Mary Quarterly*, 3d ser., 27 (1970): 546–80; John J. Waters, Jr., *The Otis Family in Provincial and Revolutionary Massachusetts* (Chapel Hill, N.C., 1968), 76–161; Heimert, *Religion and the American Mind*, 27–236; and Jack P. Greene, "Changing Interpretations of Early American Politics," in Ray A. Billington, ed., *The Reinterpretation of Early American History: Essays in Honor of John Edwin Pomfret* (San Marino, Calif., 1966), 151–84.

[20] Greene, "Changing Interpretations of Early American Politics," 159–72; Lawrence F. London, "The Representation Controversy in Colonial North Carolina," *North Carolina Historical Review* 11 (1934): 255–70; Donald L. Kemmerer, *Path to Freedom: The Struggle for Self-Government in Colonial New Jersey, 1703–1776* (Princeton, N.J., 1940), 187–236; Brooke Hindle, "The March of the Paxton Boys," *William and Mary Quarterly*, 3d ser., 3 (1946): 461–86; J. E. Crowley, "The Paxton Disturbance and Ideas of Order in Pennsylvania Politics," *Pennsylvania History* 37 (1972): 317–39; Richard M. Brown, *The South Carolina Regulators: The Story of the First Vigilante Movement* (Cambridge, Mass., 1963); Hugh T. Lefler and Paul Wagar, eds., *Orange County, 1752–1952* (Chapel Hill, N.C., 1952); and M. L. M. Kay, "An Analysis of a British Colony in Late Eighteenth Century America in the Light of Current American Historiographical Controversy," *Australian Journal of Politics and History* 11 (1965): 170–84.

[21] Heimert, *Religion and the American Mind*, 1–236; Bushman, *From Puritan to Yankee*, 147–232; J. M. Bumsted, "Religion, Finance, and Democracy in Massachusetts: The

tion also produced some unsettling effects. For one thing, it led to the appearance of an urban-rural dichotomy in many colonies. More importantly, by crowding large numbers of not fully assimilated and sometimes impoverished people together in a small area, it also created for the first time in the colonies a potential for the emergence of intraurban class and group antagonisms within the cities themselves.[22] The process of institutional differentiation that was taking place within medium-sized and large urban communities may also have contributed to the attenuation of the traditional highly personal pattern of social relations by establishing institutional barriers among groups and thereby helping to bring about a significant depersonalization of the social system.[23]

Finally, by whetting the social and economic appetites and increasing the material aspirations of people at all levels of society, the "profuse abundance" of the American environment seemed to have produced a disturbing rise in several forms of hedonistic and anomic behavior and a corresponding decline in moral standards and devotion to the public good, in direct violation of inherited norms. What was even worse, at least in some quarters, such forms of behavior appeared to be gaining

Town of Norton as a Case Study," *Journal of American History* 57 (1970–71): 817–31; Isaac, "Religion and Authority," 3–36.

[22] In the absence of specific studies of the social impact of urbanization, see Warden, *Boston*, 102–73; Henretta, "Economic Development and Social Structure in Colonial Boston," 75–92; Robert J. Taylor, *Western Massachusetts in the Revolution* (Providence, 1954); Richard D. Brown, *Revolutionary Politics in Massachusetts: The Boston Committee of Correspondence and the Towns, 1772–1774* (Cambridge, Mass., 1970); Robert Zemsky, *Merchants, Farmers, and River Gods: An Essay on Eighteenth-Century American Politics* (Boston, 1971), 255–60, 264, 281; Warner, *The Private City*, 3–21; G. B. Warden, "L'urbanisation americaine avant 1800," *Annales*, 25e année (1970), 862–79; James T. Lemon, "Urbanization and the Development of Eighteenth-Century Southeastern Pennsylvania and Adjacent Delaware," *William and Mary Quarterly*, 3d ser., 24 (1967): 501–42; Richard A. Ryerson, "Political Mobilization and the American Revolution: The Resistance Movement in Philadelphia, 1765 to 1776," ibid., 31 (1974): 565–88; Gary B. Nash, "The Transformation of Urban Politics, 1700–1765," *Journal of American History* 60 (1973): 605–32; Pauline Maier, "The Charleston Mob and the Evolution of Politics in Revolutionary South Carolina, 1765–1784," *Perspectives in American History* 4 (1970): 173–96; Carl Bridenbaugh, *Myths and Realities: Societies of the Colonial South* (Baton Rouge, La., 1952), 54–196; and Rogers, *Charleston in the Age of the Pinckneys*, 3–88.

[23] There has been almost no attention to this kind of problem in colonial America, but see the extremely suggestive analysis in Peter Laslett, *The World We Have Lost* (New York, 1965), 1–80, 150–99. See also Lockridge, "Social Change and the Meaning of the American Revolution," 405–15.

public acceptance, thus endangering the normative cohesion of colonial society.[24]

If the first hypothesis emphasizes the unsettled and chaotic state of colonial society during the mid-eighteenth century, the second suggests that it was becoming too settled. In his comprehensive investigation of *The Social Structure of Revolutionary America,* Jackson Turner Main has speculated about the existence of a general "long-term tendency . . . toward greater inequality, with more marked class distinctions throughout the colonies on the eve of the pre-Revolutionary disturbances,"[25] and several case studies of communities as diverse in size and character as Boston and Chester County, Pennsylvania, strongly suggest that during the decades just before the Revolution opportunity was declining and the social structure was becoming less open in older settled communities as a result of overcrowding brought on by a shortage of land, increasing social stratification, a greater concentration of wealth in the hands of the upper classes, rising numbers of poor, a proliferation of dependency relationships, and a pronounced tendency toward political elitism.

All of these developments, the argument runs, created deep frustrations among those who found opportunity constricting, their standard of living dropping, and their life prospects growing correspondingly dimmer. The supposed result was the creation of severe tensions between privileged and unprivileged, landed and landless, masters and servants, even fathers and sons.[26] These tensions, it has been suggested, were manifest in "a general increase in demands per capita on the political system" and a "sharpened concern over the concentration of wealth and the decline in social equality, over the concentration of political power, over

[24] Jack P. Greene, "Search for Identity: An Interpretation of the Meaning of Selected Patterns of Social Response in Eighteenth-Century America," *Journal of Social History* 3 (1970): 189–220; Perry Miller, "From the Covenant to the Revival," in James Ward Smith and A. Leland Jamison, eds., *The Shaping of American Religion,* 3 vols. (Princeton, N.J., 1961), 1:322–68; Edmund S. Morgan, "The Puritan Ethic and the American Revolution," *William and Mary Quarterly,* 3d ser., 24 (1967): 3–43; Gordon S. Wood, "Rhetoric and Reality," 24–32, and *The Creation of the American Republic, 1776–1787* (Chapel Hill, N.C., 1961), 1–24.

[25] Main, *Social Structure,* 286–87.

[26] See, especially, Kenneth A. Lockridge, *A New England Town, the First Hundred Years: Dedham, Massachusetts, 1636–1736* (New York, 1970), 139–85, and "Land, Population, and the Evolution of New England Society," 62–80; Henretta, "Economic Development and Social Structure in Colonial Boston," 75–92; Lemon and Nash, "Distribution of Wealth in Eighteenth-Century America," 1–24; and Nash, "Transformation of Urban Politics," 605–32.

increasing dependence, over the division of society by interests and over apparently declining material opportunity."[27]

Much further research will be required before we will know with some degree of certainty to what extent either or both of these two general hypotheses—the one emphasizing the destabilizing effects of rapid change and the other the frustrations created by a closing society—may be an accurate representation of some of the realities of mid-eighteenth-century colonial social development. On the basis of present knowledge, however, it is clear that there are at least three major questions that need to be confronted.

The first is simply how to resolve a number of important ambiguities about the meaning and operation of several of these specific components of social strain we have just described. For one thing, there is an apparent contradiction between the two general hypotheses. How could colonial society be becoming at once less coherent and more rigid? This problem might, of course, be resolved in one of three ways. First, it is possible that there were significant spatial variations, that there was a tendency toward less coherence in some rapidly developing areas and more rigidity in other older and more stable areas. A less likely possibility is that a generalized long-term linear process was at work with a period of intense social and economic upheaval being followed just before the Revolution by a time of declining opportunity and greater stratification. Finally, it is possible, as P. M. G. Harris has suggested,[28] that this process was cyclical, with colonial society becoming more or less flexible according to population change, community growth, institutional development, and various contingency factors, though the cycles may not have been quite so regular as Harris has posited.[29] My own suspicion is that some combination of the first and third possibilities will probably provide the most plausible resolution to this problem.

But there are many other more specific difficulties with each of these hypotheses, and this is especially true with the first. Like many of the works which can be cited in its support, it rests upon an obvious, though

[27] Lockridge, "Social Change and the Meaning of the American Revolution," 416–19.

[28] P. M. G. Harris, "The Social Origins of American Leaders: The Demographic Foundations," *Perspectives in American History* 3 (1969): 159–344.

[29] See the criticisms of Daniel Scott Smith, "Cyclical, Secular, and Structural Change in American Elite Composition," ibid., 4 (1970): 351–74.

unstated, and relatively crude application of an equilibrium theory of society. As critics of such theories have pointed out, to the extent that they assess the health or sickness of society in terms of whether or not the elements within it are in a condition of homeostasis and view change as an essentially disequilibrating force, they are potentially distorting, for it is not at all clear that the invariable price of rapid change is social instability. Obviously, change can be so well institutionalized and so widely accepted as to be itself stabilizing in its effects. Indeed, in the specific situation at hand, it can be argued that change—and increasingly rapid change at that—was at the heart of the colonial life experience and that the colonists had been forced almost from the beginning to come to terms with it.[30] Moreover, the second hypothesis suggests that it was the slowing down of change rather than its acceleration that created a potential for serious social disruption.

More particularly, it is not yet clear that the cost of rapid economic and demographic growth in combination with increasing social differentiation was always a loss of social cohesion: certainly, although there was everywhere an acceleration of the economy and the population, there does not appear to have been a movement from more to less social coherence in most of the colonies during the first three quarters of the eighteenth century. Significantly, most of the evidence for this view comes from New England, where the early settlers were reasonably homogeneous and, for most of the seventeenth century at least, generally devoted to an explicit religious and "social synthesis" that had been worked out by the leaders of the first settlements.

But each of the colonies to the south, each of the provinces from New York to Georgia, had been settled by individuals with widely divergent backgrounds, goals, interests, and orientations; and there the direction of social development during the eighteenth century was clearly toward more rather than less coherence and homogeneity as disparate groups fashioned out of diverse materials a social synthesis where none had been before.[31] Even with regard to the New England colonies, it may be ar-

---

[30] To make an intelligent judgment about this matter, we need a considerable amount of empirical evidence about individual and group reactions not only to specific social changes but to the very phenomenon of change itself. That is, we need to know in what ways the colonists' life experiences—and especially their experience with change—during the century and a half before 1760 affected their capacity to adjust to shifting social circumstances, especially whether and to what extent their earlier experience may have prepared them for the acceptance of adversity as well as opportunity.

[31] The point is obvious, but see, for example, Patricia U. Bonomi, *A Factious People: Politics and Society in Colonial New York* (New York, 1971); Gary B. Nash, *Quakers and*

gued that the breakdown of the old Puritan synthesis early in the eighteenth century was accompanied by the emergence of a new one that, while retaining a distinctly Puritan flavor, was not so dissimilar in form and character from those achieved at the same time by the colonies farther south.[32]

And there are still other problems. One problem arises out of the uncertainty that the rapid upward social mobility, the accelerated movement toward political inclusion, and the Great Awakening functioned as destabilizing rather than stabilizing forces or that the kinds of conflict they engendered did not relieve as much social strain as they created.[33] In addition, it is also possible that the widespread expression of concern about rising standards of consumption in the colonies was less an indication of fundamental discontent with existing modes of behavior than an appropriate—and necessary—device through which the colonists could fulfill an apparent need to preserve the ideal of a more static, coherent, goal-oriented, and instrumental social order without requiring them to alter their actual behavior.

There are far fewer obvious problems with the second hypothesis. But it is possible that in terms of opportunity and career chances for individuals throughout colonial society the shortage of land in older communites may have been more than offset not only by the opening up of new areas but also by new opportunities in nonfarm occupations created by the ongoing process of social differentiation and institutional development.[34] Moreover, from the evidence so far adduced, it is by no means certain that the decline in opportunity, the concentration of wealth, and the growing "Europeanization" of colonial society was sufficiently intense to be productive either of significant social malaise, even in older settled areas, or of a net increase in per capita demands on the political

---

Politics: Pennsylvania, 1681—1726 (Princeton, N.J., 1968); and M. Eugene Sirmans, *Colonial South Carolina: A Political History, 1663—1763* (Chapel Hill, N.C., 1966).

[32] For an elaboration of this argument, see Jack P. Greene, "Autonomy and Stability: New England and the British Colonial Experience in Early Modern America," *Journal of Social History* 7 (1974): 171–94, and the intriguing suggestions in Zemsky, *Merchants, Farmers, and River Gods*, 69–74.

[33] See the interesting suggestions by Edward A. Tiryakian about the relationship between religious revivals and societal revolutions in "A Model of Societal Change and Its Lead Indicators," in Samuel Z. Klausner, ed., *The Study of Total Societies* (New York, 1967), 94–95.

[34] Greven, *Four Generations*, 103–258, and James T. Lemon, *The Best Poor Man's Country: A Geographical Study of Early Southeastern Pennsylvania* (Baltimore, 1972), present a considerable amount of evidence that would seem to support this suggestion.

system. Certainly, fear of land scarcity or of declining opportunity does not seem to have been a dominant theme of social and political literature either before or during the Revolution. To be sure, there were sporadic complaints about adverse economic conditions—in the mid-1740s, the early 1760s, the early 1770s, and the mid-1780s. But these complaints are all traceable not to broad, long-term changes but to specific short-term conditions. If scarcity and economic decline were not widely manifest, moreover, abundance certainly was—in all of the colonies and at no time more than during the half century just before the Revolution—both in the literature of celebration and in expressions of anxiety over the potentially corrosive effects of galloping luxury.[35]

Nor upon a close inspection does it appear that there was much—and certainly not a "sharpened"—concern over either growing concentrations of wealth or increasing social inequality. At no time from the founding of Jamestown through the Revolution had social and economic equality been a basic goal of any sizable or strategically placed segment of colonial society. Differentiation was present from the beginning and was the only logical outcome of the colonizing impulse. As the Reverend Francis Alison told his Presbyterian congregation in 1750, all men had an equal right "to reap the benefit of honest industry."[36] But such equality implied social differences and distinctions. In James Harrington's aphorism, "Industry of all things is the most accumulative, and accumulation of all things hates leveling."[37] The colonists were thus committed to the individual's equal but unrestrained right to acquire as much as he could, to achieve the best life possible within the limits of his ability, means, and opportunity. Such a commitment meant that colonial society, like Harrington's ideal commonwealth *Oceana*, "could not only tolerate great economic inequalities but required them as a safeguard for propertied interests"[38] and that the "attempt to vanquish the inevitable differentiation of society together with all its consequences" that became manifest during the Revolution would not become central to the Revolutionary impulse.[39] To be sure, as Bernard Bailyn has pointed out, colonial Americans had a latent antagonism to privilege, to those special legal,

[35] See Greene, "Search for Identity," 189–220.

[36] As quoted by J. R. Pole, *Political Representation in England and the Origins of the American Republic* (New York, 1966), 269.

[37] *The Political Writings of James Harrington*, ed. Charles Blitzer (New York, 1955), 12.

[38] Pole, *Political Representation*, 9.

[39] Lockridge, "Social Change and the Meaning of the American Revolution," 434.

economic, social, and political advantages and exemptions that sustained the legally privileged orders of Europe.[40] But they had only respect for distinctions that had been "fairly earned" and were the legitimate fruits of "superior industry, talent, and virtue."[41]

Correlatively, there would seem to have been far less concern among the society at large over the "Europeanization" of colonial society than among some segments of the elite over its failure to become sufficiently Europeanized. The movement toward feudalism described by Rowland Berthoff and John Murrin was, insofar as it existed as either an explicit or an implicit movement, a futile and retrogressive protest against the excessive fluidity of colonial society. For one of the most fundamental facts about that society was not that it—any more than contemporary England—was becoming more feudal, but, as a long line of commentators from William Knox to Paul Lucas have pointed out, that the elite had no way to set itself apart from the rest of society as a separate, coherent, and reasonably permanent social order.[42] This is in no way to challenge the argument that colonial society was moving toward greater differentiation, but only to underline the point that resentments among some members of the elite about their inability to achieve the full fruits of membership in the elite, fruits that were enjoyed by their British counterparts (even in Ireland) as a matter of course, may have been far more intense and were certainly far more evident than discontent within other segments of society about increasing concentrations of wealth and levels of social differentiation.

Equally doubtful is the claim that there was as a function of social change a net per capita increase in demands on the political system through the middle decades of the eighteenth century. Bushman's work strongly suggests that there may have been such an increase in Connecticut, and the same may have been true for Rhode Island, which had a similar political structure; for newer and still relatively primitive political societies such as those of North Carolina, New Jersey, and perhaps

---

[40] See Bailyn, "The Central Themes of the American Revolution: An Interpretation," in Stephen G. Kurtz and James H. Hutson, eds., *Essays on the American Revolution* (Chapel Hill, N.C., 1973), 27–31.

[41] Wood, *Creation of the American Republic,* 73, 572.

[42] See Rowland Berthoff and John M. Murrin, "Feudalism, Communalism, and the Yeoman Freeholder: The American Revolution Considered as a Social Accident," in Kurtz and Hutson, *Essays on the American Revolution,* 256–88; Jack P. Greene, ed., "William Knox's Explanation for the American Revolution," *William and Mary Quarterly,* 3d ser., 30 (1973): 293–306; and Paul Lucas, "A Note on the Comparative Study of the Structure of Politics," ibid., 28 (1971): 301–9.

even New Hampshire; and for the larger urban centers.[43] Elsewhere, however, in older settled colonies and regions such as Virginia, Massachusetts, South Carolina, Pennsylvania, and Maryland, the trend seems to have been precisely the opposite, as the relationship between leaders and constituency changed from an essentially aggressive and participatory stance toward the political process on the part of the constituency to one that was much more passive and deferential. This change was reflected by declining levels of participation in elections and a seeming acceptance of the legitimacy and good policy of a more and more elitist leadership structure, developments that suggest not deepening political alienation but growing political socialization among the constituency. Thus, it is entirely possible that in the short run whatever social changes were occurring through the middle decades of the eighteenth century functioned rather more to fortify than to undermine the political position of the elite, as the constituency, at least before the 1760s, remained more latent than mobilized.[44]

The second major question raised by these two hypotheses is the extent to which there were significant variations in the nature of social development not only from colony to colony but also from region to region within a given community. From what we already know, it is clear that the differences were considerable, and the extent of these differences suggests that it is improbable that either or both of these hypotheses can subsume all of them.

The third, final, and in terms of the present discussion much the most important and pressing question posed by these hypotheses is the precise relationship between the many manifestations of social strain they have described and the American Revolution. Several scholars, especially Wood and Kenneth A. Lockridge,[45] have asserted the existence of direct causal links. But these assertions have been accompanied by what Clifford Geertz has called "a studied vagueness" that conceals the fact that as yet no one has succeeded either in establishing that such links existed or in specifying exactly what they may have been and how they

---

[43] See Bushman, *Puritan to Yankee;* and Nash, "Transformation of Urban Politics."

[44] For an elaboration of these ideas, see Jack P. Greene, "The Growth of Political Stability: An Interpretation of Political Development in the Anglo-American Colonies, 1660–1760," in John Parker and Carol Urness, eds., *The American Revolution: A Heritage of Change* (Minneapolis, 1975), 26–52.

[45] Wood, "Rhetoric and Reality," 24–32; Lockridge, *A New England Town,* 184–85, and "Social Change and the Meaning of the American Revolution."

may have functioned in the overall causal pattern of the Revolution.[46] To a large extent, this failure accounts for the perpetuation of the widespread conviction among students of the Revolution that no such links were present or that, if they were, they could not have been very important.

This conviction has been reinforced by the obvious fact that the American Revolution failed to generate a societal revolution. Note that I purposely use the term *societal revolution,* which connotes "a discontinuous process of structural innovation," rather than *social revolution,* which implies no more than some "quantitative increments" or qualitative changes within an existing structure.[47] Although the Revolution obviously helped to accelerate some long-standing tendencies within colonial society toward greater political and social inclusion and more individual autonomy, and although incremental changes in patterns of social organization, institutional arrangements, and values may be observed in many sectors of American life during the Revolution,[48] there do not seem to be any sharp discontinuities that cannot be traced primarily to exigencies created by the separation from Britain. In other words, one does not need to look for strain, frustration, and dysfunction within colonial society and one must look to the political conflict between Britain and the colonies to find a plausible explanation for these discontinuities.

But the limited character of the internal social changes produced by the Revolution can by no means be taken to mean that these various components of strain had no causal relationship to the Revolution. That social context has an important bearing upon political events is a truism, and because these components were all present to one degree or another in colonial society at the time the Revolution occurred, it may be safely assumed that they had some effect upon the Revolution. The main question, then, is not whether a causal relationship existed, but what kind of a relationship it may have been.

At least four possibilities immediately present themselves. First, from

---

[46] Clifford Geertz, "Ideology as a Cultural System," in David E. Apter, ed., *Ideology and Discontent* (Glencoe, Ill., 1964), 53.

[47] See the useful discussion by Tiryakian in "A Model of Societal Change and Its Lead Indicators," 73.

[48] See, especially, Main, *Social Structure,* and Wood, *Creation of the American Republic.*

the evidence offered in support of the first hypothesis discussed above, we may surmise that the severity of social strain was so great—the anomie, disorientation, frustration, and friction so intensive and extensive—within colonial society as to make it exceptionally prone toward revolution by creating either a single social crisis of such magnitude that it cut across and through most segments and areas of colonial life or a complex multitude of interlocking local, group, and personal crises that converged to produce severe disruption in many strategic sectors of colonial society. Something of this sort seems to have been what Wood was implying in his essay.[49]

Second, a corollary of this argument, which Alan Heimert and others have suggested, is that the Great Awakening and presumably the many other changes that contributed to the social ferment of the mid-eighteenth century prepared the colonists intellectually and emotionally for the rejection of British authority after 1763 by calling into question or otherwise undermining confidence in the authority of traditional religious, social, and political institutions and leaders.[50]

On the other hand, the findings on which the second hypothesis rests can be marshaled in support of still a third argument which is a variant of the old formula of the Progressive historians: that declining opportunity and calcifying social structure created fierce resentments among the middle and lower classes against the elite that came surging to the surface of public life during the pre-Revolutionary years and merged with the protest against Britain to generate an internal revolution.[51]

Still a fourth alternative is suggested by combining these two hypotheses: that, however upsetting it may have been to members of the older elite, the economic and demographic expansion and social ferment through the first five decades of the eighteenth century created rising economic and social expectations among the rest of society that were subsequently frustrated by a decline in opportunity beginning about midcentury. According to this formulation, which is merely an application of James C. Davies's general theory of revolution to the American Revolution,[52] the most critical element in turning American society to-

---

[49] "Rhetoric and Reality," 24–32. Lockridge is considerably more cautious: see "Social Change and the Meaning of the American Revolution," esp. 415.

[50] Heimert, *Religion and the American Mind.*

[51] Summaries of the arguments of the Progressive historians may be found in Greene, *Reappraisal of the American Revolution,* 7–17, and "Changing Interpretations of Early American Politics," 153–56.

[52] Davies, "Toward a Theory of Revolution," 1–19.

ward a revolutionary posture was not the erosion of social coherence or even the decline of opportunity but the frustrated expectations of a large segment of the population as a result of a general closing of society after a prolonged period of apparently becoming increasingly more open.

Some or all of these theories may turn out to be appropriate vehicles for relating the various components of social change in mid-eighteenth-century America to the Revolution. So far, we have been offered little more than a superficial historicism that suggests that the behavior of the generation of the Revolution somehow emerged from or was conditioned by the social environment, a suggestion that is "so general as to be truistic."[53] Before we will know which, if any, of these four theories are appropriate, we will have to be able to specify much more precisely than we can at present the ways in which those changes impinged upon and affected the actual behavior of particular groups and individuals during the 1760s and 1770s; the degree to which any discontent produced by such changes was "blamed on the political system and its agents";[54] how, when, where, why, and to what extent the uncoordinated individual and group dissatisfactions that may have been produced by those changes merged into the collective opposition to Britain; and whether, in what sense, and by what sorts of psychological mechanisms those dissatisfactions actually did find "mitigation through revolution and republicanism," as Wood has contended.[55]

In the meantime, two different categories of existing studies provide some help in this regard. By revealing, if in many cases only implicitly, the connection between particular sorts of social, economic, and religious strain and political factionalism, the rather extensive literature on political divisions within individual colonies between 1750 and 1776 and their relationship to the Revolution provides some general indications of what the answers to at least a few of these questions may be for several colonies. In particular, they make it clear that there were extensive variations from one colony to another and that virtually every colony had its own specific forms of social strain.[56] A few studies of the many symbolic representations of internal social strains in Revolutionary rhetoric have

---

[53] Geertz, "Ideology as a Cultural System," 53.

[54] Gurr, *Why Men Rebel*, 8.

[55] Wood, "Rhetoric and Reality," 30. For a persuasive argument on the necessity of providing precise answers to such questions, see James Rule and Charles Tilly, "1830 and the Unnatural History of Revolution," *Journal of Social Issues* 28 (1972): 49–76.

[56] See the discussion in Greene, "Changing Interpretations of Early American Politics," 159–72.

confronted the general question of the connection between such strains and the Revolution more directly. They have shown how colonial fears about moral declension and the increase in self-oriented behavior in their own societies merged with the opposition to Britain to turn the Revolution into a "norm-oriented movement" that looked forward to the regeneration of American society and the restoration of traditional social norms.[57] There can be no doubt that this projection of American corruption upon Britain helped to make the rejection of monarchy and the British connection and the acceptance of revolution and republicanism easier. To what extent it also relieved Americans of the guilt produced by their own moral failures and thereby helped to mitigate an important source of social strain within the colonies is not so clear. Indeed, by turning them toward republicanism with its even higher and less attainable standards, it may have exacerbated such strains.[58] Moreover, in the absence of any systematic attempt to assess the relative importance of these fears of moral declension in mobilizing widespread popular support for the Revolution, it is difficult to know what causal weight they may bear.[59]

Whenever and however these crucial problems are resolved, it is doubtful that we will be able to assign any or all of the components of social strain so far discussed a major causal role in the Revolution. To do so we would have to show that the extent of strain was infinitely greater and the degree of impingement of that strain on individuals and groups much more powerful than anyone has so far suggested or than our present

---

[57] See, especially, Miller, "From the Covenant to the Revival," 322–68; Morgan, "The Puritan Ethic," 3–43; and Wood, *Creation of the American Republic,* 1–124. On "norm-oriented movements," see Smelser, *Theory of Collective Behavior,* 109–11, 270–312, and Tiryakian, "A Model of Societal Change," 93–94.

[58] Wood's own evidence in *Creation of the American Republic* would seem to suggest as much.

[59] In *Religion and the American Mind,* Heimert has attempted to show the existence of certain continuities between the intellectual and social divisions of the Great Awakening and those of the Revolution, but enough individual exceptions to his argument have been noted to raise serious questions about its general applicability. In particular, see Bernard Bailyn, "Religion and Revolution: Three Biographical Studies," *Perspectives in American History* 4 (1970): 85–172.

knowledge seems to warrant.[60] That we will be able to say even that any or all of those components were a necessary cause of the Revolution, that is, that without them there would have been no Revolution, is extremely doubtful. In all probability, we will be able to say only that these several components—for the most part, the regular concomitants of the normal processes of incremental change within colonial society—affected the Revolution in the same sense that they would have affected any other major political event that occurred in the context of which they were a part. Thus, they may be said to have "aggravated," perhaps in some cases even "intensely," "antagonism to the imperial system" and to have "fed into the revolutionary movement."[61] But they cannot be said either to have created the movement or to have been necessary for it to occur.

Nevertheless, an understanding of the complex internal social, economic, political, and religious changes that were taking place within the colonies is essential to a comprehension of many aspects of the Revolution, and they can neither be relegated to a residual role nor eliminated from further discussions of the causes of the Revolution. Existing knowledge suggests and future investigations will surely confirm that there was a direct relationship between the degree and special character of social malintegration and the particular configuration of the Revolution in each colony and that an understanding of the nature and intensity of internal strain within a given colony during the quarter century before Independence would enable us to predict what general shape the Revolution would assume in that colony. If this suggestion is correct, then an analysis of the character and operation of various elements of social strain within the colonies is absolutely crucial to any comprehension of the many variations in the form and nature of the Revolution from one colony or one region to another.

For analytical and heuristic purposes, we might say, for instance, that only if every one of the components of strain so far identified and discussed, as well as any that may subsequently be discovered, impinged directly upon the Revolution in a given colony would we be likely to find the Revolution in its fullest and most extreme form. For simplicity, we

---

[60] If these strains had been a source of major discontent, we would expect to find a significant increase in the extent and intensity of such indices of social strain as crime, insanity, and both individual and collective violence in the colonies. No systematic study has been made of this subject, and it is obviously an area that is worth intensive investigation.

[61] Wood, "Rhetoric and Reality," 27.

can call this most extreme form of the Revolution *R*. It then follows that
the absence of one or more of these components in another colony will
result in something less than *R*. What we can finally say, then, about the
causal importance of all of these strain-producing elements—perhaps all
we can say—is that without any or all of them, we would not have all
of *R*.

The larger point is that without the conflict between Britain and the
colonies these components of social strain would not in themselves have
produced a revolution. In any explanation of the Revolution, then, what
one wants to know about such components is how they related to the
Anglo-American conflict, how they may be used to illuminate the traditional and still central question of how and why the old structure of interests, institutions, and symbols—the sacred moral order—that bound
the colonies and Britain together for the previous century broke down
so rapidly during the third quarter of the eighteenth century. For that
breakdown—as well as the frenzied rhetoric that accompanied it—can
be explained largely in terms of the anxieties deriving out of what the
vast majority of both the colonial and British political nations took to
be a series of fundamental violations of that sacred order by the other
side, without invoking whatever frustrations or resentments may have
arisen out of social strains within the colonies.

Assuming that they turn out to be correct, these conclusions raise serious doubts both about the argument—implicit in the theories of Chalmers Johnson, Neil J. Smelser, and other modern analysts of revolution—that "true revolutions," to quote Wood, must derive from "sources
lying deep within the social structure"[62] and about the utility of such
generalized theories of social change in explaining the origins of political
revolutions. Certainly, the example of the American Revolution would
seem to make it clear that social strain is a concept of limited explanatory value for at least one variety of great modern political revolution.
As James Rule and Charles Tilly have suggested in a persuasive critique
of these and other "natural history" models of revolution, the central
feature of any political revolution is "the seizure of power over a govern-
mental apparatus by one group from another," and such a development
can usually be explained largely as a result of some conflict between two
or more contenders within the polity over one or more issues of great
moment. These issues may have social or economic, religious or cultural
content, but they are invariably political because they are fought out in

---

[62] Ibid., 26.

a political arena and involve questions of basic concern to the polity. As Isaac Kramnick has remarked, "while any decent theory of the causes of revolution must take into account the political factor as well as all the others—economic, sociological, and psychological—nevertheless the political seems to play the decisive role, being forever indispensable in each of the other models."[63]

What one needs to know, then, to understand what caused a particular revolution is what specific conditions—long-term, intermediate, and short-term—led to the appearance of, first, rival contenders for authority and legitimacy; second, the acceptance of the claims of the revolutionaries by a significant or strategic segment of the politically relevant population; and third, the unwillingness or incapacity of the old regime to suppress its opponents. Usually, there is no special need to search for the existence of "anomie, strain, dysfunction or frustration" to explain these events. Wherever such evidences of disequilibration are present, they may well feed into the revolutionary situation. But because they will usually be found to exist both before and after the revolution and at any number of intervening periods when no revolution occurred, they "fail to characterize situations that are distinctly revolutionary, and thus lack [much] explanatory power."[64] Not only can they not in themselves provide a sufficient explanation for many modern revolutions, but they cannot in cases like the American Revolution even be said to have been necessary for them to occur.

The limited causal importance of the many evidences of social strain we have been discussing in this chapter does not imply that we should abandon their study, but it does suggest that they should be approached from a different and considerably broader perspective. Whatever their relationship to the American Revolution, they were obviously manifestations of fundamental, long-term social changes taking place within the colonies. To the very great extent that those changes were in the direction of more rational and less traditional patterns of social, economic, and political relations, institutional structures, and values that put ever-higher premiums upon individual autonomy, self-fulfillment, pursuit of self-interest, maximization of economic returns, accumulation, achievement rather than ascription, functional specificity of economic and social roles, and universalistic criteria for membership in the polity and society,

---

[63] Isaac Kramnick, "Reflections on Revolution: Definition and Explanation in Recent Scholarship," *History and Theory* 11 (1972): 63.

[64] Rule and Tilly, "1830 and the Un-natural History of Revolutions."

they were part of what E. A. Wrigley has described as a "revolution of modernization,"[65] a sweeping social revolution that had been in progress in western Europe since the middle of the fifteenth century and, by the time of the American Revolution, had been under way in the colonies for more than a century and a half.

This broader social revolution, which in many respects is far more crucial to an understanding of the first two centuries of American life and far more worthy of scholarly attention than the American Revolution, would have been completed with or without the American Revolution, albeit perhaps at a different rate of speed and in a somewhat different form,[66] and it would be unfortunate if it continued to be confused with the American Revolution. For, however interwoven it may have been with the American Revolution during the brief span of time between 1760 and 1790, there is always the danger that an excessive concentration upon discovering and specifying the links between the two will not only divert attention from and obscure the nature of the broader social revolution but will also contribute to prolong the unfortunate American tendency to view social history as primarily interesting for what it can tell us about politics.[67] As E. J. Hobsbawm has warned, the value of studies of "major transformations of society" may well be "in inverse proportion to our concentration on the brief moment of conflict." It is a commonplace, of course, that political revolutions, by bringing out into the open and dramatizing "crucial aspects of social structure" that would remain hidden or obscure in normal times, provide a window into the societies in which they occur.[68] But the particular phenomena thereby observed will appear in their fullest meaning only when they are fitted into the wider context of the long-term tendencies of which they are a part. Only when such a context has been established will the precise relationship between America's late eighteenth-century political revolu-

---

[65] E. A. Wrigley, "Modernization and the Industrial Revolution in England," *Journal of Interdisciplinary History* 3 (1972): 225–59. The definitions of *traditional* and *modern* implicit in my passages are derived from this paper.

[66] Jackson Turner Main, "The American Revolution as a Social Incident," paper presented on Mar. 10, 1971, at the Symposium on the American Revolution in Williamsburg, Va., p. 12, comes to a similar conclusion.

[67] Among several important recent works which attempt to break out of the prison of political history, see, especially, the general book-length essay by Rowland Berthoff, *An Unsettled People: Social Order and Disorder in American History* (New York, 1971), and the specialized study by Greven, *Four Generations.*

[68] E. J. Hobsbawm, "From Social History to the History of Society," *Daedalus* 100 (1971): 39–40.

tion and its peculiar variant of the wider social revolution of modernization that by the end of the eighteenth century was sweeping through
much of the Western world finally become clear.

The first draft of this chapter was originally written in 1971 as part of a broader and
never yet completed study of the causal pattern of the American Revolution. It was
presented at San Diego State University, California, on March 20, 1972, and at San Jose
State University, California, March 21, 1972, as the second annual lecture of The California State University and Colleges Statewide Lecture Series to Honor the Bicentennial
of the American Revolution and to The Seminar in the Department of History, The
Johns Hopkins University, Baltimore, Maryland, September 11, 1972. The published
version was the subject of a seminar on "The Dimensions of Time: Social Change in
Colonial America and the Outbreak of the Revolution" at the Newberry Library Conference on Early American History, held at the Newberry Library, Chicago, November 30,
1973. It is reprinted with permission and some additions from *Political Science Quarterly*
88 (1973): 1–22.

SEVEN

Social Structure and Political Behavior in Revolutionary America: *An Analysis of John Day's* Remarks on American Affairs

T HE THREATENING SITUATION in Anglo-American affairs following the Boston Tea Party and the coercive response of the British government[1] elicited a flood of pamphlets.[2] Few of these contain more of interest for scholars than John Day's brief and extremely rare *Remarks on American Affairs,* printed in London in a very limited edition in May 1774.[3] Day presents an unusually cogent analysis of the difficulties between Britain and the colonies and some insightful proposals for surmounting them. What gives the pamphlet unique importance, however, is the author's remarkably modern attempt to "class out and arrange the inhabitants of North America into their several orders" and to correlate political behavior with social position and economic activity.[4]

Not a man of wide contemporary prominence and even less familiar

---

[1] This situation is capably described in Bernard Donoughue, *British Politics and the American Revolution: The Path to War, 1773–75* (New York, 1964), and Benjamin Woods Labaree, *The Boston Tea Party* (New York, 1964).

[2] The many pamphlets published in Britain in 1774 are listed in Thomas R. Adams, "The British Pamphlets of the American Revolution for 1774: A Progress Report," Massachusetts Historical Society, *Proceedings* 81 (1969): 31–103.

[3] In the pamphlet, Day indicates that only three copies were printed, but Adams lists four copies, one each at the Huntington Library, Library of Congress, Historical Society of Pennsylvania, and John Carter Brown Library. Ibid., 66.

[4] Jack P. Greene, ed., "Social Structure and Political Behavior in Revolutionary America: John Day's *Remarks on American Affairs,*" *William and Mary Quarterly,* 3d ser., 32 (1975): 488. All subsequent citations to Day's pamphlet are to this edition.

to historians, the author gives only a few clues to his identity, other than his name. He tells us that he was born in England, spent his early life in the king's service, lived for twenty years in America (the last five in the middle colonies), had his family and entire estate in the colonies, and had "been a member of assembly in one of the Colonies for several years." This last piece of information has been the primary means of identifying him as the merchant John Day, whose base of operations was Halifax, Nova Scotia, where he was the most prominent member of the assembly during the latter half of the 1760s and again during the mid-1770s. He immigrated to Nova Scotia, probably with his father, a naval or military surgeon, during the early 1750s. By 1758 he had a store in Halifax and subsequently engaged in wide-ranging trading activities that stretched from Quebec to the Chesapeake. First elected to the assembly by Newport in 1765, he immediately won local political fame for his dominant role in that body's successful effort to secure control of the annual estimates of government expenses in 1765–66. Soon after the expiration of his first assembly term in 1769 he seems to have moved to Philadelphia, where, one of his political opponents charged, he "imbibed republican principles."[5]

At the time of the publication of *Remarks on American Affairs,* Day was in England, probably conducting business with John Stephenson, to whom the pamphlet was addressed. Stephenson had a contract for provisioning the king's troops in Nova Scotia, and Day, who was later referred to as "one of the Agent Victuallers to the Army," was almost certainly one of Stephenson's agents, a position that would help to account for his peripatetic activities on the American seaboard. By the summer of 1774 Day was back in Nova Scotia, where he was reelected to the assembly, this time for Halifax Town at a by-election on August 25. During the spring of 1775 he again distinguished himself in Nova Scotia politics by exercising the major hand in composing the assembly's loyal address to the crown, a document consistent with and no less remarkable than his *Remarks on American Affairs.* His career as what J. Bartlet Brebner, the foremost historian of eighteenth-century Nova Scotia, has called "the leading, perhaps the only, independent, public-spirited

---

[5] For biographical information on Day, see J. Bartlet Brebner, "Nova Scotia's Remedy for the American Revolution," *Canadian Historical Review* 15 (1934): 172n, and John Bartlet Brebner, *The Neutral Yankees of Nova Scotia: A Marginal Colony during the Revolutionary Years* (New York, 1937), 210–348, esp. 119n. Brebner was unaware of Day's authorship of *Remarks on American Affairs.*

statesman in Nova Scotia" during the era of the Revolution ended in late 1775 or early 1776 when he was killed by lightning on shipboard while taking supplies to the Boston garrison.[6]

Day's *Remarks on American Affairs* commands attention primarily because of its unusual awareness of the social bases of political behavior. The categories Day employed are considerably more refined than those of modern historians, who, like many of Day's contemporaries, conventionally divide colonial society into three broad groups: in the idiom of the times, the better, middling, and meaner sorts. Day used six more precise categories based on a combination of occupation, wealth, and "disposition." At the top were four aggrandizing classes: in descending order of "consequence," "the landed or moneyed interest"; the "commercial men"; the "practioners of the law, and the other officers of the courts of judicature"; and the "reverend . . . clergy."[7]

Each of these classes could be further divided into two groups. A small minority, Day thought, were praiseworthy people. "Many men of large property" had "acquired their fortunes in the most just and honourable manner" and possessed "the most benevolent hearts." Some merchants were willing to "forgo every prospect of private advantage for their country's good." Some lawyers were "of the most liberal sentiments in respect of government" and displayed "philanthropy in the highest degree." Even some clergy "wish[ed] well to the civil and religious liberties of mankind." But the majority of people in each class, Day was persuaded, were motivated primarily by "views . . . for their own aggrandizement," even when those views were obviously "incompatible with the peace, happiness and consequence of the great community."[8]

At the other end of the social spectrum from the aggrandizing classes were the "sailers, porters, fishermen, and other . . . appendages to large commercial towns." This group, according to Day, was still "very inconsiderable in point of property, number, consequence, or virtue to the whole community." Nevertheless, it was dangerous because it was ever ready "without thought or fear of consequence . . . to commit any acts of desperation or madness which may present."[9]

The only segment of colonial society that was not grossly deficient in character was the independent "yeomandry and peasantry." This numer-

---

[6] An edition of this document with significant elisions and revisions from an earlier manuscript draft may be found in Brebner, "Nova Scotia's Remedy," 171–81.

[7] Day, *Remarks*, 488–89.

[8] Ibid., 489–91.

[9] Ibid., 490.

ically superior group, Day wrote, obviously relying more on the model of New England or Pennsylvania than on the example of the southern plantation colonies, supplied most "members of assembly (save only in capital towns)" and "for good sense, understanding, virtue and useful learning" excelled "the same order of individuals in any part of the world."[10]

Day's effort at social classification speaks directly to two issues of continuing concern to early American historians: the direction and character of colonial social development and the nature and importance of social divisions on the eve of the American Revolution.[11] Day's remarks on the increasing number of lawyers, the proliferation of religious sects, the "rising aristocracy," and the as yet unrealized but foreseeable appearance of a "numerous vagrant poor" must be read as a commentary on a phenomenon emphasized by several recent scholars: the growing differentiation—variously referred to as the Europeanization, anglicization, or even feudalization—of colonial life.[12]

Of course, this process of what might most usefully be called metropolitanization is presumably characteristic of all successful colonial societies that have significant numbers of settlers from the parent state; in terms of current historiographical issues, what is more interesting about Day's responses to its many manifestations in early America is that they were almost entirely negative. But it is important to point out the character of his objections. Strictly speaking, his complaint was not that colonial society was becoming more feudal, that property and wealth were becoming too concentrated, or that, in the classic manner of feudal societies, dependency relationships were proliferating. Rather, echoing the

---

[10] Ibid., 489.

[11] For discussions of these issues, see Jack P. Greene, "The Social Origins of the American Revolution: An Evaluation and an Interpretation," *Political Science Quarterly* 83 (1973): 1–22 [chap. 6 above], and Kenneth A. Lockridge, "Social Change and the Meaning of the American Revolution," *Journal of Social History* 6 (1972–73): 403–39.

[12] See, especially, Kenneth A. Lockridge, *A New England Town, the First Hundred Years: Dedham, Massachusetts, 1636–1736* (New York, 1970), 167–85; John M. Murrin, "The Legal Transformation: The Bench and Bar of Eighteenth-Century Massachusetts," in Stanley N. Katz, ed., *Colonial America: Essays in Politics and Social Development* (Boston, 1971), 415–49; Jack P. Greene, "Search for Identity: An Interpretation of the Meaning of Selected Patterns of Social Response in Eighteenth-Century America," *Journal of Social History* 3 (1969–70): 189–220; and Rowland Berthoff and John M. Murrin, "Feudalism, Communalism, and the Yeoman Freeholders: The American Revolution Considered as a Social Accident," in Stephen G. Kurtz and James H. Hutson, eds., *Essays on the American Revolution* (Chapel Hill, N.C., 1973), 256–88.

bitter protests against the new monied society by Tory radicals in early eighteenth-century England,[13] he objected that the new colonial aristocracy was too mercenary and too self-oriented.[14]

According to Day, the landed interest and the monied interest were one and the same and entirely separate from the trading interest. Although the monied interest possessed "the greatest share of [landed] property, unconnected with commerce," it lived either "by Land-jobbing" or by "the interest of their money." It had a pernicious influence not because its members possessed so much property but because they were "exorbitant Usurers" and so lustful for preeminence as to be entirely heedless of the common good. So powerful was their ambition, Day thought, that it could be satisfied only by the establishment of "a nobility or distinctions . . . in America," the abolition of voting by ballot (so as to ensure their total political ascendancy), and the creation of offices "to gratify the leading families" and thereby oblige them "to support government." Such distinctions, Day believed strongly, had no place in colonies that did "not possess the extraordinary resources and commerce of Great Britain" and could therefore only lead to the creation of large numbers of poor who would be "ready instruments . . . to effect a revolution."[15]

As this last remark suggests, Day's call for the internal social reform of the colonies by the British government was only one ingredient in his larger plan to restore political harmony between Britain and the colonies. Indeed, the principal purpose of his social analysis was to impress upon the British political nation the idea that the colonies, like any "great community," were far from monolithic in political opinion and that each of the "several orders or degrees of men" was influenced in its political behavior by "its particular station, view or prospects." Thus the social situation and aspirations of the four aggrandizing classes were to an important extent determinative of each class's stance on the central political question of the day—the degree of parliamentary authority over the colonies. Members of the landed or monied interest were animated by their craving for special privileges, the merchants by "their immediate [economic] interest," the lawyers by whether they were "in the pay of Government, or in a state of expectancy," and the clerics of each

---

[13] See Isaac Kramnick, *Bolingbroke and His Circle: The Politics of Nostalgia in the Age of Walpole* (Cambridge, Mass., 1968).

[14] In effect, Day was objecting to an extreme variant of what C. B. MacPherson has called "possessive individualism." See his *The Political Theory of Possessive Individualism: Hobbes to Locke* (Oxford, 1962), 263–71.

[15] Day, *Remarks*, 488, 493.

sect by the hope for "some few persecuting powers" that would fuel their ambition to give "consequence to their several societies, and thereby to acquire weight to themselves."[16]

In Day's view, such highly self-interested behavior produced undesirable levels of social conflict. To some extent, such conflict was manifested in sectional antagonisms: he refers at one point to "the contention for pre-eminence by the several provinces." But it was primarily evident in the jarring ambitions of and the intensive "rivalship between the different orders in each community." The selfish behavior of every one of these groups, whose opinions—unfortunately, Day believed—carried undue weight in Britain because these groups were more visible and had more direct access to people in power, meant that none of them was a reliable instrument for effecting a political reconciliation between Britain and the colonies. "Their every scheme," wrote Day, had only "tended to influence Government to such measures, as would enable them to exercise a tyranny over their fellow subjects" in the colonies. The same was obviously true of the lowest social order, that volatile "banditti" which, Day testified in sharp contrast to the views of some recent scholars, had no political goals of its own and could be—and over the previous decade actually had been—easily manipulated by the four aggrandizing classes for their own political ends.[17]

In this situation Britain's best resource, as well as America's only salvation, was the independent yeomanry, who by their deep attachment to Britain and to the royal family, their common sense, their cognizance of the many mutual advantages of the British connection, and their public spirit constituted the only dependable group in colonial society. But the traditional loyalty of the yeomanry, like that of virtuous Americans of all categories, Day emphasized, had been sorely tested by Britain's behavior during the previous decade. By countenancing the "aristocratic interest" to "the injury of virtue, industry . . . and the simplicity of manners," and by permitting "his Majesty's servants" to commit "many instances of oppression, neglect, partiality, injustice and cruelty," Britain had come to appear "in the light not of a parent but of a tyrant." But the origins of disaffection, Day perceptively suggested, were traceable to

---

[16] Ibid., 488–89.

[17] Ibid., 489–90, 492. Modern positions may be found in Jesse Lemisch, "The American Revolution Seen from the Bottom Up," in Barton J. Bernstein, ed., *Towards a New Past: Dissenting Essays in American History* (New York, 1968), 3–45, and Jesse Lemisch, "Jack Tar in the Streets: Merchant Seamen in the Politics of Revolutionary America," *William and Mary Quarterly*, 3d ser., 25 (1968): 371–407.

an even deeper source than the "oppression and insult" of recent years. In contrast to "an opinion which prevails much in this kingdom," said Day, the colonists were too divided and too fearful of the upheavals that would attend a separation yet to "wish to shake off their dependence." But, he stressed in an important insight, Britain could "force" them toward independence by "leaving them in a state of uncertainty."[18]

To stop the drift toward separation, then, Day recommended that the king-in-Parliament both discountenance oppression and remove the colonists' uncertainties by devising "a proper compact or bill of rights for the American Colonies." The yeomanry especially, according to Day, were willing to accord Britain "an increasing revenue" and the "advantages of an exclusive trade" in return for military defense and constitutional guarantees of their "civil and religious freedom in the greatest extent, consistent with the good of their particular communities," guarantees that would protect them from unrestrained acts of power by either colonial officials or "any . . . individual, or body of men, . . . situated at a great distance."[19]

What was required, in Day's view, was a compact that "should be so framed, as to prevent rather than punish crimes," one that was both "equitable" and free of "speculative subtleties, which might render it uncertain." It should "abolish" the rivalry among the colonies and provide for the "due administration of justice," the "free exercise of all religions," and the collection of the king's revenue. Finally, it should appeal to the most sensible and numerous social group by encouraging the further development of an independent yeomanry while at the same time discouraging "the rising aristocracy" by forbidding any "separate privileges to any particular order of individuals" and restraining the correlative "spirit of usury, which is now extending its baneful influence over all America." "Unless highly injured," Day observed, "An independent yeomandry" was "seldom fond of change" and "consequently" made "the best subjects." "A village[,] or district, inhabited by a hundred yeoman," he wrote in reiterating his social allegiances, "will take off more British manufactures than ten Noblemen with a thousand slaves; and surely it must be a desirable object to give happiness to the many, rather than by aggrandizing a few, to render the many miserable."[20]

To "frame and grant such a constitution," Day wrote with a Boling-

---

[18] Day, *Remarks*, 490–92.

[19] Ibid., 489–90, 492.

[20] Ibid., 493.

brokean appeal and a sense of opportunity and exhilaration that approached that of the state constitution makers two years later and the members of the Federal Convention in 1787, was a work fit for "a patriot King." By conferring "happiness on the inhabitants of a vast empire to the latest period of time," such a constitution would be a "godlike act" that would be received by virtuous, sensible, and patriotic Americans with "thankfulness" and would at once transform a deplorable situation into a "glorious . . . occasion." "Once lost," Day concluded prophetically, "this opportunity . . . is lost for ever!"[21]

Of course, the opportunity was lost and Day's advice was ignored by his contemporaries. We will thus never know whether his prescription for heading off American independence, repeated a year later in the Nova Scotia assembly's address to the crown, would have been effective. But his diagnosis of the problem with its emphasis on the relationship between colonial constitutional uncertainty and the erosion of colonial affection for Britain anticipates the views of many present-day historians. More importantly, his analysis of the American social order and of the social roots of political behavior offers a series of categories and hypotheses that might profitably form the basis for further investigation and analysis. In particular, his categories might be helpful in the effort to move beyond the crude and anachronistic concepts of class we have borrowed from European social analysts. In these ways, his ideas may perhaps earn some of the recognition they did not receive, at least outside Nova Scotia, in his own day.

Written as an introduction to a documentary article for the journal in which it appeared, the chapter has been expanded modestly and is reprinted with permission from *William and Mary Quarterly*, 3d ser., 32 (1975): 481–87.

---

[21] Ibid., 492–93.

Eight

The Problematic Character of the American Union: *The Background of the Articles of Confederation*

I N THE SUMMER of 1776, during the initial debates over the Articles of Confederation, John Witherspoon, the learned president of Princeton University and a delegate to the Second Continental Congress from New Jersey, reflected upon the astonishing events of the previous two years. "Honour, interest, safety and necessity," he observed, had conspired to produce "such a degree of union through these colonies, as nobody would have prophesied, and hardly any would have expected." As a result of this startling development, Witherspoon declared, it had suddenly become clear that "a well planned confederacy among the states of America" would contribute enormously to "their future security and improvement." "A lasting confederacy," he predicted, would not only "hand down the blessings of peace and public order to many generations" of Americans. It would also serve as a model and an inspiration for the rest of the civilized world, which, he hoped, might eventually "see it prosper by some plan of union, to perpetuate security and peace" over large portions of the globe.[1]

That Witherspoon was by no means unique in his surprise at the unity achieved by the colonies in their resistance to Britain during the years from 1774 to 1776 or in his assessment of the promise of an American union has been emphasized by Jack N. Rakove, who has produced a clearheaded and persuasive analysis of the short-range developments

---

[1] John Witherspoon's Speech in Congress, [July 30, 1776], in Paul H. Smith et al., eds., *Letters of Delegates to Congress*, 18 vols. to date (Washington, D.C., 1976–), 4:584–87.

that propelled Americans in that direction. By far the most important of these developments, Rakove has shown, were the exigencies arising out of the necessity of coordinating an effective resistance and waging a war against the strongest military power then existing in the Western world. From the beginning, American leaders were aware that they had no chance of success unless they could maintain a high degree of "agreement on the principles and tactics of opposition" and avoid "the types of jealousy that had troubled American resistance in the early 1770s." Inexorably, this awareness pushed delegates to the Continental Congress in the direction of a system in which Congress exerted extraordinarily extensive power and thereby constituted a de facto national government.[2]

In this situation, Rakove has found, there was little interest during the first year of the war in creating "an enduring national state." But the surprising success of Congress in presiding over and organizing a coordinated defense effort rapidly yielded still a second short-term development that created additional pressures toward the formation of a continental union. This development was the emergence among delegates of the hope, expressed by Witherspoon, that the colonies might, despite many perceived differences among them, actually be able to achieve "a lasting Confederation." As they came to grasp the potential for such a union, especially as it was spelled out for them by Thomas Paine and others during the first half of 1776, they began to feel that it would be a great tragedy if they did not seize so favorable an opportunity to accomplish such a noble end.[3]

Yet, as Rakove has also revealed, two additional short-term developments combined both to delay codification and formal adoption of a continental confederation and to raise profound doubts about whether, as Joseph Hewes of North Carolina worried shortly after Independence, delegates would ever be able to "modell it so as to be agreed to by all the Colonies."[4] First and most decisive during the first two years after Independence was simply the press of other more urgent business. "The immensity of business created by the war," lamented the Virginia dele-

---

[2] Jack N. Rakove, *The Beginnings of National Politics: An Interpretative History of the Continental Congress* (New York, 1979), 136–45.

[3] Ibid.; Silas Deane to Patrick Henry, Jan. 2, 1775, in Smith et al., *Letters of Delegates* 1:291; Edmund Cody Barnett, *The Continental Congress* (New York, 1964), 136–37.

[4] Joseph Hewes to Samuel Johnston, July 28, 1776, in Smith et al., *Letters of Delegates* 4:555.

gate Richard Henry Lee in August 1770, necessarily meant that "the Confederation goes on but slowly."[5]

Second, and of even greater long-term significance, was the rapid identification in 1775–76 of the enormously complex issues involved in trying to bring thirteen separate political entities into a broad continental union. "In such a Period as this, Sir, when Thirteen Colonies unacquainted in a great Measure . . . with each other are rushing together into one Mass," John Adams wrote presciently in November 1775, "it would be a Miracle, if Such heterogeneous Ingredients did not at first produce violent Fermentations."[6] The coming together of representatives from the several states inevitably produced not only a sense of common purpose in resisting Britain but also a far more intense awareness of the remaining differences in interest and orientation among the several colonies. Specifically, delegates discovered that they disagreed over certain fundamental and enormously difficult issues involving representation, expenses, and western lands. By and large, the division over these issues was not sectional. Rather, as Merrill Jensen has pointed out, the "large colonies were pitted against the small ones; colonies with many slaves were in opposition to those with fewer; colonies that had no western lands contended with those that did."[7] But the delegates also quickly identified and articulated broad regional interests and contrasts between the southern and the eastern (New England) states, albeit no one initially seemed to be quite sure whether the middle states from Delaware to New York were closer to the southern or to the eastern states.[8] Invariably, the differences among the colonies in orientation, interest, and issues operated to make confederation, as John Adams predicted in May 1776, "the most intricate, the most important, the most dangerous, and delicate Business of all."[9]

If as a result of Rakove's analysis we now understand better than ever before the short-term developments beginning in late 1774 that both pushed the American colonies toward a continental union and made it difficult for them to contrive one, no one has yet considered systematically the several long-term preconditions that lay behind and shaped

---

[5] Richard Henry Lee to Thomas Jefferson, Aug. 25, 1777, ibid., 7:551.

[6] John Adams to Samuel Osgood, Nov. 14, 1775, ibid., 2:342.

[7] Merrill Jensen, *The Articles of Confederation: An Interpretation of the Social-Constitutional History of the American Revolution, 1774–1781* (Madison, Wis., 1959), 56.

[8] See John R. Alden, *The First South* (Baton Rouge, La., 1961), 33–73.

[9] John Adams to James Warren, May 15, 1776, in Smith et al., *Letters of Delegates* 3:678.

that process. This chapter is a preliminary effort in that direction. For purposes of analysis, it will divide those preconditions into two broad categories, those that inhibited and those that facilitated the formation of a permanent national union. It will conclude with some tentative observations on the ways those preconditions shaped that union in its initial form in the Articles of Confederation.

Certainly one of the most powerful of the preconditions operating to make the achievement of a permanent union extremely difficult was the obvious dissimilarities among the colonies and the nearly ubiquitous judgment that they were far more impressive than any similarities. Such a perception had prevailed through the colonial period and had received widespread expression in the decades just before the Revolution. Thus, in 1760, less than fifteen years before the first beginnings of American national union, Benjamin Franklin had informed British readers that Britain's "fourteen separate governments on the maritime coast of the [North American] continent" were "not only under different governors, but have different forms of government, different laws, different interests, and some of them different religious persuasions and different manners." These differences, Franklin observed, gave rise to mutual suspicions and jealousies that were "so great that however necessary and desirable an union of the colonies has long been, for their common defence and security against their enemies, and how sensible soever each colony has been of that necessity, yet they have never been able to effect such an union among themselves, nor even to agree in requesting the mother country to establish it for them." Franklin was writing for the express purpose of allaying rising fears in Britain that the increasingly valuable colonies might rise up and throw off British control, but he expressed the conventional wisdom of his time.[10]

Indeed, during the decades just before the Revolution, virtually every commentator on both sides of the Atlantic was entirely persuaded, with Franklin, that the extraordinary differences among the colonies made

[10] Benjamin Franklin, *Interest of Great Britain Considered* (London, 1760), in *The Papers of Benjamin Franklin*, ed. Leonard W. Labaree et al., 28 vols. to date (New Haven, 1959–), 9:90. On this point, see especially Jack P. Greene, "'A Posture of Hostility': A Reconsideration of Some Aspects of the Origins of the American Revolution," in Greene and William G. McLoughlin, *Preachers and Politicians: Two Essays on the Origins of the American Revolution* (Worcester, Mass., 1977), 5–46.

any form of union impossible. The validity of this conclusion seemed to be dramatically underscored by the fate of the Albany Plan of Union in 1754. Not a single colony ratified this proposal for a limited defensive confederation against the French. Even worse, during the Seven Years' War several colonies had shown very little concern for the welfare of their neighbors. "When their assistance had been demanded or implored by any of their distressed neighbours and fellow subjects," charged the metropolitan economist Malachy Postlethwayt in 1757, some colonies had "scandalously affected delays" and "by an inactive stupidity or indolence, appeared insensible to their distressed situation, and regardless of the common danger, because they felt not the immediate effect of it."[11] "Being in a state of separation," each of the colonies, another metropolitan writer had complained during the war, acted "solely for its own interest, without regard to the welfare or safety of the rest," a situation that unfortunately "naturally begat jealousies, envyings, animosities, and even the disposition to do one another mischief rather than good."[12] That the colonies were "all jealous of each other," Henry Frankland admitted from Boston in September 1757, was an unfortunate fact.[13]

How, contemporaries seem mostly to have thought, could it have been otherwise? In language very similar to that expressed by Franklin just four years earlier, Thomas Pownall, the former Massachusetts governor, in 1764, in his widely read treatise on *The Administration of the Colonies*, explained the deep and manifold differences among the colonies. He predicted that "the different manner in which they are settled, the different modes under which they live, the different forms of charters, grants, and frames of government they possess, the various principles of repulsion, . . . the different interest which they actuate, the religious interest by which they are actuated, the rivalship and jealousies which arise from hence, and the impracticability, if not the impossibility, of reconciling and accommodating these incompatible ideas and claims" would "obviously for ever" keep them "disconnected and independent of each other,"[14] a mere "rope of sand," in the words of another writer, the indi-

---

[11] Malachy Postlethwayt, *Britain's Commercial Interest Explained and Improved*, 2 vols. (London, 1757), in Jack P. Greene, ed., *Great Britain and the American Colonies, 1606–1763* (New York, 1970), 298.

[12] *State of the British and French Colonies in North America* (London, 1755), 54.

[13] Henry Frankland to Thomas Pelham, Sept. 1, 1757, in Additional Manuscripts 33087, f. 353, British Library, London.

[14] Thomas Pownall, *The Administration of the Colonies* (London, 1764), in Greene, *Great Britain and the American Colonies*, 306.

vidual strands of which were all too "peculiarly attached to their respective constitutions of Governments," forms of society, and interests ever "to relish a union with one another."[15]

So deep were the differences and animosities among the colonies thought to run that they became an important element in the calculations of both metropolitan officials and American resistance leaders during the controversies that preceded the American Revolution. "The mutual jealousies amongst the several Colonies," Lord Morton assured Chancellor Hardwicke in the early 1760s, "would always keep them in a state of dependence,"[16] and metropolitan officials based their strategy in the Coercive Acts, the measures that played such a crucial role in stimulating the final crises that led to war and the American decision for independence, upon the supposition that colonial opposition could easily be diffused by a policy of divide and rule, a policy the British government continued to pursue throughout the nine years of war that followed.

Before 1774 few American leaders were very sanguine about their capacity even to offer a united resistance, much less to weld themselves together into a single political society. The inability of the colonists to maintain economic sanctions against Britain during the crises over the Townshend Acts between 1768 and 1770 provided an object lesson in the difficulties of united action and exacerbated long-standing fears of internal division and disunion. These experiences and fears were certainly one of the more important deterrents to colonial revolt right down into the mid-1770s.

Nor were such fears and the perceptions of diversity that underlay them quickly dissipated once united resistance had begun in the mid-1770s. Rather, close associations in the Continental Congresses seem both to have sharpened those perceptions and to have intensified the suspicions and distrust that accompanied them. "The Characters of Gentlemen in the four New England Colonies," John Adams wrote to Joseph Hawley in November 1775, "differ as much from those in the others . . . as much as [in] several distinct Nations almost. Gentlemen, Men of Sense, or any Kind of Education in the other Colonies are much fewer in Proportion than in N. England," Adams thought, expressing his customary sectional pride: "Gentlemen, in the other Colonies have large Planta-

---

[15] "Some Thoughts on the Settlement and Government of Our Colonies in North America," Mar. 10, 1763, in Add. MSS, Liverpool Papers 38335, ff. 74–77, British Library, London.

[16] As quoted by Sir Lewis Namier, *England in the Age of the American Revolution* (London, 1963), 276.

tions of slaves, and the common People among them are very ignorant and very poor. These Gentlemen are accustomed, habituated to higher Notions of themselves and the distinction between them and the common People, than We are." Ever the realist, Adams thought that nothing less than "a Miracle" could produce "an instantaneous alteration of the Character of a Colony, and that Temper and those Sentiments which its Inhabitants imbibed with their Mothers Milk, and which have grown with their Growth and strengthened with their Strength."[17]

More cautious delegates especially continued to doubt that any effective or lasting union among such heterogeneous components could ever turn out well. "Their different Forms of Government—Productions of Soil—and Views of Commerce, their different Religions—Tempers and private Interest—their Prejudices against, and Jealosies of, each other—all have, and ever will, from the Nature and Reason of things, conspire to create such a Diversity of Interests, Inclinations, and Decisions, that they never can [long] unite together even for their own Protection," predicted Joseph Galloway. "In this Situation Controversies founded in Interest, Religion or Ambition, will soon embrue their Hands in the blood of each other."[18] Not just timid and future loyalists like Galloway but also ardent proponents of continental union like John Adams worried about the long-range prospects of a union of such apparently disparate parts. "I dread the Consequencies of this Disimilitude of Character" among the colonies, Adams wrote, "and without the Utmost Caution . . . and the most considerate Forbearance with one another and prudent Condessention . . . , they will certainly be fatal."[19]

These widespread perceptions of diversity among the separate states and regions and the many difficulties they created were not the only long-term source of anxiety that made people skeptical about the viability of a continental union. Bernard Bailyn has shown in detail the pervasiveness in early American politics of fears of the corrupting tendencies of power.[20] The long controversy with Britain after 1763 had indelibly impressed upon Americans the particular difficulties of bringing a distant power to account, and these painful lessons gave rise to a profound mistrust of central power that was readily transferable from the British

[17] John Adams to Joseph Hawley, Nov. 25, 1775, in Smith et al., *Letters of Delegates* 2:385.

[18] Joseph Galloway to [Samuel Verplanck], Dec. 30, 1774, ibid., 1:288.

[19] Adams to Hawley, Nov. 25, 1775, ibid., 2:385–86.

[20] Bailyn, *The Ideological Origins of the American Revolution* (Cambridge, Mass., 1967), 55–93, and *The Origins of American Politics* (New York, 1968), 41–58, 135–61.

government to an American national government and constituted a second precondition that delayed and affected the creation of a continental union. Having just separated from a strong central government in some major part because they had been unable to influence it in their favor, must less to control it, many American leaders were understandably wary, as Merrill Jensen has repeatedly emphasized, of creating something similar in America.[21] More recently, Rakove has pointed out that this wariness rarely rose to the surface of public life during the early years of the War for Independence.[22] But it was so deeply imbedded in public consciousness as to be easily reactivated by those who, like North Carolina delegate Thomas Burke, had an especially intense fear of power and were anxious lest, in the absence of adequate restraints, the members of a national government "would make their own power as unlimited as they please."[23] This suspicion and fear of central power meant that the grant of power to the central government in the Articles of Confederation would necessarily be a limited one.[24]

The absence of positive examples in either theory or history constituted yet a third precondition that limited expectations and shaped attitudes about the form of a continental union. By 1787–88 assiduous scholars of the science of politics such as James Madison and James Wilson had analyzed existing literature on "Ancient & Modern Confederacies" exhaustively and systematically.[25] By contrast in the mid-1770s, no one

---

[21] See Jensen, *Articles of Confederation*, and "The Articles of Confederation," in *Fundamental Testaments of the American Revolution* (Washington, D.C., 1973), 49–80.

[22] Rakove, *Beginnings of National Politics*, 1–239.

[23] Thomas Burke to Richard Caswell, Apr. 29, 1777, in Smith et al., *Letters of Delegates* 6:672.

[24] A later corollary of this fear that a central government would run roughshod over the rights and powers of the constituent components of the Union was that in America, as in Britain, not only power but wealth and talent, attracted by the great influence of a central government, would all flow from the peripheries to the center. "Agrippa" later articulated this fear succinctly during the debate over the Constitution in 1787, predicting that the northern and southern states would "in a very short time sink into the same degradation and contempt with respect to the middle state(s) as Ireland, Scotland, & Wales are in regard to England. All the men of genius and wealth will resort to the seat of government, that will be center of revenue, and of business, which the extremes will be drained to supply." Letter to Agrippa [James Winthrop], in Cecelia M. Kenyon, ed., *The Antifederalists* (Indianapolis, 1966), 157.

[25] See James Madison, "Ancient and Modern Confederacies," in *The Papers of James Madison*, ed. William T. Hutchinson et al., (Chicago and Charlottesville, Va., 1962–   ), 9:4–24; Benjamin F. Wright, ed., *The Federalist* (Cambridge, Mass., 1961), 171–85; and

was similarly prepared to put the problems of an extensive continental union in historical perspective. What American resistance leaders did know, however, discouraged all but a small minority from being very optimistic or thinking in grand terms. As Gordon S. Wood has observed, "Few Americans thought that . . . an extensive continental republic, as distinct from a league of states, was feasible."[26] This opinion derived in part from Montesquieu, the one reputable source of authority on the subject, who was of the opinion that liberty, as some later Antifederalists phrased it, could not be preserved over an extensive territory "otherwise than by a confederation of republics, possessing all the powers of internal government, but united in the management of their general and foreign concern," a theory that seemed to have been more than adequately borne out by the Americans' recent experience in the old British Empire.[27]

Just as Montesquieu taught Americans that small republics linked together in a loose confederation had a better chance of surviving and preserving their citizens' liberty than large consolidated republics, so also did both historical and contemporary examples. The people who contrived the first American national union were familiar with the confederated governments of the United Provinces of the Netherlands and the league of Swiss cantons, each of which was a limited confederacy that reserved considerable local autonomy to its constituent parts. From the works of Sir William Temple and Abbé Raynal, they understood that each of these confederations had serious deficiencies. Yet their longevity constituted a strong recommendation for their limited grant of powers to the central government and, though some questioned the extent to which the Dutch had actually managed to preserve much liberty in their limited confederacy, served as still further confirmation of the correctness of Montesquieu's belief that the only viable kind of confederation among republics was one with sharply restricted powers.[28]

A fourth precondition that inhibited the rapid formation of a perma-

---

The Works of James Wilson, ed. Robert Green McCloskey, 2 vols. (Cambridge, Mass., 1967), 1:247–69.

[26] Gordon S. Wood, The Creation of the American Republic, 1776–1787 (Chapel Hill, N.C., 1969), 58.

[27] Address and Reasons of Dissent of the Minority of the Convention of the State of Pennsylvania, 1787, in Kenyon, Antifederalists, 39. See also Wood, Creation of the American Republic, 356, 499; and Samuel H. Beer, "Federalism, Nationalism, and Democracy in America," American Political Science Review 72 (1978): 13.

[28] See Josiah Bartlett's Notes, [June 12–July 12, 1776], John Adams's Notes of Debate, July 30, Aug. 1, 1776, John Witherspoon's Speech, [July 30, 1776], and Benjamin Rush's Notes for a Speech, [Aug. 1, 1776], in Smith et al., Letters of Delegates 4:199–200, 568,

nent continental union was the almost total absence of any sense of American national consciousness. Right down to the actual break with Britain, colonial national consciousness had been intensely British. All over the colonies, Americans took pride in their incorporation into the larger Anglophone world. Their ability to identify themselves as "free Englishmen, inheriting the liberties," rights, and culture of all British subjects, was, for them, essential to the maintenance of a positive sense of identity, and this "feeling of a community of values," traditions, language, religion, manners, interests, and identity between Britain and the colonies was powerfully enhanced by the colonies' close—and growing—commercial association with the metropolis.[29] Certainly, as one contemporary observer remarked, the colonies even as late as the early 1760s were more "directly connected with their Mother Country" than they were "with each other."[30]

In view of these facts, it was scarcely surprising, as Franklin observed in 1760, that the colonies "all love[d] Britain much more than they love[d] one another."[31] By the middle decades of the eighteenth century, in fact, the colonists' pride in being British had, in Yehoshua Arieli's words, "all but obliterated" any "sense of separation and distinctiveness" that the colonists, especially New Englanders, might have felt earlier in the colonial period.[32] There was not "a single true *New England* Man, in the whole Province," exclaimed the Reverend John Barnard in 1734 from Massachusetts (the colony that had been most resistant to the benefits of metropolitan imperialism, cultural as well as economic and political, during the seventeenth century), who did not "readily" subscribe to the belief that "that form of Civil Government is best for us, which we are under, I mean the *British Constitution.*"[33]

This widespread identification with Britain and the British necessarily meant that, far from being exponents of American nationalism, the colonists exhibited "an intense personal affection, even reverence, for" Brit-

---

587, 592, 598–99; William Henry Drayton's Speech, Jan. 20, 1778, in Hezekiah Niles, ed., *Principles and Acts of the Revolution in America* (New York, 1876), 563.

[29] Yehoshua Arieli, *Individualism and Nationalism in American Ideology* (Cambridge, Mass., 1964), 45–49.

[30] "Some Thoughts on the Settlement and Government of Our Colonies," ff. 74–77.

[31] Franklin, *Interest of Great Britain Considered,* in *Franklin Papers* 9:90.

[32] Arieli, *Individualism and Nationalism,* 45–49.

[33] John Barnard, *The Throne Established by Righteousness* (Boston, 1734), as quoted by Paul A. Varg, "The Advent of Nationalism, 1758–1776," *American Quarterly* 16 (1964): 172.

ish "leaders, institutions, and culture" and the most profound feelings of British nationalism.[34] Nor were these feelings at any time more intense than in the 1760s during the wake of the Seven Years' War. That so much of that war had been fought in the colonies, that the metropolitan government had made such a major effort to defend the colonies, and that the colonies had themselves—for the very first time—made, as they were persuaded, a substantial contribution of money and manpower to such a great national cause increased the immediacy and strength of colonial ties with Britain and produced a surge of British patriotism among the colonists, a surge that found expression in the confident expectation that they were now finally—or would soon be—"upon an equal footing" with Englishmen at home.[35]

Even the long and bitter controversy during the 1760s and 1770s could not wholly eradicate this deep-seated American reverence for Britain. Throughout that controversy, as Samuel H. Beer has noted, the colonists "steadfastly claimed that they sought only freedom within the British empire, not freedom from it."[36] "So strong has been their Attachment to Britain" that "the Abilities of a Child might have governed this country," Connecticut delegate Oliver Wolcott said in May 1776 in expressing his dismay over the ineptness of the British government's handling of the colonies over the previous few years.[37]

In early 1776, Thomas Paine endeavored in *Common Sense* to make Americans aware of the many social and cultural unities among them and to articulate a vision of America's potential as a united republican political society that would serve as an example for the rest of the world. But not even Paine's persuasive rhetoric and exhilarating vision of Americans' common destiny in occupying a place of the first importance in the unfolding course of human history could immediately produce a powerful, subsuming national consciousness of the kind usually connoted by the word *nationalism*.[38] John Shy has shown that the War for Independence and, more especially, the behavior of the British army and the

---

[34] Edwin Burrows and Michael Wallace, "The American Revolution: The Ideology and Psychology of National Liberation," *Perspectives in American History* 6 (1972): 275–76.

[35] *State of the British and French Colonies*, 63–64.

[36] Beer, "Federalism, Nationalism, and Democracy," 11.

[37] Oliver Wolcott to Samuel Lyman, May 16, 1776, in Smith et al., *Letters of Delegates* 4:17.

[38] For an elaboration of this argument, see Jack P. Greene, "Paine, America, and the 'Modernization' of Political Consciousness," *Political Science Quarterly* 93 (1978): 73–92 [chap. 12 below].

widespread popular participation in the war, contributed to a kind of "hothouse nationalism,"[39] while the Revolution itself provided Americans with an instant common past. But it would be at least two further generations before most Americans would give a high priority to American, as opposed to their own state or regional, loyalties. Becoming visibly manifest only in the mid-1760s, the process by which Americans began to think of themselves as "a people" was still in a primitive stage of development between 1775 and 1787.

The fifth, last, and in many respects the most important precondition that significantly inhibited and affected the development of a continental union was the long existence of the several states as separate corporate entities. By the time of Independence, every one of the thirteen colonies except Georgia had been in existence as a distinct corporate body for at least nine decades, while the oldest colonies in the Chesapeake and in New England went back to the early decades of the seventeenth century. Consisting of a well-defined body of territory, each of these colonies had its own peculiar constitution, institutions, laws, history, and identity, to which its inhabitants were, for the most part, both well socialized and strongly attached. The thirteen colonies, Andrew C. McLaughlin has remarked, were, in fact, "thirteen distinct groups of people."[40]

Throughout the colonial period, the members of each of these distinct groups identified and defined themselves not only as members of the greater British world of which they were a part but also in terms of their common residence and collective experiences and associations as members of the clearly delineated and separate corporate bodies that each of the colonies was and long had been. If, before the Declaration of Independence, none of these colonies was independent of Britain, they were, nonetheless, as many contemporary observers pointed out, wholly independent of each other.

That Americans thought of themselves as being organized into a series of independent corporate entities, each of which had its own specific identity and characteristics that they had every intention of preserving to the fullest possible extent, was evident throughout the controversy with Britain between 1764 and 1776. From the Stamp Act crisis onward,

---

[39] John Shy, "The American Revolution: The Military Conflict Considered as a Revolutionary War," in Stephen G. Kurtz and James H. Hutson, eds., *Essays on the American Revolution* (Chapel Hill, N.C., 1973), 155.

[40] Andrew C. McLaughlin, *The Confederation and the Constitution, 1783–1789* (New York, 1962), 41.

as McLaughlin has pointed out, Americans claimed both individual liberty and "local liberty within the British empire." They demanded recognition on the part of the metropolitan government not just of the individual rights of Americans as Englishmen and as men but also "of the rights of the colonies, as bodies corporate, constituent members of the Empire."[41]

Similarly, the delegates to the First and Second Continental Congresses went off to defend not only individual rights but the corporate rights of the colonies, and they went as representatives not of the people at large but of the colonies, those ancient corporate entities which retained their distinctive identities and beings through the rapid series of changes in government—from colonial to provincial revolutionary to state—in the mid-1770s. Historians have frequently cited Patrick Henry's famous declaration at the First Continental Congress in the fall of 1774 that "the distinctions between Virginians, Pennsylvanians, New Yorkers, and New Englanders are no more. I am not a Virginian, but an American."[42] But few Americans managed to shed their provincial identities and acquire a new national one so rapidly. Rooted in their intimate associations with their native or adopted colonies, their deep local patriotism continued to be manifest during the Revolution in a strong determination to preserve the identity, authority, and distinctiveness of the several corporate entities to which they belonged. The difficulty of reconciling this determination with the desire to create a new national entity was perhaps the most perplexing single problem facing American resistance leaders in their efforts to create a lasting continental union.

Although these five preconditions—(1) the widespread tendency to emphasize the differences among the colonies with a corresponding mutuality of suspicion among them, (2) fear of the aggrandizing tendencies of a remote central power, (3) existing theory about the contemporary examples of confederated republics, (4) the primitive state of American national consciousness, and (5) a strong sense in every colony of its identity

[41] McLaughlin, *Foundations of American Constitutionalism*, 132–33, 138; Jack P. Greene, *The Quest for Power: The Lower Houses of Assembly in the Southern Royal Colonies, 1689–1776* (Chapel Hill, N.C., 1963), 438–53.

[42] John Adams's Notes of Debates, [Sept. 6, 1776], in Smith et al., *Letters of Delegates* 1:28.

as a distinctive corporate entity with an unquestioned commitment to preserve that identity—either retarded the adoption of or set definite limits upon the form and nature of a continental union during the late 1770s, still other and ultimately more powerful long-range developments helped to predispose American leaders toward some kind of permanent union.

Certainly, the most important of those was the remarkable social and cultural convergence experienced by those colonies beginning during the last decades of the seventeenth century. What makes that convergence so remarkable is the extraordinary diversity among the colonies at the time of their original settlement. Indeed, if one looks closely at the two major centers of English settlement on the North American continent during the first half of the seventeenth century, at the tobacco colonies of the Chesapeake and the Puritan colonies of New England, it would be difficult to imagine how any two areas composed almost entirely of Englishmen could have been any more different. About the only characteristics they had in common were their ethnic homogeneity, their ruralness, and, after the first few years, an abundant local food supply. In almost every other respect, they were diametric opposites.

Within a decade after the settlement of Virginia in 1607, the Chesapeake societies were oriented toward the production of a single staple crop—tobacco—for the metropolitan market, and the high profits for this product quickly made the reckless and single-minded pursuit of individual gain the central animating impulse and the chief social determinant of the region. In quest of wealth that would take them back to the civilized comforts they had left behind in England, men greedily took high risks, dispersed themselves over the land, and engaged in ruthless exploitation of labor. This highly exploitative, labor-intensive, dispersed, transient, and secular market-oriented society was composed very heavily of landless single men, most of them English bond servants. With few families, the structure of its households more closely resembled those in nineteenth-century mining boom towns than in contemporary rural England. With a high death rate and a low birth rate, population increased very slowly and largely through immigration. The differential success rates characteristic of staple economies meant that wealth was concentrated in a relatively few hands and levels of social differentiation, based almost entirely upon wealth, were high. At the same time, the fragility of life and fortune and the lack of a clear connection between wealth and the traditional attributes of leadership as they were understood by Englishmen in the home islands meant that political and social authority was weak, impermanent, and open to challenge and that the

potential for social discord was great. The last thing that seemed to interest early Virginians, a later observer remarked, was the building of "a
Country for posterity."[43]

By sharp contrast, the Puritan colonies of New England had been
settled by families in a single massive migration concentrated in the
1630s and motivated very largely by the desire to escape the religious
impurity of Albion and to establish a city upon a hill, a true religious
commonwealth that would serve as a model for the Christian world.
Highly religious, with pronounced communal impulses, the inhabitants
settled in nuclear households and in small villages organized around the
church, villages that from the very beginning were conceived of as permanent. With no profitable staple, they engaged primarily in mixed subsistence agriculture and built societies that were far more egalitarian in
terms of the distribution of wealth than those to the south. With a benign disease environment and a balanced sex ratio, mortality was low,
fecundity high, and demographic growth rapid, primarily the result of
natural increase. With a large number of visible leaders who had all the
attributes of sociopolitical authority among the initial immigrants and a
high degree of cooperation between secular and clerical leaders, lines of
authority were clear, and the potential for contention and discord was
low.[44]

At least on the surface, these strong social divergencies among the
English colonies seemed to increase over time as the Chesapeake colonies
acquired a strong biracial character with the transition from European
servant to African slave labor between 1680 and 1730 and with the establishment of two new—and also distinctive—nodes of settlement during
the last decades of the seventeenth century. The so-called Middle Colonies, consisting of New York, conquered from the Dutch in 1664, and
New Jersey, Delaware, and Pennsylvania, settled by the English between 1664 and 1681, were characterized by profound ethnic, religious,
and social diversity, rapid change, and, at least through their first de-

[43] See Edmund S. Morgan, *American Slavery, American Freedom: The Ordeal of Colonial Virginia* (New York, 1975), and Thad W. Tate and David L. Ammerman, eds., *The Chesapeake in the Seventeenth Century: Essays on Anglo-American Society* (Chapel Hill, N.C., 1979). The quotation is from John Hammond, *Leah and Rachel* (London, 1656), in Clayton C. Hall, ed., *Narratives of Early Maryland, 1633–1684* (New York, 1910), 286.

[44] For summaries of the conclusions of recent literature on colonial New England, see John M. Murrin, "Review Essay," *History and Theory* 11 (1972): 226–75, and Jack P. Greene, "Autonomy and Stability: New England and the British Colonial Experience in Early Modern America," *Journal of Social History* 7 (1974): 171–94.

cades of English control, high levels of public contention.[45] The other node, stretching out from Charleston on the South Carolina coast north into southern North Carolina and south into coastal Georgia, was similarly diverse. With rice, naval stores, and eventually indigo as enormously profitable staples, these colonies, at least at their center, were even more materialistic and far more slave and African than the Chesapeake. Many parishes in lowcountry South Carolina had a black-white ratio of from 7:1 to 9:1 and looked far more like the West Indian colonies of Barbados and Jamaica than like any colonies to the north.[46]

As noted earlier, throughout the colonial period most contemporaries continued to be far more impressed with the dissimilarities among these colonies than with the similarities. Contemporaries to the contrary notwithstanding, however, it is clear in retrospect that the colonies were becoming not less but more alike during the century after 1680. This process can be seen in the gradual diminution of the sharp divergencies that had initially distinguished the Chesapeake from New England. The slow improvement of health conditions in the Chesapeake during the seventeenth century had led by the first decades of the eighteenth century to a balance of sex ratios and a more typically European family structure. Similarly, as tobacco profits settled down to less spectacular if somewhat steadier levels, expectations among the successful colonists of returning to England all but disappeared, the commitment to the Chesapeake became stronger, settlement became more compact and expansion more measured, and the devotion to staple production was less exclusive. Concomitantly, social, religious, and political institutions acquired more vigor, society became far more stable, and the communal impulse was much more evident, as Chesapeake society cohered around an emergent and authoritative socioeconomic elite, members of which exhibited all of the traditional attributes of social leadership as they strove successfully to assimilate themselves to the powerful cultural model of the English gentry. The new sense of coherence and community which was so

[45]See Patricia U. Bonomi, "The Middle Colonies: Embryo of the New Political Order," in Alden T. Vaughan and George A. Billias, eds., *Perspectives on Early American History: Essays in Honor of Richard B. Morris* (New York, 1973), 63–92, and Douglas Greenberg, "The Middle Colonies in Recent American Historiography," *William and Mary Quarterly*, 3d ser., 36 (1979): 396–427.

[46]See Peter H. Wood, *Black Majority: Negroes in Colonial South Carolina from 1670 through the Stono Rebellion* (New York, 1974), and Converse D. Clowse, *Economic Beginnings in Colonial South Carolina, 1670–1730* (Columbia, S.C., 1971).

strikingly manifest in Virginia after 1725 was, perhaps ironically, actually intensified among the free white population by the pressures toward racial solidarity created by the transition to a heavily African slave labor force on the plantations.[47]

At the same time, in New England, the deterioration of health conditions by the mid-eighteenth century brought mortality levels not too much lower than those in the Chesapeake, while a variety of other developments pushed the region closer to the patterns of behavior and values toward which Virginians were moving. Thus, impressive population growth, the consequent dispersion of people out from the original village centers to individual farms, an increasing differentiation of society and complexity of kinship networks, a growing diversity in many aspects of town life, the acceleration of the economy as a result of rapid internal population growth and the increasing integration of the New England economy into the larger Atlantic economy, the gradual attenuation of the social and religious synthesis of the founders, a growing demand for and exhibition of autonomy among the sons of each successive generation, more individualism and more conflict within the public life of the towns, and a marked rise in geographical mobility—all of these developments weakened the bonds of community and pushed New England in the direction of greater individualism, personal autonomy, and social fluidity.[48]

Not just the Chesapeake and New England colonies but the other continental colonies as well were moving closer together in their configuration of socioeconomic and political life, the Carolinas and New York moving in the same direction as Virginia and Pennsylvania, which also began with a strong corporate and religious impulse, in the same direction as New England, only at a vastly more accelerated rate. Envision a hypothetical continuum running between the two poles of pure individualism and tight communalism at three different times—1660, 1713, and 1763—with each colonial area plotted along the line according to its dominant patterns of behavior and values. What such a continuum

---

[47] See Tate and Ammerman, *Chesapeake in the Seventeenth Century*, 206–96; Morgan, *American Slavery, American Freedom*, 131–211, 295–362; and Jack P. Greene, "Society, Ideology, and Politics: An Analysis of the Political Culture of Mid-Eighteenth-Century Virginia," in Richard M. Jellison, ed., *Society, Freedom, and Conscience: The Coming of the Revolution in Virginia, Massachusetts, and New York* (New York, 1976), 14–76, 191–200.

[48] See, especially, Murrin, "Review Essay," 240–75; Greene, "Autonomy and Stability," 187–93; Richard L. Bushman, *From Puritan to Yankee: Character and the Social Order in Connecticut, 1690–1765* (Cambridge, Mass., 1967).

shows is a steady convergence toward the center with, to take only the major continental colonies as examples, Virginia, South Carolina, and New York moving from individualism toward community, and Massachusetts and Pennsylvania moving from community toward individualism, until by the last half of the eighteenth century the differences among the colonies were less than they had ever been before.

New England was still more religious and had much lower levels of wealth concentration than the colonies to the south, while Virginia and South Carolina with their legions of slaves were certainly more strongly oriented toward acquisitiveness and more exploitative. But not even the presence of so many slaves in the southern colonies, certainly the most conspicuous difference between them and New England, was yet a crucial distinguishing feature among the colonies. Though the ratio of black slaves to the free population decreased steadily from the most southern to the most northern colonies, slavery as late as 1770 was still an expanding, not a contracting, institution in every one of the colonies that revolted except New Hampshire; and New York, Rhode Island, Pennsylvania, and New Jersey all had populations with a higher proportion of slaves than had the Chesapeake colonies as late as 1700 to 1710.[49]

The explanation for this growing convergence is to be found in two overlapping processes that were simultaneously at work in all the colonies. For purposes of analysis, they may be designated, rather crudely, as processes of Americanization and anglicization. Distance from Britain, looseness of British controls, relatively easy availability of land and other exploitable resources, and incorporation into the larger metropolitan economy and, increasingly, into the broad Atlantic trading system stretching from West Africa to the Caribbean in the south and from North America to western Europe in the north—all of these conditions combined to produce levels of prosperity sufficient to support societies that were everywhere becoming more and more pluralistic, complex, differentiated, and developed. They also worked to stimulate the high levels of individual activity and expansiveness that underlay the remarkable economic and demographic growth that characterized all of the North American colonies through the middle decades of the eighteenth century.

These developments and the conditions that lay behind them also seem to have led throughout the colonies to the development of "more autonomous personality types," impatient with authority and jealous of

---

[49] Population figures may be found in *Historical Statistics of the United States, Colonial Times to 1757* (Washington, D.C., 1960), 756.

the personal independence that was the chief defining quality of any fully competent man,[50] a fact appreciated by perceptive British officials for many decades before the American Revolution. In his analysis of Britain's difficulties in America during the 1760s and 1770s, William Knox, undersecretary for the colonies with experience as a royal officeholder in Georgia, declared that conditions of both private and public life in America had strongly militated against the development of "all [of those] ideas of subordination and dependence" that had traditionally been thought to be requisite for the successful functioning of the British political system.[51] South Carolina lawyer Charles Pinckney testified to the truth of Knox's observation during the Philadelphia Convention of 1787, when he noted that the societies of all of Britain's former colonies exhibited "fewer distinctions of fortune and less of rank, than among the inhabitants of any other nation."[52]

Along with the failure to establish a proper religious hierarchy and the total absence of a middle or aristocratic estate, the wide distribution of property referred to by Pinckney had all along served to inhibit the emergence, as Knox and many others pointed out, of whatever feelings "of subordination that property, ancestry or dignity of station . . . naturally excited" among Britons in the home islands. The weakness of such feelings had inevitably meant that the political systems of the colonies had been thoroughly "tinctured with republicanism." In all the colonies, "the Democracy had the leading influence and the general tendency," Knox thought, was to ward off the "adoption of the commonwealth-mode," a general tendency that only "increased with their wealth, & . . . their prosperity."[53] In the words of J. R. Pole, "The American Colonies [had] developed the characteristics of what would later be known as a republican form of government many years before they were to claim to be republican in principle."[54]

Throughout the free segments of the Anglo-American population, from one region to the next and from the cradle to the grave, visitor

<hr/>

[50] See Burrows and Wallace, "American Revolution," 287–88.

[51] Jack P. Greene, ed., "William Knox's Explanation for the American Revolution," *William and Mary Quarterly,* 3d ser., 30 (1973): 299.

[52] Speech of Charles Pinckney, June 25, 1787, in Max Farrand, ed., *The Records of the Federal Convention of 1787,* 4 vols. (Washington, D.C., 1911–37), 1:398.

[53] Greene, "Knox's Explanation," 297–306.

[54] J. R. Pole, *The Seventeenth Century: The Sources of Legislative Power* (Charlottesville, Va., 1969), 69.

after visitor reported, people in the colonies seemed to exhibit very little respect for authority. "A fierce spirit of liberty," Edmund Burke, echoing a common opinion, declared in March 1775, was "stronger in the English colonies, probably, than in any other people of the earth."[55] This pervasive and deeply ingrained commitment to personal freedom and independence, said Samuel Williams, whose *History of Vermont*, published during the last decade of the eighteenth century, constitutes one of the first systematic analyses of the configuration of the emerging American society, "had been the constant product and effect, of the state of society in the British colonies" for "a century and a half" and, he might have added, of the social, economic, and physical forces that produced that society.[56]

If, as Williams observed, a "similarity of situation and conditions" had gradually pushed the colonies toward a similitude of society and values, more specifically, toward "that natural, easy, independent situation, and spirit, in which the body of the [free] people were found, when the American war came on," still a second major influence—growing anglicization—was important in helping to erode differences among the colonies.[57] Partly, this development was the result of deliberate efforts by metropolitan authorities to bring the colonies under closer control, including the gradual conversion of the vast majority of the colonies into royal provinces directly under the supervision of the crown; the imposition of a common political system, at least at the provincial level, upon those colonies; strong pressures upon the five remaining private colonies to assimilate to that system; and the largely successful attempt, beginning in the 1650s, to subordinate the economies of the colonies to that of the metropolis. These efforts led both to the establishment of a common pattern of political institutions among the colonies and to an ever more intense involvement between metropolis and colonies in both the political and economic spheres. This growing involvement, together with an increasing volume of contacts among individuals and the improved communications that accompanied them, drew the colonists ever closer into the ambit of British life during the eighteenth century, provided them

---

[55] Edmund Burke, "Speech on Moving Resolutions for Conciliation with the Colonies," Mar. 22, 1775, in *Edmund Burke: Selected Writings and Speeches on America*, ed. Thomas H. D. Mahoney (Indianapolis, 1964), 131–32.

[56] Samuel Williams, *The Natural and Civil History of Vermont*, 2 vols. (Walpole, N.H., 1794), 2:431.

[57] Ibid., 429–30.

with easier and more direct access to English, Irish, and increasingly, Scottish ideas and models of behavior, and tied them ever more closely to metropolitan culture.

As the ties with the metropolis thus tightened, the pull of metropolitan culture increased, and the standards of the metropolis more and more came to be the primary model for colonial behavior, the one certain measure of cultural achievement for these provincial societies at the outermost peripheries of the British world. Throughout the colonies, and especially among the emergent elites, there was a self-conscious effort to anglicize colonial life through the deliberate imitation of metropolitan institutions, values, and culture. Thus, before the mid-1770s, Anglo-Americans thought of themselves primarily as Britons, albeit Britons overseas, and, contrary to the dominant opinion among earlier historians, colonial comparisons of the colonies with Britain did not usually come out in the colonies' favor. Quite the contrary. The colonists were far less interested in identifying and finding ways to express and celebrate what was distinctively American about themselves than, insofar as possible, in eliminating those distinctions so that they might with more credibility think of themselves—and by people in Britain be thought of—as demonstrably British.[58]

As each of the colonies had during the century before the American Revolution become both more American and more British, as they increasingly assimilated to a common American social and behavioral pattern and to British cultural models, they became more and more alike. They shared similar institutions, a common identity as Britons overseas, a similar historical experience, a common political inheritance, the same political and social ideology, and similarly, though by no means equally, fragile structures of social and political authority. They were all becoming, to one degree or another, ever more complex and pluralistic societies, and they all had an upward trajectory of demographic and economic growth. As William Grayson would later remark, they also displayed a conspicuous "similarity of laws, religion, language, and manners."[59]

There were still obvious differences, many of them rooted in the dis-

[58] A fuller discussion of this subject may be found in Jack P. Greene, "Search for Identity: An Interpretation of the Meaning of Selected Patterns of Social Response in Eighteenth-Century America," *Journal of Social History* 3 (1970): 189–224. The contrary view is succinctly stated in Max Savelle, "Nationalism and Other Loyalties in the American Revolution," *American Historical Review* 57 (1962): 904.

[59] Grayson's observation may be conveniently found in Kenyon, *Antifederalists*, 282.

tinctions between the slave-powered staple economies of the South and the mixed agricultural and commercial economies of the North, albeit when John Dickinson worried in July 1776 about the eventual dissolution of the American union, he drew the line not between north and south but between New England and the rest of the states.[60] Whatever the continuing variety among the new American states and to whatever extent that variety continued to impress contemporaries, their interests, "Trade, Language, Customs, and Manners," Benjamin Rush could credibly insist in congressional debate during the summer of 1776, were by no means "more divided than they are among . . . people in Briton."[61]

This growing convergence was the first and most important precondition for either the American Revolution or the emergence of an American national government and an American nationality. As David Potter reminded us, however, social and "cultural similarities alone will not provide a basis of affinity between groups." Nationalism and similar collective loyalties, he pointed out, have to rest on "two psychological bases": the "feeling of a common culture *and* the feeling of common interest." "Of the two," he posited, "the concept of culture is, no doubt, of greater weight," but it cannot have its full effect without a mutual awareness of common interests.[62]

In the American case, it must be said, an awareness of a common interest was a second necessary precondition even for a clear and full recognition of the existence of a common culture. As several scholars have argued, the emergence during the middle decades of the eighteenth century of intercolonial trading patterns and communications networks, an interlocking elite, closer interurban ties, and common participation between 1739 and 1763 in two wars against the neighboring colonies of foreign metropolitan powers resulted in the colonies' becoming increasingly more interested in one another and perhaps, even, in the development of some rudimentary sense of American community. The metropolitan penchant, especially evident during the midcentury intercolonial wars, for treating the continental colonies as a unit and describing them under the common rubric *American*, to some degree stimulated this de-

---

[60] "John Dickinson's Notes for a Speech in Congress," July 1, 1776, in Smith et al., *Letters of Delegates* 4:356.

[61] John Adams's Notes in Debates, Aug. 1, 1776, ibid., 592; Benjamin Rush's Notes for a Speech in Congress, [Aug. 1, 1776], ibid., 592, 599.

[62] David M. Potter, "The Historians' Use of Nationalism and Vice Versa," *American Historical Review* 67 (1962): 935, 949.

velopment.[63] Perhaps the most important point that can be made about
the Albany Plan of Union in the early 1750s, in fact, a point that seems
not to have been appreciated by anybody at the time, was not that it
was universally rejected but that it had been proposed and adopted by a
conference of leaders in the first place. For its mere initiation manifested
at least a rudimentary consciousness of the existence of some bases for
an "American" union.

But Americans did not yet fully understand or attach any special importance to their many and growing commonalities—as opposed to the
similarities that linked them all to Britain—until the metropolis vividly
impressed upon them that they had a common interest by challenging
their pretensions to an equal status with Britons at home by new, restrictive measures between 1763 and 1776. In pointing out the seemingly vast
differences among the colonies and stressing the extent to which those
differences made united action improbable, Benjamin Franklin had
warned metropolitans in 1760, in words that both he and many later
observers would echo, that a "grievous tyranny and oppression" might
very well drive the colonies to unite.[64] During the 1760s, many Americans had pointed out, in the words of Richard Henry Lee of Virginia,
that the colonists' attachment to Britain could be preserved "on no other
terms . . . than by a free intercourse and equal participation of good
offices, liberty and free constitution of government."[65] But Lee's point
was appreciated, virtually alone in Britain, by Burke when he pointed
out that America's affection for Britain had always been conditional
upon its continuing ability to carry "the marke of a free people in all"
its "internal concerns" and to retain at least "the image of the British
constitution."[66]

Britain's insistence upon treating the colonies as separate and unequal
in the 1760s and 1770s was thus the contingent development that, in the

---

[63] See Albert Harkness, Jr., "Americanism and Jenkins' Ear," *Mississippi Valley Historical Review* 37 (1950): 61–90; Richard L. Merritt, *Symbols of American Community, 1735–
1775* (New Haven, 1966); Michael Kraus, *Intercolonial Aspects of American Culture on
the Eve of the Revolution with Special Reference to the Northern Towns* (New York, 1928);
and Carl Bridenbaugh, *Cities in Revolt: Urban Life in America, 1743–1776* (New York,
1955).

[64] Franklin, *Interest of Great Britain Considered,* in *Franklin Papers* 9:90.

[65] Richard Henry Lee to Arthur Lee, July 4, 1763, in *Letters of Richard Henry Lee,* ed.
James C. Ballagh, 2 vols. (New York, 1912–14), 1:11. See also, among many expressions
of similar beliefs, Robert M. Calhoon, "William Smith, Jr.'s Alternative to the American
Revolution," *William and Mary Quarterly,* 3d ser., 22 (1965): 117.

[66] Burke, "Speech on American Taxation," Apr. 19, 1774, in *Edmund Burke,* 79.

words of Arieli, provided the "point of observation and comparison from which" the colonists could finally come to appreciate the many unities among them.[67] Increasingly during those years, they came to comprehend that, given existing attitudes among those in power in Britain, membership in the British Empire did not mean, for them, the equality as freeborn Englishmen to which they had so long aspired. Rather, it meant an inferior status equivalent, in the bitter words of Alexander Hamilton in 1774, only to those unworthy people in Britain who were "*in so mean a situation*" that they were "supposed to have no will of their own" and, according to Sir William Blackstone, therefore deserved no role in governing themselves.[68]

As the colonists slowly came to this comprehension, they gradually began to lose their British nationalism and to develop, as grounds for asserting their own worthiness against their metropolitan antagonists, an awareness of their common interest in resisting metropolitan efforts to place them in a subordinate, unequal, and un-British status. They developed as well an understanding of the common histories of the colonies as asylums for the oppressed and places where unfortunates could make new beginnings and of the many social and cultural similarities among them. Only then did they begin to acquire some sense of their possible "future power and imperial greatness" as a separate American people and to glimpse the potential for a comprehensive American political union.[69]

Still a third precondition that predisposed leaders of American resistance toward a national union was their deep-seated and residual fear of disorder. Almost to a man, they took pride in the Anglo-American devotion to liberty. But they knew from history and their own experience that the line between liberty and licentiousness was thin, and they worried that the notorious weakness of authority in America might under certain conditions lead to the breakdown of political institutions. Although the extent and depth of such fears varied from place to place according to the strength of local political institutions and the cohesiveness of local elites,[70] they clearly had been behind the powerful anglicizing impulses among the colonies' emerging elites throughout the eighteenth century

---

[67] Arieli, *Individualism and Nationalism*, 45.

[68] Hamilton, *The Farmer Refuted*, [Feb. 23], 1774, in *The Papers of Alexander Hamilton*, ed. Harold C. Syrett and Jacob E. Cooke, 19 vols. (New York, 1961–73), 1:106–7.

[69] Arieli, *Individualism and Nationalism*, 67–68.

[70] See on this point Jack P. Greene, "Social Context and the Causal Pattern of the American Revolution: A Preliminary Consideration of New-York, Virginia and Massachu-

and had functioned as a strong deterrent to revolution during the period from 1763 to 1776.

One of the most evident manifestations of these fears in the pre-Revolutionary period had been the belief that the British connection was essential to the continued political stability of the colonies. "We think ourselves happier . . . in being dependent on Great Britain, than in a state of independence," said an anonymous writer in the *New York Mercury* in 1764, "for then the disputes amongst ourselves would throw us into all the confusion, and bring on us all the calamities usually attendant on civil wars."[71] Given the weakness of authority in the colonies, many people feared with John Dickinson that without Britain's central controlling power, Anglo-America would quickly degenerate into "a multitude of Commonwealths, Crimes and Calamities—centuries of mutual Jealousies, Hatreds, Wars and Devastations, till at last the exhausted Provinces shall sink into Slavery under the yoke of some fortunate conqueror."[72]

During the uncertain situation that obtained after 1774, such anxieties quickly translated into powerful fears of division and disunion and pushed congressional delegates more and more toward the view that a national union was essential not simply to coordinate resistance and war against Britain but to prevent internal chaos. At the time of the First Continental Congress, Joseph Galloway, the later loyalist, was one of the few to voice openly his anxieties about the ill effects that might arise from the absence of a central authority, without which, he observed in urging his fellow delegates to support his proposed plan of union, the colonies would be "destitute of any supreme direction or decision whatever, even to the settlement of differences among themselves."[73]

With war and independence, however, virtually all delegates from the most cautious to the boldest agreed that "Disunion among ourselves," as Witherspoon declared, was "the greatest Danger We have"[74] and that a formal union was absolutely essential not just to prosecute the war but,

setts," in *Le Revolution Américaine et l'Europe: Colloques Internationaux du Centre National de la Recherche Scientifique* (Paris, 1979), 25–63.

[71] *New York Mercury*, Aug. 27, 1764, as quoted by Burrows and Wallace, "American Revolution," 191.

[72] John Dickinson to William Pitt, Dec. 21, 1765, in Chatham Papers, PRO 30/8/97, Public Record Office, London.

[73] Joseph Galloway, *Historical and Political Reflections on the Rise and Progress of the American Rebellion* (London, 1780), 77, as quoted by Jensen, *Articles of Confederation*, 69.

[74] Adams's Notes of Debate, July 30, 1776, in Smith et al., *Letters of Delegates* 4:568.

in the words of Richard Henry Lee, to secure "internal peace."[75] In the existing situation, complained Edward Rutledge, a delegate from South Carolina, "the Inhabitants of every Colony consider[ed] themselves at Liberty to do as they please upon almost every occasion."[76] Only a formal and lasting continental union, as Gouverneur Morris had earlier suggested, could be certain to "restrain the democratic spirit, which the constitutions and the local circumstances of the country had so long fostered in the minds of the people" throughout the colonies.[77] If the colonies remained "separate and disunited, after this war," predicted Witherspoon in urging a formal confederation upon Congress, "we may be sure of coming off the worse." Victory over Britain would surely be followed by "a more lasting war, a more unnatural, more bloody, and more hopeless war, among the colonies themselves."[78]

A fourth—and final—precondition that strongly predisposed American resistance leaders toward a permanent continental union was their long-standing involvement with the de facto federal system of government in the old British Empire. According to metropolitan theory, Britain and its colonies constituted a single unitary state in which sovereignty—ultimate unqualified authority—lay in the metropolitan government, more specifically, following the working out of "revolution principles" during the Revolutionary Settlement between 1688 and 1715, in king, Lords, and Commons in Parliament assembled. This theory rested on strong medieval precedents involving the relationship between England and the crown's dominions outside the realm, including the Channel Islands, Anjou, Aquitaine, Gascony, Ireland, Wales, and the Isle of Man,[79] and virtually all metropolitan commentators on the governance of the empire during the colonial period subscribed to it. Black-

---

[75] Richard Henry Lee to Landon Carter, June 2, 1776, in *Letters of R. H. Lee* 1:198.

[76] Edward Rutledge to John Jay, [June 8, 1776], in Smith et al., *Letters of Delegates* 4:175.

[77] Jared Sparks, *The Life of Gouverneur Morris*, 3 vols. (Boston, 1832), 1:26–27, as cited by Jensen, "Articles of Confederation," 57.

[78] Speech of Witherspoon, [July 30, 1776], in Smith et al., *Letters of Delegates* 4:584–85. On the generalized extent of how the fear of disunion operated in favor of continental confederation in the mid-1770s, see the excellent analysis in Rakove, *Beginnings of National Politics*, 135–215.

[79] A. F. M. Madden, "1066, 1776, and All That: The Relevance of English Medieval Experience of 'Empire' to Later Imperial Constitutional Issues," in J. E. Flint and G. Williams, eds., *Perspectives of Empire* (London, 1973), 9–26. See also the earlier exchange on this subject by C. H. McIlwain, *The American Revolution: A Constitutional Interpretation* (New York, 1924), and Robert L. Schuyler, *Parliament and the British Empire* (New York, 1929).

stone in his authoritative *Commentaries on the Laws of England* provided "its classic formulation" in 1765 during the first stages of the colonists' quarrels with Britain.[80]

Whatever the theory, the old empire, "as a practical working system," as the doyen of American constitutional historians Andrew C. McLaughlin pointed out almost fifty years ago, was "marked by the distribution rather than by the concentration of authority." "In the actual workings of the Empire, during several generations," McLaughlin argued cogently, "there had been an Empire in which powers were parceled out among governments," with the metropolitan government exercising general powers "that could not well be exercised by the colonies—the post-office, naturalization, war and peace, foreign affairs, intercolonial and foreign commerce, establishment of new colonies, etc."—and the colonial governments exerting de facto and virtually exclusive jurisdiction over almost all matters of purely local concern, including taxation. In "actual *practice*, the empire of the mid-eighteenth century was [thus] a diversified empire; powers were actually distributed and exercised by various governments."[81] As William Smith, Jr., the noted New York lawyer, had pointed out in the mid-1760s, political arrangements within the British Empire had gradually drifted into a situation in which there was in fact a "*manifold . . . Partition,* of the *Legislative* Authority of the Empire."[82]

A failure to rationalize the existing imperial system in a way that satisfied both colonists and metropolitan officials was the constitutional rock on which the old empire split apart. As it had gradually taken shape during the last decades of the seventeenth century, this "problem of imperial organization" had been primarily discussed in terms not of the locus of sovereignty but of the question, as an anonymous Virginian put it in 1701, of "how far the Legislative Authority is in the Assemblies,"[83] that is, to what extent—and in what cases—the jurisdiction of colonial legislatures was limited by the authority of the metropolitan govern-

[80] See H. T. Dickinson, "The Eighteenth-Century Debate on the Sovereignty of Parliament," Royal Historical Society, *Transactions*, 5th ser., 26 (1976): 189–210; Bailyn, *Ideological Origins*, 201.

[81] Andrew C. McLaughlin, *Foundations of American Constitutionalism* (New York, 1961), 133–38, and *A Constitutional History of the United States* (New York, 1935), 14.

[82] Calhoon, "Smith's Alternative to Revolution," 114.

[83] Louis B. Wright, ed., *An Essay upon the Government of the Plantations on the Continent of America* (San Marino, Calif., 1945), 15–17, 23.

ment. Before the 1760s, the debate over this question focused not upon Parliament's authority over the colonies, which was, in any case, usually exerted only in very limited spheres relating to trade and other economic concerns of the empire as a whole, but upon whether the authority of the king and his ministers to bind the colonies by executive orders was limited by the requirement of colonial legislative consent. No theoretical resolution of this problem was ever achieved. In the meantime, however, the empire continued to function with a rather clear demarcation of authority. In practice, virtually all internal matters were handled by the governments of the respective colonies and most external affairs by the metropolitan government.[84]

That this was indeed the proper line and that it ought to have explicit constitutional recognition was the argument of Americans of almost all political persuasions in the debate with Britain after 1764. Increasingly in this debate, they endeavored to demarcate the jurisdictional boundaries between Parliament and the colonial assemblies according to external and internal spheres of authority, with the former belonging to Parliament and the latter to the colonial assemblies. Regarding colonial demands as a direct challenge to metropolitan theory about the location of sovereignty within the empire, spokesmen for the metropolitan government, by contrast, insisted upon reducing the controversy to the single issue of sovereignty. They insisted that the logic of the indivisibility of sovereignty rendered any suggestion of qualifications upon Parliament's authority wholly absurd. The colonists resisted such reductionism and endeavored, unsuccessfully, to focus debate upon the seemingly more tractable and certainly less abstract problem of how power was or should be allocated in a political system composed of several related but nonetheless distinct corporate entities. For the colonists, resolution of their dispute with Britain seemed to require little more than the rationalization of existing arrangements with the empire.

But the continued insistence by metropolitan protagonists that the issue was nothing short of the location of ultimate authority eventually forced Americans in the late 1760s and early 1770s to consider their relationship with Britain in these terms. By 1774, they had agreed that, if indivisibility of sovereignty required that Parliament have either total authority over the colonies or none, it had none. The colonies, they argued, were separate states, each with its own sovereign legislature, and

---

[84] See the discussion in Greene, *Great Britain and the American Colonies,* xi–xlvii, and Greene, "Posture of Hostility," 41–46.

the British Empire was therefore "an imperial federation of sovereign states sharing and establishing unity in a single monarch."[85] In the later words of John Witherspoon, it was "a federal" and not "an incorporating Union," the colonies having always been independent "of the people or Parliament of England."[86]

In contrast to their metropolitan protagonists, however, American resistance leaders never seem to have attached central importance to the abstract question of the locus of sovereignty as opposed to the more immediate issue of the allocation of power. Thus, when they took their first concrete steps toward the creation of a continental political system in 1774–76, they made it abundantly clear by their actions that they had no intention, in the words of the North Carolina lawyer James Iredell, of permitting "the happiness of millions" to be sacrificed to so "narrow and pedantic . . . a point of speculation."[87] If, as Beer has noted, "theory . . . powerfully directed" the work of the people who fashioned and pushed through the Federal Constitution of 1787,[88] experience and exigency were much more evident in shaping the earliest national political system under both the Continental Congress and the Articles of Confederation. The Americans' experience in the old empire had accustomed them to living in a political system in which there were functionally two interdependent levels of government, each with its own sphere of authority. Reinforced beginning in 1775 by the palpable fact that resistance and war, general activities that "from the *necessity of the case*, . . . could not well be exercised" by the individual states, required central direction, this experience also produced a strong disposition to re-create in their new national situation a system in which political authority was similarly allocated.[89]

In view of their long experience with a divided structure of authority, it is not surprising, as Rakove has found, that, far from being "central to the burgeoning Revolutionary . . . controversy between anti-Federalists

[85] Bailyn, *Ideological Origins*, 223–25.

[86] Thomas Jefferson's Notes of Proceedings in Congress, [June 1776], and John Adams's Notes of Debates, Aug. 1, 1776, in Smith et al., *Letters of Delegates* 4:161, 593.

[87] Don Higginbotham, "James Iredell and the Origins of American Federalism," in George G. Suggs, Jr., *Perspectives on the American Revolution: A Bicentennial Contribution* (Carbondale, Ill., 1977), 107.

[88] Beer, "Federalism, Nationalism, and Democracy," 12.

[89] McLaughlin, *Foundations*, 138. See also John C. Ranney, "The Bases of American Federalism," *William and Mary Quarterly*, 3d ser., 3 (1946): 8–9.

and continentalists," as Merrill Jensen and, more recently, Richard B. Morris have affirmed,[90] the question of sovereignty "was never directly raised" in 1775–76. In fact, "political exigency imposed [such] powerful limits on the sweep [and, one might add, the depth] of formal constitutional thought" that not even the problem of the proper allocation of authority "was at first . . . carefully examined": "basic issues were neither clearly posed nor well understood," and congressional discussions of confederation "tended, like other issues, to be more deeply influenced by the demands of resistance."[91]

In this situation, the federal structure of the new nation simply evolved out of the colonists' experience in the old empire and the need to meet the conditions of the war. Much as in the history of the old British Empire, a working division of power between Congress and the states, a division along the very lines that had obtained in the empire, quickly took shape. In view of the intense suspicion of a remote central power that American leaders had exhibited both during the years before Independence and in the 1780s, they showed remarkably little aversion to endowing Congress with "legislative and administrative responsibilities unprecedented in the colonial past." Not even the intense theoretical discussion in 1776–77 of the form of the new republican state governments included much consideration of the relationship of those governments to Congress or to a permanent national union. At that point, Rakove has noted, Congress still commanded a degree of deference that "left it immune from close theoretical scrutiny." Perhaps more important, resistance leaders of all political persuasions seem to have assumed, virtually without question, that the pragmatic division of power that had taken shape during the early years of resistance, a division that had evolved, like that of the British Empire, without formal codification and that saw the states handling all matters internal to them while Congress was "endowed with substantial authority over matters of general concern," should continue.[92] The difference between a formal confederation and the existing union, John Adams blithely declared in April 1776, would be no greater than "that between an express and an implied Contract."[93]

---

[90] Richard B. Morris, "The Forging of the Union Reconsidered: A Historical Refutation of the State Sovereignty over Seabeds," *Columbia Law Review* 74 (1974): 1062; Jensen, *Articles of Confederation.*

[91] Rakove, *Beginnings of National Politics*, xvi, 136, 162, 190.

[92] Ibid., 136, 148–49, 151, 172, 184–85.

[93] John Adams to James Warren, Apr. 16, 1776, in Smith et al., *Letters of Delegates* 3:536.

In the mid-1770s, three powerful long-range preconditions—growing social and cultural convergence among the colonies, a more recently discovered awareness of a common interest in opposing metropolitan efforts to curtail colonial rights and privileges, and fears of both disunion and the fragility of authority in American society—thus combined with short-term pressures created by war and the colonists' earliest experiences with united action to push American resistance leaders in the direction of a permanent national continental union, while a fourth precondition—their experience with a multitiered government under the old empire—predisposed them toward a federal union. Simultaneously, the five preconditions discussed in the previous section—mutual suspicions and sharpened perceptions of differences, mistrust of distant power, available theories and models of federal organization, absence of national consciousness, and the long-standing existence of the states as distinctive corporate entities—made the actual codification of the ad hoc federal structure that had taken shape in 1774–76 extremely difficult.

Precisely how difficult was revealed with the very first effort to devise a suitable plan of confederation beginning in June 1776. On the surface, immediate issues involving representation, expenses, and western lands seemed to be most troublesome. Lurking behind all of these issues, however, was the old imperial problem of specifying a clear division of power among the two existing spheres of authority, a division that would give the central government sufficient power to meet its responsibilities without compromise to the political integrity of the individual states. Although it clearly did not, as Edward Rutledge charged, destroy "all Provincial [state] Distinctions" and by no means sought to consolidate the states "into one unitary polity," the original plan of confederation drawn up by John Dickinson was a plan which, in Rakove's words "clearly intended to use confederation as a vehicle . . . for defining the powers of Congress to satisfy the majority of the delegates."[94]

During most of the present century, of course, historians have assumed that the national government was actually the creation of thirteen sovereign states which retained all those powers they did not dele-

---

[94] Edward Rutledge to John Jay, June 29, 1776, ibid., 4:338; Rakove, *Beginnings of National Politics,* 155–57.

gate to Congress.[95] Since the publication of a seminal article by Curtis P. Nettels in 1960, however, a new orthodoxy has replaced this "contract theory" of the formation of the American national union.[96] Following Nettels, Richard B. Morris, Samuel H. Beer, and Jack N. Rakove have each in turn recently attested to the validity of a national theory of the origins of American federalism according to which the national government "existed and functioned before the birth of any state," and "the source of authority for the various acts initiated by the congress was 'the inhabitants of the several colonies, whom we represent.'" According to this interpretation, Congress as well as the states was the creation of "a single sovereign power, the people of the United States," and Congress "alone possessed those attributes of external sovereignty which entitled" the United States "to be called a state in the international sense[,] while the separate States, possessing a limited or internal sovereignty, may rightly be considered a creation of the Continental Congress, which preceded them in time and brought them into being."[97]

But neither the old nor the new orthodoxy on this point seems to be an adequate description of what happened. To be sure, Congress existed before any of the new independent state governments. But these new state governments were merely the creations and the newest political instruments of old corporate entities, each of which preserved its own well-defined territory and collective legal identity as it moved rapidly in 1775–76 through a series of statuses from colony to provincial revolutionary society to independent state. These distinctive corporate entities certainly preceded the existence of a new continental one.

Of course, Congress portrayed itself in various public documents from September 1774 onward as representing "the inhabitants of the several colonies,"[98] and during the debates over confederation a few delegates even argued that Congress should represent people rather than states.[99]

---

[95] See, especially, in addition to Jensen, *Articles of Confederation,* C. H. Van Tyne, "Sovereignty in the American Revolution: An Historical Study," *American Historical Review* 12 (1907): 529–45.

[96] Curtis P. Nettels, "The Origin of the Union and of the States," Massachusetts Historical Society, *Proceedings,* 72 (1957–60): 68–83.

[97] Morris, "Forging of the Union," 1067, 1089; Beer, "Federalism, Nationalism, and Democracy," 12; Rakove, *Beginnings of National Politics,* 173–74.

[98] Morris, "Forging of the Union," 1067.

[99] John Adams's Notes of Debates, Aug. 1, 1776; Benjamin Rush's Notes for a Speech, [Aug. 1, 1776], in Smith et al., *Letters of Delegates* 4:592–93, 599–601. See also "Of the

But those who, with Roger Sherman, insisted that "we are rep[resenta-tive]s of States, not Individuals," strongly and successfully opposed this view at the time. Behind this conception of Congress as an assemblage of representatives of the states and not of the people at large was the assumption, made explicit by John Witherspoon, that "Every Colony is a distinct Person."[100] Congress may have directed the colonies to form new state governments. But each of them retained, Witherspoon thus implied, its ancient legal identity as a distinct corporate entity. In all probability, this view was strongly reinforced by the actual process of state constitution making in 1776 and 1777, a process that had given explicit definition to and reaffirmation of the authority and legal identity of the states.[101]

The triumph of the view represented by Sherman and Witherspoon was evident in the fact that delegates to Congress continued to be se-lected by the state governments both before and after the adoption of the Articles of Confederation, which were ratified not by the people at large but by the states. The "Provincial Distinctions" cherished by so many of the delegates would not be obliterated by the Articles of Confed-eration,[102] and the first American national union would thus be not, as Beer has argued, representational but territorial and corporate, its source of authority lying not, as recent scholars have suggested, in the people of the United States but in the states as corporate entities which retained their separate identities and legal authority throughout the transition from colonies to states, from membership in the British Em-pire to membership in the new United States. As it had developed within the colonies before 1770, American government, as Beer has argued, was "fundamentally government by consent as opposed to the Old Whig con-stitution" in England, which was not representational but hierarchical and corporatist. To an important degree, however, America's first na-tional government was to be a throwback to the old Whig constitution. It would represent the territorial and legal corporations of the states, not the people at large.[103]

But this is emphatically not to suggest that the older compact theory

Present State of America," Oct. 10, 1776, in Peter Force, comp., *American Archives*, 5th ser. (Washington, D.C., 1837–53), 2:967–70.

[100] John Adams's Notes of Debates, July 30, Aug. 1, 1776, in Smith et al., *Letters of Delegates* 4:568, 592.

[101] Rakove, *Beginnings of National Politics*, 167; "Of the Present State of America," 967.

[102] Edward Rutledge to John Jay, June 29, 1776, in Smith et al., *Letters of Delegates* 4:338.

[103] Beer, "Federalism, Nationalism, and Democracy," 10, 12.

of the origins of American federalism, whereby a group of sovereign states came together to create a national government, is correct. If few in Congress before the early 1780s intended to annihilate the identities of the individual states, yet, as Rakove has argued with great cogency, Congress had all along been "a national government" exerting an extraordinary degree of authority over the separate states. Moreover, the framers of the Articles of Confederation revealed their conscious intention to perpetuate this arrangement by vesting "certain sovereign powers in Congress" and subordinating "the states to its decisions."[104] During the war, most delegates probably agreed with William Henry Drayton that Congress should have no power that could, "with propriety, be exercised by the several states."[105]

But the declaration in Article 2 of the Articles of Confederation that "Each State retained its sovereignty, freedom and independence," was, ultimately, a fiction.[106] As Rufus King pointed out in the Philadelphia Convention in 1787, the states, under the Articles, lacked many of the fundamental attributes of sovereignty. "They could not," King said, "make war, nor peace, nor alliances, nor treaties."[107] On paper at least, the Articles of Confederation, as Gordon Wood has correctly remarked, "made the league of states as cohesive and strong as any similar sort of republican confederation in history."[108] In doing so, the Articles simply gave formal sanction to an existing arrangement.

The process by which the American Union was formed is thus too complicated to support either a national or a compact theory of its origins. The Continental Congress gathered to itself broad powers at the same time that the colonies as old and continuing corporate entities were changing themselves into states. What was clear throughout was that from the First Continental Congress on, the national union had involved a division of power in which, "in their separate spheres, both Congress and the states were to exercise certain functions of sovereign government." Inherited from the British Empire, such a division was thus "inherent in the nature of American union from the start"[109] and, as McLaughlin long ago pointed out, was perpetuated by the Articles of

---

[104] Rakove, *Beginnings of National Politics*, xvi, 184–85.

[105] William Henry Drayton's Speech, Jan. 20, 1778, in Niles, *Principles and Acts*, 363.

[106] Jensen, *Articles of Confederation*, 263.

[107] Morris, "Forging of the Union," 1064.

[108] Wood, *Creation of the American Republic*, 359.

[109] Rakove, *Beginnings of National Politics*, 162, 172.

Confederation, which sought to specify the boundaries between Congress and the state governments "with considerable precision."[110]

Throughout this initial phase in the creation of an American national union, the issue of the location of sovereignty that has received so much stress from modern historians was remarkably little emphasized by contemporaries. Much more interested in the practical problem of allocating power between the national and the state governments, members of Congress simply failed "to give serious attention" to the question of sovereignty. Even when Thomas Burke, the North Carolina delegate, raised it explicitly in Congress in early 1777, few of his colleagues exhibited much interest in pursuing it. Before the end of the War for Independence, Rakove concludes on the basis of these facts, few Americans seemed to be "deeply interested in the nature of the union they were forming." Not only, as Gordon Wood has noted, did the war years yield no theoretical advance over the formulations of Blackstone, but the question of the locus of sovereignty remained "imperfectly understood" and a potential source of conflict and confusion.[111]

Although the problem of sovereignty "remained academic" in the late 1770s, it quickly became an important "practical issue" in the 1780s.[112] Wood has shown that the end of the war produced a reassertion of state authority and a corresponding diminution of central power, a development marked by a revival of that traditional distrust of remote power that had been so evident in the controversy with Britain in the 1760s and early 1770s and would be such a conspicuous feature of the debate over the Constitution of 1787. Ignoring the extraordinary power Congress had exercised during the war, observers in the mid-1780s could describe it, as did John Adams, as neither "a legislative assembly, nor a representative assembly, but only a diplomatic assembly." From this new and later perspective, Congress by no means appeared to be, as Ezra Stiles observed, "a body in which resides authoritative sovereignty." There had obviously occurred, said Stiles, "no real cession of dominion, no surrender or transfer of sovereignty to the national council[,] as each state in the confederacy" had remained "an independent sovereignty."[113]

The steady diminution in the actual power and status of the Confeder-

---

[110] McLaughlin, *Foundations of American Constitutionalism*, 140.

[111] Rakove, *Beginnings of National Politics*, 164, 174, 185; Wood, *Creation of the American Republic*, 353.

[112] Willi Paul Adams, *The First American Constitutions: Republican Ideology and the Making of the State Constitutions in the Revolutionary Era* (Chapel Hill, N.C., 1980), 50.

[113] Wood, *Creation of the American Republic*, 355, 464, 580.

ation Congress during the 1780s provides yet further vivid testimony to the continuing strength of the states and to the determination of their leaders to preserve their ancient identities as distinct corporate entities. What was new and radical about the Federal Constitution of 1787, Wood has shown, was its embodiment of the new American theory that sovereignty resided in the people at large and its incorporation of the idea of consent into the national government through the institution of direct election of members of the House of Representatives. These steps made American federalism, the "new" federalism of 1787, representational. What was old about the Federal Constitution was its endorsement of the continued sanctity of the identity of each of the states as separate territorial and corporate entities and their representation in the Senate. That provision ensured that American federalism would continue to be, as it had been entirely under the Articles of Confederation, territorial as well as representational and not, as Beer recently argued, merely representational.[114]

This chapter was written for a conference on "The Continuing Legacy of the Articles of Confederation" sponsored by the Center for the Study of Federalism of Temple University and held in Philadelphia, August 30-September 1, 1981. In abbreviated form it was presented as a paper entitled "The Cultural Roots of American Union" at the 42d Annual Meeting of the American Association for State and Local History, at Hartford, Connecticut, September 24, 1982, and formed the core of one of three lectures given in the series "Power, Authority, and the Problem of Center-Periphery Relations in Anglo-American Constitutional Development, 1607–1789," given as the Richard B. Russell Lectures at the University of Georgia, Athens, February 28–March 2, 1983. Previously reprinted in Peter S. Onuf, ed., *The New American Nation, 1775—1820*, 12 vols. (New York, 1991), 4: *Congress and the Confederation*, 1–44, it is here included with permission and minor corrections from "The Background to the Articles of Confederation," *Publius* 12 (1982): 15–44.

---

[114] Beer, "Federalism, Nationalism, and Democracy," 12, 14–15.

—NINE—

"Virtus et Libertas": *Political Culture, Social Change, and the Origins of the American Revolution in Virginia, 1763–76*

> *Oh Britain how thou suffered thy renowned Arms to be degraded, by employing them in the cause of Tyranny and Oppression, when* Virtue and Liberty *was the Sheild and Spear which made them formidable!*
> —Edmund Pendleton to Richard Henry Lee, April 20, 1776

O N MAY 6, 1776, the elected delegates of the people of Virginia met in convention in Williamsburg to determine the political future of their "Country." Over the next two months they took a series of momentous decisions. On May 15 they committed Virginia to independence by voting to instruct the colony's delegates to Congress to propose independence for all of the thirteen colonies then in arms against Great Britain. On June 12 they approved the Virginia Declaration of Rights, the prototype for all later American bills of rights. On June 29 they adopted a constitution for the independent Commonwealth of Virginia and elected a governor and privy council. On July 5, the last day of the convention, they settled on the design for "a great Seal" for the new commonwealth.[1] Adopted as the capstone of the new political edifice and as the final step in a sustained and intense process of corporate self-redefinition, the de-

---

[1] The best modern study of the work of the Virginia Convention of May–June 1776 is Keith B. Berwick, "Moderation in Crisis: The Trials of Leadership in Revolutionary Virginia," Ph.D. diss., Univ. of Chicago, 1959.

sign of this seal could scarcely have been more revealing of the contemporary meaning of the Revolution in Virginia.

Both sides of the seal would bear engravings. On the first was "Virtus, *the genius of the Commonwealth*, dressed like an Amazon, resting on a spear with one hand, and holding a sword in the other, and treading on *tyranny*, represented by a man prostrate, a crown fallen from his head, a broken chain in his left hand, and a scourge in his right." Over the head of Virtus was "the word 'Virginia' . . . and underneath, the words 'Sic semper tyrannis.'" On the reverse side was a group: in the center was "Libertas, with the cornucopia in one hand and an ear of wheat in the other; on the other side Altemitas . . . with the globe and phoenix." Beneath the group were the words "'Deus nobis hoc otia fecit.'"[2]

This juxtaposition of virtue and liberty was not novel;[3] indeed, it was a cliché of eighteenth-century Anglo-American political thought. The two qualities, or conditions, were thought to be inextricably intertwined: to separate them was to unravel the whole political fabric. A people's virtue was a certain measure of the extent of its liberty; liberty without virtue was licentiousness. The composition of the obverse of the seal was less conventional, albeit the symbolism was as appropriate for the other twelve colonies as for Virginia. It emphasized the dependence of civil liberty, as represented by Libertas, upon the bountifulness of the American environment, as depicted by Ceres, the goddess of agriculture, and the hope, as illustrated by Aeternitas, the goddess of permanence, both for the "timeless sovereignty of the new commonwealth" and for the perpetuation of the civil liberty and the bounty on which it was based.[4] The Latin motto, meaning "God endowed us with these retreats," was simply an invocation of another familiar eighteenth-century cultural theme: the association of virtue and liberty with retirement in a country setting, a theme that was especially appropriate to Virginia, perhaps the most rural of all of the colonies.[5]

---

[2] Edmund Randolph describes the great seal virtually verbatim from the original resolution in *History of Virginia*, ed. Arthur H. Shaffer (Charlottesville, Va., 1970), 276.

[3] See the important discussions in Gordon S. Wood, *The Creation of the American Republic, 1776–1787* (Chapel Hill, N.C., 1969), 65–70; Gerald Stourzh, *Alexander Hamilton and the Idea of Republican Government* (Stanford, Calif., 1970), 63–75; and J. G. A. Pocock, *The Machiavellian Moment: Florentine Political Thought and the Atlantic Republican Tradition* (Princeton, N.J., 1975), 406–552.

[4] W. Edwin Hemphill, "The Symbolism of Our Seal," *Virginia Cavalcade* 2 (1952): 27–33, analyzes the meaning of the seal.

[5] See especially Maynard Mack, *The Garden and the City* (Toronto, 1969), and Maren-Sofie Rostvig, *The Happy Man*, 2 vols. (Oslo, 1958–62).

But it was the other side of the seal that was freighted with the most profound emotional content. If almost every segment of the emerging American political community emphasized the intimate connection between virtue and liberty and if Boston could claim a special affinity for the "generous Principles of *Liberty*," which, as one earlier Bostonian had asserted, had "always distinguish'd this METROPOLIS,"[6] only Virginia claimed virtue "as the genius of the Commonwealth." Nor was this a new claim, a utopian vision evoked by the exhilarating contemplation of the possibilities of revolution. Rather, it represented a dramatic restatement of a self-conception—an elusive aspiration—that stretched back at least two generations and had been sharpened vividly over the previous fifteen years by the counterexample of Britain, whose behavior seemed to make patent that it had followed the tragic example of Rome and, as Edmund Pendleton remarked, abandoned "virtue and Liberty . . . the Sheild and the Spear" that had made it "formidable" for "Tyranny and Oppression." But this self-conception also had been seriously shaken over the previous twenty-five years by a series of ominous social and political developments within Virginia that seemed to portend moral and social decline of the most disturbing variety.[7]

The claim of virtue as the special characteristic of Virginia was thus an expression—in the midst of revolution—both of a continuing commitment to a political and social ideal that long had animated the leaders of the Virginia polity and of deep-seated fears, grounded in experience, about the present and future moral state of the commonwealth. The design of the seal thus suggests that revolution and independence were ways of overcoming two powerful threats to Virginia's corporate self-image as it had taken shape over the previous half century. One threat, external, was represented by the tyrannical acts of the metropolitan government; the other, internal, was manifest in the frightening decline of virtue in Virginia. Vividly evident in the heavy symbolism of the new seal of the commonwealth, the intense anxieties arising from these two challenges—the interlocking fears of the loss of both liberty and virtue as well as the determined commitment to preserve both—underlay and to a considerable extent determined the behavior of Virginia's political

---

[6] *The Invitation* (Boston, 1755), 3.

[7] Pendleton to R. H. Lee, Apr. 20, 1776, *The Letters and Papers of Edmund Pendleton,* ed. David J. Mays, 2 vols. (Charlottesville, Va., 1967), 1:164. The background to these developments is discussed in Jack P. Greene, "Society, Ideology, and Politics: An Analysis of the Political Culture of Mid-Eighteenth-Century Virginia," in Richard M. Jellison, ed., *Society, Freedom, and Conscience: The American Revolution* (New York, 1976), 14–76.

leaders during the dozen years immediately preceding the Declaration of Independence. The nature and origins of Virginia's corporate self-image and the emerging dialectic between the self-image and these two formidable challenges during the crucial years 1764–66, at the very beginning of the pre-Revolutionary crises, are the subjects that will be explored in this chapter.

By 1760 a large native oligarchy had dominated the political life of Virginia at both the local and provincial levels for over a century. Until near the end of the second decade of the eighteenth century, public affairs had been riven with strife and discord, the stability that had obtained under Governor Sir William Berkeley between the Restoration in 1660 and Bacon's Rebellion in 1676 being only the exception that proved the rule. The seemingly endless struggles for ascendancy in an extremely fluid social and economic environment that had characterized political life from the founding of the colony in 1607 to the Restoration was followed in the wake of Bacon's Rebellion by a series of recurrent conflicts over the crown's efforts to gain more control over the economic and political life of the colony. For the next forty years, these conflicts both split the gentry—a combination of leading tobacco magnates, overseas merchants, professional men, and the colony's political elite—into warring factions and led to the expulsion or removal of one royal governor after another. Not until 1718, when, following the failure of a vigorous and sustained attempt to undermine the extraordinary power of the Virginia council, Lieutenant Governor Alexander Spotswood (1710–22) reached an accommodation with local leaders, was this pattern finally broken.[8]

By casting themselves in the role of "patriot" governors and carefully cultivating the gentry as well as the new Walpolean emphasis upon harmony and cooperation among all branches of government, Spotswood's immediate successors, Hugh Drysdale (1722–26) and, especially, Sir William Gooch (1727–49), joined with the leading local politicians to fashion a new political stability that remained essentially intact for the rest of

---

[8] See, especially, Bernard Bailyn, "Politics and Social Structure in Virginia," in James Morton Smith, ed., *Seventeenth-Century America: Essays in Colonial History* (Chapel Hill, N.C., 1959), 90–115; John C. Rainbolt, "The Alteration in the Relationship between Leadership and Constituents in Virginia, 1660–1720," *William and Mary Quarterly*, 3d ser., 27 (1970): 411–34; and Jack P. Greene, "The Opposition to Lieutenant Governor Alexander Spotswood, 1718," *Virginia Magazine of History and Biography* 80 (1962): 35–42.

the colonial period. Political factions disappeared, and, unlike their counterparts in many other colonies, Virginia legislators routinely supported the administration and increasingly took special pride in the colony's intense British patriotism and loyalty to the crown. With the exception of Robert Dinwiddie during the first years of his tenure in the early 1750s, subsequent governors, including Francis Fauquier (1758–67) and Norborne Berkeley, Baron de Botetourt (1767–70), obtained similar results by following the successful example of Gooch.[9]

From 1720 through the early 1760s, Virginia politics was a classic model of what Samuel P. Huntington has described as a situation of "traditional stability." In the absence of large or important urban centers, with overall economic prosperity, and without serious social divisions, the countryside was dominant, and the rural elite governed unchallenged by endogenous opposition. The tenantry and yeomanry assumed a largely passive or only marginally active role in politics, and the numerically weak intermediate class of merchants and lawyers allied itself with the dominant elite. Virginia, as Sir John Randolph, speaker of the House of Burgesses, informed that body in August 1734, had attained a degree of public "Happiness, which seems almost peculiar to our selves, of being under none of the Perturbations which we see every where else arising from the different Views and Designs of Factions and Parties."[10]

The central figures in this political nirvana during the early 1760s were Francis Fauquier, the lieutenant governor, and John Robinson, since 1738 speaker of the House of Burgesses and treasurer of the colony. The council included several "very respectable [and politically influential] characters," including its aging president, John Blair, Sr.; William Nelson, perhaps the colony's largest resident merchant; Thomas Nelson, William's brother and a prominent lawyer; and Richard Corbin, receiver general and scion of an old gentry family. But none of these men approached Fauquier and Robinson in political power and popularity. Fauquier, the urbane and cosmopolitan Englishman, and Robinson, the ami-

---

[9] For a discussion of the social and political conditions that underlay this new political stability, see Greene, "Society, Ideology, and Politics," and, more broadly, Jack P. Greene, "The Growth of Political Stability: An Interpretation of Political Development in the Anglo-American Colonies, 1660–1760," in John Parker and Carol Urness, eds., *The American Revolution: A Heritage of Change* (Minneapolis, 1975), 26–52.

[10] Samuel P. Huntington, *Political Order in Changing Societies* (New Haven, 1978), 76; Randolph's Speech, Aug. 24, 1734, in Henry R. McIlwaine and John P. Kennedy, eds., *Journals of the House of Burgesses of Virginia*, 13 vols. (Richmond, 1906–15), *1727–40*, 75–76 (hereafter cited as *Burgesses Journals*).

able "native, educated wholly in Virginia," were the same age—in 1763, fifty-nine years old—and very much alike in political personality: judicious, conciliatory, pragmatic, and benevolent. At the time of his appointment in 1758, Fauquier had been advised by Lord Anson, who knew the "people you are going to preside over well," that Virginians were a "good Natured people whom you may lead but whom you cannot drive." Fauquier found this advice extraordinarily congenial. Although he had been charged by his political superiors in London to obtain Robinson's resignation from one of his two powerful offices and to secure the permanent separation of the offices of speaker and treasurer, Fauquier instead proceeded, to the great displeasure of London officials, to form an intimate alliance with Robinson. By this action he securely established his reputation among Virginians as a "kind benevolent patriot Governor" who could be counted on to defend the colony's established constitution and fundamental interests against all external enemies, whether metropolitan officials or British mercantile interests, and who helped to ensure the perpetuation of the colony's traditional internal political stability. Robinson was equally devoted to the politics of moderation and compromise. He took his seat in the House of Burgesses in 1727, the first year of Gooch's gubernatorial tenure, and subsequently received his political tutelage from Gooch and Sir John Randolph, his predecessor as speaker and, next to Gooch, the principal architect of Virginia's remarkable political stability. During his long tenure in office, Robinson had acquired such extraordinary political popularity that by the early 1760s he could be described by Fauquier as the "darling of the Country."[11]

Robinson's enormous popularity, and power, derived in part from the "weight and influence" of the "Speaker's . . . Chair" among "those, who" were "candidates for his countenance and favour" and in part, it was discovered after his death in 1766, from the liberal disposition of public funds entrusted to him as treasurer. But his power and popularity were much too general to be explained entirely in these terms. Far more important were his "sound political knowledge," his public reputation as a man of "great integrity, assiduity, and ability in business," and his per-

---

[11] Randolph, *History of Virginia*, 173; Fauquier to Earl of Egremont, May 19, 1763, Egremont Papers, PRO 30/47/14, bundle 1, Public Record Office, London; Jack P. Greene, "The Attempt to Separate the Offices of Speaker and Treasurer in Virginia, 1758–1766," *Virginia Magazine of History and Biography* 71 (1963): 11–18; Fauquier to Board of Trade, May 12, 1761, CO 5/1330, ff. 129–35, PRO; James Maury to John Camm, Dec. 12, 1763, *Burgesses Journals, 1761–65*, li–liii; James Horrocks, *Upon the Peace* (Williamsburg, Va. 1763), iii–iv; St. George Tucker to William Wirt, Sept. 25, 1815, *William and Mary College Quarterly*, 1st ser., 22 (1914): 253.

sonification of the politics of prudence and restraint so much admired by the gentry. Contemporaries found his "acquaintance with parliamentary forms" and the grace with which he filled the speaker's chair remarkable. "When he presided," wrote Edmund Randolph,

> the decorum of the house outshone that of the British House of Commons, even with Onslow at their head. When he propounded a question, his comprehension and perspicuity brought it equally to the most humble and the most polished understanding. To committees he nominated the members best qualified. He stated to the house the contents of every bill and showed himself to be a perfect master of the subject. When he pronounced the rules of order, he convinced the reluctant. When on the floor of a committee of the whole house, he opened the debate, he submitted resolutions and enforced them with simplicity and might. In the limited sphere of colonial politics, he was a column.

No less important as an ingredient of Robinson's political power was an extraordinary warmth of personality, "a benevolence which created friends and a sincerity which never lost one," qualities that won for him wide applause and admiration as "a jewil of a man" whose "opinions must [always] be regarded."[12]

Around Robinson in the house revolved an impressive array of political talent that was broadly representative of the ruling gentry and genuinely and, in most cases, effectively responsive to the needs of the larger society. Among the leading members were several men who were closely attached to Robinson, including Attorney General Peyton Randolph, who would succeed him as speaker in 1766; his special protégé Edmund Pendleton, a lawyer of great probity and stature; and Benjamin Harrison and Archibald Cary, two James River planters from prominent gentry families. But Robinson never tried to use his associates as the nucleus of a political machine or to prefer them to the exclusion of other "qualified" members. He distributed committee assignments widely, and not only among such relatively independent, if usually supportive, men as Richard Bland, Benjamin Waller, George Wythe, Robert Carter Nicholas, and Dudley Digges—all, like Randolph and Pendleton, members of that "constellation of eminent lawyers and scholars" who practiced be-

---

[12] Randolph, *History of Virginia*, 173–74; Robert Carter Nicholas to the Printer, *Virginia Gazette* (Purdie and Dixon), June 27, 1766; entry of Oct. 9, 1776, in Jack P. Greene, ed., *Diary of Colonel Landon Carter of Sabine Hall, 1752–1778*, 2 vols. (Charlottesville, Va., 1965), 2:738.

fore the General Court. He also utilized the talents of those who most frequently opposed his policies and were potential political rivals, including the two brothers Charles Carter of Cleve, the last person to contest Robinson for the speakership in 1742, and Landon Carter, the petulant squire of Sabine Hall, and, more recently, Richard Henry Lee, the brilliant, ambitious, and hot-tempered young planter from Westmoreland County. Until his death in 1764, Charles Carter of Cleve was, next to Robinson, the most powerful and prominent man in the house, while Robinson repeatedly assigned Lee to major committee posts even though Lee had launched his career in the burgesses in 1758 with a vigorous attack upon the speaker.[13]

Several historians have discussed mid-eighteenth-century Virginia politics in terms of a split between a James River faction under the leadership of Robinson and his associates and a Northern Neck interest revolving around the Carters, Lees, Masons, and other prominent families from the Rappahannock and Potomac river valleys. During the 1740s, competition over western lands by rival speculating groups roughly corresponded to such a division, and the fact that Northern Neck representatives such as the Carters and Lee were among Robinson's most consistent critics lends some plausibility to such a categorization. But if such a factional split existed, it does not seem to have been very serious or to have had any major impact upon the politics of the house. Both the house and the council frequently divided over such fundamental issues as the extent of Virginia's contribution to the Seven Years' War and any of the myriad questions involved with the several paper money emissions made during that war. But these divisions, as St. George Tucker, still another prominent member of the Virginia bar who emigrated from Bermuda to Virginia in 1772, later testified, were the results not "of *party spirit*" but "only" of such "differences of opinion . . . as different men, coming from different parts of our extensive Country might well be expected to entertain." Before the mid-1760s, at least, no issue arose of sufficient force to create deep or lasting political divisions.[14]

---

[13] Jack P. Greene, "Foundations of Political Power in the Virginia House of Burgesses, 1720–1776," *William and Mary Quarterly*, 3d ser., 16 (1959): 485–506; Randolph, *History of Virginia*, 174–79.

[14] Tucker to Wirt, Sept. 25, 1815, *William and Mary College Quarterly*, 1st ser., 22 (1914): 253. Historians who have treated Virginia politics in terms of a north-south split include David Alan Williams, "Political Alignments in Colonial Virginia," Ph.D. diss., Northwestern Univ., 1959; Joseph Albert Ernst, "The Robinson Scandal Redivivus: Money, Debts, and Politics in Revolutionary Virginia," *Virginia Magazine of History and Biogra-*

To have organized themselves into parties would in any case have constituted a serious and disturbing violation of a clear and proud corporate
self-image that Virginians had carefully nurtured over the previous half
century. "The pride of Virginia," later wrote Edmund Randolph, who
had grown to manhood during the years when that self-image was assuming concrete and durable shape,

> had so long been a topic of discourse in the other colonies that it had
> almost grown into a proverb. Being the earliest among the British
> settlements in North America, having been soon withdrawn from the
> humiliation of proprietary dependence to the dignity of a government
> immediately under the crown, advancing rapidly into wealth from her
> extensive territory and the luxuriant production of her staple com-
> modities, the sons of the most opulent families trained by education
> and habits acquired in England and hence perhaps arrogating some
> superiority over the provinces not so distinguished, she was charged
> with manifesting a cons[c]iousness that she had more nearly ap-
> proached to the British model . . . of excellence, and what was
> claimed as an attribute of character in a government readily diffused
> itself among the individuals who were members of it.[15]

Among the attributes of character thus assigned by Virginians to their
political system, six were primary. The first was *unanimity*, the successful
transcendence, celebrated by Sir John Randolph in a quotation given
earlier, of "private Broils" and "Party-Rancour." A second was *moderation*. Virginia, said Edmund Randolph, had "received from the parent
country an original stamina, perhaps I might add something phlegmatic
in her temper, which inclined her to regulated liberty by saving her from
those ebullitions which teem with violence and insubordination." Virginians took special pride in the "spirit of mildness" that both pervaded
social relations among whites and animated the colony's uniformly "cool
and deliberate" political counsels. A third was hardheaded *pragmatism*.
The "happiness of Virginia character," according to Edmund Randolph,
was "hardly ever to push to extremity any theory which by practical
relations may not be accommodated." Believing, as Edmund Pendleton
later remarked, that "perfection in any institute devised by *man*, was as
vain as the search for a philosopher's stone," Virginians were willing

phy 77 (1969): 146–73; and J. A. Leo Lemay, "Robert Bolling and the Bailment of Colonel Chiswell," *Early American Literature* 6 (1971): 99–142.

[15] Randolph, *History of Virginia*, 177.

when, "as in all . . . Political cases," they could not "get the very best" to "take the best we can get."[16]

Moderation and practicality were closely related to *virtue*, the fourth and, for contemporary Virginians, central defining attribute of Virginia's political character. Virginians, said the German traveler Johann David Schoepf, conceived of themselves as having "an inborn higher morality" that had infused itself into the political system. Because it was composed of fallible men, that system might occasionally make mistakes. But its leaders prided themselves upon always trying to work for the corporate welfare of the whole community rather than the particular interests of any of its parts and upon keeping the polity almost totally free from the corruption that had tainted and eventually destroyed so many other political systems. "The possession of soil," said one observer, "naturally turns the attention to its cultivation, and generally speaking, men who," like Virginians, "are occupied by labor in the country are more exempt from the vices prevailing in towns." But the virtue of a political system also depended upon a fifth attribute of political character and an extremely important component of Virginia's corporate self-image: the vaunted *independence* of its leaders. A "high sense of personal independence," said Edmund Randolph, "was universal" among white Virginians. Nourished by the "system of slavery, however so baneful to virtue," a "quick and acute sense" of personal liberty, a disdain for every "abridgement of personal independence," was, thought Randolph, the "ornament" of the "real Virginia planter." A sixth and final attribute of the character of the Virginia political system was its *loyalty*. "Every political sentiment, every fashion in Virginia," Randolph said, "appeared to be imperfect unless it bore a resemblance to some precedent in England." Virginians liked to think that this "almost idolatrous deference to the mother country" was reciprocated by "a particular regard and predilection for Virginia." Obviously, a polity thus characterized by its unanimity, moderation, pragmatic realism, virtue, independence, and loyalty was, said Randolph proudly, "in a political view inferior to [that of] no other colony."[17]

Events during the early 1750s and 1760s both sharpened and rein-

[16] Ibid., 157–58, 247–48; John Markland, *Typographia: An Ode to Printing* (Williamsburg, Va., 1730), 9–10; David Mossum, Jr., "Ode," *Virginia Gazette*, Nov. 26, 1736; Pendleton, "Address to the Va. Ratifying Convention," June 12, 1788, in *Pendleton Papers* 2:528.

[17] Johann David Schoepf, *Travels in the Confederation [1783–1784]*, trans. and ed. Alfred J. Morrison, 2 vols. (Philadelphia, 1911), 1:91–95; Randolph, *History of Virginia*, 161, 176, 178, 193, 197, 257; marquis de Chastellux, *Travels in North America in the Years*

forced—if also somewhat shook—this image. Between 1752 and 1764, various actions by the metropolitan government and its servants had called into question the confident assumption that Britain "had a particular regard and predilection" for Virginia and had eaten away at the foundations of the colony's celebrated British patriotism. Having found, said one anonymous bard, probably the respected Stafford County lawyer John Mercer,

> . . . This loyal land in peace
> nor striving nor contending
> than how to prove its loves increase
> tow'rds one of George's sending,

Lieutenant Governor Robert Dinwiddie, through his unilateral imposition in 1752 of a fee of a pistole for signing and sealing all land patents, had raised the specter of arbitrary royal power in the colony for the first time in nearly thirty-five years. The pistole fee controversy was only the first in a trio of political contests through which "Virginians hitherto distinguished for their loyalty" found themselves "shamefully traduced, were Oppressed, Insulted, & treated like rebells, by the very persons from whom they" had been so "long taught to expect Succour."[18] The other two disputes erupted in 1759 and commanded the intermittent attention of the Virginia political community for the next five years. They revolved around the British merchants' opposition to the colony's wartime paper money emissions and the Virginia clergy's attack upon the Two-Penny Acts, measures that enabled people to pay public obligations, including the salary of the established clergy, in money instead of tobacco in two years of extremely short crops.[19]

1780, 1781, and 1782, ed. Howard C. Rice, Jr., 2 vols. (Chapel Hill, N.C., 1963), 2:428–30.

[18] [Mercer], "Dinwiddianae," in Richard Beale Davis, ed., *The Colonial Virginia Satirist: Mid-Eighteenth-Century Commentaries on Politics, Religion, and Society* (Philadelphia, 1967), 21, 27. On the pistole fee controversy, see Jack P. Greene, ed., "The Case of the Pistole Fee," *Virginia Magazine of History and Biography* 66 (1958): 406–22. The points covered in this and the following three paragraphs are developed more fully in Greene, "Society, Ideology, and Politics."

[19] These disputes are treated in detail by Thad W. Tate, "The Coming of the Revolution in Virginia: Britain's Challenge to Virginia's Ruling Class, 1763–1776," *William and Mary Quarterly*, 3d ser., 19 (1962): 324–35; Rhys Isaac, "Religion and Authority: Problems of the Anglican Establishment in Virginia in the Era of the Great Awakening and the Parsons' Cause," ibid., 30 (1973): 3–36; and Joseph Albert Ernst, "Genesis of the Currency

As in the case of the pistole fee controversy, in both of these disputes metropolitan officials had supported a person or a group that the vast majority of Virginia political leaders believed was trying to extend its power or gain private advantage at the expense of the general welfare of the colony. In the classic manner of British colonial administration, crown officials never sided wholly with the colony's opponents in any of the three controversies. But the cumulative effect of their behavior was to persuade Virginia's political leaders that Virginia's political institutions, specifically the elected House of Burgesses, were the only agencies that could be trusted to act in the best interests of the colony and to make them, for the first time in almost fifty years, especially sensitive to a dangerous defect in the Virginia political system: the vague constitutional arrangements that obtained under the empire made the Virginia polity particularly vulnerable to the awesome might of the parent state. To remedy this defect, Virginia's political leaders vigorously sought to secure precise constitutional limitations upon royal power that would provide the colony with permanent protection against any ill-considered or corrupt exertion of metropolitan authority.

The anxiety arising from their inability to achieve such limitations, which haunted Virginians through the early 1760s and fed a mounting suspicion of the intentions of the metropolitan government, had, however, been tempered by two other developments: first, the intensification of British patriotism as a result of the justifiable pride Virginians took in their impressive contribution to the great British victory in the Seven Years' War and the conciliatory behavior of Dinwiddie's successor, Francis Fauquier; and, second, the perpetuation of the belief, fostered by the few concessions extended to the colony by metropolitan officials in each of the controversies, in the essential justice of the mother country and its basic goodwill toward Virginia.

Moreover, the behavior of the colony's political leaders throughout these disputes could only reinforce the colony's corporate self-image. They had behaved, said Edmund Randolph, with a "loyalty debased by no servile compliance and . . . a patriotic watchfulness never degenerating into the mere petulance of complaint" and had displayed "an elevation of character" that would render Virginians "incapable of being seduced by the artifices" of any set of men, however corrupt or designing, who might gain control of the metropolitan government. Besides, if the British government was in fact as just and benignly disposed toward Vir-

---

Act of 1764: Virginia Paper Money and the Protection of British Investments," ibid., 22 (1965): 34–59.

ginia as Virginians wanted to believe, "to know when to complain and how to complain with dignity" was all that was necessary to avoid any evils that might descend upon the colony as a result of a deleterious exertion of its power.[20]

More disturbing by far to the Virginia political community and potentially far more damaging to the colony's corporate self-image were the abundant signs of rampant internal moral decay that had become increasingly manifest in the years after 1740. Slavery, some observers noted, had had a vicious effect "upon the Morals & Manners of our People," undermining a respect for labor and feeding lamentable "Habits of Pride, and Cruelty in . . . Owners."[21]

Even more serious, in their view, and much more widely condemned, was a perceptible falling away from the old values of industry, thrift, and sobriety and an exorbitant increase in luxury, gambling, and drunkenness. More and more after 1745, travelers and native Virginians alike remarked on the "extravagance, ostentation, and . . . disregard for economy" in the colony, especially, and most menacingly, among the wealthy. Fauquier expressed great alarm in 1762 at the planters' rising indebtedness to British merchants, which he attributed to the planters' unwillingness to "quit any one Article of Luxury." In a sermon celebrating the peace of 1763, the Reverend James Horrocks of the College of William and Mary warned the colony in moderate Anglican tones against too "great a Tendency amongst us to Extravagance and Luxury" and admonished his readers to eschew the "insignificant Pride of Dress, the empty Ambition of Gaudy Furniture, or a splendid Equipage . . . which must undoubtedly serve more for Ostentation and Parade, than any real Use or valuable Purpose." Equally sinister in its meaning, an uncontrollable "spirit of gaming" had broken "forth . . . in ways destructive of morals and estates." This "prevailing Passion and Taste for Gaming . . . Racing, Cards, Dice and all other such Diversions," "wretched practice[s]" that, said one critic, "fifty years ago [were] . . . scarcely . . . known," had devastating effects upon the character of Virginians at all levels of society, especially the young, and thus carried a potentially "fatal Tendency" for Virginia society. Said one poet:

---

[20] Randolph, *History of Virginia*, 160–61, 163, 248. See Greene, "Society, Ideology, and Politics," for a fuller discussion of these points.

[21] George Mason, "Scheme for Replevying Goods, [Dec. 23, 1765], in *The Papers of George Mason*, ed. Robert A. Rutland, 3 vols. (Chapel Hill, N.C., 1970), 1:61–62. See also the citations in note 65 of Greene, "Society, Ideology, and Politics."

> Honor it stabs; religion it disgraces,
> It hurts our trade, and honesty defaces.
> But, what is worse, it so much guilt does bring,
> That many times distraction thence does spring.

Many thought that Virginia was already too far "infatuated & Abandoned" to feel any guilt. "The Vice and Wickedness of a Nation," the Reverend William Stith, also of the college, told the colony's political leaders in a sermon before the House of Burgesses in 1752, "are the certain Forerunners and Cause of its Disgrace and Destruction." Clergymen of every religious stamp agreed that all indications suggested that the destruction of Virginia was imminent and could be averted only by an uncompromising and permanent return to the solid virtues of earlier generations.[22]

If this widespread moral declension obviously had touched some of the colony's first families, and if it constituted an omnipresent and menacing threat to several aspects of the colony's corporate self-image, especially its belief in its own moderation, prudence, virtue, and independence, there were still in the early 1760s no ostensible signs that it had touched—much less damaged—the colony's political system. The system was dominated by men who had been performing capably in positions of power and responsibility for at least a generation. Thirteen of the most powerful members of the House of Burgesses between 1750 and 1764 were still active and alive in the mid-1760s and had a combined total of over two hundred years of legislative service. The median number of years of service was fifteen, ranging from thirty-six for Speaker Robinson to five for Richard Henry Lee, and the median age was forty-two, with Robinson, at fifty-nine, being the oldest, and Lee, at thirty-one, the youngest. Men reached such positions of top leadership, moreover, not from the "vanity of pedigree" but from the "positive force of character." "Fortune, birth, and station" might be sufficient to get a man elected to the house but not to gain for him a place of leadership and the confidence of his colleagues that such a position represented. Such places were re-

---

[22] See Andrew Burnaby, *Burnaby's Travels through North America*, ed. Rufus Rockwell Wilson (New York, 1904), 55; Fauquier to Board of Trade, Nov. 3, 1762, CO 5/1330, ff. 339–40, PRO; Horrocks, *Upon the Peace*, 9–10, 14; "My Country's Worth," [1752], in *The Poems of Charles Hansford*, ed. James A. Servies and Carl R. Dolmetsch (Chapel Hill, N.C., 1961), 62–64; William Stith, *The Sinfulness and Pernicious Nature of Gaming* (Williamsburg, Va., 1752), 11–12; Randolph, *History of Virginia*, 61.

served for men of "Ability and Distinction." And not just Robinson but the whole group enjoyed wide public esteem. These men, said Charles Hansford, a blacksmith turned poet, in 1752, were "stars of the first magnitude" who "in their several stations" combined

> The great support and ornament to be
> Of Britain's first and ancient colony.[23]

Satisfaction with the colony's political system was not, of course, universal. There were occasional complaints about the growth of corruption in elections, of ambition and demagoguery among politicians, and of the number of men standing for elections "who have neither natural or acquired parts to recommend them."[24] Far more importantly, perhaps, an increasing number of people began to worry about the excessive power lodged in the hands of John Robinson in his joint capacity as speaker and treasurer. "How unhappy must a Country be," Landon Carter confided to his diary in March 1752 after witnessing Robinson's extraordinary influence upon the members of the House of Burgesses, "should such a man be byased with vitious Principles." "The gentleman who has filled that chair for several Assemblies, I hope is a good man and very worthy of his promotion," Alexander White wrote to Richard Henry Lee in 1758, "but still he is but a man, and so much power lodged in one man's hands, seems to me to be inconsistent with the freedom and independency of an English Legislature." One writer, perhaps Landon Carter, circulated a piece in manuscript entitled "*Lady Virginia*, to prove the . . . Speaker's great influence, and arbitrary conduct, in the House of Burgesses," a piece, Richard Bland later declared, "that stood very high in the opinion of most men . . . [and] must have made [a] deep impression on those to whom he communicated" it, "to the Speaker's disadvantage." There were even widespread "suspicions . . . among the people" that Robinson was converting public funds to private uses, and Arthur Lee charged in a private letter from Britain in November 1763 that Robinson was "a Man, more mercenary & abandoned, but far less able, than S[i]r. Robert Walpole." But Robinson met these rumors by

---

[23] Randolph, *History of Virginia,* 177–78; Greene, "Foundations of Political Power," 485–506; "My Country's Worth," *Poems of Charles Hansford,* 58.

[24] Alexander White to R. H. Lee, [1758], "Selections and Excerpts from the Lee Papers," *Southern Literary Messenger* 286 (1858): 118; Landon Carter, *The Rector Detected* (Williamsburg, Va., 1764), 8. See also Gordon S. Wood, "Rhetoric and Reality in the American Revolution," *William and Mary Quarterly,* 3d ser., 22 (1965): 27–28.

placing his most vocal critic, Richard Henry Lee, on a committee to investigate the state of the treasury, and the failure of this committee to turn up any irregularities only confirmed people in their "high opinion of" Robinson's "good conduct and" in their belief in his honesty in "complying with the laws relating to the management of the Treasury."[25]

From all appearances in the early 1760s, Sir John Randolph's 1734 remark that the Virginia political system as "yet [had] no Footsteps of Corruption" within it still applied.[26] But the general moral declension in Virginia nevertheless had created residual fears among many of the colony's political leaders for the continuing virtue of the political system.

Beginning in the spring of 1764 and continuing over the next thirty months, a series of developments revealed just how justified had been the anxieties of the early 1760s, anxieties arising from the conjoint fears of external oppression from the metropolitan government and internal corruption within the Virginia political system. In quick succession, Virginia's political leaders had to face a grave external challenge and a severe internal shock. The external challenge was posed by the Stamp Act and the threat of taxation by the British Parliament; the internal shock derived from two separate sources: first, the disclosure at the death of Speaker John Robinson in May 1766 that he had loaned over £100,000 from public funds to members of the gentry, and, second, the special treatment accorded a member of the gentry, Robinson's son-in-law Colonel John Chiswell, by other gentlemen on the General Court when he was accused of murdering a social inferior in a tavern in a fit of anger. The Stamp Act made it abundantly clear, as Richard Bland, Landon Carter, and others had been warning over the previous five years, that the colony had no certain protection against the overpowering might of the metropolitan government, while the Robinson and Chiswell affairs constituted a powerful blow to the colony's traditional corporate self-image. Both

[25] Entry of Mar. 13, 1752, *Diary of Landon Carter* 1:85, and, generally, 1:65–124; White to Lee, [1758], and Richard Bland to R. H. Lee, May 22, 1766, "Lee Papers," 116–17; "The Freeholder" [Richard Bland] to Printer, *Virginia Gazette* (Purdie and Dixon), Oct. 17, 1766; Arthur Lee to Philip Ludwell Lee, Nov. 5, 1763, Arthur Lee Papers, MS Am 811 F, I, f. 2, Houghton Library, Harvard University, Cambridge, Mass.; Robert Carter Nicholas to Printer, *Virginia Gazette* (Purdie and Dixon), Sept. 1, 1766. On Lee's challenge to Robinson, see Ernst, "Robinson Scandal Redivivus," 149–50.

[26] Randolph's Speech, Aug. 24, 1734, *Burgesses Journals, 1727–40*, 175–76.

demonstrated the inadequacy of constitutional safeguards within the colony and raised serious doubts about the health of the Virginia body politic and, more especially, about the extent of the devotion of its gentry leaders to its hallowed political beliefs.

The immediate result of this simultaneous display of the evils of unbounded power from both without and within was a political, moral, and psychological crisis that might have destroyed a less stable and adaptable political system. Out of this crisis, however, emerged a new reformist impulse in Virginia politics that called for a purification of the political system and the uncompromising reaffirmation of the gentry's commitment to the old political values. Only by bringing political reality into harmony with the colony's traditional corporate self-image, the proponents of the new impulse insisted, would the colony be able to combat either the challenge from Britain or the internal moral laxity that, temporarily they hoped, had seized the Virginia polity.

News that the House of Commons had resolved on March 10, 1764, that it was proper to levy stamp duties on the colonies reached Virginia within six weeks and appeared in the *Virginia Gazette* on April 27.[27] The immediate reaction was widespread alarm, and the response of Richard Henry Lee was a preview of the collective sentiments the colony's leaders would express over the next two years. A "very clever Man" of great spirit and driving ambition, Lee was the son of Thomas Lee of Stratford, who had been president of the council and in 1749–50 acting governor of the colony. The son had early chosen politics as the best means to gratify a boundless passion for fame and in 1758 at age twenty-six had entered the House of Burgesses as representative from his native county of Westmoreland. By 1764, after six years of service in the house, he had made his reputation as a brilliant, polished, and impassioned orator—"one of the first Speakers in the House of Burgesses"—and "an ornament to his Country."[28]

Reacting with characteristic warmth to the news of the Commons' resolutions, Lee expressed his alarm in a letter to a friend in Britain in May 1764. The "free possession of property, the right to be governed by laws made by our representatives, and the illegality of taxation without

---

[27] According to John Mercer in a letter of Sept. 12, 1766, to the *Virginia Gazette* (Purdie and Dixon), Sept. 26, 1766. Because the issue for Apr. 27, 1764, is no longer extant, there is no way to verify Mercer's statement. But there is no reason to doubt it, although no announcement appeared in the *Maryland Gazette* (Annapolis) until May 24, 1764.

[28] Harry Piper to Dixon and Littledale, May 29, 1773, Henry Piper Letter Book, 1767–76, University of Virginia Library, Charlottesville.

consent," he declared, were "such essential principles of the British constitution, that it is a matter of wonder how men, who have imbibed them in their mother's milk, whose very atmosphere is charged with them, should be of opinion that the people of America were to be taxed without consulting their representatives." That Britons could treat the colonists, "by whose distress and enterprise they saw their country so much enlarged in territory, and increased in wealth, as aliens to their society, and meriting to be enslaved by their superior power" was hard to believe. But Lee thought he had an explanation. In combination with many other "late determinations of the great" in Britain, the Commons' vote seemed to him "to prove a resolution, to oppress North America with the iron hand of power, unrestrained by any sentiment, drawn from reason, the liberty of mankind, or the genius of their own government" to keep the colonists "low, in order to secure our dependence." Although Lee did not counsel open resistance, he did express the hope that the scheme would be subversive of the ends it was intended to effect. "Poverty and oppression, among those whose minds are filled with ideas of British liberty," he warned, "may introduce a virtuous industry, with a train of generous and manly sentiments, which, when in future they become supported by numbers, may produce a fatal resentment of parental care being converted into tyrannical usurpation."[29]

Lee's letter indicated both how devoted Virginia's leaders were to the preservation of their constitutional rights as Englishmen and what a highly charged emotional issue parliamentary taxation might be, at least among less temperate Virginia politicians; equally important, it put forth two important ideas about the meaning of Parliament's behavior and its possible effects upon Virginia society. The first was the—in my view, essentially correct—perception that parliamentary taxation was part of a design formed by the "great" in Britain not to establish an internal tyranny in Britain by beginning gradually with the distant colonies, as a few nervous American observers would later charge, but to secure colonial dependence by keeping the colonies "low." The second, an idea that would be amplified and become increasingly attractive to Virginians in response to developments over the next decade, was the notion that British oppression might be the means for recovering the lost, or at least the declining, virtue of the colony. By depriving Virginians of the means to gratify their increasing passion for luxury and pleasure, such a severe economic blow as that to be expected from the Stamp

[29] R. H. Lee to ——, May 31, 1764, in *The Letters of Richard Henry Lee*, ed. James C. Ballagh, 2 vols. (New York, 1911–14), 1:5–7.

Act might force them to return to the old values, produce that moral regeneration being called for by Anglican and dissenting clergy alike, and endow the old dominion with renewed vigor.

The official response was somewhat more measured but no less emphatic. On June 15, 1764, the committee of correspondence (a joint committee composed of four councillors and most of the leading members of the House of Burgesses and charged with corresponding with Edward Montague, a London barrister who represented Virginia in London) met to consider Montague's March 10 letter informing the committee of Parliament's resolutions on the proposed stamp duties. The committee immediately and emphatically declared its opposition to the duties and ordered George Wythe and Robert Carter Nicholas, two of the colony's most respected lawyers and prominent leaders in the House of Burgesses, to draft a reply. Raising all of the obvious objections to the duties, Wythe and Nicholas, as moderate in their politics as Lee was warm, attacked them as being both unjust and economically unwise. Such duties, they complained, would be "an additional heavy burthen . . . upon a People already laden with Debts, contracted chiefly" they reminded the agent, "in Defense of the Common Cause" during the Seven Years' War. They found the proposal the "more extraordinary" in view of the part taken by the colony during the war, when "with the greatest Cheerfulness" it had "always . . . submitted to & comply'd with every Requisition . . . made . . . with the least Colour of Reason or Pretence of Necessity."[30]

But the main focus of Wythe and Nicholas's objections was constitutional. Going right to the heart of the constitutional problem that had plagued Virginia's relations with the metropolitan government over the previous twelve years, they expressed the "wish that our just Liberties & Privileges as free born British Subjects were once properly defin'd." What those liberties and privileges might be, they did not spell out in detail, and they carefully disavowed any intention of trying to put a "restraint upon the controlling Power of Parliament." But they did assert that the "most vital Principle of the British Constitution" was the exemption of the subject from laws made "without either their personal Consent, or the Consent by their representatives" and suggested that for Parliament to "fix a Tax upon such Part of our Trade & concerns as are merely inter-

[30]Committee of Correspondence to Edward Montague, July 28, 1764, "Proceedings of the Virginia Committee of Correspondence," *Virginia Magazine of History and Biography* 12 (1905): 5–14.

nal, appears . . . to be . . . a long & hasty Stride . . . of the first importance."[31]

Before the committee met to approve this letter of July 28, it had
received a subsequent letter from Montague informing it of the ministry's determination "to carry their Intentions of taxing the Colonies at
pleasure into Execution." Now that the threat of parliamentary taxation
seemed more certain, the committee felt compelled to make its constitutional claims both more explicit and more emphatic. In a postscript to
the Wythe and Nicholas letter, it applied the traditional distinction between power and right to the case. That Parliament had the power to
do what it pleased, that it was mighty enough even to give the king
power to tax the "people of England by Proclamation," it did not deny.
"But no man surely dare be such an Enemy to his Country," it argued,
"as to say they have a Right to do this." "We conceive," the committee
declared, "that no Man or Body of Men however invested with power,
have a right to do anything that is contrary to Reason & Justice, or that
can tend to the Destruction of the Constitution."[32]

Over the next few weeks, Richard Bland, the colony's most respected
political writer, worked out exactly what was reasonable and just in this
situation and which constitutional rules applied. Like Wythe and Nicholas, Bland was an outstanding lawyer, noted for his political moderation.
In 1764 he was fifty-four years old, had been a representative for Prince
George County for twenty-two years, and was widely respected for his
scholarship, especially his knowledge of political theory and Virginia history: "staunch & tough as whitleather," one observer later remarked,
with "something of ye look of musty old Parchme'ts w'ch he handleth &
studieth much."[33]

Although he was a member of the committee of correspondence, Bland
had not been at either of the meetings at which it had considered the
proposed stamp duties. However, he made it clear that he approved of
the committee's proceedings in *The Colonel Dismounted,* his last salvo
against the clergy in the polemic over the Two-Penny Acts. To counter
the clergy's claim that royal instructions were binding upon the Virginia
legislature, Bland argued in this pamphlet that Virginians, like all Englishmen, were subject only to laws made with their own consent, that

---

[31] Ibid.

[32] Ibid.

[33] Roger Atkinson to Samuel Pleasants, Oct. 1, 1774, in A. J. Morrison, ed., "Letters of
Roger Atkinson, 1769–1776," ibid., 15 (1908): 356.

only the House of Burgesses could give the consent of Virginians, and that instructions could not have the force of law because the house had not approved them.[34]

Upon learning of the proposed stamp duties, Bland simply extended his argument to include acts of Parliament as well as royal instructions. Because Virginians had no voice in the decisions of Parliament, it could not, he insisted, "impose laws upon" them "merely relative to" their "INTERNAL Government" without depriving them of the "most valuable Part" of their "Birthright as *Englishmen,* of being governed by Laws made with" their "own Consent." Bland was careful to point out that the "Term INTERNAL Government" excluded "from the Legislature of the Colony all Power derogatory to their Dependence upon the Mother Country." He declared, in fact, that Virginians could never withdraw their "Dependence without destroying the Constitution" and that in "every instance" of "EXTERNAL Government" they were, and "must be, subject to the Authority of the *British* Parliament." But, he argued, just as "all Power . . . is excluded from the Colony of withdrawing its Dependence from the Mother Kingdom, so is all Power over the Colony excluded from the Mother Kingdom but such as respects its EXTERNAL Government."[35]

By thus assigning to the House of Burgesses exclusive jurisdiction over Virginia's internal affairs and limiting Parliament's authority over the colony to matters of "EXTERNAL Government," Bland sought to define the constitutional relationship between Virginia and Great Britain in a way that would protect Virginia from the overwhelming power of Parliament—as well as the crown—without lessening the colony's dependence upon the parent state. Characteristically, Bland had attempted to find a reasonable and moderate solution, but he left no doubt about where the logic of his argument led. "Parliament, as the stronger Power," he observed, could certainly "force any Laws it shall think fit upon us." But the question, he added with a firm and gentle warning, was "not what it can do, but what Constitutional Right it has to do so. And if it has not any constitutional Right, then any Tax, respecting our INTERNAL Polity, which may hereafter be imposed upon us by Act of Parliament, is arbitrary, as depriving us of our Rights, and may be opposed."[36]

Bland published his pamphlet on October 27, 1764, just three days

[34] Richard Bland, *The Colonel Dismounted* (Williamsburg, Va., 1764), esp. 21–23.
[35] Ibid.
[36] Ibid.

before the House of Burgesses convened for the first time since news of the proposed stamp duties had reached the colony.[37] On November 7, Peyton Randolph in behalf of the committee of correspondence placed the various communications with the agent before the house. Denunciation of the duties in the house seems to have been universal, and Speaker Robinson appointed a committee to draw up formal protests to the king, Lords, and Commons. Composed of eight of the most distinguished members and broadly representative of the spectrum of political tempers in the house, including such moderates as Randolph, who acted as chairman, Wythe, Edmund Pendleton, Benjamin Harrison, and Archibald Cary and such firebrands as Landon Carter, Richard Henry Lee, both of whom seem to have taken the lead in opposing the duties, and John Fleming, a Cumberland County lawyer, the committee submitted on November 30 an address to the king, a memorial to the Lords, and a remonstrance to the Commons. After making a number of amendments, both the house and the council unanimously adopted all three documents on December 18.[38]

These documents, by which the Virginia assembly joined the New York assembly as the first American legislatures to protest the constitutionality of the proposed stamp duties, were a model of moderation—but moderation expressed "with decent Firmness." To authorities in London, Fauquier described them as merely "praying that Virginians be permitted to tax themselves." In fact, they went considerably beyond that. Citing the colony's "ready Compliance with Royal Requisitions during the late War" as evidence of its "firm and inviolable Attachment to your sacred Person and Government," the address to the king implored him "to protect your People of this Colony in the Enjoyment of their ancient and inestimable Right of being governed by such Laws respecting their internal Polity and Taxation as are derived from their own Consent, with the Approbation of their Sovereign or his Substitute"—an official endorsement of Bland's claim that the Virginia legislature had exclusive jurisdiction over all of the internal affairs of Virginia, including matters

[37] Virginia Gazette Daybook, 1764–66, Oct. 24, 27, 1764, 108, 110, University of Virginia Library.

[38] *Burgesses Journals, 1761–65*, Nov. 7–Dec. 18, 1764, esp. 240, 254, 257, 279, 293, 299, 300, 301, 302–4. For the roles played by Carter and Lee, see entries for July 14, 25, 1776, Feb. 23–24, 1777, *Diary of Landon Carter* 2:1057, 1063, 1082–84; Jack P. Greene, *Landon Carter: An Inquiry into the Personal Values and Social Imperatives of the Eighteenth-Century Virginia Gentry* (Charlottesville, Va., 1967), 85–86; and R. H. Lee to William Rind, *Virginia Gazette* (Rind), July 25, 1766.

of legislation as well as taxation. The address thus committed the legislature of the colony to a claim of constitutional jurisdiction that went way beyond that advanced by the assembly of any other colony during the Stamp Act crisis. Like the statements of the Stamp Act Congress, these documents claimed no more than exclusive jurisdiction over matters of taxation.[39]

The memorial to the Lords and the remonstrance to the Commons pointed out the adverse economic consequences such duties might have upon a colony already overburdened with a large war debt and threatened by a renewal of Indian hostilities on its frontiers at a time of "Scarcity of circulating Cash," "little Value of their Staple at the *British* Markets" to which it was confined, and the "late Restrictions upon the Trade of the Colonies"—a reference to other aspects of the Grenville program. Stamp duties would render the "Circumstances of the People extremely distressful." But the memorial and remonstrance also firmly denied that Parliament had any right to exercise "a Power never before constitutionally assumed" of taxing the colonists "without the Consent of Representatives chosen by themselves" and asked "by what Distinction" Virginians could "be deprived of that sacred Birthright and most valuable Inheritance by their Fellow Subjects" in a "Parliament, wherein they are not, and indeed cannot, constitutionally be represented." For Parliament to exercise such a power would be to "establish this melancholy Truth, that the Inhabitants of the Colonies are Slaves of *Britons,* from whom they are descended, and from whom they might expect every Indulgence that the Obligations of Interest and Affection can entitle them to."[40]

But the evil consequences to be expected from parliamentary taxation were not limited to the colonies. By reducing the colonists to such "extreme poverty" that they would be compelled to manufacture most of the items they customarily bought from Britain, parliamentary taxation would prove destructive of that "happy Intercourse of reciprocal Benefits" that had so much advanced "the Prosperity of both" the colonies and Britain. Nor would it be wise, said the remonstrance to the Commons, for "*British* patriots" ever to "consent to the Exercise of anticonstitutional Power, which even in this remote Corner may be dangerous in its Example to the interiour Parts of the *British* Empire." To prevent all such measures for the future and to achieve constitutional security,

---

[39] Fauquier to Board of Trade, Dec. 24, 1765, CO 5/1331, 1–2, PRO; Address, Memorial, and Remonstrance, Dec. 18, 1764, *Burgesses Journals, 1761–65,* 302–4.

[40] Address, Memorial, and Remonstrance, Dec. 18, 1764, *Burgesses Journals, 1761–65,* 302–4.

the lack of which Virginians had lamented over the previous five years, the memorial asked the assistance of the Lords in the Virginians' endeavors "to establish their Constitution upon its proper foundation"—a "Necessity" required by the "Duty" the memorialists "owed to themselves and their Posterity."[41]

If these documents put the Virginia legislature unequivocally on record in behalf of the principles that no society should be subject to power beyond its control, that Parliament was beyond the control of Virginia society, and that, therefore, Parliament could have no legitimate claim to jurisdiction over the internal concerns of Virginia, they did so in the traditional Virginia mode: "in a respectful Manner" and amid great, and doubtless sincere, protestations that their conduct had been animated by "Principles . . . of the purest Loyalty and Affection as they always endeavoured by their Conduct to demonstrate that they consider their Connexions with *Great Britain,* the Seat of Liberty, as their greatest happiness." Not so the next official Virginia statement on the stamp duties. By the time the assembly met again on May 24 for the primary purpose of trying to resolve a financial crisis arising out of the treasury's inability to redeem paper money whose currency ended on March 1, unofficial news had reached the colony of Parliament's passage of the Stamp Act on February 17.[42]

For whatever reason—ostensibly because the colony had received neither an official answer to its earlier protests nor official news of passage of the Stamp Act, but probably because the established leaders, in the absence of both Landon Carter and Richard Henry Lee, the "warmest" patriots among them, were genuinely ambivalent about what course to adopt—house leaders failed to take any notice of the matter. This failure opened the way for several "young hot and giddy members," as Fauquier described them, "whose habits and expectations had no relation to men in power," to seize the initiative. The group included three young lawyers: John Fleming, George Johnston of Fairfax County, and Patrick Henry. Henry, who was barely twenty-nine years old and had just been returned at a by-election as a new member for Louisa County, had the primary role in the drama that unfolded in the chambers of the house on May 29. Son of an Anglican vestryman and militia colonel, Henry was an "improving" young lawyer with a brilliant vernacular speaking style and a boundless ambition for fame and popular applause. Having already achieved some renown for his work in the county courts, specifi-

---

[41] Ibid.

[42] Ibid.

cally his bold defense of his clients in the Parsons' Cause, Henry was now anxious both to shine in the colony's highest political counsels and to obtain recognition from the colony's political establishment.[43]

Henry achieved these objectives and more by his actions on May 29. After the main business of the session had been aborted and many of the members had left for home, he succeeded, with the help of Johnston and against the opposition of the established leaders, in pushing through five resolutions roundly and unequivocally condemning the Stamp Act as illegal and destructive of "British as well as American Freedom." Asserting that Virginians possessed all of the rights of Englishmen and that those rights had been guaranteed to them by two royal charters, the resolutions argued that of all of those rights no taxation without representation was the "distinguishing Characteristic of British Freedom," that Virginians had "uninterruptedly enjoyed the Right of being thus governed by their own Assembly in the Article of their Taxes and internal Police," and that their assembly had the *"only and sole exclusive* Right and Power to lay Taxes upon" them. The last resolution declaring the assembly's exclusive right of taxation passed by one vote and was rescinded the next day after Henry, perhaps anticipating Fauquier's dissolution of the House in response to the resolutions, had left for home. But the resolutions, including a sixth and a seventh that Henry apparently had not introduced, had already been transmitted, by whom is not certain, to the other colonies, where they were widely reprinted, applauded, and copied. Indeed, by providing the rallying call for strong resistance to the Stamp Act and serving as a model for similar resolutions from most of the other colonies, they placed Virginia at the forefront of the continental protests against the Stamp Act.[44]

---

[43] Fauquier to Board of Trade, June 25, 1765, CO 5/1331, PRO; Randolph, *History of Virginia,* 167; Robert Douthat Meade, *Patrick Henry,* 2 vols. (Philadelphia, 1957–69), 1:169–82. On the Parsons' Cause, see Glenn C. Smith, "The Parson's Cause, 1755–1765," *Tyler's Quarterly Historical and Genealogical Magazine* 21 (1940): 140–71, 291–306; Richard R. Beeman, *Patrick Henry: A Biography* (New York, 1974), 11–43; and Tate, "Coming of the Revolution in Virginia," 323–43. The interpretation of Henry's motivations is my own. The continued opposition but ambivalence of the establishment leaders is suggested by Edmund Pendleton to James Madison, Sr., Apr. 17, 1765, in *Pendleton Papers* 1:20.

[44] Henry's resolutions are conveniently reprinted in William J. Van Schreeven, comp., and Robert L. Scribner, ed., *Revolutionary Virginia: The Road to Independence* 1 (Charlottesville, Va., 1973): 17–18. The circumstances surrounding their passage are discussed by Ernst, "Robinson Scandal Redivivus," 152–57. Their transmission to and reception in other colonies is discussed in Edmund S. Morgan and Helen M. Morgan, *The Stamp Act Crisis: Prologue to Revolution* (Chapel Hill, N.C., 1953), 88–98.

The absence of substantive differences between the Henry resolutions and the protests adopted by the unanimous vote of both house and council the previous December has made it difficult for historians to understand why the established leadership opposed them and strongly suggests that it was not the content but the tone, source, and circumstances of the passage of the resolutions that elicited establishment opposition. For such immoderate resolutions, introduced by surprise and passed precipitously, diverged sharply from the customary Virginia mode of firm but considered, sober, and judicious protest combined with profuse expressions of loyalty and affection and therefore constituted an obvious deviation from the political system's corporate self-image. Equally important, perhaps, the introduction of such resolutions by a man with a public reputation for emotional oratory and their hasty passage on the basis of a highly emotional appeal without the establishment's considered approval carried ominous portents for the future of Virginia politics.

For Henry's resolutions and the circumstances of their passage raised the specter of emotionalism and unreason. Were they a harbinger of a totally new, and frightening, political mode that would replace the politics of self-control and disinterest with the politics of passion and ambition, a new style of politics in which the electorate would be more widely involved in the political process, the distinctions between rulers and ruled would become hopelessly blurred, and men of mean intentions would, in the manner of Henry, manipulate the people for their own self-interests by appealing to their emotions rather than to their reason? This was not to say that Henry was such a man, but only that his success could be interpreted as a potential challenge to the elevated politics of moderation, restraint, and enlightened upper-class leadership to which Virginians of all categories long had been committed.[45]

Henry's resolutions turned out to be only a temporary lapse from the traditional moderation of Virginia politics. Fauquier did not again call a meeting of the General Assembly until the fall of 1766, after he had received official word of the repeal of the Stamp Act, because he feared that it could not be controlled, as in the past, by "cool reasonable men." In the meantime, the several public meetings that subsequently assumed

---

[45] An alternative explanation for the division over the Henry resolutions, interpreting it in terms of a "democratic," "outside," or sectional challenge to an entrenched, aristocratic, and eastern elite runs through most of the literature on the subject from Randolph, *History of Virginia*, 167–68, to Ernst, "Robinson Scandal Redivivus," 152–57. Closer to my own view is Tate, "Coming of the Revolution in Virginia," 323–43.

responsibility for preventing enforcement of the Stamp Act were not taken over by men from the middle and lower orders, but, as in most of the other colonies, were dominated by the gentry. "This Concourse of People, I should call a Mob," Fauquier wrote of the group who forced stamp distributor George Mercer's resignation in Williamsburg in late October 1765, "did I not know that it was chiefly composed of Gentlemen of Property in the Colony—some of them at the Head of their respective Counties, and the Merchants of the Country whether English, Scotch, or Virginians, for few absented themselves."[46]

Similarly, the 115 signers of the Westmoreland Association, the nucleus of the group of 400 men who marched the following February 28 to Hobb's Hole in neighboring Essex County to force Archibald Ritchie, a Scottish merchant who had publicly threatened to use stamps, to sign the association, included virtually every prominent resident of Westmoreland and surrounding counties. Finally, the movement to defy the Stamp Act and to conduct judicial and commercial business without stamped paper was led by the county magistrates upon the advice of the colony's leading lawyers, who, concerned to "convince the people that there is not a total end of laws," ruled that the act was invalid "for want of . . . constitutional authority . . . in the Parliament to pass it."[47]

Indeed, the gentry emerged from the Stamp Act crisis with its position as strong as ever. At new elections to replace the House of Burgesses dissolved by Fauquier following passage of Henry's resolutions, the turnover of members was less than one-third, which was about normal for a house that had been sitting for several years. All of the old leaders who were still alive were returned, and none of the known opponents of the Henry resolutions lost his seat.[48]

The traditional leadership was in fact united with the vast majority of the public in opposition to a common enemy and around a clearly articulated intellectual position vis-à-vis Parliament's constitutional au-

---

[46] Fauquier to Board of Trade, June 25, 1765, CO 5/1331, PRO; and Nov. 3, 1765, in *Burgesses Journals, 1761–65,* lxviii-lxxi.

[47] Resolutions of the Westmoreland Association, Feb. 27, 1766, and Declaration of Magistrates of Northampton Co., Feb. 11, 1766, in Van Schreeven and Scribner, *Revolutionary Virginia,* 20–26; *Maryland Gazette* (Annapolis), Oct. 17, 1765; Edmund Pendleton to James Madison, Sr., Dec. 11, 1765, Feb. 15, 1766, in *Pendleton Papers,* 1: 23, 30; *Virginia Gazette* (Rind), May 16, 1766. On the the Ritchie affair, see John C. Matthews, "Two Men on a Tax: Richard Henry Lee, Archibald Ritchie, and the Stamp Act," in Darrett B. Rutman, ed., *The Old Dominion: Essays for Thomas Perkins Abernethy* (Charlottesville, Va., 1964), 100–108.

[48] See *Burgesses Journals, 1761–65,* 5–9.

thority in the colony. In the months following Henry's resolutions, Virginians, in private letters, newspaper essays, and pamphlets, revealed a remarkable consensus in both the tone and the content of their opposition to the Stamp Act. Although they continued to complain about the economic distress that would result from the enforcement of the act, especially in view of the large, and largely unpaid, public debt accumulated by Virginia during the war, the "matter of right," said a "Gentleman in Virginia" to his Bristol correspondent, was what really "Tingles in every vein of Americans." For "If the p[arliamen]t have a right to tax Americans, to speak in their favor, it thence must follow, that Americans have no benefit of the British constitution, or the great charter, which says, 'No man's life, liberty, or property, shall be taken from him, or harm'd, but by known and established laws, made by his own consent, or the consent of his representatives chosen by himself!'"[49]

Virginians continued to insist that parliamentary taxation was a constitutional innovation, an "extension of arbitrary unconstitutional power"; to deny, in elaborate treatises by Richard Bland and Landon Carter, that Parliament had any jurisdiction over the internal government of the colony; and to demand that the constitutions of the colonies be defined in such a way as to safeguard American liberty and thereby ensure that "men who derive their original from Britons" would not "become slaves." "I know of no civilized people, in like situation with the Americans, at this time," wrote one Virginian. "All have some constitution, but I really cannot find a name for ours. We seem to be entirely at the mercy of the m[inistr]y for the time being, and are considered only as a machine to be made useful to Britain, without the least regard how we may be affected ourselves." Clearly, the Stamp Act was "arbitrary" and unconstitutional and was a part, as John Mercer put it, of those "Chains forging for us" across the Atlantic. Less obvious was why the ministry and Parliament would deal such a "fatal blow to American liberty." What was to account for the sudden transformation of "the mother country . . . into an arbitrary, cruel, and oppressive stepdame"? No one in Virginia, at this early date, seems to have attributed that transformation to a conspiracy of power "to reduce," as Landon Carter later said, "the subjects of Great Britain" to "slavery . . . though beginning only by degrees with those in America." Many explained it as the result of simple malice, the roots of which were never explained, on the part of George

---

[49] Letters from a Gentleman in Virginia, June [Sept.] 5, 1765, in Walter E. Minchinton, ed., "The Stamp Act Crisis: Bristol and Virginia," *Virginia Magazine of History and Biography* 73 (1965): 147–51.

Grenville and his followers. But the most rational, and widespread, explanation was the one offered by Richard Henry Lee when the Stamp Act was first suggested. By keeping the colonies low through taxation and other restrictive measures, the British hoped to keep them dependent and, as Landon Carter surmised, thereby increase the profits annually derived from them.[50]

Whatever the explanation, Virginia's active and undeviating determination "to convince the world that we are as firm and unanimous in the cause of Liberty, as so noble and exalted a principle demands" was enormously reinforcive of the colony's corporate self-image. However enervated by luxury and pleasure, the colony's political system still had vigor—and virtue—enough to dare "to despise power, when that power was opposed to Liberty." Its leaders had not yet become so "unmanly [and] . . . ignominious, [as] to yield to such impositions, which confirms on us the condition of slavery," but had shown by their rejection of "passive obedience" and their pursuit of active opposition that in the manner of free, independent, and virtuous men, true Virginians, they despised "sycophants, and all kinds of servility." Indeed, said George Washington, the Stamp Act had opened the "Eyes of our People" to the fact that "many Luxuries which we lavish our substance to Great Britain for, can well be dispensed with whilst the necessaries of Life are (mostly) to be had within ourselves." This recognition, he predicted, would inevitably "introduce frugality, and be a necessary stimulation to Industry" and a means of reviving the declining virtue of Virginia.[51]

Indeed, in but short retrospect, even Henry's resolutions, though they deviated from the colony's customary political moderation, seemed to have been a fitting exertion of Virginia's firmness against a flagrant exertion of arbitrary power. Many moderates did continue to condemn those resolutions, chiefly for their redundancy and emotionalism. But the favorable reception they received in the other colonies clearly placed Vir-

---

[50] Anglo-Americanus (John Mercer) to Printer, *New York Gazette, or, The Weekly Post-Boy* (New York), July 4, 1765; Richard Henry Lee to ——, July 4, 1765, and to Arthur Lee, July 4, 1765, in *Letters of R. H. Lee* 1:9–10; Jack P. Greene, ed., "'Not to Be Governed or Taxed, But by . . . Our Representatives': Four Essays in Opposition to the Stamp Act by Landon Carter," *Virginia Magazine of History and Biography* 76 (1968): 259–30, esp. 294; Greene, *Landon Carter*, 53.

[51] R. H. Lee to Landon Carter, June 22, 1765, in *Letters of R. H. Lee* 1:8; Northamptoniensis to Printer, Mar. 24, 1766, in *Virginia Gazette* (Purdie), Apr. 4, 1766; Algernon Sydney to Printer, May 16, 1766, ibid., May 30, 1766; George Washington to Francis Dandridge, Sept. 20, 1765, in *The Writings of George Washington*, ed. John C. Fitzpatrick, 39 vols. (Washington D.C., 1931–44), 2:425–26.

ginia in the vanguard of opposition to the Stamp Act and thereby nourished Virginian pride in taking the lead in the essential concerns of the
American colonies, a position the colony would assiduously seek to maintain throughout the next twenty-five years. To be "a part of that colony,
who first, in General Assembly, openly expressed their detestation" to
the Stamp Act, said the Norfolk Sons of Liberty in March 1766, was
extremely gratifying.[52]

So pleased were Virginians with their manly and virtuous opposition
to a flagrant attempt to "rivet the shackles of slavery and oppression on
ourselves, and millions yet unborn" that they openly chided the British
upon the impurities of their political system and contrasted it with the
more virtuous system of Virginia. "The unequal representation of the
people of England has long been called the *rotten* part of the constitution," said one writer, and, said Richard Bland, was certainly "a great
Defect in the present part of the Constitution, which has departed so
much from its original Purity." "It would," Bland suggested condescend-
ingly, "be a Work worthy of the best patriotick Spirits in the Nation to
effectuate an Alteration in this putrid Part of the Constitution; and by
restoring it to its pristine Perfection, prevent any 'Order of Rank of the
Subjects from imposing upon or binding the rest without their Consent.'"
"But," he added, "I fear, the Gangrene has taken too deep Hold to be
eradicated in these Days of Venality." And in an open letter to the British
press, George Mason reminded "our fellow-Subjects in Great Britain . . .
that We are still the same People with them, in every Respect; only not
yet debauched by Wealth, Luxury, Venality & Corruption."[53]

Within a matter of weeks after the Stamp Act had been repealed and
almost contemporaneously with these pious lectures, the death of
Speaker Robinson on May 10, 1766, revealed the existence of the deepest
and most extensive example of government corruption in any of the British colonies in America up to that time—and in the proud colony that
claimed virtue as the special attribute of its political system. Immedi-

---

[52] Resolutions of Norfolk Sons of Liberty, Mar. 31, 1766, in Van Schreeven and Scribner, *Revolutionary Virginia,* 46.

[53] Ibid.; Richard Bland, *An Inquiry into the Rights of the British Colonies* (Williamsburg, Va., 1766), as reprinted ibid., 33–34; Gentleman in Va. to —, [Sept.] 1765, in Minchinton, "Stamp Act Crisis," 149; George Mason to Committee of Merchants in London, June 6, 1766, in *Mason Papers* 1:68.

ately after his death there was no hint of scandal. The newspapers praised Robinson as a "worthy Member of Society," the "greatest of human kind," and the "best of men," who had been always "animated with every Social Virtue." But the old rumors of the diversion of public funds soon resurfaced, and Fauquier's appointment of Robert Carter Nicholas, a respected lawyer with impressive family connections and a reputation for impeccable honesty, as interim treasurer until the burgesses met to make a permanent election led to the discovery of great irregularities, the extent of which was not immediately clear and the exact nature not made public until the 1950s! By late June, Nicholas had speculated in the newspapers that the total might approach £1,000,000.[54]

Within a month after Robinson's death, a second and equally appalling scandal broke upon the public. Colonel John Chiswell, burgess from Williamsburg and a prominent and well-connected member of the gentry (John Robinson was his father-in-law, and he had been married to a Randolph), during a tavern brawl in Cumberland County on June 3, 1766, ran his sword through and killed Robert Routledge, a local merchant who, in the heat of argument and deep in his cups, had thrown some wine in Chiswell's face. Chiswell was immediately committed to the county jail, from which the local examining court ordered him to public prison without bail to be tried for murder. But three judges of the General Court and members of the governor's council—including the council president, John Blair, Sr., William Byrd III, and Pressly Thornton, all of whom were closely attached to Chiswell through family or friendship—took him out of the custody of local officials and gave him bail—without looking at the record of the examining court that had confined him or hearing a single witness. This flagrant display of favoritism elicited an enormous outcry of public disapproval.[55]

The newly opened press in Williamsburg facilitated this outcry and an intense public discussion of the implications of both it and the Robinson scandal. Virginia had no newspapers until 1736 and only one from then until May 1766. The refusal of its publisher, Joseph Royle, who was also public printer to the colony, to publish several essays against the Stamp

[54]Obituary, *Virginia Gazette* (Rind), May 16, 1766; Nicholas to Printer, ibid. (Purdie), June 27, 1766. The best published treatments are Ernst, "Robinson Scandal Redivivus," 146–73, and David J. Mays, *Edmund Pendleton*, 2 vols. (Cambridge, Mass., 1952), 1:174–208, 358–85.

[55]Carl Bridenbaugh, "Violence and Virtue in Virginia, 1766: or, The Importance of the Trivial," Massachusetts Historical Society, *Proceedings* 76 (1964): 3–29, and Lemay, "Robert Bolling," 99–142, are the best published accounts.

Act had forced several writers, including John Mercer and Landon Carter, to send their essays to newspapers in neighboring colonies and had
provided dramatic evidence of the "undue influence the press, in Virginia, has long laboured under" by being too "complaisant" to the royal
administration. To remedy this situation, "some of the hot Burgesses
invited a printer from Maryland" to set up a rival and "uninfluenced"
newspaper. Published by William Rind, the new paper first appeared on
May 16 on the very eve of the Chiswell murder case and the first revelations of the Robinson scandal. Over the next several months, the fierce
competition between Rind and Alexander Purdie and John Dixon, who,
Royle having died in December 1765, together had resumed publication
of the old *Gazette* the previous March with promises that their newspaper
would "be as free as any Gentleman can wish or desire," stimulated a
wide-ranging canvass of the meaning of both the Chiswell and Robinson cases.[56]

For the first time in nearly forty years, this debate created a fundamental rift of opinion among the ruling gentry. The upholders of Robinson, now headed by Peyton Randolph and firmly defending the old
Robinson system of personal government, a system, they pointed out,
that had provided the colony with a long period of uninterrupted stability and public peace, emphasized the necessity of tempering the constitution and the letter of the law with "lenient applications and the good
offices of men of virtue." An opposing group, consisting of many previously independent leaders including Robert Carter Nicholas, Richard
Bland, Richard Henry Lee, Severn Eyre, and Robert Bolling, demanded
disinterested, impartial, and impersonal government and an uncompromising return to and rigorous implementation of the traditional values
of the Virginia political system.[57]

The latter group considered the special treatment accorded Chiswell
by the judges of the General Court especially ominous. Robert Bolling
and James Milner spearheaded public discussion of the case. Bolling was
a member of an old, if no longer quite so prominent, gentry family. He
had studied law in Britain and Virginia but had become a planter in
Buckingham County. A member of the Burgesses, he was also, in the
judgment of a modern scholar, "probably the most prolific poet of Pre-

---

[56] See Bridenbaugh, "Violence and Virtue in Virginia," 14–16; Jack P. Greene, *The Quest for Power: The Lower Houses of Assembly in the Southern Royal Colonies, 1689–1776* (Chapel Hill, N.C., 1963), 288–90; Greene, "'Not to Be *Governed* or *Taxed*,'" 268–69; *New York Gazette,* July 4, 1765; and Lemay, "Robert Bolling," 102, 119–20.

[57] Nicholas to Printer, *Virginia Gazette* (Purdie and Dixon), Sept. 5, 1766.

Revolutionary America." Milner was a young lawyer who practiced in the county courts in the western piedmont. A new man on the Virginia political scene, Milner had credentials that, had he not later moved to North Carolina, would have enabled him to enter the ranks of the politically influential.[58]

As Bolling put it, the behavior of the judges in the Chiswell case posed the questions whether the judges' action was legal and, if it was not, whether it did not have "a tendency to overturn the laws and constitution of the country, by their exercising an extrajudicial power and controuling the course of law in a case of the highest consequence to the safety of the subject." Bolling's principal contention was that the action was not legal and that it was "in fact a [mere] rescue" of a powerful man by his powerful friends, "a most flagrant injury, both to Prince and people" that reserved to the judges of the General Court "nothing less than a power of licensing homicides." John Blair offered a weak public defense of the judges' behavior. Because the murder was not premeditated but the result of "a most unhappy drunken affair," he declared, leniency was justifiable. But Bolling mockingly replied that the judges clearly had violated the letter of the law and that if the judges could so behave then "your fellow subjects in Virginia live only at discretion of your sublime Board; a Board," he added, "which having an unreasonable power by law already, should at least be prevented from usurping one, subversive both of law and reason." Blair had indicated that making a public defense had required him to waive "the dignity of our [the judges'] stations." To Bolling, the very suggestion that the dignity of office should exempt any group from public accountability was outrageous. "I begin to think myself an inhabitant of some other country than Virginia," he wrote. "Is there a *dignity* in this land which exempts any person whatever from a duty to satisfy, if possible, a people which conceives itself injured? Methinks I hear a general negative from every part of Virginia."[59]

But the man who first spelled out the full, and sobering, implications of the judges' misbehavior was not Bolling but Milner, writing under the pseudonym Dikephilos—a lover of justice. That behavior gave rise to the suspicions that the "influence of Mr. Chiswell's friends" would "prevent the truth from being published," that "justice" would be "perverted, and law trampel[l]ed on." But for "an atrocious murderer" to be thus

---

[58] Lemay, "Robert Bolling," 103.

[59] Bolling's letters, all published anonymously, are printed in *Virginia Gazette* (Purdie), June 20, July 11, 25, 1766. For Blair's defense, see ibid., July 4, 1766.

"screened from justice," to be "cleared, by means of great friends," said Milner, was not only "an act of wonderful partiality" but an "opprobrius stain . . . on our colony" that justifiably had enraged Routledge's family and friends and deeply alarmed "Patriots, . . . foreigners, [and] the middle and lower ranks of men, who are acquainted with the particulars." "They said," according to Milner, "that one of the worthiest of men had been not only murdered, but defamed; and that the murderer was treated with indulgence and partiality inconsistent with our constitution, and destructive of our security and privileges." "People in general," wrote Milner, said that "every true American justly detested the late intolerable Stamp Act" and laudably expressed willingness to risk their lives and fortunes to prevent so dreadful an attack on American liberty and property. "But now they apprehend that this partiality may be attended with still more dreadful consequences than ever that detestable Act of power could have been, because this must affect our lives, while that could only affect our estates."[60]

Milner agreed with one of the anonymous defenders of the judges, a defender who had objected to the public outcry against the judges on the grounds that "men in power should be treated with great deference." But this deference, said Milner, "should be consistent with British freedom, and not like slaves to a [Turkish] Bashaw. If British subjects know the power of men in high stations, and if men in high stations will exceed their due bounds, has not the meanest subject a right to mention his apprehension and grievance?" No man deserved British privileges, Milner declared, "who would not protect them." Obviously, added Bolling, the country had to be preserved "from a stretch of jurisdiction, which, if allowed, may probably, one day or other, form its greatest infelicity." "To pass over, without attention," such an obvious violation of the constitution, he declared, "would be a proof of great deficiency in public virtue, insomuch as to leave us but a melancholy prospect of futurity." Virginians had to make sure that "some Virginians" could not "massacre other Virginians (or sojourners among them) with impunity." Bolling summarized the issue acidly and succinctly in verse:

> The Laws, in Vulgar Hands unkind,
> The worthy Gentleman confined;
> But in the hands of Gentlemen
> Politer, they released again.
> But then began a strange Fracas:

---

[60] Dikephilos [James Milner] to Printer, ibid., July 18, Aug. 29, 1766.

> Some swore it was, some 'twas not, Law.
> 'Twas not for common Men, 'twas plain;
> But was it not for Gentlemen?

Did Virginia, that ancient repository of virtue, have a double standard in the law, one for the rich and powerful and another for the rest of society?[61]

Public debate over the Chiswell case came to an abrupt end on October 15 when Chiswell was found dead on the eve of his murder trial. Friends attributed his death to "Anxiety of Mind." But suspicions ran so deep that many believed that the report of Chiswell's death had been fabricated to permit him to escape punishment, and a mob insisted upon opening the casket to verify the identity of the corpse before it was interred.[62]

The charge of murder was not the only source of Chiswell's "Anxiety of Mind," for he had been one of the principal beneficiaries of Robinson's largesse with the public funds, and the public debate over the Chiswell case paralleled a vigorous discussion of the significance of Robinson's default at the treasury and how such behavior might be prevented in the future. Outrage at this notorious "shock to the constitution" was balanced by a widespread reluctance to condemn the man responsible for it, and the general consensus seems to have been, as William Nelson put it, that a "good . . . man . . . in private Life" had been "prevail'd upon by a set of men he was connected with, & who pretended to be his Friends" to engage in conduct that stained "a character otherwise so amiable." "The Truth is," said Nelson, Robinson "had a Benevolence for all Mankind & so great a Desire to please everybody & make them happy, that he never could resist an application to him for money which he hoped to be able to replace before he should be called upon for it. This humane Disposition of his they took Advantage of. Therefore on them lay the Balance: his was the Error, or rather let me say the Weakness of carrying even his Virtues to too great an Excess."[63]

---

[61] Ibid.; [Bolling] to Printer, ibid., July 11, 1766; Marcus Fabius and Marcus Curtius [Bolling] to Metriotes, ibid., Sept. 12, 1766; Bolling, "The Gentleman, 1766," as quoted by Lemay, "Robert Bolling," 100–101.

[62] *Maryland Gazette* (Annapolis), Oct. 30, 1766.

[63] Nicholas to Printer, *Virginia Gazette* (Purdie), June 27, 1766; William Nelson to Edward and Samuel Athawes, Nov. 13, 1766, Nelson Letter Book, 19, Library of Virginia, Richmond.

Even the most vociferous critics of Robinson's actions conceded that the old speaker had always intended "to charge himself with every shilling, which came into his hands, or for which he ought to have been accountable." Some defenders even contended that Robinson's actions were "a publick good." Given the prevailing shortage of specie and Parliament's prohibition of further emissions of paper money by the Currency Act of 1764, Robinson's loaning out paper money instead of retiring it, they said, was a patriotic action that "immediately relieved many worthy families from ruin and indigence." What was good for indigent "worthy families" was good for Virginia![64]

But the drift of opinion seems to have run strongly in the opposite direction. "Private virtues, amiable as they are," said Nicholas in turning Bernard Mandeville's famous aphorism on its head, easily could "become publick vices, and prove the means of destroying a whole country." Although he praised Robinson's "humane disposition" and "many brilliant virtues," Landon Carter expressed the predominant view when he declared that "charity . . . is certainly condemnable when extended out of any office of trust." Many others took an even less charitable view of Robinson's charity. "To metamorphose a notorious breach of the publick confidence into charity and munificence," sputtered Robert Bolling, was to subvert "all ideas of virtue and morality."[65]

Far from being praised for his private generosity with public funds, he had to be condemned, said an anonymous and uncompromising critic writing under the pseudonym Elizabeth Barebones, for what he was: "a misapplier of the publick revenues, a destroyer of his country's credit, [and] . . . a subverter of its liberty." Robinson had not acted in behalf of the public welfare, as many of his defenders had seemed to imply: he had only contributed to hasten Virginia's ruin by helping some of the colony's "untowardly degenerate brats, who would not be ruled, nor satisfied with a wholesome allowance; but by intemperance, and a rich diet, quite unsuitable to [either] their constitutions" or their resources, enmeshed themselves ever further in "an impoverished luxury."[66]

Consider, warned Elizabeth Barebones,

---

[64] Nicholas to Printer, *Virginia Gazette* (Purdie), June 27, 1766, and ibid., (Purdie and Dixon), Sept. 5, 1766; Philautos [Peter Warren?] to Printer, ibid. (Purdie), July 25, 1766.

[65] Nicholas to Printer, *Virginia Gazette* (Purdie), Sept. 5, 1766; Honest Buckskin [Carter] to Printer, ibid., Aug. 1, 1766; Marcus Fabius and Marcus Curtius [Bolling] to Metriotes, ibid., Sept. 12, 1766.

[66] Elizabeth Barebones to Printer, ibid., Nov. 27, Dec. 11, 1766.

What convulsions were produced in old Rome by the ambitious com-
passion of proud and luxurious debtors for their dear selves. Is it not
the judicious *Sallust* who puts these words into the mouth of *Cato?*
. . . *And shall any one talk to me in this case of mildness and mercy? We
have long since indeed lost the right names of things from amongst us. The
giving what belongs to other people is called generosity, and the courage to
venture upon wickedness is named fortitude, by which it is that the state
has been brought upon the very brink of destruction.* Is it not the mild
and good natured *Addison* who, after he had caused Decius to assert
that the *virtues of humanity are Caesar's,* makes Cato reply, with a
proper vehemence and resentment, *Curse his virtues, they have undone
his country. Such popular humanity is treason!*[67]

Robinson's behavior, wrote Richard Hartswell, revealed "vices of a
very deep die," and the gentry, whose role it was to provide a laudable
example for the rest of society, could not possibly afford "to connive at
vices that ought to be punished" or in any way "give . . . a sanction to
any thing that may be injurious to their country." Once it was revealed,
said "A Planter," quoting Alexander Pope, that

> . . . beneath the patriot's Cloak
> From the crack'd Bag the dropping Guinea spoke,
> And gingling down the Back Stairs told the Crew,
> "Old Cato is as great a Rogue as you,"

and it became clear to the public that the gentry was willing to tolerate
the corruption of which Robinson was guilty, social disaster could be the
only result. Inferiors would rush to imitate their superiors, and the last
vestiges of the vaunted virtue of Virginia would be swept away in a tide
of social corruption. Clearly, the stakes were too high for Virginians to
be content with merely "shinning over our ulcers." Far more drastic remedies were required: "probing to the bottom, . . . laying *bare* the bone,
and scraping it . . . to obtain a real and unequivocal cure." "Neither the
interest of any individual, while alive, nor his posthumous fame, when
dead," could be suffered to prevent "an impartial attention to the true
interests of the colony" at such a critical juncture in its history.[68]

Obviously, Robinson had been tempted into his excesses because of

---

[67] Ibid.

[68] Richard Hartswell to Printer, ibid., Sept. 19, 1766; A Planter to Printer, ibid. (Rind),
Aug. 8, 1766; Anonymous to Editor, ibid. (Purdie and Dixon), July 4, 1766.

his extraordinary power, which shielded him from immediate discovery. Robinson, charged Nicholas, "knew he had a power superiour to the whole Legislature; and that he could dispense with . . . laws made to regulate his own steps." But no man could be permitted to put himself above the law. "With what face," asked Hartswell, "can any one deny the absolute necessity of executing the laws with the utmost vigour upon *all* who" chose to live under them? "No rule ought ever to be more regarded, than the law of equality" before the law, declared Nicholas, "this being equity and justice itself."[69]

As in the Chiswell case, this demand for powerful remedies to cleanse the colony of political corruption came largely from within the gentry itself, as the proponents of impersonal government and a return to the traditional political values of the colony spearheaded a movement to separate the offices of speaker and treasurer as the only means to prevent similar abuses in the future. Nicholas, who hoped for appointment as treasurer on a permanent basis, as well as Richard Bland and Richard Henry Lee, who were both candidates for the speakership, led a spirited campaign against the supporters of Peyton Randolph, who hoped to succeed Robinson as both speaker and treasurer.

Randolph received support from many who were probably indebted to the Robinson estate, who hoped that he would take a more lenient view of his predecessor and feared that Nicholas might insist upon rapid repayment so as to "distress many familys," as well as from close connections like Benjamin Grymes and his brother John Randolph, who professed themselves to be, in principle, "enemies to [all] innovations in Government, which" tended—as a general rule—"to destroy liberty." He also was favored by independent men who, like Landon Carter, predicted that separation might produce an even "greater evil" by presenting the crown with an opportunity to do what it had been endeavoring to do for nearly a decade: wrest the power to appoint the treasurer "out of controul of the House of Burgesses." "I see," said Carter, "a power somewhere too apt to be abused, and fond of extending the right to lucrative employments." Should the crown succeed in such a venture, Carter declared, "Then farewell Dear Liberty."[70]

---

[69] Nicholas to Printer, ibid., (Purdie), Sept. 5, 1766; Richard Hartswell to Printer, ibid., Sept. 19, 1766.

[70] Richard Bland to Printer, June 20, 1766, ibid., July 11, 1766; Nicholas to Printer, ibid., June 27, 1766; ibid. (Purdie and Dixon), Sept. 5, 1766; Honest Buckskin [Carter] to Printer, ibid. (Purdie), Aug. 1, 1766; Benjamin Grymes to Printer, ibid., Sept. 15, 1766; Philautos [Peter Warren?] to Printer, ibid., July 25, 1766; Nicholas to William Preston,

But the traditional values of the gentry made the arguments in favor of separation far more powerful. "Whenever . . . the publick happiness can be promoted by abrogating a *constitutional custom*," said Bland, "it is the duty of the national Council to banish such a custom from the constitution, which by its continuance might prevent that happiness, and the establishment of the perfection of the State upon the firmest foundation." Old customs, said Nicholas, "if found inconvenient . . . surely ought to be abolished." That the union of the two offices had indeed proved inconvenient seemed obvious to the proponents of separation. Under Robinson, the union demonstrably had given so "much weight and influence to the Chair" as to permit the "weight of dignity" to "intrude itself into the place of reason and just argument and bear everything before it," thereby destroying that "just . . . equilibrium" that "in every state . . . is necessary for the publick weal." Such a union had the unfortunate effect of setting in motion "a kind of action and reaction, that the one [office] might become almost unbounded in its influence and the other placed almost out of reach of publick controul." "Where two such offices are enjoyed by one person," said the freeholders of James City County, "it must convey a great degree of power and superiority, which may lay a foundation for such undue influence as is inconsistent with the liberty of a free people." Clearly, the legislature had to consider "how far the power of any single man in authority ought to be limited" and take proper steps to eliminate "too exhorbitant [a concentration] of power" in the hands of any man and all possibility of his obtaining an "undue influence."[71]

Moreover, opposition to separation in the face of such an extravagant misuse of power as that of which Robinson had been guilty only lent credence to "a strong suspicion that there was *and is* an influence or something very much like it, still [even after Robinson's death] prevailing." Should "a man destitute of any real Goodness of Heart, and Benevolence of Disposition" ever succeed both to the chair, "the greatest Post of Honour conferr'd on him in the Power of the Country to give," and

May 21, 1766, Preston Papers 2QQ97, State Historical Society of Wisconsin, Madison; Bland to R. H. Lee, May 22, 1766, and Nicholas to Lee, May 23, 1766, in "Lee Papers," 116–17; John Wayles to John T. Ware, Aug. 20, 1766, American Loyalist Claims, PRO T.79/30, PRO. See also Greene, "Attempt to Separate the Offices of Speaker and Treasurer."

[71] Nicholas to Printer, *Virginia Gazette* (Purdie and Dixon), June 27, 1766; ibid., Sept. 5, 1766; The Freeholder [Richard Bland] to Honest Buckskin [Carter], ibid. (Purdie and Dixon), Oct. 17, 1766; Address of Freeholders of James City County to Lewis Burwell, ibid., Oct. 30, 1766.

the treasury, "what dreadful Things may we not fear from him?" asked "A Planter" in the *Gazette*. "Is it not in his Power (if not to breed Convulsions in the State) at least to dispose [as had Robinson] of our Property by his own Will, and build his Greatness on his Country's Ruin?" "Will ye then, O ye Guardians of the People, any longer suffer Things to remain in a Channel that so evidently does and must tend to produce great Hardships and Inconveniences on Ourselves and Posterity?" queried "A Planter," who called upon the voters "not to suffer" their representatives to depart from their "respective Counties without positive Instructions, not only to separate those two Offices, but to fix that of Treasurer in such a Manner" that public monies no longer could be misapplied. This and other similar appeals to the public had their effect: one of the few occasions in colonial Virginia politics up to that time when meetings of constituents publicly instructed their representatives.[72]

When the House of Burgesses convened in November 1766 for the first time since it had been dissolved for passage of the Henry resolutions in the late spring of 1766, the reform impulse was running very strong. The reform group carried a motion to separate the offices of speaker and treasurer "by a great majority," and the house chose Robert Carter Nicholas as treasurer, put him under severe penalties for any mismanagement at the treasury, authorized him to conduct a thorough investigation of the scandal, and insisted upon immediate repayment from the forced sale of Robinson's estate.[73]

Yet the Burgesses did not reject the old Robinson system in its entirety. Perhaps in part because it was not clear that all of the borrowers from Robinson had known they were dipping into public funds and in part because Robinson's records were sufficiently confused as to prevent immediate verification of the names of debtors and the amounts owed, the Burgesses did not insist upon a full public relation of the details of the scandal. Despite the diligent efforts of Edmund Pendleton as trustee for Robinson's estate, the difficulty of verifying details and of collecting many of the debts prevented full repayment to the treasury for several decades.

For speaker, the house selected Peyton Randolph, Robinson's chief protégé. In temperament and political style, the new speaker could

---

[72] Nicholas to Printer, *Virginia Gazette* (Purdie and Dixon), Sept. 5, 1766; A Planter to Printer, ibid. (Rind), Aug. 8, 1766; see also Philautos to Printer, ibid., Aug. 15, 1766; Principal Inhabitants of Accomack Co. to Thomas Parramore and Southy Simpson, Oct. 1, 1766, ibid., Oct. 17, 1766; Anonymous to Printer, Nov. 11, 1766, ibid. (Rind), Nov. 27, 1766.

[73] *Virginia Gazette* (Purdie and Dixon) Nov. 27, 1766; *Maryland Gazette*, Nov. 27, 1766.

scarcely have been more similar to Robinson, though Randolph was widely respected for his honesty and untainted by the scandal. To compensate Randolph, who had to give up the attorney generalship to accept the speakership, for the loss of income resulting from the separation of the treasury from the speakership, the house, against the strong wishes of one segment of the reform group that argued against giving the speaker a salary that not only would "burthen the people" but might "hereafter . . . tempt men of corrupt minds, or mercenary principles, to solicit the honour for the sake of the profit," voted, for the first time ever, an annual salary to the speaker.[74]

In the manner of Robinson, Randolph quickly moved to mollify discontent by diffusing political power within the Burgesses. He increased the size and thereby broadened the base of membership on the powerful standing committees in the house and distributed assignments to major committees much more widely than Robinson had done. Although a relatively few talented and influential men continued to dominate the work of the burgesses, this diffusion of committee assignments slightly increased the number of burgesses who thenceforth played a visible role in the proceedings of the house.[75]

Because of their temporal relationship to the Stamp Act crisis and their simultaneous revelations, the Robinson scandal and the Chiswell case hit the Virginia political community much harder than either might have done in isolation. Only a few weeks before these two developments broke, political writers had drawn a sharp contrast between the corruption of the British polity and the virtue of the Virginian. But these two developments, one on top of the other, strongly suggested both that the Virginia gentry was guilty of the same inner corruption and suffering from the same decay of public virtue as Britain's governing classes had so recently been charged with and that Virginia's liberty was at least as much endangered from the unrestrained lust for gain and social privilege among its own gentry as from the wanton exertion of imperial power by greedy and designing politicians in Britain.

The many questions raised by these developments constituted a profound and disturbing challenge to the colony's flattering corporate self-

---

[74] Inhabitants of Accomack Co. to Parramore and Simpson, Oct. 1, 1766, ibid. (Purdie and Dixon), Oct. 17, 1766; Greene, Quest *for Power*, 248; *Pendleton Papers* 1:174–208, 358–85.

[75] Greene, "Foundations of Political Power," 486.

image. Had, as these developments both implied, Virginia already and "so early quit the paths of wisdom" and virtue and degenerated into a base aristocratic oligarchy in which mere "family and fortune" raised men to such a "superiority" above the rest of society that they could, without fear of retribution, place themselves entirely beyond the law? Had the government of the colony fallen into the hands of "men, who had more influence than merit, and men who have patronized villains (or have been duped by them) and defended what they ought to have detected," men "whose vices, extravagances, and follies" were of that very species that had always been "inconsistent with the prosperity of any society" and had "formerly brought ruin and desolation upon the most powerful states and kingdoms"? Had the celebrated public virtue of the gentry so far declined as to prevent them from making any distinction between their own private interests and the public welfare?[76]

The rising fear throughout the summer and fall of 1766 was that the answer to all of these questions was yes, but the fear finally was allayed by the vigorous and self-critical reaction of the gentry itself. This reaction made it abundantly clear that the gentry would not condone unconstitutional and corrupt actions by any of its members, not even the powerful and popular John Robinson, much less, as one earlier historian has suggested, "present a solid, silent phalanx to the rest of society whether" or not the cause was "just or unjust, good or bad, right or wrong."[77]

Far from uniting in a cover-up, some members of the gentry inaugurated and dominated both the public protest against the favoritism extended to Chiswell and the successful campaign to get to the bottom of the Robinson scandal and to prevent similar occurrences in the future by detaching the treasury from the speakership. And when William Byrd III, one of the judges who had granted Chiswell bail, and John Wayles, a lawyer friend of Chiswell's who had given evidence in Chiswell's behalf at the hearing, sued Robert Bolling and all three of the colony's printers for libel, a grand jury in Williamsburg including such well-known gentry figures as Mann Page, John Page, and Lewis Burwell, Sr., threw out the actions on the grounds that they were "NOT TRUE BILLS" and, for doing so, were celebrated publicly as "GOOD MEN AND TRUE, FRIENDS TO LIBERTY."[78]

---

[76] Speech of R. H. Lee, 1766, in "Lee Papers," 121; Anonymous to Printer, *Virginia Gazette* (Purdie and Dixon), Feb. 27, 1766; Dikephilos [Milner] to Printer, Sept. 1766, ibid., Nov. 6, 1766; [R. R.] John Camm to Printer, ibid.; [Thomas Burke], "A Prophecy from the East," ibid. (Rind), Aug. 15, 1766.

[77] Bridenbaugh, "Violence and Virtue in Virginia," 27–28.

[78] *Maryland Gazette*, Oct. 30, 1766.

Moreover, the full and open discussion of both matters by the gentry and others in the press, as one writer remarked, "had the salutary Effect of correcting the haughty Spirits of some of our great Men, who, from their Fortunes, Connections, and Stations, had conceived very high Ideas of Self-Importance,—but who are now convinced, that *a Bashaw opposed against a Man, is but a Man*." Even more important, perhaps, the very conception of *"great men"* had been restored to its ancient Virginia meaning: great men were identifiable not through their "outward grandeur" but through their vigorous and honest "service to the publick."[79]

By all these actions in behalf of reform, as well as by the obvious moral outrage that underlay them, the gentry, or at least those many "worthy patriots" among them, put itself firmly on record as opposed to the "confederacy of the great in place, family connections, and that more to be dreaded foe to public virtue, warm and private friendship," and left no doubt that it was not yet ready to "seal [the] . . . ruin" of the colony either by continuing to unite "in one person the only two great places in the power of her assembly to bestow" or by countenancing special treatment under the law for wealthy and well-connected inhabitants. Thenceforth, personal government was to be replaced by impersonal government. Merit and virtue, not wealth and family, would be the central criteria for political leadership. Behavior and practice once again would be brought into harmony with the colony's cherished corporate self-image. Old ideas would be revitalized. The malignant humors that gradually had taken hold of the body politic during Robinson's thirty-year domination of public life would be purged. Public virtue once again would become the central defining quality of the Virginia political system.[80]

The reformist impulse generated within the ranks of the gentry by the events of 1764–66 continued to have a strong, and ramifying, influence in Virginia politics for at least another generation. In combination, those events had intensified the movement for constitutional security, first generated during the late 1750s by the growing recognition of the inadequacy of existing constitutional safeguards for the colony's rights and liberties against the extraordinary might of the imperial state, and had stimulated a searching examination of the entire structure of constitutional arrangements within Virginia. The excessive concentration of

[79] Lemay, "Robert Bolling," 115, 120; *New York Journal* (New York), Nov. 27, 1766; Richard Hartswell to Printer, *Virginia Gazette* (Purdie and Dixon), Sept. 19, 1766.

[80] Richard Hartswell to Printer, *Virginia Gazette* (Purdie and Dixon), Sept. 19, 1766; David Boyd to R. H. Lee, Nov. 17, 1766, in "Lee Papers," 118.

power in the council, each of whose members united the "discordant and heterogeneous dignities of Privy Councillor, Judge of the General Court, and Member of the intermediate body of the Legislature"; the total absence of that "one very essential security, namely the Right of" the voters to choose a new House of Burgesses to meet "in a certain time after being dissolved, as in Britain"; and the crown's excessive influence through its appointment of both the governor and council which together constituted "⅔ of the Legislature & all the judicial power"—these were all identified in 1764–66 as serious "imperfection[s] in the constitution" that put the liberty and property of Virginians "on a very precarious footing."[81] Even the ancient and rarely criticized economic restrictions imposed on the colony's trade by the navigation system, restrictions that, however quietly, had "ever been regarded here as oppressive in many Respects," received modest criticism.[82]

Perhaps the most important result of this new critical posture, however, was the increasing sensitivity of Virginia's leaders to any indications of corruption within their political system, as they subsequently watched each other's conduct and the operation of their own polity with the same jealous avidity that they accorded to distasteful measures of the metropolitan government. From this new critical posture, the Virginia gentry was in a position both to continue to "claim the Honour of" taking "the Lead" in the opposition to Britain over the next decade and to assert, once again with some measure of credibility, that, as one writer put it in 1769, "the prevailing principle of *our* government is *virtue*," albeit the continuing proliferation of luxury, gaming, and other forms of vice among large segments, and within every stratum, of Virginia society contributed to feed the powerful currents of anxiety about the moral health of the society that were so vividly manifest in the symbolism of the new state seal in 1776.[83]

---

[81] See Greene, *Quest for Power*, 386–87; R. H. Lee to Arthur Lee, Dec. 20, 1766, in *Letters of R. H. Lee* 1:19–21; Lee, "State of the Constitution in Virginia," n.d., Lee-Ludwell Papers, Virginia Historical Society, Richmond; Marcus Fabius and Marcus Curtius [Bolling] to Metriotes, *Virginia Gazette* (Purdie and Dixon), Sept. 12, 1766; Letter of Phileleutheros, Apr. 10, 1769, Va. Misc. MSS, Library of Congress, Washington, D.C.; George Mason, "Comments on the Va. Charters," 1773, in *Mason Papers* 1:174–75.

[82] A Virginian to Printer, *Virginia Gazette* (Rind), Dec. 11, 1766.

[83] Benjamin Franklin's marginalia in Israel Mauduit, *A Short View* . . . (London, 1769), in *The Papers of Benjamin Franklin*, ed. Leonard W. Labaree et al., 28 vols. to date (New Haven, 1959–), 16: 296–97; Brutus to Printer, *Virginia Gazette* (Rind), June 1, 1769, as printed in Jack P. Greene, ed., *Colonies to Nation: A Documentary History of the American Revolution, 1763–1789* (New York, 1975), 156–57.

Despite the vigor of the gentry's response to the Stamp Act, developments within Virginia—the Robinson scandal and the special treatment accorded Chiswell—had called into question the legitimacy of the gentry's claim both to public virtue and to political leadership and had generated a strong movement, within the gentry, toward self-reform, a movement that received its strength less from the gentry's desire to perpetuate its political power as a corporate group than from the devotion of individual members of the gentry to the traditional ideals and the ancient corporate self-image of the Virginia political system.

Through self-reform, through the powerful reassertion of an active commitment to the preservation, and exemplification, of the hallowed values of the Virginia polity, the reformist group among the gentry managed in 1766 to reestablish, more firmly than ever perhaps, the viability of the gentry's long-standing claim to political dominance. The success of the reform effort and the rededication of the gentry to *virtus et libertas* represented by that effort may, moreover, have been the primary reason why the Revolution in Virginia constituted not a rejection but an endorsement of government by the gentry, of a set of political arrangements under which, as Edmund Pendleton later put it, "those of more information on political subjects" instructed the "classes who have not otherwise an opportunity of acquiring that knowledge . . . in their *rights* and *duties* as freemen, and taught [them] to respect them."[84]

In the midst of a revolutionary upheaval, a political gentry regenerated by events a decade earlier managed to infuse the traditional Virginia political modes and the old ideals into a new state government, to carry out still further reforms in the political and social system without altering in any fundamental way the existing structure of politics, and to retain the confidence of the politically relevant segments of Virginia society.

This chapter was written for presentation on September 25, 1975, at a one-day session on "Origins of the Revolution in the South," held at the University of North Carolina in Chapel Hill, as the first of the three-part "The Experience of Revolution in North Carolina and the South: A Symposium." It was one of three papers on eighteenth-century Virginia politics considered at a seminar held in the Department of History at La Trobe University, Bundoora, Victoria, Australia, August 20, 1976. It is here reprinted with some minor editing and permission from *The Southern Experience in the American Revolution,* ed. Jeffrey Crow and Larry E. Tise (Chapel Hill: Copyright © 1978 by The University of North Carolina Press), 55–102. Used by permission of the publisher.

---

[84] Pendleton to Citizens of Caroline, Nov. 1768, in *Pendleton Papers* 2:650.

—TEN—

Character, Persona, and Authority:
A Study of Alternative Styles of Political Leadership in Revolutionary Virginia

. . . this part [of the patriot], it is well known, is played in very different styles.
> —Alexander Grayden, *Memoirs of His Own Time*

I F THE NUMBER and quality of leaders produced by a political culture are an important measure of its vitality, the political culture of Revolutionary Virginia must be judged as one of the most vital in modern history. No other political society in Revolutionary America, or, indeed, at any later time in American history, has produced so many gifted leaders. Patrick Henry and George Washington, George Mason and Thomas Jefferson, James Madison and John Marshall are only the most conspicuous of a whole galaxy of leaders contributed by Virginia to the Revolutionary era. Various scholars have considered the intriguing question of why this particular political culture produced such a profusion of talent. They have, at least in a preliminary way, analyzed the social, institutional, and intellectual framework out of which it came.[1] To date, how-

---

[1] See, especially, Charles S. Sydnor, *Gentlemen Freeholders: Political Practices in Washington's Virginia* (Chapel Hill, N.C., 1952); Daniel J. Boorstin, *The Americans: The Colonial Experience* (New York, 1958), 99–143; Robert E. and B. Katherine Brown, *Virginia*,

ever, there has been no systematic examination of the character of political leadership, of how politicians acquired the cloak of prominence—and authority—and how they wore it. This essay seeks to illuminate these "inner compulsives of politics" in Revolutionary Virginia through an examination of the relationship between styles of leadership and the foundations of individual authority as revealed by the careers of three men: Richard Henry Lee, Edmund Pendleton, and George Mason.[2]

These three men meet five important criteria for inclusion in this study. First, each belonged to the political generation that, born between 1721 and 1735, entered public life during the two decades before the Revolution and assumed a large role in the direction of public affairs during the 1760s. George Washington, Peyton Randolph, Robert Carter Nicholas, George Wythe, John Blair, Jr., Archibald Cary, Joseph Jones, and Benjamin Harrison V all fall within the same generation. This generation can be distinguished from an older one which included Speaker John Robinson, Richard Bland, Landon Carter, Charles Carter of Cleve, William and Thomas Nelson (the elder), and Benjamin Waller, all of whom died or retired during the 1760s and 1770s. It can be differentiated as well from a younger group, including Patrick Henry, Thomas Jefferson, James Madison, Thomas Nelson (the younger), Severn Eyre, Edmund Randolph, John Marshall, and James Monroe, all of whom entered politics after the Revolutionary controversy had begun. Second, each of the three men had a career that spanned the entire era of the Revolution from 1760 to 1790, unlike Peyton Randolph or Nicholas, who were either more or equally prominent during the 1760s and early 1770s. Third, each achieved extraordinary success and widespread acclaim as a political leader. Fourth, unlike Wythe, each left behind a body of papers large enough to permit consideration of the problem at hand, but, unlike Washington, not so large as to defy analysis in an essay of confined

---

1705–1786: Aristocracy or Democracy? (East Lansing, Mich., 1964); Keith B. Berwick, "Moderates in Crisis: The Trials of Leadership in Revolutionary Virginia," Ph.D. diss., Univ. of Chicago, 1959; Jack P. Greene, *The Quest for Power: The Lower Houses of Assembly in the Southern Royal Colonies, 1689–1776* (Chapel Hill, N.C., 1963); Jack P. Greene, "Foundations of Political Power in the Virginia House of Burgesses, 1720–1776," *William and Mary Quarterly*, 3d ser., 16 (1959): 485–506; and Jack P. Greene, *Landon Carter: An Inquiry into the Personal Values and Social Imperatives of the Eighteenth-Century Virginia Gentry* (Charlottesville, Va., 1967).

[2] The quotation is from J. H. Grainger, *Character and Style in English Politics* (Cambridge, Eng., 1969), 11. This volume is one of the few systematic studies of styles of political leadership for any past society.

length. Finally, in both personality and role they were sufficiently different from one another to reveal divergent styles of leadership.

This essay employs four concepts—*role, persona, character,* and *style* of leadership—that have no very precise definitions or generally agreed-upon meanings. The definitions used herein are set forth in the following propositions, which consist of an elaboration of the major assumptions on which the subsequent analysis is based.

1. Each political system has standards of conduct by which leaders may be evaluated and traditional roles which incorporate those standards. The term *role* is here employed in its vernacular sense and not in its technical sociological one.

2. These political roles—usually drawn from the past or from an admired contemporary model—exist independently of the actors who fill them and have readily identifiable functions within the political system. Each of these in turn prescribes a certain familiar posture or stance, here referred to as *persona,* which constitutes the external representation—the face—of a particular political role. These personae have two important functions in the political process.

3. Quite as much as institutional structures, established procedures, or underlying ideologies, they help to give coherence to the "ragged world of politics." Because they have the sanction of tradition, they link the participants in the political process to the larger sweep of history and thereby provide an escape from the "mundane present."[3] They provide leaders with identity models through which they can explain to themselves and their audience who they are, what they stand for, and what their function is in the public realm. These personae also supply audiences with visible symbols of authority, symbols whose power rests upon their familiarity and acceptability and which provide an ideal standard against which the performance of individual leaders may be measured. Thus, to act coherently and to command authority each leader must assume and maintain an approved persona.

4. These personae provide a link—that is, they help to mediate—between role, which exists outside the individual actor, and *character,* which may be defined for the purposes of this essay as that complex of salient mental and ethical traits that give distinctive configuration to each individual personality.

5. Force of personality is not a sufficient condition for political leadership. For a leader to achieve and maintain credibility among an audience

---

[3] Ibid., 4, 33–34.

throughout the course of prolonged and intimate exposure (e.g., his peers in a legislative body or his constituents in a small electoral district), for his public behavior to carry conviction, a leader must find a persona that is—or can be made—congruent with his character.

6. The successful internalization of a persona may thus require a significant modification of character (e.g., the suppression of disapproved traits or the cultivation of approved ones) to achieve the necessary degree of congruity between character and the imperatives of the persona. At the same time, exigency may also necessitate or stimulate character modification in individual leaders.

7. Exigency may also require the alteration of an old or the creation of a new persona, for to be viable a persona must have not only the sanction of—or at least congruence with—tradition but also contemporary relevance. A leader with a powerful personality may therefore significantly expand or change the shape and content of any given persona.

8. What is customarily referred to as *style* in a political leader may be defined as his distinctive "lustre" and his peculiar "form or mode of functioning" in the public realm: that is, his "characteristic way of performing duties," speaking, responding to problems, handling work assignments, and interacting with other participants in the political arena. Style is thus "a form of conduct created by an actor in communication with other actors." From the outside, it "is the observed quality and character of his performance"; from the inside, it is the leader's "bundle of strategies" for eliciting sympathetic resonances from other participants for the purpose of enhancing his self-esteem by adding to his public reputation or his record of political achievement.[4]

9. Because a leader can elicit sympathetic resonances most easily by incorporating an approved persona into his style, an individual's style of leadership is ordinarily a product of the interaction between his character and his chosen persona, an interaction that takes place within and is shaped by the exigencies of the general context of his time.

May the cause of liberty be ever conducted with prudence, but never benumbed by too frigid estimates of difficulty or danger.
—Richard Henry Lee to the Virginia Convention, 1775

[4] Ibid., 4; David Shapiro, *Neurotic Styles* (New York and London, 1965), 1; Hugh Dalziel Duncan, *Symbols and Social Theory* (New York, 1969), 33; James D. Barber, "Classifying and Predicting Presidential Styles: Two 'Weak' Presidents," *Journal of Social Issues* 24

Richard Henry Lee was born to public service. No member of his political generation had a more distinguished or longer lineage. Three generations of Lees, dating back to the 1640s, had played a prominent role in the colony's affairs, while his mother's family, the Ludwells, had exercised a powerful voice in Virginia politics since the 1660s. Each of his five brothers had distinguished political careers. Of the two who were older than Richard Henry, Philip Ludwell Lee was a member of the Virginia council, while Thomas Ludwell Lee, a lawyer, took a leading role in the Revolutionary conventions and committees during 1775–76 and was a judge of the General Court under the new state government. Of the three younger brothers, Francis Lightfoot Lee represented Virginia in the Continental Congress, while William and Arthur Lee, after a decade of vigorous and conspicuous activity as opposition politicians in London, held important diplomatic posts on the Continent for the new United States government.

Richard Henry himself became a justice of the peace for Westmoreland County in 1757 when he was only twenty-five years old, and the following year the freeholders of that county elected him one of their two representatives to the House of Burgesses, a post that he held for the next eighteen years. Despite his youth, he quickly—within a year—distinguished himself as one of the most active and prominent members of the house. Selected as a delegate to the First Continental Congress in 1774, he represented Virginia in Congress from 1774 to 1779 and again from 1784 to 1788, serving as president of Congress in 1784, and, in between his two stints in Congress, representing his county in the Virginia House of Delegates. The capstone to this long political career was his appointment as one of the first two senators from Virginia in the new federal government in 1789, a post that he held until his retirement in 1792.[5]

His "antient and honorable family" was not, however, the only or even a very important ingredient in Richard Henry Lee's long-lasting prominence in Virginia politics. Among his own generation, there were many men of equally distinguished ancestry. Of them all, however, only Peyton Randolph and Robert Carter Nicholas carried a political weight that exceeded or matched that of Lee. Clearly, one has to look elsewhere for

(1968): 52–53; Alexander L. George, "Assessing Presidential Character," *World Politics* 26 (1974): 242–45.

[5] See Burton J. Hendrick, *The Lees of Virginia* (Boston, 1935); Oliver Perry Chitwood, *Richard Henry Lee: Statesman of the Revolution* (Morgantown, W.Va., 1967); and Greene, "Foundations of Political Power in the Virginia House of Burgesses."

the primary sources of Lee's political authority. In his brief description of Lee in his *History of Virginia,* written two decades after Lee's death, Edmund Randolph, Lee's younger contemporary, offered some important suggestions. Lee, said Randolph,

> had gained the palm of a species of oratory rare among a people backward in refinement. He had attuned his voice with so much care that one unmusical cadence could scarcely be pardoned by his ear. He was reported to have formed before a mirror his gesture, which was not unsuitable even to a court. His speech was diffusive, without the hackneyed formulas, and he charmed wheresoever he opened his lips. In political reading he was conversant, and on the popular topics dispersed through the debates of Parliament, his recollection was rapid and correct. Malice had hastily involved him in censure for a supposed inconsistency of conduct upon the Stamp Act; but the vigor and perseverence of his patriotism extorted from his enemies a confession that he deserved the general confidence which was afterwards conceded to him.[6]

As Randolph's description suggests, much of Lee's appeal as a political leader and an essential component of his style of leadership derived from his eloquence as a public speaker. He was widely admired for his "unique oratorical and histrionic talents" and was early "reckoned one of the first Speakers in the House of Burgesses." He had, said one contemporary, "all the advantages of voice[,] . . . the fine polish of language[,] . . . and all the advantages of gesture which the celebrated Demosthenes considered as the first, second, and third qualifications of an orator."[7] At the First Continental Congress, John Adams testified that "the Virginians" justly spoke "in Raptures" about the oratory of "Richard Henry Lee and Patrick Henry—one the Cicero and the other the Demosthenes of the age." Like the rhetoric of Demosthenes, that of Henry "did not smell of lamp-wicks . . . but of water-drinking and anxious thought." It was not informed by "the artifice of scholastic rhetoric": no "rules and forms and niceties of elocution" intervened to choke "his native fire" or blunt the

---

[6] Richard Henry Lee to Silas Deane, Jan. 22, 1779, in *The Letters of Richard Henry Lee,* ed. James Curtis Ballagh, 2 vols. (New York, 1912), 2:16; Edmund Randolph, *History of Virginia,* ed. Arthur H. Shaffer (Charlottesville, Va., 1970), 184.

[7] Grainger, *Character and Style,* 67; Harry Piper to Dixon and Littledale, May 29, 1773, Henry Piper Letter Book, 1767–76, University of Virginia Library, Charlottesville; William Wirt, *The Life of Patrick Henry* (Philadelphia, 1836), 109.

natural power of his eloquence. By contrast, Lee's oratory was studied—
"chaste—classical—beautiful"—so cultivated and harmonious as to
make his hearers "sometimes fancy that" they were "listening to some
being inspired with more than mortal powers of embellishment." When
he spoke, it was "as if elegance had been personified."

Lee's striking appearance—his "aquiline nose, and Roman profile" being "too remarkable not to have been noticed" at a great distance—and
the "gracefulness of his attitude (generally) leaning a little with his hat
in his hand on the back of the front seat" enhanced his effectiveness as a
speaker. As his younger contemporary St. George Tucker remarked,
Lee's manner of speaking may have "approach'd more nearly to that of
Cicero . . . than any other I ever heard." But Lee also seems to have had
another more contemporary model in William Pitt, earl of Chatham.
Like Chatham, Lee strove for theatrical effect. The Great Commoner
stood before the House of Commons "with the eye that could 'cut a diamond,' the black velvet, the bandages, the huge boot," while Lee, having
"lost the use of one of his hands," kept it constantly covered with a *black
silk Bandage*, very neatly fitted to the palm of his hand, but leaving his
thumb free."[8]

Not only Lee's self-conscious and dramatic presence as a speaker but
also what he said and did commanded the attention and admiration of
his fellow legislators. He was "a very clever Man," said one Virginia contemporary, "& an ornament to his Country"; "a masterly man," added
John Adams, a "sensible and deep thinker," who, like both Cicero and
Chatham, prevailed not simply "by reason of his eloquence" but by the
power of his reason and his intellectual acuity: he seems both to have
"reasoned well" and to have "had a quick sensibility and a fervid imagination." Like Cicero's, his rational powers were informed by extensive
learning and a good memory. Educated at Wakefield Academy in Yorkshire, he was widely read in the classics, science, the Bible, the law, constitutional and political theory, parliamentary debates, and the polemics
of contemporary politics.[9]

---

[8] *Diary and Autobiography of John Adams,* ed. L. H. Butterfield et al., 4 vols. (Cambridge, Mass., 1962), 2:113; *Plutarch's Lives,* trans. Bernadotte Perrin, 11 vols. (London,
1914–26), 7:211; Wirt, *Patrick Henry,* 109, 125; St. George Tucker to William Wirt, Sept.
25, 1815, *William and Mary Quarterly,* 1st ser., 22 (1914): 256; Randolph, *History of Virginia,* 213; Grainger, *Character and Style,* 67.

[9] Harry Piper to Dixon and Littledale, May 29, 1773, Piper Letter Book, University of
Virginia Library; Page Smith, *John Adams,* 2 vols. (Garden City, N.Y., 1962), 1:170;
Plutarch's Lives 7:211, 215; R. H. Lee to [Thomas Shippen Lee], Apr. 7, 1787, in *Letters
of R. H. Lee* 1:418–19.

Sensibility, learning, and affecting oratory were, however, only the most conspicuous of Lee's talents as a legislator: he also had a remarkable capacity for business. Regarding self-discipline as essential "for the depraved heart of man," he never shrank from hard work. Unlike Patrick Henry, who seems to have had an "insuperable aversion" to "the labours of the closet" and, according to Jefferson, "was the laziest man in reading I ever knew," Lee was an industrious and effective committeeman who at every stage of his political career wrestled with the most intricate problems and drafted large numbers of committee reports, state papers, and laws. During his long service in Congress, he was such a workhorse that "excessive writing and constant attention to business" left him "little time for the ordinary offices of life." To Henry, in October 1777, he complained of "the want of time to discharge with propriety an hundreth part of the business with which I am crowded. My eyes fail me fast, and I believe my understanding must soon follow this incessant toil." His contemporaries admired Lee's capacity for work. "Fine parts," Henry wrote Lee the following December, "are seldom joined to industry, and very seldom accompany such a degree of strength and toughness" as Lee had exhibited in his devotion to the American cause.[10]

Henry's reference to Lee's "strength and toughness" calls attention to still another and even more important source of Lee's political authority. With Lee, as with Chatham, the "very vigour of his policies" was the *numen*, the presiding spirit, of his political personality. Within a year after his first entry into the House of Burgesses, he donned the mantle of the vigorous, independent "country" patriot who, ever suspicious of power, blew the whistle on corruption in the political establishment by demanding a strict examination of the treasury, the preserve of John Robinson, who, as speaker of the house and treasurer, was the most powerful politician in Virginia and so enormously popular as to be described as "the darling of the Country." By this act Lee quickly established his reputation as a man "hot, violent, and supercilious, in party; [and] very tenacious of his opinion."[11] Beginning in the mid-1760s, the contest with

---

[10] Lee to George Washington, Nov. 13, 1775, to Samuel Adams, Feb. 7, 1776, to Charles Lee, May 21, 1776, to Patrick Henry, Oct. 8, 1777, in *Letters of R. H. Lee* 1:156, 167, 192, 325; *The Writings of Thomas Jefferson*, ed. A. A. Lipscomb and Albert Ellery Bergh, 20 vols. (Washington, D. C., 1903), 1:12; Hugh Blair Grigsby, *The Virginia Convention of 1776* (Richmond, 1855), 132, 142.

[11] Grainger, *Character and Style*, 68; Francis Fauquier to Board of Trade, May 12, 1761, CO 5/1330, ff. 129–35, Public Record Office, London; Jack P. Greene, "The Attempt to Separate the Offices of Speaker and Treasurer in Virginia, 1758–1766," *Virginia Magazine of History and Biography* 71 (1963): 11–18; David John Mays, *Edmund Pendleton, 1721–*

Britain provided Lee with a stage and a setting that could scarcely have been better contrived for the elaboration of a role that was so congenial to his personality. The Stamp Act, that wanton application of "the iron hand of power," so "warmed" his mind, he declared, as to produce "a fixt determination to exert every faculty I possessed both in public and private life, to prevent the success of a measure" that was "in the highest degree pernicious to my Country." For the next decade, he was the ever-vigilant patriot, sounding the clarion to alert his countrymen to the "unjust and destructive" measures of a "tyrannous administration" to impose its "slavish system" of "Colony Administration" upon the colonies.[12]

A vigorous advocate of firm and uncompromising resistance, Lee was an early and consistent proponent of a "union of counsel and action among" the "lovers of liberty in every province." "Whilst men in general, are thoughtless and indolent," he wrote John Dickinson in 1768, "spirit and wisdom are necessary to rouse and inform minds," and the special role of Lee and men like him was to "rouse a spirit that proving fatal to an abandoned Ministry may save the whole Empire from impending destruction."[13] "If the people will submit to abuse," he wrote Landon Carter in 1771, "let them do it with their eyes open; if they will pursue the wrong, after having been shown the right way, they will have only themselves to blame." The patriot at least would have the satisfaction of having done his duty: "Who fails in doing right," Lee later told John Adams, "fails nobly, because Virtue is its own and a very great reward." Indeed, the cause of virtue would be lost without "the strongest exertions," perseverance, and "vigor" on the part of patriots such as himself. He wanted to believe that virtue would ultimately "drive vice & folly off the ground," but his political experience taught him that "the cause of virtue, without proper means to support it, must often fail."[14] Hence, he

---

1803: A Biography, 2 vols. (Cambridge, Mass., 1952), 1:174–208; Joseph A. Ernst, *Money and Politics in America, 1755–1775: A Study of the Currency Act of 1764 and the Political Economy of Revolution* (Chapel Hill, N.C., 1973), 63, 74–75; An Enemy of Hypocrisy [James Mercer] to *Virginia Gazette* (Purdie and Dixon), Oct. 3, 1766.

[12] Lee to ——, May 31, 1764, to Landon Carter, June 22, 1765, to *Virginia Gazette*, July 25, 1766, to [Edmund Jenings], May 31, 1769, to William Lee, July 7, 1770, and to Samuel Adams, Feb. 4, 1775, in *Letters of R. H. Lee* 1:5–7, 17, 36, 46, 128.

[13] Lee to Landon Carter, June 22, 1765, to John Dickinson, July 25, 1768, to ——, Mar. 27, 1768, to Samuel Adams, Feb. 4, 1773, and to Arthur Lee, Feb. 24, 1775, in *Letters of R. H. Lee* 1:8, 26–27, 29, 82, 131.

[14] Lee to William Lee, July 7, 1770, Landon Carter, Apr. 18, 1771, to William Lee, Sept. 20, 1774, to John Adams, Apr. 24, 1779, to Patrick Henry, Feb. 14, 1785, ibid., 1:52, 56, 124, 2:47, 333.

had no use for the practitioners of "pedantic politics," for "time-serving Men," for the "Dealer in Expedients," or for "timid senseless politics." The stakes were too high for principle to be sacrificed to expediency: the colonies had to be as adamant in "the cause of Liberty, as so noble and exalted a principle demands." The "blessings of Liberty," he was persuaded, "flow not from timid and selfish policy."[15]

Vigor, for Lee, did not mean impetuosity. Although he introduced the motion for independence in Congress in June 1776, he was not an early advocate of a complete break with Britain, and throughout the years of war and Confederation he was vigorous in support of a moderate rather than a radical approach to most major political issues, including especially the movement to strengthen the federal government. "I remember when I once detested the moderate character [during the long political contest with Britain before Independence]," Lee wrote Samuel Adams in the fall of 1784, but at "this moment I think that moderation, wisdom, firmness, and attention, are the principles proper for our adoption: and highly becoming the dignity of our successful situation." And Lee could be—and was—vigorous in support of unpopular measures. During the 1770s and 1780s, he strongly opposed large paper money issues and advocated a program of vigorous taxation, payment of British debts, and mild treatment of Tories—all positions that were unpopular with large segments of the Virginia political community and especially with the localist followers of Patrick Henry.[16]

Lee endorsed John Adams's view "that persons & property in America" should "be held sacred." "I too love Liberty," he wrote his cousin in the year of his death, "but it is a regulated Liberty, so that ends & principles of society may not be disturbed by the fury of a Mob or by the art, cunning, and industry of wicked, vicious & avaricious Men." During the Stamp Act crisis, he played a conspicuous role in the "out-of-doors" opposition in Virginia's Northern Neck. He staged a public demonstration against the Stamp Act at Westmoreland Court House in September 1765 and the following winter organized the Westmoreland Association, a vigilante group dedicated to preventing the use of stamps,

---

[15] Lee to Landon Carter, June 22, 1765, to John Dickinson, Nov. 26, 1768, to William Lee, July 7, 1770, to Landon Carter, Apr. 18, 1771, to William Lee, Sept. 20, 1774, to George Washington, Oct. 22, 1775, to Charles Lee, Apr. 22, 1776, to Samuel Purviance, May 1, 1776, and to Patrick Henry, Feb. 14, 1785, ibid., 1:8, 30–31, 52, 56, 124, 183, 186, 2:333.

[16] Lee to Thomas Jefferson, Aug. 25, 1777, Aug. 10, 1778, to Patrick Henry, Nov. 15, 1778, to Samuel Adams, Nov. 18, 1784, Mar. 14, 1785, ibid., 1:319, 431, 452–53, 2:294,

and personally led a massive march to Hobb's Hole in Essex County to force Archibald Ritchie, a Scottish merchant who had announced his intention of complying with the Stamp Act, to make a humiliating public recantation. Except for these early episodes in his career, however, Lee eschewed the part of the country patriot "who will be popular, right or wrong." Unlike John Wilkes or Patrick Henry, he seems to have lacked the inclination or the necessary breadth of appeal to secure a broad following among the public at large and become a demagogue. His proper forum was the legislative chamber; his audience, his fellow legislators. Like Chatham and Charles James Fox, he was not the ideologue who would take his case to the country but a "parliamentary politician" who preferred to operate inside the legislative halls and within the small circles of the politically powerful. Even his newspaper essays were primarily directed toward his peers.[17]

Perhaps as much as anything Lee's insatiable desire for approval—his ambition for fame—among those he admired in the political arena underlay his powerful devotion to public life. It "has ever been my wish," he wrote Patrick Henry in 1777 while defending himself against attacks from his enemies in the Virginia legislature, "to deserve the esteem of virtuous men, and to stand well in their opinion." This yearning for esteem, wrote Landon Carter, made him "always open to flattery" and, in William Maclay's opinion, overly "ambitious and vainglorious." Indeed, his hunger for public fame was so great as to evoke distrust among his associates. He was a man, said James Mercer in 1766, "very happy in FACE, and good in expression" but "too great a slave to his ambition and desire" to be speaker of the house. Moreover, that distrust seemed to be given some credence by his inconsistent behavior during the crisis over the Stamp Act. At the suggestion of a friend, Lee rashly, as he later explained, applied for the post of stamp collector before he had "reflected in the least on the nature and tendency of such an Act." He claimed to have recognized his error "a few days after" he had sent off his application and to have embarked upon his vigorous opposition to the measure "long before" his "application could possibly" have reached Britain. But the application and the prominent role he later took in opposition to the

---

342–43; Grigsby, *Virginia Convention of 1776*, 142. The political divisions of the 1780s in Virginia are analyzed by Jackson Turner Main, *Political Parties before the Constitution* (Chapel Hill, N.C., 1973), 244–65.

[17] Lee to ——, Oct. 10, 1785, and to Thomas Lee Shippen, Feb. 12, 1794, in *Letters of R. H. Lee* 2:390, 576; Grainger, *Character and Style*, 47, 68–77; Chitwood, *Richard Henry Lee*, 36–42.

Stamp Act left him open to the charge that he did not discover the evil "consequences of the act until he was assured his application was not attended with success, so it is to be presumed his patriotick spirit was set on fire by envy and disappointment." Only after having failed in the closet, the charge went, did Lee feel compelled to seek his account with the people.[18]

To moderate men such as Edmund Pendleton, not only did a man thus compromised seem to be an "improper leader" of such an "incendiary stigma" as the march on Archibald Ritchie, "but the [excessive] number emploied" on that march—"about 600 men"—as well as the "Parade and noise on the Occasion," seemed to betray, on Lee's part, a willingness to sacrifice public order to personal ambition. No matter how intense his later patriotism, Lee's motives were thereafter always somewhat suspect. "As true a trout as ever swam, as staunch a hound as ever ran" was the Petersburg merchant Roger Atkinson's estimation of Lee ten years later. But he added, as if he were not entirely sure of the accuracy of his evaluation, that he hoped it would be "possible [to] keep this gentleman firm & faithful in his country's cause & I think he will be so kept." The distrust arising out of Lee's ambition may have been deepened by his attitude of reserve. While he interacted easily with other people, he kept all but a very few at some distance, and by his own testimony, he "endeavored not to take up friendships lightly." Though he always managed to vindicate himself and regain his authority, this distrust helped to lend plausibility to a number of vicious attacks on Lee during the late 1770s both in Congress and in Virginia.[19]

From the point of view of the public, however, Lee's ambition was entirely functional. No man seems to have striven harder to achieve some congruence between his public persona—as the vigorous, unselfish

---

[18] Lee to *Virginia Gazette*, July 25, 1766, to Patrick Henry, May 26, 1777, in *Letters of R. H. Lee* 1:16–18, 298; Chitwood, *Richard Henry Lee*, 39, 225; Jack P. Greene, ed., *The Diary of Colonel Landon Carter of Sabine Hall, 1752–1778*, 2 vols. (Charlottesville, Va., 1965), 2:1102–3; An Enemy to Hypocrisy [James Mercer] to *Virginia Gazette* (Purdie and Dixon), Oct. 3, 1766.

[19] Edmund Pendleton to James Madison, Apr. 21, 1790, in *The Letters and Papers of Edmund Pendleton, 1734–1803*, ed. David John Mays, 2 vols. (Charlottesville, Va., 1967), 2:566; Atkinson to Samuel Pleasants, Oct. 1, 1774, in A. J. Morrison, ed., "Letters of Roger Atkinson, 1769–1776," *Virginia Magazine of History and Biography* 15 (1908): 356; Lee to William Whipple, July 1, 1783, to Samuel Adams, Apr. 7, 1785, in *Letters of R. H. Lee* 2:246, 283. See also *Diary and Autobiography of John Adams* 3:367–68, for another, less credible analysis of the reasons for distrust of Lee.

patriot—and his political behavior. For what he craved was not merely praise but praiseworthiness. He wanted not merely to be famous but to deserve fame, and this consuming "spur of fame," as the men of the Revolution phrased it, repeatedly seems to have driven Lee to sacrifice personal and family concerns to his political career. He began talking about retirement from elective office—which he "found . . . an hard service"—as early as 1770 after only twelve years as a legislator, and the wish to retire was a persistent theme in his correspondence for the remaining twenty-two years of his career. His complaints about overwork, the loss of "private enjoyments," and the adverse affects of his public obligations upon his "health . . . fortune, and . . . domestic happiness" were incessant. His long service in Congress took him away from home for as long as six to seven months at a stretch, with the result that his plantation affairs were often in a "distracted state" and his family—he had nine children—suffered "immensely by my absence." He had only the utmost contempt for and resentment toward those "avaricious plunderers" among his colleagues in public life who used their position for personal enrichment, and his public service may actually have contributed to the diminution of a fortune that was never "very ample" for his large family. Indeed, he found himself forced to live with "the truest republican economy" when he was at Congress, at one point during the winter of 1777 being reduced to living upon the "scanty fare" of "wild pigeons" which were "sold for a few cents per Dozen."[20]

As a consequence of the "distressing pressure" created by these and similar adversities, Lee "long panted for retirement." Whenever he came under attack from his political enemies in either Virginia or Congress, as he did in 1777, 1778, and 1779, this threat to retire became strident. "Where a man by being honest is sure to be oppressed—Where disgrace & ruin are to reward the most faithful services. When the discharge of duty raises up the angry and malignant passions of envy, malice, and all uncharitableness— It is best to retire until necessity has pointed out proper men and proper measures," declared Lee in 1779. As Cato in Joseph Addison's play had said in lines that struck deep resonances among

---

[20] Lee to William Lee, July 9, 1770, to Landon Carter, Apr. 18, 1771, to Charles Lee, May 21, 1776, to Thomas Jefferson, Nov. 2, 1776, to Patrick Henry, Dec. 3, 1776, May 13, May 26, Oct. 8, 1777, to William Lee, Jan. 25, 1778, to Arthur Lee, May 27, 1778, to Patrick Henry, Nov. 15, 1778, to Arthur Lee, Feb. 11, 1779, to William Shippen, Jr., Apr. 18, 1779, to Thomas Jefferson, May 3, 1779, and to Samuel Adams, Apr. 6, 1783, Virginia Delegates to George Pyncheon and John Bradford, Oct. 16, 1777, in *Letters of*

eighteenth-century Virginians, "When vice prevails, and impious men bear sway, the post of honor is a private station."[21]

But Lee would never retire "absolutely" until his health forced him to do so. The true and virtuous patriot Lee aspired to be could not retire without violating both his public persona and his own self-image. For such men, duty demanded that comfort be sacrificed for great public ends. For one who had made the "generous, Roman resolution . . . at the hazard of life, fortune and domestic happiness, to contribute, by every means to the perfect establishment of our Independence," it was impossible to "quit the service . . . untill . . . a proper peace upon proper principles" had been established, lest such an important work fall into the hands of "weak, ambitious, avaricious and wicked men." Having once put his "hand to the plough," he was "bound to go through" no matter what the difficulties. In the cause of "public liberty," he was fond of remarking, "nothing is done whilst any thing remains to be done." Only after the "independence of America" had been fixed "on wise and permanent foundations" could Lee "with infinite pleasure . . . return to" his "farm and eat the bread of industry in freedom and ease."[22]

His sense of identity was, in fact, too deeply bound up with the public realm ever to permit him to be content in a private station. He might occasionally denounce politics as "the Science of Fraud" and politicians as "the Professors of that Science." He might sometimes think "that the life of a private Citizen is more desirable than any public character whatever," or that "taking care of a large family" was an "important concern" that could justifiably consume his total attention. But for Lee, neither sentiment was a true measure of his deepest feelings. After spending so many years "in the busy scene of politics," he found private life dull and vapid. Within less than a year after he left Congress in 1779, he had returned to politics as a representative from Westmoreland to the Virginia House of Delegates, and on those occasions when illness forced him home he could scarcely wait until he was "in a state to venture on the stormy sea of politics & public business." Whatever his profession, no

---

R. H. Lee 1:52, 56, 192, 222, 228, 290, 302, 325, 332, 384–85, 410, 453, 2:30–31, 35, 44–45, 54–55, 381.

[21] Lee to John Page, May 26, 1777, to Francis Lightfoot Lee, July 27, 1778, to William Shippen, Jr., Apr. 18, 1779, to F. L. Lee, Apr. 26, 1779, in ibid., 1:295–96, 429, 2:45, 49–51; Joseph Addison, *Cato* 4.4.140–51.

[22] Lee to Thomas Jefferson, Nov. 3, 1776, to Patrick Henry, May 13, 1777, to Landon Carter, June 25, 1777, to George Wythe, Oct. 19, 1777, to William Lee, Jan. 25, 1778, to

man could, in fact, have been more eager to surrender "private ease to public service."[23]

Moreover, his years in Congress encouraged a distinct preference for public service on a larger and more conspicuous stage. Even as a young legislator, Lee had shown his ambition for higher office and status by repeatedly seeking appointment to the Virginia council, and his early initiation of correspondence with John Dickinson, Samuel Adams, and other prominent opponents of British policy in the other colonies revealed his orientation toward the political world outside Virginia. Moreover, his contacts with his two younger brothers, William and Arthur, who lived in London, the center of the Anglo-American public world, and were deeply involved in British politics in the years before Independence, greatly enhanced that orientation. Beginning with the First Continental Congress, he identified more and more with the national political scene. He was proud of Virginia's preeminent contribution to the Revolution, of "the spirit, wisdom, and energy of her councils," and, though he once thought of moving to Massachusetts, where he thought the genius of the people might be more consistent with his "ideas of what must constitute social happiness and security," he retained an intense loyalty to "my own country." Furthermore, he occasionally grew sick of "Congress wisdom." But once he had returned to Virginia he missed the "hurry of business" and longed for "the patriotic inhabitants of Liberty Hall" and the "sensible social evenings they pass there."[24] Not rural and remote Virginia but "Philadelphia or Boston," he wrote his brother Arthur in 1780, "seem to be the only Theatres [in America] for great Actors to play upon." His primary identification was with "those proved Patriots with whom I early toiled in the vineyard of American liberty," with

---

John Adams, May 13, 1778, to Francis Lightfoot Lee, July 27, 1778, to Henry Laurens, Dec. 26, 1778, to John Adams, Oct. 8, 1779, to Samuel Adams, Jan. 18, 1780, to Arthur Lee, Aug. 31, 1780, in *Letters of R. H. Lee* 1:222, 290, 304, 337, 385, 405, 429, 467, 2:155, 170, 197.

[23] Lee to John Page, May 26, 1777, to John Adams, Oct. 8, 1779, to William Shippen, Jr., May 7, 1780, to Samuel Adams, Apr. 6, 1783, to James Monroe, Jan. 5, 1784, to Thomas Lee Shippen, Apr. 17, 1787, Sept. 21, 1791, ibid., 1:296, 2:155, 179, 281, 386–87, 417, 544.

[24] Lee to James Abercromby, Aug. 27, 1762, to William Lee, Dec. 17, 1769, to Landon Carter, Apr. 18, 1771, to George Washington, Nov. 13, 1775, to Patrick Henry, Apr. 20, 1776, to William Whipple, Nov. 29, 1778, to *Pennsylvania General Advertiser*, Dec. 16, 1778, to Francis Lightfoot Lee, Apr. 26, 1779, to John Adams, Oct. 8, 1779, and to George Wythe, Feb. 28, 1783, ibid., 1:1–2, 40, 52, 156, 176, 454, 457, 2:51, 155, 279.

those "original friends to the just rights of America, whose wise and firm perseverance . . . secured to the United States at last the blessings [of freedom], without which there is little difference between men and brutes."[25]

The elegant, dramatic, and persuasive orator, the cogent political analyst, the attentive and hardworking legislator—these were all important ingredients of Lee's political personality. But his most distinctive quality and the one which gained for him the "general confidence" conceded to him by the Virginia political nation, as Edmund Randolph observed, was the "vigor and perseverence of his patriotism." He was the "active" man who "vivified" the politics of restraint practiced by so many of his equally prominent colleagues. Always "earnest for the public," he was "a *scarecrow of violence* to the gentle warblers of the grove, the moderate Whigs and temperate statesmen."[26] Lee thus found his identity in the public realm as an active cultivator in the "vineyard of Liberty," as one of those "Republican spirits who . . . labored for the liberty of their Country, and whose sole object" was "the security of public happiness." He stood for energy and activity. He was the Virginia epitome of the classic English patriot as exemplified by a long line of heroic figures from Sir John Eliot and Shaftesbury in the seventeenth century to Bolingbroke and Chatham in the eighteenth. Like them, he strove to be the independent and incorruptible man who stood for a strenuous—but responsible—exertion of public spirit, one of those "grave sensible Men" who came to the rescue of his country when liberty was in jeopardy, roused his countrymen to a spirited resistance against tyranny, and never quit the public stage until liberty was secure and virtue ascendant in the public counsels. In "concert with other generous friends to human liberty and the rights of America," he remained adamantly and "uniformly warm for the freedom, happiness, and independence of my Country" and yielded to no one in "zeal for the American cause, and industry to promote its success."[27]

---

[25] Lee to John Adams, June 20, 1778, to Arthur Lee, Aug. 31, 1780, to William Whipple, July 17, 1782, to Patrick Henry, Feb. 14, 1785, ibid., 1:417, 2:197, 274, 331.

[26] Randolph, *History of Virginia*, 184; Grainger, *Character and Style*, 59, 64, 68.

[27] Lee to Arthur Lee, Feb. 24, 1775, to Patrick Henry, May 26, 1777, to George Wythe, Oct. 19, 1777, to John Adams, June 20, 1778, to *Pennsylvania General Advertiser*, Dec. 16, 1778, to Silas Deane, Jan. 22, 1779, and to William Whipple, July 1, 1783, in *Letters of R. H. Lee* 1:131, 300, 337, 417, 457, 2:25, 283.

> *I opposed and endeavoured to moderate the violent and fiery, who*
> *were plunging us into rash measures, and had the happiness to*
> *find a majority of all public bodies confirming my sentiments.*
> —Edmund Pendleton's "Autobiography," July 20, 1793

Edmund Pendleton brought to the political arena none of the social advantages enjoyed by Richard Henry Lee.[28] Indeed, although he received considerable help from the powerful Robinson family, he was to a large degree a self-made man. The fifth son of a father who died before he was born in 1721, a decade earlier than Lee, Pendleton was descended from "a good family, fallen to decay" in England. His grandfather, the immigrant, had been "well educated" and "respectable" for his "piety and moral virtue," but the Pendletons had not made much of a mark upon Virginia society. Thus, Edmund Pendleton, as he later remarked in a brief autobiography, had to make his way "without any classical education—without patrimony—without what is called the influence of Family Connection." But he had natural advantages—in his words, "a docile and unassuming mind, a retentive memory, a fondness for reading, a clear head, an upright heart, with a calm temper, benevolent to all"— that were a sufficient foundation for a spectacular career in law and politics. For a young man of fine parts but small fortune in Virginia during the middle of the eighteenth century, the law provided the readiest access to wealth, status, and fame, and Pendleton, admitted to the bar when he was only nineteen years old, practiced his "profession with [such] great approbation and success . . . at the County Courts" that he moved up to the General Court of the colony when he was barely twenty-four years of age. Within less than two years following his appointment as justice of the peace for Caroline County, he won—in his thirtieth year—election from the same county to the House of Burgesses, in which he served with distinction for the rest of the colonial period. Beginning with the Revolutionary disturbances of 1774–75, Pendleton, as he proudly noted in his autobiography, attained "without solicitation . . . the highest offices in my Country." He was one of the Virginia delegates to the First and Second Continental Congresses in 1774–75, was elected president of the Virginia Committee of Safety in August 1775, succeeded

---

[28] Portions of this section are adapted from Jack P. Greene, "Virginia Political Culture in the Era of the American Revolution," *Virginia Quarterly Review* 44 (1968): 302–10.

Peyton Randolph as president of the Virginia Convention in December 1775, served as the first speaker of the House of Delegates under the new constitution, and presided over the Virginia ratifying convention in 1788. For a quarter century, from the creation of the state court system in 1778 until his death in 1803, Pendleton served as the "head of the Judiciary Department" of the state, a post to which he was initially elected "by an unanimous vote."[29]

Superficially, the ingredients of Pendleton's political authority were similar to those of Richard Henry Lee. Like Lee, Pendleton was "a very pretty smoothtongued speaker." Unlike Lee, however, he was "not eloquent" and not histrionic. Though "elegant . . . in style and elocution," he was essentially a debater rather than an orator. "He had not indeed," Jefferson later wrote, "the poetical fancy of Mr. Henry, his sublime imagination, his lofty and overwhelming diction." But, continued Jefferson, Pendleton

> was cool, smooth and persuasive, his language flowing, chaste and embellished; his conceptions quick, acute and full of resource; never vanquished: for if he lost the main battle, he returned upon you, and regained so much of it as to make it a drawn one, by dexterous manoeuvres, skirmishes in detail, and by the recovery of small advantages which, little singly, were important all together. You never knew when you were clear of him, but were harassed by his perseverance, until the patience was worn down of all who had less of it than himself.

"Taken all in all," Jefferson concluded, Pendleton "was the ablest man in debate I ever met with."[30]

Pendleton's ability as a debater was enhanced by his appearance and manner. The Petersburg merchant Roger Atkinson compared him "to old Nestor in Homer—in the words of Pope:

> Experienced Nestor, in persuasion skill'd
> Words sweet as honey from his lips distilled."

---

[29] "Autobiography," July 20, 1793; Pendleton's Notation, 1801, *Pendleton Papers* 2:605–7, 700; Greene, "Foundations of Political Power in the Virginia House of Burgesses." The standard biography is Mays, *Edmund Pendleton*.

[30] Roger Atkinson to Samuel Pleasants, Oct. 1, 1774, in "Letters of Roger Atkinson," 357; Jefferson, "Autobiography," in *Writings of Jefferson* 1:54–55; Mays, *Pendleton* 1:283.

A man "of easy and cheerful countenance," he was, as Edmund Burke wrote of Sir Robert Walpole, "straightforward, bold, and open, and the least addicted to scheming and cabal." Though by his own testimony he was, like Lee, "particular in friendship with but a few," this openness, joined with an "amiablenness [that] bordered on familiarity without detracting from personal dignity," gained him the trust even of his opponents. Pendleton, said Jefferson, one of his most persistent adversaries, "was one of the most virtuous and benevolent of men, the kindest friend, the most amiable and pleasant of companions, which ensured a favorable reception to whatever came from him." His amiability and honesty guaranteed as well that he would end his life, as another observer noted, with "not only the esteem but the love, the admiration, nay even the veneration of his countrymen."[31]

In his capacity for business Pendleton matched and probably even exceeded Lee. "Labor," said Edmund Randolph, "was his delight." His life, according to another contemporary, "approached the nearest to constant employment in useful occupations . . . of any I ever knew." This "great industry" in public affairs derived in some large part from an acute awareness of his own limitations, a recognition that he was not a man of broad learning or unusual brilliance: as he phrased it, he was "not equal to Mansfield or Franklin" in mental abilities and not likely to achieve the high "Character of a Statesman." Thus cognizant of his own limitations, Pendleton could and did compensate for them by a constant effort both to "stretch . . . his mental powers" and to apply himself thoroughly to any task that came before him. "If I had uncommon merit in public business," he observed in his autobiography, "It was that of superior diligence and attention."[32]

Such devoted attention quickly made Pendleton the master of all forms of legislative business. His reputation as a committeeman and draftsman of legislative papers was equal to his stature as a debater. "With a pen which scattered no classical decorations," wrote Edmund Randolph, "he performed the most substantial service by the perspicuity and comprehensiveness of his numerous resolutions, reports, and laws."

---

[31] Mays, *Pendleton* 1:283, 2:347; Grainger, *Character and Style*, 62; Pendleton, "Autobiography," July 20, 1793, in *Pendleton Papers* 2:607; Randolph, *History of Virginia*, 186; Jefferson, "Autobiography," in *Writings of Jefferson* 1:55; Grigsby, *Virginia Convention of 1776*, 127; Atkinson to Pleasants, Oct. 1, 1774, in "Letters of Roger Atkinson," 357.

[32] Grainger, *Character and Style*, 21; Randolph, *History of Virginia*, 186; Pendleton, "Autobiography," July 20, 1793, and Pendleton to George Washington, Sept. 11, 1793, in *Pendleton Papers* 2:607, 615; Mays, *Pendleton* 1:122, 261.

His chief political tutors and patrons, speakers John Robinson and Peyton Randolph, who had themselves built their political power on reputa-
tions for "great integrity, assiduity and ability in business," had taught
him to put "every question so . . . as to be well understood, and free as
might be from embarrassment or complexity." He learned his lesson so
well that his colleagues sent him as a delegate to the First Continental
Congress for the express purpose of being "the penman for business."
"With his habits [and extensive knowledge] of business," Pendleton as-
sisted "every burgess who was a stranger to parliamentary forms or unacquainted with debate." As in the case of Sir Robert Walpole, extensive
training and experience in "the craft of politics" and an impressive mas-
tery "of parliamentary business, of ready argument" gave Pendleton "a
glare of confidence," an appearance of wisdom, and enormous political
authority.[33]

If Lee was the exponent of vigorous and uncompromising patriotism,
Pendleton was the voice of moderation. Not that he was in any sense a
"quietist." On the contrary, he was an early and firm opponent of parliamentary taxation and, as Edmund Randolph noted, was throughout the
period from 1764 to 1776 a "master of the principles of opposition to the
ministry." But the politics he found personally so congenial and the politics he had learned from his mentors John Robinson and Peyton Randolph was the politics of the possible, the politics of prudence and restraint, of "circumscribed dissidence" and "political lenity," "of dispute
within safe limits with blunted weapons, within the consensus." In the
Anglo-American world of the eighteenth century, the primary models for
this type of political posture were Sir Robert Walpole, that penultimate
master of "humane, civilized and realistic politics," and George Savile,
marquis of Halifax, the "Trimmer." J. H. Grainger has written that Halifax's adversary, Shaftesbury, "stood for violence, emerging causes,"
while Halifax was the advocate of "poise, some inactivity, consensus, a
delimitation of politics, a minimization of rule"—a characterization
that, with some softening of the language used to describe Shaftesbury,
is equally descriptive of the contrasting political stances of Lee and Pendleton.[34]

Indeed, although there is no evidence that he consciously modeled

---

[33]Grainger, *Character and Style*, 24, 41, 61; Randolph, *History of Virginia*, 185–86, 206;
Pendleton to Thomas Jefferson, June 17, 1800, in *Pendleton Papers* 2:675–76; Fauquier
to Board of Trade, May 12, 1761, CO 5/1330, ff. 129–35, PRO.

[34]Grainger, *Character and Style*, 47–49, 59, 61; Randolph, *History of Virginia*, 186; Pendleton to James Madison, Sr., Apr. 17, 1765, in *Pendleton Papers* 1:20.

himself after either Halifax or Walpole or that he thought of himself in terms of the Halifax prescription—for then, as now, the term *trimmer* was one of political opprobrium—Pendleton was, in fact, a classic example of the public-spirited trimmer as originally described by Halifax. He strove always to keep the political system on an even keel by discouraging dispute over fundamentals and seeking the pragmatic adjustment of lesser conflicts of interest, personality, and opinion. Realizing, as he put it in an address before the Virginia ratifying convention in 1788, that "perfection in any institute devised by *man*, was as vain as the search for a philosopher's stone," he was willing when—"as in all . . . Political cases"—he could not "get the very best," to "take the best we can get," "to relax in some matters in order to secure those of greater moment," and to work for compromise among "the different Jarring Interests" for the purpose of bringing things "as near the Centre of General good" as possible. The "good of the common cause" could not "be interrupted by Punctilios of no real consequence." Whenever there was a "Variety of Opinions" in politics, "Compromise," the search for "proximate solutions," was the wisest and "most Equitable" course. Prudence dictated that such matters be "as little Agitated as may be, lest differences of Sentiment should be wrought into dissentions, very injurious to the common Cause." It was invariably better for the contestants to "yield, rather than interrupt for a moment the general good."[35]

Like Halifax, Pendleton was "a sceptic about political passion," extremely wary of "mere speculative opinions," and distrustful of "the patriot with virtuous politics who would break up the unity of the country." The true patriot should put aside "his zeal and work for prizes within the system." He should also seek to foster unanimity and maintain the "strength and Vigor" of the political system by "watching and breaking the Spirit of Party" and "all Private, dirty, unjust and ingrateful Cabals" and standing up against "Noise," "dissipation," and "dissentions"—those "stated enemies to wisdom and deliberation," to "*social*, as well as *private* happiness." He had to spurn "all Intrigues, Finesse and Stratagems in Government, as well as in Private transactions" and, deeply aware that

---

[35] Pendleton to William Woodford, May 30, 1775, Dec. 7, 1775, to Thomas Jefferson, Aug. 26, 1776, to James Madison, Sept. 25, 1780, June 17, 1782, Dec. 19, 1786, and Address to the Va. Ratifying Convention, June 12, 1788, in *Pendleton Papers* 1:103, 136, 201, 309, 2:399, 491, 528; Grainger, *Character and Style*, 8. An instance of the popular usage of "trimmer" in a negative sense in Pendleton's Virginia may be found in Isaac Wilkins to David Griffith, July 21, 1771, David Griffith Papers, Virginia Historical Society, Richmond. I am grateful to Rhys Isaac for this reference.

"Selfish Party regards" were the "bane of all Public Councils," attach himself to "no party" and act under no "influence, but the true interest and real happiness" of the whole society. He should strive to be a man "in Pursuit of Right[,] . . . Uninfluenced by anything but the real difference between *that* and *Wrong*," a man ever on the alert against any ill-considered or "destructive popular measures" that might be a threat to liberty, property, and stability or any tendencies that might lead to the development of "a dangerous aristocracy." In times of uncertainty and stress, when the authority of existing institutions was in doubt, times of possible disruption such as in 1775-76, men like Pendleton had to seize every "opportunity to erect new barriers against folly, fraud, and ambition" and insert themselves between the "Sanguine" politicians, who stood for "rash Measures without consideration," and the "Flegmatic," who, paralyzed by their own fears, were "afraid to move at all." He was the one who took "the middle way" and attempted "by tempering the first sort and bringing the latter into action to draw all together to a Steddy" political course. "He recommended moderation under all circumstances," said Philip Mazzei of Pendleton, "so that [his opponents] . . . called him 'Moderation' instead of Pendleton." Moderation required lenity—not "drawing the reins too tight"—toward political opponents. "I have ever been on the side of lenity," Pendleton wrote in reference to "pretended Neutrals" in 1777.[36]

But moderation and lenity were not appropriate in all cases. Treason or open opposition to the common cause during the War for Independence could not be tolerated. Moreover, Pendleton was an unswerving advocate of a close "Obedience to the Laws" and a strict regard for justice, even for Tories and British creditors. Thus, he opposed closing the courts both in 1765-66 and 1775-76 lest such an action "fix an eternal Stigma on the Country, introduce Anarchy and disorder and render Life and property here precarious." "Laws should be mild and gentle," Pendleton declared in 1782, "but rigidly Executed." A satisfactory government had to have energy. Having spent all of his political life on the inside of Virginia politics, he was far less suspicious of power than was Lee. "I am not overjealous of power," he declared in 1781 in arguing for

---

[36]Grainger, *Character and Style*, 47-48; Mays, *Pendleton* 2:136; Pendleton to Joseph Chew, June 15, 1775, to Va. Convention of 1776, May 6, 1776, to Thomas Jefferson, July 22, Aug. 26, 1776, to Richard Henry Lee, Dec. 6, 1776, Sept. 27, 1777, to William Wood-ford, Mar. 13, 1778, Nov. 8, 1779, to Joseph Jones, Feb. 10, 1781, to James Madison, Aug. 27, 1781, to Richard Henry Lee, Apr. 18, 1785, to Va. Ratifying Convention, June 12, 1788, to Harry Innes, Nov. 9, 1791, to George Washington, Sept. 11, 1793, to Citizens of Caroline, Nov. 1798, Pendleton's Account of the Case of the Prisoners, Oct. 29, 1782,

giving every "public body so much [power] as is necessary to their appointment." A corollary of this deep veneration for law and belief in vigorous government was a zealous attachment to "ancient establishments," and during the Revolution Pendleton was the primary spokesman in Virginia for the desire for continuity. As Jefferson later recalled, Pendleton was one of those men who "from their natural temperaments . . . were more disposed generally to acquiesce in things as they are, than to risk innovations." He always preferred, he wrote Jefferson in August 1776, the "old terms, which custom has made easy and familiar." Yet, his "habits of mind," a later historian remarked, "insensibly attached him to the new state of things," and, as Jefferson hastened to point out, "whenever the public will had once decided," none "was more faithful or exact" in obeying and carrying out a measure he had opposed. For a man whose only personal ambition in public life was to be "esteemed by the great and the good of my acquaintance," friend and foe alike, maintenance of the system was vastly more important than political victory. "Ever since I had any power," Pendleton declared to the Virginia ratifying convention in 1788, "I was more anxious to discharge my duty than to increase my power."[37]

For Pendleton, this concern with maintaining order, keeping the political system on an even keel, making sure that justice always prevailed, and preserving the ideal of government by the virtuous, enlightened, and experienced was a means for achieving the larger objectives of Virginia society, which he defined as securing "substantial and equal liberty to the people" and fostering "Prosperity to the Community and Security to Individuals." With most Virginia leaders of his political generation, Pendleton believed that the role of the people in the polity should be limited, that the suffrage ought to be confined to "those of fixed Permanent property," and that unqualified and untrustworthy men who in their lust for acclaim used open demagoguery and irresponsible promises to excite the people's political passion or raise their political pretensions should be firmly opposed. But he had an equally strong commitment to the ideal of preserving an open society in which every free man should

Pendleton, "The Danger Not Over," Oct. 5, 1801, in *Pendleton Papers* 1:110, 176, 188, 200–201, 204, 225, 251, 306, 334, 370, 2:422, 478, 519, 580, 615, 651, 695–97.

[37] Grigsby, *Virginia Convention of 1776*, 47; Jefferson, "Autobiography," in *Writings of Jefferson* 1:54–55, 59; Pendleton to James Madison, Sr., Feb. 15, 1766, to Ralph Wormeley, Jr., July 28, 1774, to William Woodford, June 14, 1775, to Va. Delegates in Congress, Oct. 28, 1775, to Carter Braxton, May 12, 1776, to Thomas Jefferson, Aug. 10, 26, 1776, to James Madison, July 6, 1781, to Va. Ratifying Convention, June 20, 1788, to James Madison, Apr. 7, 1789, Pendleton's Opinion on Fees, May 4, 1774, Pendleton's

have an equal and unrestrained right to acquire property and rise as high in society as he could within the limits imposed upon him by his ability, resources, and opportunities and be secure in the knowledge that he would be protected "in the enjoyment of" his "honestly and industriously acquired property": the people had a fundamental right to be left "at liberty to pursue their labour in peace, and acquire wealth." Thus, as Pendleton argued after Independence, future land grants should be made in "small quantities" so as "to give the Poor a chance with the Rich of getting some Lands"; "all employments" should be kept "free and open to such as chuse them . . . without clog or restraint"; and "equal liberty" should be accorded to "all [free] men, from the palace to the cottage, without any other [legal] distinction than that between good and bad men."[38]

An outsider who had prospered materially and fulfilled himself personally under the old political and social system, Pendleton had no illusions that his success was attributable entirely to his own efforts. Rather, he understood clearly that it depended as well upon the opportunities available in the American environment and the existence in Virginia of a fluid social and political system that permitted new men such as himself to rise to the highest echelons of wealth, prestige, and leadership. Pleased by his success and appreciative of the "grateful smiles" the Virginia political system had repeatedly bestowed upon him, Pendleton developed a deep veneration for that system and had an especially strong stake in maintaining it, in making sure that the underlying structures and values on which it depended should be transferred intact to the post-Revolutionary world. Precisely because other leaders and potential leaders were to varying degrees less well adjusted to the system and for that reason were potentially disruptive influences in a fluid political situation during the Revolution, Pendleton, Robert Carter Nicholas, and others like them had to assume the responsibility for upholding that system, for serving not merely as its conservators but as its active protagonists against internal as well as external enemies.[39]

In Virginia, as in Britain, rank-and-file politicians seemed "on the

---

Account of the Case of the Prisoners, Oct. 29, 1782, in *Pendleton Papers* 1:22–23, 82–85, 97, 104, 125, 177, 198, 200, 366, 2:423, 544, 556.

[38] Resolutions of Va. Convention, May 15, 1776, Pendleton to Thomas Jefferson, May 24, Aug. 3, 10, 1776, to James Madison, May 28, 1781, to Richard Henry Lee, Feb. 21, Mar. 18, 1785, to Va. Ratifying Convention, June 12, 1788, to Harry Innes, Nov. 9, 1791, to ——, Dec. 4, 1792, in *Pendleton Papers* 1:179, 180, 196, 198, 359, 2:473, 477, 521, 580–81, 593.

[39] Pendleton to William Woodford, Oct. 4, 1778, ibid., 1:271.

whole" to have "preferred men of prudence to 'those confounded men of genius.'" Pendleton's prudence and moderation, his dedication to the pragmatic resolution of political problems, his "deeply considered patriotism" and devotion to the Virginia political system, earned for him a degree of trust and responsibility withheld from the more flamboyant, widely acclaimed, and personally ambitious Richard Henry Lee. Like Lee, Pendleton had found his identity in the public realm. Unlike Lee, he never felt a compulsion to move onto the larger political stage provided by the national government, never experienced any sense of rejection by his peers in politics, and never felt any urge to retire. On rare occasions, he complained about the ardors of politics or hoped for "some leisure to attend [to] . . . private affairs." Once he even remarked that "true pleasure" was "not to be found in a Public bustle." In fact, however, Pendleton was a public man who clearly relished and was devoted to public service. With no children, he took an almost paternal interest in the state of the Virginia political system. Besides, as he wrote Jefferson in 1779, no real friend of his country could retire until he had "taught the rising Generation, the Forms as well as the Substantial principles" of that system.[40]

That Pendleton could write in his autobiography that throughout his long political career he had "had the happiness to find a majority of all the public bodies confirming my sentiments" on both the values and objectives of politics is a testimony to the influence that he and others like him had in Virginia politics. "From the experience of nearly sixty years in public life," Pendleton wrote in 1798, "I have been taught to . . . respect this my native country for the decent, peaceable, and orderly behaviour of its inhabitants; justice has been, and is duly and diligently administered—the laws obeyed—the constituted authorities respected, and we have lived in the happy intercourse of private harmony and good will. At the same time, by a free communication between those of more information on political subjects, and the classes who have not otherwise an opportunity of acquiring that knowledge, all were instructed in their *rights* and *duties* as freemen, and taught to respect them." The perpetuation of that system, Pendleton justifiably liked to think, depended to some significant degree upon the dedication to stability, moderation, and compromise of levelheaded and patriotic men such as himself.[41]

---

[40]Grainger, *Style and Character*, 46, 58; Pendleton to William Preston, Dec. 18, 1773, to Thomas Jefferson, Nov. 16, 1775, to James Mercer, Mar. 19, 1776, and to Thomas Jefferson, May 11, 1779, in *Pendleton Papers* 1:80, 130, 160, 284.

[41]Pendleton, "Autobiography," July 20, 1793, Pendleton to Citizens of Caroline, Nov. 1798, in *Pendleton Papers* 2:607, 650.

I recommend it to my sons, from my own Experience in Life, to prefer the happiness of independence & a private Station to the troubles and Vexations of Public Business.
                              —George Mason's will, March 20, 1773

Among the generation of Virginia political leaders considered in this essay, only George Washington achieved a greater degree of respect among his contemporaries than his neighbor George Mason.[42] To later historians, however, Mason's prominence and authority in the public realm have remained something of an enigma. Unlike every other famous Virginian of his generation, he had been only a minor figure on the provincial political stage before the Revolutionary crisis. Born in 1725, four years after Pendleton and seven years before Richard Henry Lee, he was, like Lee, a fourth-generation Virginian and a member of a prominent Northern Neck family. But the Masons, unlike the Lees, had not played a major role in provincial politics. Three generations of George Masons had concerned themselves primarily with building up their estates and had concentrated their political energies in their home county. Each of them had served several terms in the House of Burgesses, the second George Mason representing Stafford County continuously from 1720 to 1735. But each generation seems to have had less impact than the previous one upon that body. As of 1765, Mason himself seemed to represent a continuation in this trend. Though he evidenced an early interest in provincial politics by an unsuccessful bid to represent Fairfax County in the Burgesses in 1748 when he was only twenty-three years old, for the next fifteen years he devoted himself largely to his family and estate. He was active on the Truro parish vestry and the Fairfax County court, was a trustee for the new town of Alexandria, and served one undistinguished three-year term as a member of the House of Burgesses. But his greatest visibility probably derived from his activities as one of the leading spirits in, and treasurer of, the Ohio Company of Virginia, a massive scheme of speculation in western lands.[43]

---

[42] Portions of this section are adapted from my review essay on *The Papers of George Mason, 1725–1792*, ed. Robert A. Rutland, 3 vols. (Chapel Hill, N.C., 1970), in *South Atlantic Quarterly* 72 (1973): 159–62.

[43] See Robert Rutland, *George Mason: Reluctant Statesman* (Williamsburg, Va., 1961); Kate Mason Rowland, *The Life of George Mason, 1725–1792*, 2 vols. (New York, 1892); and Greene, "Foundations of Political Power in the Virginia House of Burgesses." For

Only with the pre-Revolutionary crisis was Mason gradually drawn into a more active involvement in public life, and even that involvement was limited and idiosyncratic. Like most other prominent members of his political generation, he took a strong stand against Parliament's attempt to tax the colonies and other "oppressive" British measures. But his platform was not the House of Burgesses, the main school of Virginia politics, to which he made no effort to return, but the library at his plantation at Gunston Hall. His anonymous letter to the "Committee of Merchants in London," apparently published in the *Public Ledger* in London following the Stamp Act crisis, is one of the best short statements of the American view of the relationship between Britain and the colonies and the American case against parliamentary taxation of the colonies. In 1769 and 1770 Mason worked privately through George Washington and others to help shape the Virginia nonimportation agreements against the Townshend Acts, and in the summer of 1774 he wrote the Fairfax Resolves, which in twenty-four resolutions reviewed American grievances against Britain, condemned the Coercive Acts, and advocated a broad program of resistance to secure "Restoration of our just Rights and Privileges." Not until the summer of 1775 did Mason, apparently with extreme reluctance, return to the provincial political arena as a delegate to the Virginia Convention from Fairfax County to replace George Washington, who had gone to Boston to take command of the new American army. Despite his lean and unremarkable political record, Mason exercised an immediate and powerful voice in the Virginia Convention, which chose him as a member of the Committee of Safety, and he vaulted into provincial—and international—prominence during the late spring of 1776 as the principal architect of the Virginia constitution and Declaration of Rights—the first American bill of rights. Subsequently he played a major role in Virginia politics as a representative from Fairfax to the House of Delegates until his retirement in 1781 and, coming out of retirement, was one of the most conspicuous members of the Federal Convention of 1787 and a leader of the opposition to the Federal Constitution at the Virginia ratifying convention in June 1788.[44] What has been so puzzling about Mason's meteoric political ascendance in 1775-76 is that it was the accomplishment of a man who previously had pointedly avoided political responsibility at the provincial level in a

the fullest recent study, see Helen Hill Miller, *George Mason: Gentleman Revolutionary* (Chapel Hill, N.C., 1975).

[44] Fairfax Co. Resolves, July 18, 1774, in *Mason Papers* 1:206; Rutland, *George Mason*, 30–110.

political culture that placed extremely heavy and explicit stress upon the obligation of men of ability to serve the public.

Part of the explanation for Mason's sudden political success may be found in a cluster of personal talents and traits that especially fitted him to play a central role in the tense and exigent political circumstances of 1775–76. A man who "concentrated on relatively few endeavors with a patient thoroughness," Mason, as some of his earlier writings reveal, had obviously read deeply in classical and modern English history and, as Edmund Randolph had reported, "was behind none of the sons of Virginia in knowledge of her history and interest." Educated at home by private tutors, Mason had clearly made excellent use of his access to the library of his uncle and neighbor John Mercer of Marlborough, one of the leading lawyers in Virginia, whose collection of books was among the largest in the colonies. The result was that, although Mason was not a lawyer, he was an avid and learned student of the law. Thus, when "the People of" his "County" "much against" his "Inclination drag'd [him] out of . . . Retirement" to serve in the Conventions of 1775 and 1776, the extensive learning he brought gave him an authority and an expertise that stood out among a group of men who, with the possible exception of the older Richard Bland, were, though politically more experienced and publicly more visible, considerably less learned in such matters.[45]

Moreover, as his writings and his contemporaries also attest, Mason combined this knowledge with a clear and penetrating intellect. He had few peers as a political analyst: "At a glance," said Randolph, "he saw to the bottom of every proposition." He was a man, avowed Jefferson, "of the first order of wisdom among those who acted on the theatre of the revolution, of expansive mind, profound judgment, cogent in argument, learned in the lore of our former constitution." "Among the many profound statesmen Virginia had produced," said Henry Lee, Mason "was perhaps second to none in wisdom and virtue, and by many of the most renowned of his contemporaries was regarded as the wisest of them all." "The Political Cooks are busy in preparing the dish," wrote Pendleton to Jefferson in May 1776 during the deliberations on the Virginia constitution, "and as Colonel Mason seems to have the Ascendancy in the great work, I have sanguine hopes it will be framed so as to Answer it's end." So formidable were his learning and his intellectual gifts that "his opinions on a great political question had almost a conclusive authority." As Edmund Randolph put it in reference to Mason's contribution in 1776,

[45] Mason to Mr. Brent, Oct. 2, 1778, in *Mason Papers* I:cxiii, 434; Randolph, *History of Virginia*, 192; Rutland, *George Mason*, 60–67.

Mason's proposals carried such cogency that they simply "swallowed up all the rest."[46]

But the authority of his opinions rested not only upon their cogency but also upon his ability to articulate them with force and persuasion. In the judgment of James Madison, who had ample opportunity to witness Mason's performance, Mason "was the soundest & clearest reasoner that he ever listened to." Unlike Richard Henry Lee, Mason was not a dramatic or polished orator. Preferring a manner of exposition that was "learned & elegant without the Vanity of seeming so," he had no taste for "the florid Ciceronian Style." Rather, his manner of speaking seems to have been modeled upon that of his classical hero, Cato the Younger, whose speech, according to Plutarch, "had nothing about it that was . . . affected, but was straightforward, full of matter, and harsh." Thus, Mason's "elocution," Jefferson testified, "was neither flowing nor smooth; but his language was strong, his manner most impressive, and strengthened by a dash of biting synicism, when provocation made it seasonable."[47]

Jefferson's description suggests still another source for Mason's political authority: his extreme moral rectitude. He seems to have cultivated—virtually to have personified—the Catonic model. Like Cato, he sought to be—and by his entire bearing to appear as—a man of "unbending character and absolute integrity," who, as his grandson remarked, staked "his life upon the truth." Mason possessed, Edmund Randolph said, "that philosophical spirit which despised the adulterated means of cultivating happiness." In his "habits generally he was severe and strict," displaying extraordinary discipline and self-control as well as a Spartan simplicity and disdain for ostentation. An "inflexible, imperturbable, and altogether steadfast" supporter of his conception of colonial rights before 1776, he was a "stern . . . Republican" thereafter, the constant opponent of any measures or social tendencies—including a general "Depravity of Manners and Morals" that seemed to be sweeping the states— that might render the Revolution a "Curse" rather than a "Blessing," and an exponent of unpopular measures—such as payment of British

---

[46] Randolph, *History of Virginia*, 192, 252, 258; Grigsby, *Virginia Convention of 1776*, 155; Jefferson, "Autobiography," in *Writings of Jefferson* 1:60; Rowland, *George Mason* 2:374; Pendleton to Jefferson, May 24, 1776, in *Pendleton Papers* 1:180.

[47] *Plutarch's Lives* 8:247; Randolph, *History of Virginia*, 192, 252; Mason to George Brent, Dec. 6, 1770, in *Mason Papers* 1:127; Jefferson, "Autobiography," in *Writings of Jefferson* 1:60; St. George Tucker to William Wirt, Sept. 25, 1815, *William and Mary College Quarterly*, 1st ser., 22 (1914): 256.

debts, security of paper money, and the remedying of defects in the administration of justice—that seemed necessary to fulfill the "Obligations of Morality & Justice" and guarantee "the sacred Rights of . . . Citizens."[48]

For Mason, the cause of liberty and virtue, "the Principles of Justice & Equity," the "Security of private-Property," could never be sacrificed to popularity or exigency. Eager, like Cato, to take "a course directly opposite" to "practices of the time . . . that . . . were bad and in need of great change," he was more alert than most of his contemporaries to the pernicious effects of existing institutions within his own society, as was revealed by his early—for Virginia—condemnation of Negro slavery as a "slow Poison, which is daily contaminating the Minds & Morals of our People" and unjustly debasing "a part of our own Species . . . almost to a Level with the Brute Creation."[49]

In the political arena, Mason, in sharp contrast to Pendleton, had little patience with anything that smacked either of selfishness or foolishness and no taste for the routine interchange—the hum—of day-to-day politics. The "Partys & Factions" that he encountered at the Virginia Convention in 1775, his first legislative session in over a dozen years, produced so much "Vexation & Disgust" as to throw him "into such an ill state of Health that" he "was sometimes near fainting in the House." Only after weeks of tedious irrelevance were "the Bablers . . . pretty well silenced" so that "a few weighty Members" such as himself could begin "to take the Lead" in fashioning "several wholsome Regulations." By himself or in company with a few peers, Mason could accomplish the most demanding legislative tasks. But he was too proud, too persuaded of the rectitude of his own opinions and productions, to accept opposition gracefully. Mason's austere, elevated, and forbidding public persona might have alienated his colleagues had his "steadfast and zealous" Virginia patriotism been insincere or had he not applied the same high standards to himself as to others. But his success, as measured by the posi-

---

[48] Rowland, *George Mason* 2:367; Randolph, *History of Virginia*, 192; *Plutarch's Lives* 8:245, 253, 259; Mason to George Washington, Apr. 5, 1769, to Arthur Lee, Mar. 25, 1783, to Patrick Henry, May 6, 1783, to Thomas Marshall, Oct. 16, 1789, Petition of Prince William Co. Freeholders, Dec. 10, 1781, Address of Fairfax Co. Freeholders to Delegates, May 30, 1783, and Mason, Speech on Sumptuary Laws, Aug. 20, 1787, in *Mason Papers* 1:99–100, 2:711, 766, 770–72, 779–80, 861–62, 3:962, 1175.

[49] Mason, Scheme for Replevying Goods, Dec. 23, 1765, Abstracts from Virginia Charters, July 1773, and Petition of Prince William Co. Freeholders, Dec. 10, 1781, in *Mason Papers* 1:61–62, 173, 275, 2:711; *Plutarch's Lives* 8:249–51.

tive response of his colleagues, in his strivings to personify those values of "pristine Englishry" that had been so long and so carefully cultivated by the Virginia elite—"justice, moderation, temperance, frugality, and virtue," he called them in the Virginia Declaration of Rights—was instead one of the primary sources of his political appeal and both established him as the conscience—the veritable superego—of Virginia politics and helped to win him the respect and admiration of his colleagues in the public arena, even as they earlier impressed his friends and neighbors in private life.[50]

But Mason's spectacular rise and continued exercise of leadership in Revolutionary Virginia are also traceable to a still deeper, and probably much more important, source. A persistent and powerful tension ran through the elite culture of eighteenth-century Virginia between the individual's obligation to serve the public and his responsibility to preserve his personal independence.[51] Most men, like Pendleton and Lee, managed to achieve some balance between the two, but with Mason the pull of the latter was always infinitely stronger. Unlike Richard Henry Lee, Washington, or younger colleagues such as Jefferson, Madison, or Henry, all of whom found their identities in the public realm, Mason was an intensely private man. His main concerns were overwhelmingly personal: the education of his numerous family, the management of his plantations and the money he had loaned out at interest, and his involvement with western lands. In his own eyes, his most important accomplishment was not the authorship of the Virginia Declaration of Rights but the ample provision he had made for his five children: "the Payment of my Daughter's Fortune, the building for, & setling two of my Sons, and raising Capitals in trade for two others." His self-image, as he declared in 1766, was of "a Man, who spends most of his Time in Retirement, and has seldom med[d]led in public Affairs, who enjoys a moderate but independent Fortune, and content with the Blessings of a private Station, equally disregards the Smiles & Frowns of the Great"; and the death of his wife in March 1773 only strengthened his determination to "spend the remainder of my Days in privacy & Retirement with my Children." From his "own Experience in Life," he recommended to his sons in a will written shortly after his wife's death, "to prefer the

---

[50] Mason to George Washington, Oct. 14, 1775, Virginia Declaration of Rights, June 12, 1776, in *Mason Papers* 1:255, 289; Grainger, *Character and Style*, 63; Jefferson, "Autobiography," in *Writings of Jefferson* 1:60.

[51] See Greene, *Landon Carter*, esp. 70–92.

happiness of independance & a private Station to the troubles and Vexations of Public Business."[52]

Government, for Mason, was, more than anything else, an instrument to protect men in the peaceful and unfettered pursuit of their own and their posterity's private fortunes and interests and to preserve to them the fruits of their endeavors; and what eventually pulled him out of retirement in 1775—perhaps the only thing that could have done so—was his growing perception that a corrupt government in Britain was bent on denying this invaluable blessing to Americans, a blessing that they had "received from" their "Ancestors" and were obliged "to transmit to" their own "posterity," if America, "the only great nursery of freedom" still "left upon the face of the earth," was not to become "a sink for slaves." "When the Subject is of such Importance as the Liberty & Happiness of a Country," he had written to Richard Henry Lee in 1770, "Every Member of Society is in Duty bound to contribute to the Safety & Good of the Whole," and "every inferior Consideration, as well as the Inconvenience to a few Individuals, must give place to it, nor is this any Hardship upon them; as themselves & their Posterity are to partake of the Benefits resulting from it."[53] When anything less was at stake, however, public service, as Mason petulantly declared in attempting to cut off a movement to elect him to the Virginia House of Delegates in 1784, could only be considered "an oppressive & unjust Invasion of my personal Liberty." Only a dangerous and malevolent threat to that liberty, to the right of every individual to enjoy the "Sweets of domestic Life" at "Ease under the Shade of his own vine & his own fig-tree," could justify a society in forcing a man to abandon his "Quiet & Retirement."[54]

For at least a half century before 1775, the Virginia gentry had assiduously cultivated the image of the retired life of virtue, privacy, and independence, free from the bustle and care of public life, at the same time that they were actively participating in that life. For most Virginians, this arcadian image seems to have served as a psychological balm for the pain and anxiety they felt at being so far removed from the really great

[52] Mason to Committee of Merchants in London, June 6, 1766, Will, Mar. 20, 1773, to Mr. Brent, Oct. 2, 1778, and to John Francis Mercer, Aug. 26, 1791, in *Mason Papers* 1:71, 159, 433, 3:1235–36.

[53] Mason to Richard Henry Lee, June 7, 1770, Remarks on Election for Fairfax Independent Co., Apr. 17–26, 1775, to George Washington, Apr. 2, 1776, and William Lee to Mason, July 29, 1775, ibid., 1:118, 231, 244, 267.

[54] Mason to George Washington, Apr. 2, 1776, to Edmund Randolph, Oct. 19, 1782, to Martin Cockburn, Apr. 18, 1784, ibid., 1:267, 2:747, 799.

affairs of state in the metropolis across the Atlantic. For Mason, however, the power of this image in giving coherence to his own identity seems to have depended more upon personal inclination than cultivation: his genuine and deeply rooted preference was always for "the happiness of independance & a private Station" rather than "the troubles and Vexations of Public Business." This intense commitment to private life, this deep aversion to all public service except that undertaken in behalf of the most fundamental—the deepest—concerns of society, gave Mason a degree of detachment from the concerns of day-to-day politics that most Virginia leaders admired and wanted for themselves, at least in theory, but could never achieve because of their intense devotion to and involvement in public life. Mason's detachment freed him both "from the entanglements, political and personal, of party and passion" and from the ambition for office that together circumscribe the independence of most political leaders. Just as, much later, Mason would decline appointment to the United States Senate, during the seven years he served in the legislature he was "at different times . . . chosen a Member of the Privy Council, & of the American Congress," but, because of "his indifference for distinction," "constantly declined acting in any other public character than that of an independent Representative of the People, in the House of Delegates." Perhaps more than anything else—more than his learning, intelligence, ability in debate, or moral rectitude—this extreme independence, which he valued more highly than "the approbation of any man, or all the men upon earth," accounted for his rapid ascendancy in 1775–76 and his continuing authority in Virginia political counsels. As in the case of Cato, Mason's carefully nurtured position as "the only man who was [entirely] free" brought him "in greatest measure" that to which he "gave least thought[,] . . . namely, esteem, favour, surpassing honour, and kindness" from his associates in the political arena.[55]

When Mason retired from the legislature in 1781 with the firm intention of spending "the Remnant of my Life in Quiet & Retirement," he did so not only because of the economic costs—"the no small Neglect & Injury of my private Fortune"—of such a heavy commitment of "Time to public Business" but also, and much more importantly, because he had lost some of his authority and, as he saw it, "was no longer able to do any essential Service." "Some of the public Measures have been so con-

---

[55] *Plutarch's Lives* 8:257, 407; Grigsby, *Virginia Convention of 1776,* 155; Randolph, *History of Virginia,* 192; Mason, Will, Mar. 20, 1773, to Mr. Brent, Oct. 2, 1778, to John Mason, Mar. 13, 1789, and to Beverley Randolph, Mar. 27, 1790, in *Mason Papers* 1:159, 434, 3:1142, 1192.

trary to my Notions of Policy and of Justice, that I wished to be no further concern'd with, or answerable for them." In Addison's famous quotation of Cato again: "When vice prevails, and impious men bear sway, The post of honor," for Mason, indeed, was "a private station." But Mason was too deeply engaged in the great cause of ensuring that "the American Union" would be "firmly fixed, and free Governments well established in our western world" ever to withdraw completely. He wrote to his son in January 1783, "My Anxiety for my Country, in these Times of Danger, makes me sometimes dabble a little in Politicks, & keep up a Correspondence with some Men upon the public stage," and he professed his willingness to "sacrifice my own Ease & domestic Enjoyments to the Public-Good," whenever, as had been the case in 1775–76, some great public business required the exertions of "a few Men of Integrity & Abilitys, whose Countrys Interest lies next their Hearts." He was thus waiting when the call came to go as a Virginia delegate to the Federal Convention in Philadelphia in the summer of 1787. To contrive a workable political system for the "American Union" was indeed a task worthy of Mason's talents: one that was capable, for the first time in his sixty-two years, of drawing him beyond the environs of the Chesapeake Bay. In his own words, it was "an Object of such Magnitude, as absorbs, & in a Manner suspends the Operations of the human Understanding." That this proud man failed to gain support for many of his ideas in Philadelphia probably accounts in large degree for his subsequent opposition to the Constitution: he could not bring himself to support a document that was adopted over his opposition without admitting to himself that he had been unable to live up to his self-image as the virtuous patriot of deep understanding, "*independent* Circumstances and Principles," who, when duty called, could come out of retirement to give fundamental law to his country. George Washington thought that Mason's pride and "want of manly [self-]candour" were largely responsible for preventing him from admitting "an error in his opinions" on the Constitution.[56]

Whatever his disappointments in 1787–88—and the narrow margin by which the Virginia Convention ratified the Constitution was in some part a measure of the continuing respect for Mason's opinions—Mason had indeed played an extremely important role and commanded extraordi-

---

[56] Mason to R. H. Lee, May 18, 1776, to Mr. Brent, Oct. 2, 1778, to Edmund Randolph, Oct. 19, 1782, to George Mason, Jr., Jan. 8, 1783, to Arthur Lee, Mar. 25, 1783, and to George Mason, Jr., June 1, 1787, in *Mason Papers* 1:271, 434, 2:747, 759–61, 766, 3:892–93; Addison, *Cato*, 4.4.140–50.

nary authority in the political life of Virginia after 1775. As he wrote his son John in 1789, his "conduct as a public man, through the whole of the late glorious Revolution," had "been such as . . . will administer comfort to me in those moments when I shall most want it, and smooth the bed of death": insofar as he was aware, he had always "acted from the purest motives of honesty, and love to my country, according to that measure of judgment which God has bestowed on me." But the key ingredient in his political authority was not his moral rectitude, his patriotism, or even his judgment and learning. Rather, it was his cherished independence. He was the epitome of the bucolic image, which struck so many positive resonances among the Virginia elite, of the "private man living in the ordered *patria*" of the Virginia countryside, who in emergencies could be an effective servant of the public precisely because he was in the political debt of no man. What Mason's remarkable political success would seem to suggest about the larger system of values and patterns of behavior among the extraordinary group of which he was a member is that, however deeply committed the Virginia gentry may have been to the traditional ideals of stewardship and the obligation of public service, a commitment that is well illustrated by the careers of Richard Henry Lee and Edmund Pendleton, they valued individual independence—personal liberty—and the detachment it carried with it even more.[57]

> . . . *a high sense of personal independence was universal.*
> —Edmund Randolph, *History of Virginia*

Each of the three men analyzed in this essay represents a distinctive mode of political leadership in late colonial and Revolutionary Virginia. By focusing on what they had in common, we can delineate more clearly those essential qualities demanded of all leaders in a political culture in which leaders were selected not by the political community at large but by a small group of peers on the basis of day-to-day performance. Those qualities were summarized succinctly in 1761 by Lieutenant Governor Francis Fauquier in his explanation, previously quoted, for the extraordinary popularity of Speaker John Robinson. What gave Robinson such great authority, said Fauquier, were his "great integrity, assiduity, and ability in business," qualities exhibited in substantial measure by all

---

[57] Mason to John Mason, Mar. 13, 1789, in *Mason Papers* 3:1142; Grainger, *Character and Style*, 26.

three men here considered. Although Lee was required on more than one occasion to offer public proof of the rectitude of his conduct, each was a man of cultivated and recognized virtue in both the private and the public spheres, a man of genuine independence of mind who was devoted to and could be trusted to act in accordance with what he took to be the best interests of the whole society. Each was also a man of great diligence who performed his duties thoroughly. And each had a remarkable "capacity for business," an impressive learning, especially in the law, that informed his analysis of political issues, and an ability to define those issues clearly, devise strategies for coping with them, and elicit support for those strategies from among his peers in the political arena.

As the examples of all three men testify, the ability to elicit such support in a political culture like that of Revolutionary Virginia required great skill in speaking and debate. With virtually no infrastructure—no organized parties, factions, clientage system, or bureaucracy—to serve as a basis for mobilizing opinion, leaders had to depend very heavily upon force of personality and cogency of argument to gain support for their views from within the political community. Finally, the widespread acclaim extended to all of these men was the result not merely of their manifest abilities in these several areas but also of the achievement, in each case, of a remarkable—and demonstrable—congruity between character and persona.

But the divergencies among the three leaders—the particular way each of them gave expression to and utilized the essential qualities of leadership—are perhaps even more revealing of the characteristics, priorities, and responsiveness of eighteenth-century Virginia political culture than the commonalities. Together, the three distinct modes of political leadership represented by Lee, Pendleton, and Mason would seem to cover the complete range of leadership styles available in that culture. With relatively minor qualifications, every leader can be fitted into one of them.

Throughout the whole period, the persona of the trimmer as characterized by Pendleton was dominant. This role, with its emphasis upon accommodation, moderation, deliberation, and control and its commitment, above all else, to the continuing stability of of the polity, had been hammered out and given definition in Virginia by a long line of earlier political leaders, including John Holloway, Governor Sir William Gooch, Sir John Randolph, John Robinson, Charles Carter of Cleve, and Richard Bland. For a polity in which there was virtually no disagreement over the fundamental objectives of society, one in which government was expected to do little more than provide maximum scope for individual enterprise by guaranteeing the liberty of its members to pursue their own private interests in a stable and orderly context and by securing to them the fruits of their enterprise, the authority of this persona rested upon its appropriateness: the political nation demanded no more of its leaders than that they maintain a stable political environment. That most leaders among Pendleton's contemporaries—Peyton Randolph, George Washington, Robert Carter Nicholas, George Wythe, Archibald Cary, Benjamin Harrison V—as well as many of the most prominent members of the next generation—James Madison, Edmund Randolph, John Marshall—adopted a similar persona and continued to command authority throughout the Revolutionary era is a testimony both to the commitment of the political culture to the values that this persona embodied and was designed to facilitate and to its heightened appropriateness in a time of political upheaval and change.

As long as none of the fundamental values of the polity were threatened from either internal or external sources, there was little room for the emergence of either of the two alternative personae characterized by Lee and Mason. Hence, albeit during the early stages of the Seven Years' War Landon Carter seems to have prefigured the posture exhibited by Lee, there was no precise counterpart to either Lee or Mason among either of the two previous political generations. The persona of the vigorous and uncompromising defender of the basic values and beliefs of the society was thus the creation—in Virginia—of Richard Henry Lee and some of his young contemporaries, notably Patrick Henry and Thomas Jefferson. Initially, its authority was directly dependent upon the exigencies of the mid-1760s, the internal corruption represented by the Robinson scandals and the external challenge posed by the Grenville program, and it was provided wide scope for development as the deepening quarrel with Britain seemed to demand activity, energy, and resolution to prevent the subversion and loss of the most cherished possessions of the community: liberty, property, and autonomy. That so few of the major leaders adopted this new persona even in the midst of the Revolutionary crisis is a measure of the extent to which the trimmers, while advocating different tactics, were committed to the same basic goals and a further indication of the extraordinary and continuing power of the traditional model of the trimmer in Virginia politics.

The persona represented by George Mason and shared by no other Virginia leader of the Revolutionary era reveals even more emphatically the depth and extent of the Virginia commitment to those basic goals. The intensely private and talented man who could not tolerate the banalities of politics in ordinary times and would abandon his private station only when his independence and with it the deepest values of his country were in jeopardy, Mason personified the personal independence, the honest and uninterrupted pursuit of private happiness, objectives to which Virginians had always—since the very beginning—given the highest possible personal and social priority. As the personification of that independence which Virginians cherished so deeply, Mason—in the critical moments at the founding of the independent state of Virginia—was accorded the exalted role of giver of fundamental law.

This chapter was written early in 1975 for the volume in which it appeared. It was offered at The Seminar, Department of History, The Johns Hopkins University, March 3, 1975, and at the seminar in American History, Churchill College, Cambridge, England, on February 24, 1976. It was one of three papers on eighteenth-century Virginia politics considered at a seminar held in the Department of History at La Trobe University, Bundoora, Victoria, Australia, August 20, 1976. It is here reprinted with permission and minor corrections from W. Robert Higgins, ed., *The Revolutionary War in the South: Essays in Honor of John Richard Alden* (Durham, N.C.: Duke University Press, 1979), 3–42.

—ELEVEN—

The Alienation of Benjamin Franklin, British American

O N SATURDAY, January 29, 1774, "thirty-five Lords of the Privy Council" assembled at their usual meeting place at the Cockpit. The ostensible purpose of this assemblage was to hear counsel on a petition from the House of Representatives of the colony of Massachusetts Bay praying the removal of Governor Thomas Hutchinson and Lieutenant Governor Andrew Oliver for having sought "to excite the resentment of the British Administration" against the colony.[1] Both the number and the mood of the Lords in attendance dramatically indicated that this was not a routine meeting. They had gathered, as if "invited . . . to a Bull-baiting," to witness the ritual humiliation of Benjamin Franklin, agent for the Massachusetts house, by Alexander Wedderburne, the king's solicitor general. Franklin was extremely vulnerable. To prevent a duel between two innocent parties, he had only a few weeks earlier admitted responsibility for transmitting to a select group of Massachusetts political leaders a series of letters that had mysteriously come into his possession from Hutchinson and Oliver to Thomas Whateley, George Grenville's political confidant. By this action, Franklin hoped to convince "that Country that the sending of Troops and other Measures they complained of, did not take their Rise from an inimical Disposition towards them here, but were originally planned and recommended by some of their own People"—namely, Hutchinson and Oliver. Despite Frank-

---

[1] Bernhard Knollenberg, *Growth of the American Revolution, 1766–1775* (New York, 1975), 113–16, treats this petition concisely.

lin's enjoinder to his correspondents not to circulate the letters outside
the innermost circles of the colony's political counsels, someone published the letters, and they formed the basis for the petition to remove
Hutchinson and Oliver.[2]

But the "virulent invective" and "Ribaldry," the scurrilous personal
abuse with which Wedderburne savaged Franklin "for near an hour," and
the raucous response of the Lords, who "generally appeared much delighted, chuckling, laughing, and sometimes loudly applauding," were
greatly out of proportion to the magnitude of Franklin's offense, which
was, in any case, already under consideration in the courts and only tan-
gentially relevant to the matter under consideration. Indeed, this *"pre-
concerted"* public humiliation of Franklin, a man of letters celebrated for
his scientific achievements throughout Britain and Europe, America's
most distinguished citizen, and, for much of the previous two decades,
the most prominent spokesman for the colonies in Britain, was expressive of some of the deepest psychological tensions within the British political nation. Occurring only a matter of days after the arrival in London
of news of the unexpected and daring tea party that had taken place in
Boston in mid-December, it provided an occasion for the British political
community to vent its building hostility toward its errant and rebellious
children in America, children who for a decade had been seemingly refus-
ing obedience to the mother country by defying the authority of its sovereign institution, the king-in-parliament assembled.[3]

The *"entertainment"* served as well to offer a temporary release from
the deep anxieties, increasingly manifest over the previous quarter of a
century, arising from the fear that these growing and valuable possessions might become independent and thereby lost to Britain, anxieties
that had only been intensified by the colonial challenge to parliamentary
authority after 1765. As Wedderburne excoriated Franklin as little better
than a common thief and, cleverly playing upon some of Franklin's most
notable achievements, charged him with being the "first mover and
prime conductor[,] . . . the actor and secret spring[,] . . . the inventor
and first planner," who had provided the "materials for dissensions" and
systematically sought "to irritate and incense the minds of the king's
subjects against the king's governor" in Massachusetts, Franklin became
for Wedderburne's hearers both a surrogate for and the palpable per-

[2] Franklin's own descriptions of this episode may be found in *Benjamin Franklin's Letters
to the Press*, ed. Verner W. Crane (Chapel Hill, N.C., 1950), 240–46.

[3] Ibid., 242, 245–46.

sonification of all of "their" rebellious subjects in America and a convenient scapegoat onto whose eminent shoulders could be loaded, for the moment at least, all of the responsibility for the convulsions in America.[4]

Franklin offered no defense. Standing passively throughout, he let Wedderburne—and his audience—have their day. What seemed to be an easy victory that winter afternoon at the Cockpit was, in actuality, a costly defeat for the future of British authority in America, yet another in a long series of official miscalculations in dealing with the American problem. In return for the immediate gratification of their hostilities, Franklin's abusers had only helped further to alienate the man who was perhaps the best friend they had from America. For Franklin, far from being a plotter of sedition and rebellion, had been a consistent exponent of imperial harmony and union. He was not by nature a revolutionary. If he had been the leading spokesman for the colonies in Britain, he had also repeatedly put the most charitable construction possible on offensive British policies and been one of the most prominent and effective advocates of a moderate colonial response. Indeed, no American had greater or deeper affection for Britain or had worked harder over the previous decade to preserve its connection with the colonies. How his efforts were aborted and his deep affections gradually alienated provides a vivid insight into the origins of the American Revolution.

Franklin's public personality and his political orientation and priorities were, of course, already well formed before he went to Britain in July 1757 to begin the first phase of his long career as agent, first for Pennsylvania and then for other colonies, in the metropolis. They were an external manifestation of his most basic character traits as they had been modified by experience. Franklin had always had a burning desire for recognition. In his early years, he tells us in his *Autobiography*, he expressed this desire through a "disputacious turn." After reading Xenophon's *Memorable Things of Socrates* in adolescence, however, he determined to drop the "abrupt contradiction and positive argumentation" that had formerly been his manner "and put on the humble inquirer and doubter." Thenceforth, he "made it a rule to forbear all direct contradiction to the sentiments of others, and all positive assertions of my own"

---

[4] Ibid., 240–46. See also Carl Van Doren, *Benjamin Franklin* (London, 1939), 469–72.

and to cultivate a public persona of "modest diffidence" and "evenness of temper" that, he remarked in 1784, "became at length so easy, and so habitual to me, that perhaps for these fifty years past no one has ever heard a dogmatical expression escape me."[5]

But this public posture was a strategy not for suppressing his hunger for fame and attention but for gratifying it. He had early learned that men only lessened "their power of doing good by a positive, assuming manner, that seldom fails to disgust, tends to create opposition, and to defeat everyone of" their "purposes." A "positive and dogmatical manner" might bring "victory sometimes, but . . . never . . . good will." *Exemplum adest ipse homo*—"The example presents the man himself"—was the Franklin family motto, and, by disguising his "overbearing and rather insolent" pride with "the *appearance*" of "*Humility*," for as he himself suggested, he could not "boast of much success in acquiring the *reality* of" that virtue, Franklin was able to shelter himself from much unpleasant hostility—"of all things, I hate hostility," he wrote Arthur Lee in April 1778—and, infinitely more important, to maximize both his effectiveness in persuading his associates in the public realm to accept his opinions and the acclaim and self-esteem that accompanied their acknowledgment of his leadership and endorsement of his measures.[6]

In pursuit of the same objectives, Franklin sought to reinforce his image as a "moderate prudent man" by cultivating a whole congeries of related behavioral characteristics. Having "a tolerable character to begin the world with," he was determined to value "it properly, and . . . to preserve it," and he was always careful of his reputation for temperance, industry, frugality, honesty, justice, sincerity, independence, contempt for narrowly self-interested behavior, and conspicuous dedication to the public good. Early "convinced of the folly of being on ill terms with those one is to live with continually," he never departed radically from prevailing social norms, and he sought to maintain a "cheerfulness in conversation, which" made "his company . . . agreeable." To the "character of integrity" that he was able to achieve through the diligent, if not invariably constant or successful, pursuit of such virtues, Franklin attributed

---

[5] *Benjamin Franklin's Autobiography,* ed. W. MacDonald (London, 1908), 14, 17, 81–83.

[6] Ibid., 17, 82, 118; *The Papers of Benjamin Franklin,* ed. Leonard W. Labaree, et al., 28 vols. to date (New Haven, 1959–), 12:63; Richard L. Bushman, "On the Uses of Psychology: Conflict and Conciliation in Benjamin Franklin," *History and Theory* 5 (1966): esp. 234, 237–38.

his "early . . . weight with my fellow-citizens when I proposed new institutions, or alterations in the old," and his considerable "influence in public councils when I became a member; for I was a bad speaker, never eloquent, subject to much hesitation in my choice of words, hardly correct in language, and yet I generally carried my points."[7]

Franklin's behavior in public life was almost wholly congruent with this carefully nurtured image. The politics he practiced was the politics of prudence and restraint, of "circumscribed dissidence" and "political lenity," of "dispute within safe limits with blunted weapons within the [existing] consensus." The primary model for this type of "humane, civilized and realistic politics" in the Anglo-American world of the eighteenth century was George Savile, marquis of Halifax, the "Trimmer," that staunch enemy to zealous patriotism and the politics of violence. A "sceptic about political passion," Halifax was the quintessential advocate of "poise, some inactivity, consensus, a delimitation of politics, a minimization of rule." Indeed, although there is no evidence that Franklin consciously modeled himself after Halifax, for in his lifetime, as now, *trimming* was a term of political opprobrium, Franklin was, in fact, the classic public-spirited Trimmer as originally limned by Halifax. Like the trimmer, Franklin was fundamentally concerned to keep the political system on an even keel by forgoing all debate over basic issues and seeking pragmatic solutions to conflicts among major contending interests.[8]

Franklin abhorred "Rashness" and always recommended "Coolness and Steadiness" in politics. The common welfare, he believed, should not be interrupted by too punctilious an insistence upon adherence to principle; the basic principles of the constitution itself might even be safely suspended in times of real necessity. Nothing of fundamental importance, he was persuaded, could be relinquished through the sort of compulsive "*force*" that operated on such occasions. He thought it better, in the short run, to yield to a superior power, to acquiesce in the inevitable, than to risk a greater evil by running "fast into Anarchy and Confusion." The operation of reasoned self-interest, Franklin believed, would usually lead in time to the correction or amelioration of gross political evils for the simple reason that the distress of one segment of the

---

[7] Franklin, "On the Candidacy of Barlow Trecothick," Mar. 8, 1768, in *Franklin's Letters to the Press*, 113; *Autobiography*, 42, 52–53, 80–83; Franklin to Peter Collinson, Nov. 12, 1756, in *Franklin Papers* 7:14.

[8] On the persona of the Trimmer, see J. H. Grainger, *Character and Style in English Politics* (Cambridge, Eng., 1969), 8, 47–49, 58–59, 61.

political community must ultimately affect adversely all other portions of that community.[9]

Moreover, Franklin was always willing to give even his staunchest political opponents the benefit of the doubt—and not only, as he wrote Peter Collinson in 1754, because "An Appearance of Impartiality in general, gives a Man sometimes much more Weight when he would serve in particular Instances" but also, as he was persuaded, because compromise among discordant groups was absolutely essential for the smooth functioning and preservation of the political system. In most cases, the middle way was the best way in politics because it was the most equitable. Thus, in his later years, the plan of union for the American continental colonies which he had proposed at the Albany Congress in 1754, a plan that had been rejected by the colonists because "there was too much *prerogative* in it" and by British officials because it contained "too much of the *democratic*," seemed to Franklin to have been "the true medium" which might, if adopted, have prevented the subsequent disintegration of the British Empire.[10] For Franklin, as Gerald Stourzh has written, the "mutual adjustment of interests would always remain the chief remedy of political evils." "Moderation and equity," his experience had taught him, constituted the "true political wisdom."[11]

If, however, Franklin's most fundamental political commitment was to moderation, harmony, and order in the public arena, he was unwilling to purchase them at any price. He would sacrifice neither his "Consciousness of [his own] Rectitude in Action and Intention" nor his ultimate devotion to the perpetuation of British liberty. Thus, he despised narrow mercenary behavior in public life and took pains to preserve his own sense of personal independence from the hand of official power, whether that of the Pennsylvania proprietors or that of metropolitan ministers in Britain. Especially fortunate in the fact that his personal circumstances were such that "proprietary favours [were] unnecessary" to him and he had "nothing to ask or expect of Ministers," he insisted that his place as deputy postmaster general of North America, a post he filled

[9] See Franklin, *Plain Truth*, 1747, Franklin to John Fothergill, Mar. 14, 1764, to Richard Jackson, June 1, 25, 1764, to Charles Thomson, July 11, 1765, to John Hughes, Aug. 9, 1765, to Joseph Fox, Mar. 1, 1766, and Arthur Lee to Samuel Adams, June 10, 1771, in *Franklin Papers* 3:191–203, 11:101–5, 214–18, 234–39, 12:207–8, 234–35, 13:186–87, 18:128–29; *Autobiography*, 142.

[10] Franklin to Collinson, Dec. 29, 1754, in *Franklin Papers* 5:453; *Autobiography*, 117.

[11] Gerald Stourzh, "Reason and Power in Benjamin Franklin's Political Thought," *American Political Science Review* 43 (1953): 1115.

with efficiency and profit from 1753 until his abrupt dismissal the day after Wedderburne's scathing attack upon him in 1774, should in no way limit his free expression of political views.[12]

Ever the thoroughgoing Whig, he was similarly determined to do everything in his power to ensure that "sentiments of Liberty . . . would . . . always . . . prevail," not only in his home colony of Pennsylvania but, increasingly, as he came more and more to assume a larger Anglo-American perspective in the 1760s and 1770s, throughout the whole of the British Empire.[13] Indeed, this devotion to liberty lay at the heart of Franklin's deep veneration for Britain and the British political system, a veneration that underlay and informed all of his central political activities from the 1750s through the mid-1770s and survived, in a somewhat attenuated form, even Wedderburne's vicious attack.

That same veneration derived, of course, from a variety of sources. In part, it was the product of that profound yearning, so strong among aspiring people on the peripheries of social and political systems, for incorporation into the life of the center. Like most aspiring provincials, Franklin had an acute sense of cultural remove, even deprivation. Philadelphia might very well be "the Seat of the *American* Muses," but Franklin was under no illusion that it was anything more than a "remote Part" and pale imitation of the larger metropolitan world. "We have seldom any News on our Side [of] the Globe that can be entertaining to you on yours," he wrote the London printer William Strahan in 1744. "All our Affairs are *petit*. They have a miniature Resemblance only, of the grand things of Europe. Our Governments, Parliaments, Wars, Treaties, Expeditions, Factions, &c. tho' Matters of great and Serious Consequence to us, can seem but trifles to you."[14]

For Franklin, any anxieties that might have derived from his isolation in Philadelphia were quickly mitigated by his experiences in Britain.

---

[12] Franklin to Jane Mecom, Mar. 1, 1766, in *Franklin Papers* 13:188; Franklin to Samuel Cooper, Jan. 13, 1772, in *The Writings of Benjamin Franklin*, ed. Albert Henry Smyth, 10 vols. (New York, 1905–7), 5:357; *Autobiography*, 140.

[13] Franklin to Collinson, Dec. 29, 1754, Nov. 12, 1756, to Isaac Norris, June 9, 1759, to Jane Mecom, Apr. 27, 1769, and to Lord Le Despencer, July 26, 1770, in *Franklin Papers* 5:453, 7:14, 8:402, 16:120–21, 17:200–201.

[14] See Franklin, preface to James Logan's *Cato Major*, Feb. 29, 1744, Franklin to Strahan, July 4, 1744, to Sir Alexander Dick, Jan. 3, 1760, ibid., 2:405, 411, 9:3. For a general discussion of the cultural dependence of the British-American elite upon Britain, see Jack P. Greene, "Search for Identity: An Interpretation of the Meaning of Selected Patterns of Social Response in Eighteenth-Century America," *Journal of Social History* 3 (1970): 189–220.

There, he found both "an opportunity of displaying his talents among virtuosi of various kingdoms and nations" and "Friendship, and Friends whose Conversation" was "agreeable and . . . improving." There, "the most famous universities" and learned societies celebrated his scientific accomplishments. He received honorary doctorates from St. Andrews in 1759 and Oxford in 1762.[15]

Indeed, for a man of ravenous appetite for public recognition, Franklin's situation in Britain could scarcely have been more agreeable. As he wrote his son William in the summer of 1772, he had in Britain

> a general respect paid me by the learned, a number of friends and acquaintance among them, with whom I have a pleasing intercourse; a character of so much weight, that it has protected me when some in power would have done me injury . . . ; my company so much desired, that I seldom dine at home in winter, and could spend the whole summer in the country-houses of inviting friends, if I chose it. Learned and ingenious foreigners, that come to England, almost all make a point of visiting me; for my reputation is still higher abroad than here. Several foreign ambassadors have assiduously cultivated my acquaintance, treating me as one of their *corps,* partly I believe . . . that they may have an opportunity of introducing me to the gentlemen of their country who desire it.[16]

So attached was Franklin to the active life in the metropolis that it was difficult for him to leave it, and, when he did so for two years in the early 1760s, he thirsted for news from London and yearned to return. So strong was his "*Inclination*" for the British "Side of the Water" that he had decided, he wrote Strahan in 1762, "to settle all my Affairs [in America] in such a Manner, as that I *may* then conveniently remove to England, provided we can persuade the good Woman [his wife Deborah] to cross the Seas." His intention was to settle in Britain "for ever."[17]

If the gratifying attentions he received in Britain strongly reinforced Franklin's firm attachment to Britain, that attachment was also, to an important extent, a function of the general and, increasingly through

---

[15] James Hamilton to Jared Ingersoll, July 8, 1762, Franklin to David Hume, May 19, 1762, in *Franklin Papers* 10:84, 113.

[16] Franklin to William Franklin, Aug. 19, 1772, in *Franklin Writings* 5:414.

[17] Franklin to Strahan, Aug. 23, Dec. 7, 1762, June 28, Dec. 19, 1763, in *Franklin Papers* 10:149, 166, 304, 406–7.

the 1740s and 1750s, prevailing colonial belief in the essential justice and
equity of the British political system and in its basic goodwill toward the
colonies. Distance tended to filter out or to dim most negative aspects
of the system. Franklin's characterization of the Americans' attitudes
toward the British literary world could have been applied with almost
equal force to their assessment of the political. The works of British authors, said Franklin in 1745, were read in the colonies "with perfect Impartiality, being at too great a Distance to be bypassed by the Fashions,
Parties and Prejudices that prevail among you. We know nothing of
their personal Failings; the Blemishes in their character never reach us,
and therefore the bright but amiable part strikes us with its full Force.
They have never offended us or any of our Friends, and we have no Com-
petitions with them, and therefore praise and admire them without Restraint."[18]

Franklin often wrote about the sources of the colonial attachment to
Britain. The almost universal "respect for the mother country, and admiration of every thing that is British" on the part of the colonists, Franklin wrote in the *London Chronicle* in 1759, was "a natural effect" not only
"of their constant intercourse with England, by ships arriving almost
every week from the capital," but also, and more importantly, of an ingrained loyalty to a country that, for the vast majority of settlers of
European descent, was their country of origin and that, for all free
whites, permitted far more liberty than was enjoyed by the colonists of
any European power.[19]

"Delegates of [British] Power" in the colonies might indeed lose the
respect of—and "give Jealousy to"—the colonists, either by their corrupt
behavior or by "continually abusing and calumniating the People." But
such actions did not diminish colonial faith in metropolitan institutions.
"Confidence in the Crown" remained, Franklin believed, "as great as
ever," and colonists, no less than residents of the home islands, held Parliament in the highest esteem as the ultimate protector of British liberty—in the colonies as much as in Britain. There was "no Doubt,"
Franklin wrote in 1756, "but the Parliament understand the Rights of
Government." Ministers might, through either ignorance or malice, take
up oppressive measures against the colonists. Thus, in 1749, "the ministry proposed to make the king's instructions laws in the colonies, but
the clause was thrown out by the Commons, for which," Franklin later
recalled, "we adored them as our friends and friends of liberty." So much

[18] Franklin to Strahan, Feb. 12, 1745, ibid., 3:13.
[19] Franklin to Strahan, Dec. 19, 1763, ibid., 8:343.

regard did the Parliament seem to have for liberty that, said Franklin, the colonists had "an implicit Confidence" in its "Wisdom" that caused them to take it "for granted, that no Regulation was likely ever to be made by it, which should materially injure them." Because the colonists could never be deprived of their ancient rights and privileges except by "act of Parliament," Franklin believed, they could therefore rest relatively secure, as he put it in April 1764, in the expectation that "the united Justice of King, Lords, and Commons" would prevent passage of any such act while the colonists continued "loyal and dutiful Subjects."[20]

Yet neither Franklin's implicit confidence in the collective wisdom of British political institutions nor his enthusiasm for life in London blinded him to metropolitan faults. He had, indeed, long been critical of some aspects of metropolitan colonial policy. The deliberate and systematic transportation of convicted felons to the colonies, Franklin complained bitterly in 1751 and repeatedly thereafter, was a cruel and contemptuous insult that could scarcely "be equal'd by emptying their jakes on our tables." "We call Britain the *mother* country; and what *good* mother . . . would introduce thieves and criminals into the company of her children, to corrupt and disgrace them?" Firsthand observation beginning in 1757 provided Franklin with some explanation for why the metropolitan government could persist in such a "cruel" policy. The British nation, he wrote his young protégé Joseph Galloway in early 1758, seemed to be almost "universally corrupt and rotten from Head to Foot."[21]

But it was not primarily corruption that so frequently prevented the metropolitan government from doing what was "right and reasonable" toward the colonies. Franklin was appalled to find, as his son remarked, "little Knowledge of (or indeed Inclination to know) American Affairs" and strong "Prejudices against the Colonies in general." Moreover, many people in power seemed to entertain deep "suspicions and jealousies" of the colonies, suspicions and jealousies nourished by the conviction that the colonies were "not sufficiently obedient" and manifest in fears that they might begin to "feel their own strength" and either enter into com-

[20] Pennsylvania Assembly to Governor, Sept. 12, 1755; Franklin, "A Dialogue between X, Y, and Z," 1756, Franklin to *London Chronicle*, May 9, 1756, "A Letter to a Friend in the Country," Apr. 12, 1764, ibid., 6:203, 300, 10:406–7, 11:157–73; *Autobiography*, 149; Franklin, "The Colonist's Advocate," no. 3, Jan. 11, 1770, in *Franklin's Letters to the Press*, 176.

[21] See Franklin to *Pennsylvania Gazette*, Apr. 11, May 9, 1751, to Galloway, Feb. 18, 1758, to *London Chronicle*, May 9, 1759, in *Franklin Papers* 4:130–33, 7:375, 8:351.

petition with the metropolis or throw off their political dependence and divert their lucrative trade to one of Britain's European rivals.[22]

The results were both a widespread feeling within the British political nation that the growth of the colonies should be stunted, lest "the children might in time be as tall as their mother," and strong sentiments for reducing "the People's Privileges" in the colonies. "The Prevailing Opinion, as far as I am able to collect it, among the ministers and great Men here," Franklin wrote the Pennsylvania political leader Isaac Norris in March 1759, after he had been in Britain for almost twenty months, "is, that the Colonies have too many and too great Privileges; and that it is not only the Interest of the Crown but of the Nation to reduce them" and in particular to clip "the wings of [the colonial] Assemblies in their Claims of all the Privileges of a House of Commons." Only the fear that "Parliament would establish more Liberty in the colonies than is proper or necessary," Franklin was told by a friend in government, prevented the ministry from trying to enlist it in this scheme. Although Franklin found it "some Comfort" that the ministry was "doubtful of Parliament," he also understood perfectly well "that if the Ministry make a Point of carrying *any thing* in Parliament, they can carry it." Within a year after his arrival in England in 1757, he had become convinced that the colonies would not be entirely invulnerable to a "general Attack" upon them by the metropolitan government until their constitutions had been "settled firmly on the Foundations of Equity and English Liberty."[23]

Virtually from the beginning of his first mission to London, his own suspicions and fears concerning metropolitan intentions toward the colonies tempered Franklin's deep veneration for Britain; from a much earlier period, a proud sense of the past achievements and future promise of the American colonies counterbalanced that veneration. Colonial rusticity and cultural underdevelopment notwithstanding, the relative equality of free white society, the independent circumstances of most free men, and the widespread "Possession & Enjoyment of the various Comforts of Life" in the colonies were, for Franklin, vastly preferable to the extremes of "Magnificence" and "Wretchedness" he encountered in the Old World. During his agency for the Pennsylvania assembly in the

---

[22] See Franklin to Galloway, Jan. 9, 1760, to Isaac Norris, Mar. 19, 1759, and William Franklin to Elizabeth Graeme, Dec. 9, 1757, ibid., 7:290, 8:295, 9:17; *Autobiography*, 120.

[23] See Franklin to Galloway, June 10, 1758, to Isaac Norris, Mar. 19, 1759, to *London Chronicle*, Dec. 27, 1759, in *Franklin Papers* 8:96, 293–96, 450.

late 1750s, he assumed the mantle he would wear in Britain for much of the next eighteen years as primary spokesman in Britain for all of the colonies. In pamphlets, letters to newspapers, letters to friends and acquaintances, and conferences with influential political figures, he carried on a broad and intensive campaign of education on behalf of the colonists, the main objectives of which were to correct misconceptions about them, counteract prejudice against them, allay "visionary" fears of colonial independence, and persuade the British political nation not only that the colonies were of profound economic importance to Britain but also "that Dominion" was "founded in Opinion, and that if you would preserve your Authority among us, you must preserve the Opinion we . . . have of your Justice."[24]

As was revealed in 1751 by his brilliantly original *Observations concerning the Increase of Mankind,* perhaps no one on either side of the Atlantic appreciated earlier or more fully the significance of the remarkable and hitherto unparalleled demographic growth of the colonies. "I have long been of Opinion," he wrote Lord Kames in January 1760, "that the Foundations of the future Grandeur and Stability of the British Empire, lie in America; and tho', like other Foundations, they are now low and little seen, they are nevertheless, broad and strong enough to support the greatest Political Structure Human Wisdom ever yet erected." The recent expulsion of the French from Canada during the Seven Years' War, he predicted, would mean that "all the Country from St. Laurence to Missisipi, will in another Century be fill'd with British people; Britain itself will become vastly more populous by the immense Increase of its Commerce; the Atlantic Sea will be cover'd with your Trading Ships; and your naval Power thence continually increasing, will extend your Influence round the whole Globe, and awe the World!" So much prominence did Franklin accord the colonies in this scene of future British grandeur that he laid himself open to the ridicule of Josiah Tucker, who later charged that "his constant plan" had been "to remove the seat of government [of the British Empire] to America." Few people in America, much less in Britain, appreciated the prescience of Franklin's vision of America's future.[25]

---

[24] See Franklin, "Observations," 1751, Franklin, *The Interest of Great Britain Considered,* 1760, Franklin to *London Chronicle,* May 9, 1759, to Richard Jackson, Mar. 14, 1764, ibid., 4:227–34, 8:341–42, 9:74–97, 107; Franklin to Joshua Babcock, Jan. 13, 1772, in *Franklin Writings* 5:361–63.

[25] See Franklin, "Observations," 1751, Franklin to Kames, Jan. 3, 1760, to William Franklin, Nov. 25, 1767, in *Franklin Papers* 4:227–34, 9:6–7, 14:325.

As much as he savored the stimulation and adulation he found in Britain, Franklin was in fact never thoroughly comfortable there and often longed for home. At times, he felt in Britain "like a thing out of its place, and useless because it is out of its place." The pace of life and the frustrations of trying to deal with the metropolitan bureaucracy were exhausting, and he grew "weary of Business," "anxiously" desired "once more the happy Society of Friends and Family in Philadelphia," and "languish[ed] after Repose and my America." He was "too old to think of changing Countries." When, after five years in Britain, he finally did return to Pennsylvania in 1762, he took enormous delight in "the kind Reception," "hearty Welcome, and" great "Cordiality" he "met with from my old and many new Friends." But just as his vision of America's future glory was a vision of British greatness, so his memories of that "happy Island and my Friends in it" ensured that he would thenceforth keep one ear cocked toward Britain. During his five years there between 1757 and 1762, he had become in the fullest sense of the term a British American, almost as much British, perhaps, as American.[26]

Throughout the early and mid-1760s, Franklin's mood about the future of the British Empire was buoyant. Though he fretted in Philadelphia about the factional strife and "civil Dissensions" of the first years of the reign of George III, he was "not much alarm'd" by either the new restrictions on colonial trade in 1763–64 or George Grenville's proposals for parliamentary taxation of the colonies. Self-interest, he confidently believed, provided the colonies with sufficient security against persecution by the metropolitan government. "We are in your Hands as Clay in the Hands of the Potter," he wrote Peter Collinson in April 1764, "and so in one more Particular than is generally consider'd: for as the Potter cannot waste or spoil his Clay without injuring himself; so I think there is scarce anything you can do that may be hurtful to us, but what will be as much or more so to you."[27]

Franklin was much more inclined to stress "the Greatness and Stability of . . . Empire" to be expected from the mild reign of "our virtuous

---

[26] Franklin to Galloway, Apr. 7, 1759, Jan. 9, 1760, to Kames, Aug. 17, 1762, to Strahan, July 20, Dec. 7, 1762, May 1, 1764, ibid., 8:310, 9:15–17, 10:133, 147, 166, 11:189.

[27] Franklin to Jackson, Jan. 16, June 25, 1764, to John Fothergill, Mar. 14, 1764, and to Collinson, Apr. 30, 1764, ibid., 11:19–20, 101–5, 183–84, 234–39.

young King" and the "broad and strong Foundation" for "the most beneficial and certain Commerce" provided by the "truly glorious" peace of
1763. "The Glory of Britain" had never been "higher than at present."
Britons could now be "as happy as their moderate Share of Virtue will
allow them to be," and, Franklin declared in a fit of patriotic exuberance,
"as to their Quantity of Virtue, I think it bids fair for Increasing."[28]

Thus, once he had concluded in early 1764 that the "Breach . . . between the Proprietaries and the Province [was] irreconcilable" and that it
was "impossible [for Pennsylvania] to go on longer with the Proprietary
Government," he did not hesitate to support an application to the metropolitan government to convert Pennsylvania into a royal colony. Refus-
ing to credit rumors that some crown officials had indicated that they
would welcome such a petition so that they might use the opportunity
to abridge the colony's generous privileges of self-government, Franklin
argued that only the crown could provide Pennsylvanians with "a Government . . . that we can respect." So destructive of "Peace and Order"
were the "continual Jarrs" and perpetual "Obstructions to all necessary
Business" that had for over a decade been the result of an "ill-will" between proprietors and people that was "as fix'd as it is mutual" that,
Franklin was persuaded, Pennsylvania would "soon have no Government
at all" unless the crown took "the Government into its own Hands."[29]

While Franklin was masterminding the campaign for royal government in Pennsylvania through the spring and summer of 1764, the British ministry was committing itself to an American policy that would produce the first general rupture ever in Anglo-American politics and raise
serious doubts in Franklin about in the beneficence of the metropolitan
government toward the colonies. By the time Franklin arrived in Britain
in December to present the Pennsylvania petition for royal government,
George Grenville's proposed Stamp Act had already been "fram'd at the
Treasury" and was ready for consideration by Parliament. Franklin, as
he later wrote his Pennsylvania associate Charles Thomson, opposed the
act "sincerely and Heartily" and "took every Step in my Power, to prevent" its passing. But, he reported, he might just "as well [have] hinder'd
the Suns setting." The "Tide was . . . too strong," "Provok'd by Ameri-

---

[28] See Franklin to John Whitehurst, June 27, 1763, to Strahan, Dec. 19, 1763, ibid.,
10:302–3, 406–7.

[29] Franklin to Fothergill, Mar. 14, 1764, to Jackson, Mar. 31, June 25, Sept. 1, 1764,
Franklin, "Preface to Joseph Galloway's Speech," 1764, ibid., 11:101–5, 150–51, 234–39,
294, 326–29.

can Claims of Independence, . . . all Parties join'd in resolving by this Act to Settle the Point."[30]

So respectful was he of the authority of Parliament that, once the act had passed, he seems to have expected that the Americans would accept it, albeit with much groaning and complaining, and he in fact counseled acquiescence to his American correspondents and even recommended his friend John Hughes to be stamp master in Philadelphia. By these actions, which later seemed to lend credibility to charges circulating in the colonies that he had been instrumental in passing the Stamp Act, "his Credit suffered" enormously in the colonies. By the fall of 1765 massive colonial resistance had made clear the extent of his miscalculation, and he "was in great Anxiety" for the future of the empire. Although he abhorred the violence of the colonial Sons of Liberty, he was even more offended by the uninformed and unreasoning response of the British political nation to the American objections to the Stamp Act, and he quickly "retrieved his Char[acter]" in America by spearheading a vigorous movement for repeal through the fall and winter of 1765–66.[31]

Franklin now resumed in earnest the campaign he had inaugurated five years earlier to educate the British political nation about the colonies; in the process, he revealed himself to be a far more militant apologist for the colonies than his recent behavior might have suggested. Through conversations with political figures and a plethora of anonymous essays in the newspapers, he sought to combat the torrents of anti-American abuse that filled the pages of the London press. Specifically, he pointed out that "excepting the yet infant colonies of Georgia and Nova Scotia, *none of them* were settled at the expence of *any money* granted by parliament"; that the Seven Years' War had been "begun, *not* for 'the immediate protection' of the Americans, but for the protection of the *British trade*, carried on with *British manufactures* among the Indians in America"; that the colonists had contributed money and men in that war "*far beyond* their *proportion*," incurring in the bargain "a Load of Debt" and "heavy Taxes" that they would not escape for years; that they were not ungrateful to the parent state; and that they "had not the least desire of independence." In fact, Franklin argued, they had invariably been "thankful for the favours they have received" from home and

---

[30] See Franklin to Thomson, July 11, 1765, to Hughes, Aug. 9, 1765, to David Hall, Sept. 14, 1765, to Jane Mecom, Mar. 1, 1766, Hall to Franklin, Sept. 6, 1765, ibid., 12:207–8, 234–35, 259, 267, 13:187–88.

[31] Ezra Stiles, "Memoir and Conjecture," May 1, 1769, ibid., 16:122–25.

had "always had a great respect for the Parliament." Far from being examples of a rebellious spirit, colonial protests against the Stamp Act,
Franklin declared, merely revealed that Americans had the same "strong
sense of liberty" and the same "determination to risque every thing
rather than submit voluntarily to what they deem[ed] an unconstitutional act" that were the distinguishing characteristics of Britons everywhere.[32]

In this campaign against the Stamp Act, Franklin hammered hard at
a fundamental point that would totally escape all but a few members of
the British political nation both at the time of the Stamp Act crisis and
later. "No people under easy circumstances ever desire a change of Government," said Franklin, paraphrasing John Locke. "It is not a thing
ever wantonly undertaken; and even if some ambitious men, from selfish
views should desire it; unless there be some great grievance, they can
have no handle to make use of for the purpose; so nothing but some
violent measure here, such as the abolition of their assemblies, will produce any such defection."[33]

Given the determined opposition of the colonists to the Stamp Act,
the government had three alternative courses of action open to it: formal
union, force, or conciliation. Of the three, Franklin preferred union. "If
you chuse to tax us," he had written Richard Jackson as early as May
1764, "give us Members in your Legislature, and let us be one People."
But this "People," he later lamented, referring to the British, "is too
proud, and too much despises the Americans, to bear the Thought of
admitting them to such an equitable Participation in the Government of
the whole." To execute the act by force, a policy widely advocated in the
press, would be total "Madness" and bring nothing but "Ruin to the
whole." "Military arguments, used in a political controversy," Franklin
warned, "though they may *silence,* are extremely improper to *convince.*"
Moreover, "by totally alienating the Affections of the Americans from
this Country," such severe measures would inevitably set off a chain of
"mutual Violences, Excesses and Severities" that would produce "a total
separation of affections, interest, political obligations, and all manner of

---

[32] Franklin to *Gazeteer and New Daily Advertiser,* May 2, 1765, to Pacificus, Jan. 2, 1766,
ibid., 12:120, 13:4–6; Charles Thomson to Franklin, Sept. 24, 1765; Franklin to Tom
Hint, Dec. 19, 27, 1765; to Vindex Patriae, Dec. 28, 1765, Franklin, "On the Tenure of
the Manor of East Greenwich," Jan. 11, 1766, in *Franklin's Letters to the Press,* 37–41,
43–44, 48.

[33] Franklin to *Lloyd's Evening Post,* Sept. 5, 1765, in *Franklin Papers* 12:120, 253–55.

connections[,] . . . by which the whole state" would be "weakened, and perhaps ruined for ever!"[34]

Obviously, the "best thing" in this situation was conciliation, and Franklin urged that the Stamp Act be repealed and the colonies left "in the quiet Enjoyment of their separate Constitutions," with money for imperial purposes to be raised through "the Long establish'd Custom" of "Requisatorial Letters from the Crown." Such a course, Franklin predicted, would fill the colonists "with Joy and Gratitude, reestablish their respect and Veneration for Parliament, [and] restore at once their ancient and natural love for this Country, and their regard for every thing that comes from it." A general redress of grievances intended to guarantee the colonists "an *equal* dispensation of protection, rights, privileges, and advantages" might then be undertaken. Such "an Instance of the Considerateness, Moderation, and Justice of this Country towards its remote Subjects," Franklin asserted, "would contribute more towards securing and perpetuating the Dominion, than all its Force, and be much cheaper."[35]

When the Rockingham administration, at the urging of British merchants who were suffering from colonial economic boycotts of British goods and partly on the basis of Franklin's public testimony in Parliament, did repeal the Stamp Act in early 1766 and seemed bent upon making even further concessions toward the colonies, Franklin was jubilant. His faith in the basic goodwill of Britain toward the colonies seemed to have been vindicated. "We now see," he wrote his younger colleague David Hall in Philadelphia, "that tho' the Parliament may sometimes possibly thro' Misinformation be misled to do a wrong Thing towards America, yet as soon as they are rightly inform'd, they will immediately rectify it, which ought to confirm our Veneration for that most august Body, and Confidence in its Justice and Equity." The Declaratory Act, which accompanied repeal and asserted Parliament's jurisdiction over the colonies in all cases whatsoever, was, he assured his American correspondents, "Merely to save Appearances, and to guard against the Effects of the Clamour made by the late Ministry [of George Grenville] as if the Rights of this Nation were sacrificed to America: And I think

---

[34] Franklin to Jackson, May 1, 1764, to William Franklin, Nov. 9, 1765, to _____, Jan. 6, 1766, and Franklin, "The Moral," Jan. 1766, ibid., 11:185–88, 12:361–65, 13:23–26, 71; Franklin to Tom Hint, Dec. 27, 1765, in *Franklin's Letters to the Press*, 41.

[35] Franklin to William Franklin, Nov. 9, 1765, to _____, Jan. 6, 1766, and Franklin, "The Moral," Jan. 1766, in *Franklin Papers* 12:361–65, 13:23–26, 71.

we may rest secure notwithstanding such Act, that no future Ministry will ever attempt to tax us, any more than they venture to tax Ireland." The colonies and Britain could thenceforth march arm in arm under the guidance of a benign Parliament into a future of unparalleled British greatness, the colonists secure in the knowledge that their liberties and property were wholly safe.[36]

That Franklin's assessment of the situation was infinitely too sanguine quickly became apparent. Within a year after the repeal of the Stamp Act, further challenges of parliamentary measures by the colonial assembly of New York had produced fresh demands for the exertion of parliamentary authority over the colonies. In the spring of 1767 the Townshend Acts levied new taxes upon the colonies and threatened the New York legislature with suspension if it failed to comply with parliamentary regulations concerning the quartering of metropolitan troops in the colony. These measures provoked another major crisis in imperial affairs, a deadlock that, despite the efforts of Franklin and others, persisted for three years. Again, Franklin, believing "that one man of tolerable abilities may work great changes, and accomplish great affairs among mankind" by diligent application, played an active and conspicuous role in trying to effect a reconciliation. Ever the negotiator, Franklin thought of himself, as he wrote of his fellow American Barlow Trecothick, as a man "well acquainted with the interests of both countries, a moderate prudent man, and so a fit instrument to conciliate jarring interests, and restore harmony" between Britain and the colonies, a person fit "to be consulted upon the great Objects . . . and . . . Grounds of Dispute."[37]

Again, Franklin cast himself in the part of the explicator and defender of the colonies, elaborating upon themes employed and positions taken during the Stamp Act crisis and earlier. He appealed to metropolitan self-interest by repeatedly emphasizing the importance of the colonies to the British economy and its consequent dependence upon the colonies, dilating upon the depth of the colonists' "Affection and Respect" for

---

[36] Franklin to Hall, Feb. 24, 1766, to Joseph Fox, Mar. 1, 1766, ibid., 13:170, 186–87.

[37] *Autobiography*, 86; Franklin, "On Candidacy of Trecothick," Mar. 8, 1768, in *Franklin's Letters to the Press*, 113; Extract of Letter from London, June 5, 1771, in *Franklin Papers* 18:119.

Britain and the degree to which those feelings were rooted in "opinion" rather than force, and stressing the danger that harsh measures would "alienate" the colonists' "Affections." His constant object, as in the earlier crisis, was "the restoration of harmony."[38]

To that end, he was, characteristically, the consistent exponent of moderation, prudence, and restraint on the part of the colonists as well as the British. To his American correspondents, he put the best gloss possible on British behavior and urged a concerted effort "to lessen the present Unpopularity of the American Cause; conciliate the Affections of the People here towards us; increase by all possible Means the Number of our Friends, and be careful not to weaken their Hands and strengthen those of our Enemies, by rash Proceedings on our side, the Mischiefs of which are inconceivable." "Every offensive thing done in America," he lamented, "is charged upon all, and every province though unconcerned in it, suffers in its interests through the general disgust and the little distinction here made." Thus, he strongly disapproved of the adulation "indiscreetly" accorded to John Wilkes in the colonies and vigorously endorsed nonimportation, a peaceful device which, by creating economic difficulties for British merchants, could be expected ultimately to pressure them into throwing their weight behind the movement to repeal the Townshend taxes.[39]

Franklin's strategy for saving the empire was merely an adaptation of his ancient strategy for public life. It was the strategy of the Trimmer: accommodation, restraint, goodwill, avoidance of basic issues that would invariably be divisive, and a clear sense of priorities that placed immediate tangible benefits far ahead of distant anticipated evils. After 1766, Franklin himself had moved rapidly and well ahead of most colonials to the radical position that the colonies were really distinct states, each state with its own parliament and united to Britain only through the crown. But, given the universal commitment of the British political nation, including even the friends of the colonies, to the beliefs in the indivisibility of sovereignty and the omnipotence of Parliament throughout the crown's dominions, he thought it best that "a public Discussion

---

[38] Franklin, "On Candidacy of Trecothick," Mar. 8, 1768, Franklin, "Answers to Late Queries on the Colonies," Sept. 24, 1768, Franklin, "The Colonist's Advocate," nos. 4, 7, 10, Jan. 15, Feb. 1, 19, 1770, in *Franklin's Letters to the Press*, 115–16, 130, 177–79, 193, 204–5; Franklin, Preface to "Votes and Proceedings," 1773, Franklin to William Franklin, Nov. 3, 1773, in *Franklin Writings* 5:452–53, 6:152–53.

[39] Franklin to Galloway, Aug. 6, 1767, to William Franklin, Nov. 25, 1767, Oct. 5, 1768, to Thomas Wharton, Feb. 20, 1768, to Samuel Cooper, Feb. 24, Sept. 30, 1768, to Timo-

of [such] Questions" should be avoided because it was bound to throw "all into Confusion." Had Parliament not attempted to tax the colonies, he was persuaded, the colonists would never have begun "seriously [either] to consider their situation, and to resolve afresh in their minds grievances which from their respect and love for this country, they had long borne and seemed almost willing to forget" or to deny Parliament's authority over them. Franklin's "real Idea," said one critic in 1769, had always been the same from his first entry into Pennsylvania politics through the latest crisis: a "coalition of parties" for the purpose, the critic cynically added, of "gaining honour from all."[40]

But Franklin was not merely trying to gratify his prodigious passion for fame and recognition by his feverish activity during the crisis over the Townshend Acts: he was desperately attempting to find some way to save the British Empire from self-destruction, to contrive some instrument that would "destroy those seeds of disunion" so that "both countries might thence much longer continue to grow great together, more secure by their united strength, and more formidable to their common enemies." "I have lived so great a Part of my Life in Britain, and have formed so many Friendships in it, that I love it and wish its Prosperity," he wrote Lord Kames in February 1767, "and therefore wish to see that Union on which alone I think it can be secur'd and establish'd." Indeed, he never completely ceased toying with the idea of contriving "a consolidating Union of the whole," one based on "a clear, intelligible constitution" that would prevent subsequent misunderstandings by specifying "what we are henceforth to do and expect for and from each other." But there were so many forces working against the devising, much less the acceptance, of such a plan that he ultimately concluded that the old "Mode of letting" the colonists "govern themselves by their own Assemblies [was] much preferable. They will always be better governed; and the Parliament has Business enough here with its own internal Concerns." Thus, when "a noble Lord" asked him if he did not have a plan of conciliation in 1769, he replied succinctly: "*Repeal* the Laws, *Renounce* the Right, *Recall* the Troops, *Refund* the Money, and *Return to the old Method of Requisition.*" And he was even willing to forgo Parliament's "renouncing the Right," provided no attempt was ever made to exercise

---

thy Folger, Sept. 29, 1769, to Charles Thomson, Mar. 18, 1770, in *Franklin Papers* 14:230, 326, 15:55–56, 224, 16:53, 208–11, 18:113.

[40] See Franklin to *London Chronicle*, Jan. 5–7, 1768, to *Public Advertiser*, Oct. 21, 1768, and Stiles, "Memoir and Conjecture," May 1, 1769, ibid., 15:9–10, 241, 16:123.

it and the colonists could regard it "in the same Light with the Claim of the Spanish Monarch to the Title of King of Jerusalem."[41]

What Franklin was working to forestall, but what seemed in the late 1760s to be rapidly approaching, if indeed it had not already arrived, was a situation in which repeated "Imprudencies on both Sides" would "Step by Step . . . bring on the most mischievous Consequences." In his analysis of the situation, Franklin revealed great insight into the psychology of contention. When "a Quarrel is once on foot," he wrote Galloway in March 1770, "even those who are at first *least in the wrong*, are often provok'd to do something that makes them *most so;* and the mutual Injuries are apt to increase Animosity till the worst of Remedies become[s] the only one, the Sword." Once such a process was under way, moreover, it was difficult to interrupt it. Thus, a failure to redress the grievances of the colonists further inflamed them and produced "further rash Measures there" that created "more Resentments" in Britain and evoked even harsher responses from the ministry. To "justify the Measures of Government," "Ministerial Writers" would then further "revile the Americans . . . as Miscreants, Rogues, Dastards, Rebels, &c. which" tended further "to alienate the Minds of the People here from them, and diminish their Affections to this Country." "Mutual Provocations," Franklin observed, "will thus go on to complete the Separation; and instead of that cordial Affection that once so long subsisted, and that Harmony so suitable to the Circumstances, and so Necessary to the Happiness, Strength, Safety and Welfare of both Countries; an implacable Malice and Mutual Hatred, (such as we now see subsisting between the Spaniards and Portuguese, the Genoese and Corsicans, from the same Original Misconduct in the Superior Government) will take place."[42]

That the primary responsibility for the controversy did indeed lie in an "Original Misconduct in the Superior Government," Franklin never had the slightest doubt. "There was no Posture of Hostility in America," he fumed at a suggestion in an anonymous pamphlet that the causes of the dispute were rooted "in a posture of hostility against Great Britain"

---

[41] See Franklin to Kames, Feb. 25, 1767, to Galloway, Apr. 14, 1767, Jan. 9, 1767, Jan. 11, 1770, to Massachusetts House of Representatives Committee of Correspondence, May 15, 1771, Franklin, marginalia in *An Inquiry. . .* (London, 1770), ibid., 14:69, 125, 16:17–18, 17:24, 322–23, 18:104; Franklin, "On Partial Repeal," in *Franklin's Letters to the Press,* 199.

[42] Franklin to Galloway, June 13, 1767, Mar. 21, 1770, to Strahan, Nov. 29, 1769, in *Franklin Papers* 14:184, 16:248–49, 17:119.

on the part of the colonists. Rather, said Franklin, "Britain put herself in a Posture of Hostility against America." The folly of such behavior seemed obvious. The "Seeds of Liberty," he kept trying to explain to the British political nation, were so "universally sown" in the colonies that "nothing can eradicate them. And yet there remains among that People so much Respect, Veneration and Affection for Britain, that, if cultivated prudently, with kind Usage and Tenderness for their Privileges, they might be easily govern'd still for Ages, without Force or any considerable Expence." All harsh measures had to be avoided. For the metropolis to send troops to protect the customs officers in Boston, as they did in 1768, was obviously like "setting up a smith's forge in a magazine of gunpowder." "I do not pretend the gift of prophecy," wrote Franklin, but "History shows, that, by" such "steps great empires have crumbled heretofore." "Government is not established merely by *Power,*" he often asserted; "there must be maintain'd a general Opinion of its *Wisdom* and *Justice,* to make it firm and durable." "The true Art of governing the colonies lies in a Nut-Shell," he said tersely. "It is only letting them alone."[43]

Why the metropolitan government should have embarked upon such a disastrous and, to Franklin, patently irrational course of behavior in the first place and should have persisted in it long after its ill effects had become obvious was a question that obsessed Franklin. Unlike some of his more nervous countrymen, in Britain as well as in the colonies, Franklin did not find the explanation in a malign conspiracy of power-hungry ministers to subvert British liberty by beginning first with that of the colonies. But he did trace at least some of the colonists' difficulties to the corruption of British public life. Some objectionable measures seemed to be directly attributable to ministerial designs calculated "not for the good of Great Britain or her colonies, but for an American establishment, whereby" the ministers could create "a few Places for our needy Court-Danglers." "The Irish establishment," Franklin wrote acidly, "has been much talked of as a sinecure for friends and favourites, and cast-off mistresses; but this American establishment promises a more ample provision for such-like purposes."[44]

---

[43] Franklin to Kames, Feb. 25, 1767, to Galloway, Jan. 9, 1769, to George Whitefield, Sept. 2, 1769, and to Massachusetts House of Representatives Committee of Correspondence, May 15, 1771, Franklin, marginalia in *Good Humour* (London, 1766), ibid., 14:70, 16:12, 192, 283, 18:102–04; Franklin, "Colonist's Advocate," no. 8, Feb. 5, 1770, in *Franklin's Letters to the Press,* 197.

[44] Franklin, "Sinecures for Friends and Favourites," Sept. 28, 1768, Franklin, "The Colonist's Advocate," nos. 4, 11, Jan. 15, Mar. 2, 1770, in *Franklin's Letters to the Press,* 133–34, 177–79, 208–9.

Not only the ministry was animated by such mercenary designs, however. Parliament itself, Franklin had decided by the late 1760s, had become thoroughly corrupt. "Luxury," he wrote Thomas Cushing, speaker of the Massachusetts House of Representatives, "introduces necessity even among those that make the most splendid Figures here; this brings most of the Commons as well as Lords to Market; and if America would save for 3 or 4 Years the money she spends in [the] Fashions and Fineries & Fopperies of this Country she might buy the whole Parliament, Minister and all." At elections, he complained to his son in 1768, the "whole venal nation" put itself on the block, would "be sold for about Two Millions; and might be bought out of the hands of the present bidders (if he would offer half a million more) by the very devil himself." "The general Corruption and Servility of Parliament is now so generally seen and known to all the Nation, that it is no longer respected as it used to be." Franklin reported to Galloway in 1771: "Its Censures are no more regarded than Pope's Bulls. It is despis'd for its Injustice. And yet it is not clear that the People deserve a better Parliament, since they are themselves full as corrupt and venal; witness the Sums they accept for their Votes at almost every Election." So dependent was Parliament upon the ministry that he began "to think a Parliament here of little Use to the People."[45]

The ministry's desire to create an American establishment could account for some unwise measures and Parliament's base dependence for its servile adherence to the dictates of the ministry, but such dramatic evidences of corruption were not the most important components of Franklin's explanation for metropolitan behavior. The absence of effective channels for communicating American sentiments to British political leaders, the "perpetual mutations" of British political life, "a want of attention to what passes in such remote Countries as America," a general want of "a sufficient Quantity of . . . Wisdom" within the British political nation, and what Franklin referred to as "the present very polite disorder of being short-sighted" were also significant. So also was the too general presence of "Toryism," of "Unjust and Tyrannical Notions of Colony Government," even among the friends of the colonies. Further, the "Malice against us in some powerful People," the supporters and spiritual adherents of those "unnatural and churlish-hearted Men . . . who, needlessly, wickedly, and madly sowed the first seeds of Discontent

---

[45] Franklin to William Franklin, Mar. 13, 1768, to Galloway, Mar. 13, 1768, Apr. 20, 1771, in *Franklin Papers* 15:77–79, 18:78, Franklin to Cushing, Oct. 10, 1774, to Galloway, Oct. 12, 1774, in *Franklin Writings* 6:251–54.

between Britain and her Colonies," also helped to "prevent those healing Measures that all good Men [should] wish to take place."[46]

But there were still other and much more important explanations for metropolitan behavior. These included especially what Franklin called "the Pride natural to so great a Nation, the Prejudices that have so universally prevail'd here with regard to the Point of [Britain's] Right[s over the colonies], and the Resentment at our disputing it." Britons had such "a pride, a haughtiness, and an insolent contempt for all but" themselves that such opposition from a group of whom they already had "the most unfavourable idea . . . as unworthy the name of Englishmen, and fit only to be snubb'd, curb'd shackled, and plundered," incurred only their "*implacable resentment*" and their fixed determination to put such upstarts in their proper place. Thus, the "National Honour" as well as the self-esteem of individual members of the political nation was seen to depend upon the exertion of the authority of Parliament over the colonies. Not to exert that authority would be to reveal that Britain was not "master of its Colonies," a revelation that could only bring self-loathing within the British political nation and contempt from "all the Nations round."[47]

By far the most important element in explaining metropolitan behavior, however, appeared to Franklin to be the widespread belief, arising out of the "groundless jealousy" that Americans wanted independence, that the metropolitan government had "an Interest in keeping us down and fleecing us." Thus, Britons, Franklin wrote in one of his satires, charged Americans with "*dreaming*" that they would so increase in "strength and prosperity . . . that the seat of government" would "be transported to America, and Britain dwindle to one of its provinces. And, because Joseph's brethren hated him for a dream he *really* dreamed," Britons, "for a dream you never *dreamed,* and which we only

---

[46] Franklin to Kames, Feb. 25, 1767, to Galloway, Aug. 8, 1767, July 2, 1768, June 11, 1770, Franklin, "On Civil War," Aug. 25, 1768, in *Franklin Papers* 14:64–70, 228–31, 15:164–65, 191–93, 17:168–71; Franklin to James Bowdoin, Jan. 13, 1772, to Noble Wymberly Jones, Apr. 2, 1772, to Mecom, July 7, 1773, in *Franklin Writings* 5:358–59, 390–91, 6:93; Franklin, "Sinecures," Sept. 28, 1768, "Colonist's Advocate," no. 8, Feb. 5, 1770, "An Observation concerning Corsica," July 3, 1770, "Reply to a Friend of Lord Hillsborough," Sept. 7, 1772, in *Franklin's Letters to the Press,* 134, 196–97, 213, 223–34.

[47] Franklin to Galloway, Jan. 9, 1769, to Noble Wymberly Jones, June 7, 1769, in *Franklin Papers* 16:10–11, 152; Franklin, "Defense of Indian Corn," Jan. 15, 1766, "Extract from a Pamphlet," Apr. 9, 1767, "Arguments Pro and Con," pt 2, Oct. 29, 1768, "On Humbling Our Rebellious Vassals," May 21, 1774, in *Franklin's Letters to the Press,* 51–52, 82–83, 141, 263.

dream you *dreamed*, are to hate you most cordially" and to gratify their hate by inequitable schemes of persecution, malice, and mistaken policy.[48]

Whatever the proper weight to be given to each of these manifold factors that combined to produce all the "Insults and Oppressions" to which the colonists were being subjected in the late 1760s, Franklin continued to hope that, as he wrote the Reverend Samuel Cooper of Boston in April 1769,

> nothing that has happened or may happen will diminish in the least our Loyalty to our Sovereign, or Affection for this Nation in general. I can scarcely conceive a King of better Dispositions, of more exemplary Virtues, or more truly desirous of promoting the Welfare of all his Subjects. The experience we have had of the Family in the two preceding Reigns, and the good Temper of our Princes so far as can yet be discovered, promise us a Continuance of this Felicity. The Body of the People too is of a noble and generous Nature, loving and honouring the Spirit of Liberty, and hating arbitrary Power of all Sorts.

With the king and the people thus so favorably disposed to what America stood for, surely Parliament could not persist much longer in oppressing the colonies. "I have indeed, no doubt," he wrote a French correspondent, "that the parliament . . . will finally abandon its present pretensions, and leave us to the peaceable enjoyment of our rights and privileges."[49]

The "favourable Sentiments towards us, which apparently begin to take place in the Minds of his Majesty and his Ministers" and a seemingly growing disposition on the part of "Government . . . to be . . . more moderate with regard to America" encouraged Franklin, as he assessed the situation in 1769, to believe that, if the colonists could "prudently, as you have lately done, continue q[uiet,] avoiding Tumults, but still resolutely keeping up your claims and asserting your Rights," they would "finally obtain all our important Points, and establish American Liberty on a clearer and firmer Foundation." Yet, throughout the crisis over the Townshend Acts, Franklin's optimism existed in a state of high tension with the fear that the British government would not change its

---

[48] Franklin to Samuel Cooper, June 8, 1770, in *Franklin Papers* 17:160–65; Franklin, "Right, Wrong, Reasonable," Apr. 18, 1767, in *Franklin's Letters to the Press*, 96–97.

[49] Franklin to Cooper, Apr. 27, 1769, to Jacques Barbeu-Dubourg, Oct. 2, 1770, in *Franklin Papers* 16:118–19, 17:234.

behavior, that through ignorance, contempt, suspicion, and pride, it would continue its "Posture of Hostility" toward the colonies and, as he had earlier written to his son during the Stamp Act crisis, "from Punctilios about Form" continue to "refuse hearing Complaints and Redressing Grievances" and thereby give "great Handle to those turbulent factious Spirits who are ever ready to blow the Coals of Dissension" in every society.[50]

Such pessimism was accompanied by a deepening alienation from Britain. Increasingly after 1767, Franklin seems to have become more and more critical not only of the metropolitan political system but also of the nation as a whole. He found the Wilkite demonstrations profoundly disturbing. They had turned London into a "daily Scene of lawless Riot and Confusion. Mobs are patrolling the Streets at Noon Day, some knocking all down that will not roar for Wilkes and Liberty: Courts of Justice afraid to give Judgment against him." But it was not only the Wilkites that were responsible for the chaos: "Coalheavers and Porters [were] pulling down the Houses of Coal Merchants that refuse to give them more Wages; Sawyers destroying the new Sawmills; Sailors unrigging all the outwardbound Ships, and suffering none to sail till Merchants agree to raise their Pay; Watermen destroying the private Boats and threat'ning Bridges; Weavers entring Houses by Force, and destroying the Work in the Looms; Soldiers firing among the Mobs and killing Men, Women and Children."[51]

Nothing angered Franklin more than condemnation of the Americans for their allegedly "riotous" opposition to British measures. "Do you Englishmen then pretend to censure the Colonies for Riots?" he wrote angrily in the margins of an English pamphlet in 1770. "Look at home!!! I have seen within a Year, Riots in the Country about Corn, Riots about Elections, Riots about Workhouses, Riots of Colliers, Riots of Weavers, Riots of Coalheavers, Riots of Sawyers, Riots of Sailors, Riots of Wilkites, Riots of Government Chairmen, Riots of Smugglers in which Customhouse Officers and Excisemen have been murdered, the King's armed Vessels and Troops fired at; &c &c." So common were riots in Britain, said Franklin, that "one would [almost] think" them "part of the Mode of Government." Thus were the British "ungratefully abusing the best

---

[50] Franklin to William Franklin, Nov. 9, 1765, to Cooper, Apr. 27, 1769, to Noble Wymberly Jones, June 7, 1769, to James Bowdoin, July 13, 1769, Franklin, marginalia in *Good Humour* (London, 1766), ibid., 12:364, 16:118–19, 151, 176, 283.

[51] Franklin to John Ross, May 14, 1768, ibid., 15:128–29.

Constitution and the best King any Nation was ever blest with, intent on nothing but Luxury, Licentiousness, Power, Places, Pensions, and Plunder." The picture was sufficiently bleak to evoke some obvious, if never fully articulated, ambivalence about the long-term desirability of the connection between Britain and the colonies but not so bleak as to destroy Franklin's continuing desire for a reconciliation. His mood during the late 1760s was poignantly illustrated in the first three verses of a song he composed, entitled *The Mother Country:*

> We have an old Mother that peevish is grown,
> She snubs us like Children that scarce walk alone;
> She forgets we're grown up and have Sense of our own;
>
> . . . . .
>
> If we don't obey Orders, whatever the case;
> She frowns, and she chides, and she loses all
> Patience, and sometimes she hits us a Slap in the Face.
>
> . . . . .
>
> Her Orders so odd are, we often suspect
> That Age has impaired her sound Intellect;
> But still an Old Mother should have due Respect.[52]

Franklin's continuing attachment to England meant that he would respond to Parliament's repeal of all the Townshend duties except a token tax on tea in the spring of 1770 with enormous optimism. The British government seemed at last to have acted decisively to break the vicious cycle of action and reaction that had plagued metropolitan-colonial relations for the past six years, and he rejoiced at the prospect of "a perfect happy Union between Great Britain and the colonies." There appeared, he reported to Galloway in June 1770, to be "a general Disposition in the Nation (a particular Faction excepted) to be upon good Terms with the Colonies, and to leave us in the Enjoyment of our Rights." Indeed, he wrote, a general act was "talk'd of, revising all the Acts for regulating Trade in America, wherein every thing that gives just Cause of Offence to the Colonists may be omitted, and the Tea [tax] with its odious Pre-

---

[52] Franklin to William Franklin, Apr. 16, 1768, to John Ross, May 14, 1768, Franklin, "The Mother Country," [1765–72], Franklin, marginalia in *An Inquiry* . . . (London, 1770), ibid., 12:431–32, 15:98–99, 128–29, 17:341–42.

amble may be dropt, without hurting the Honour of Parliament."
Whether or not such a measure was passed, Franklin wrote, it was "universally thought that no future Impositions on America" would "ever be
attempted here." Franklin fervently wished that this "Disposition . . .
to treat us more equitably" would "increase and prevail."[53]

Yet, Franklin remained skeptical. "Some powerful People" bore so
much "Malice against" the colonies, he warned, that they wished for
"nothing more . . . than that by Insurrections we should give a good
Pretence for increasing the Military among us, and putting us under
more severe Restraints." For that reason, he counseled his American correspondents that it was most "prudent to be quiet, to stir no new Questions, to let Heats abate; and when Minds are cooler Reason may be
better heard." For the time being, the colonists "should carefully avoid
all tumults and every violent measure, and content themselves with ver-
bally keeping up their claims, and holding forth their rights whenever
occasion requires; secure, that, from the growing importance of
America, those claims will ere long be attended to and acknowledged."
The increasing strength of the colonies, Franklin was persuaded, "must
give such Weight in time to our just Claims, as no selfish Spirit in this
Part of the Empire will be able to resist." In the meantime, he thought
it best "to indulge the Mother Country in" her "concern for her own Honour" by maintaining "a steady dutiful Attachment to the King and his
Family" while only "declining," with as little militancy as possible, "the
usurped Authority of Parliament."[54]

Franklin's hopes were once again disappointed, however. Lord Hillsborough, the colonial secretary, appeared to have such a "settled Malice
against the colonies" that, Franklin concluded, "the Colonies could expect neither Favour nor Justice during his Administration," while "the
Arbitrary Proceedings of Governors & other Crown officers [in the colo-
nies] countenanc'd by their Protectors here," he feared, were "daily di-
minishing" the "Affections of the Americans to this Country . . . and
their Attachment to its Government." "Having naturally no Respect for
the People, but abundance for Ministers," the crown's servants in the
colonies, charged Franklin, took far "greater Liberties" than the crown

---

[53] Franklin to Galloway, June 11, 1770, to Samuel Cooper, Dec. 30, 1770, ibid., 17:168,
170, 310.

[54] Franklin to Galloway, June 11, 1770, to Samuel Cooper, Dec. 30, 1770, to James Bowdoin, Feb. 5, 1771, to Thomas Cushing, Feb. 5, June 10, 1771, ibid., 17:168–70, 310–11,
18:23, 27–28, 122–23; Franklin to Cushing, Jan. 5, Mar. 9, 1773, to William Franklin,
Sept. 1, Oct. 6, 1773, in *Franklin Writings* 6:3–4, 22, 117, 144.

would dare take in Britain, and, instead of being responsible to those they were governing, were the mere tools of the ministry at home.[55]

To make matters worse, Franklin's own influence in government circles—never, except at the time of the repeal of the Stamp Act in 1766, as great as he would have preferred—seemed to be declining. In part, this decline was a function of Franklin's long and persistent advocacy of the American cause, an advocacy that had saddled him with a reputation in some circles as "a Republican, a factious, mischievous Fellow." "I am now thought here too much an American," Franklin wrote his fellow printer Peter Timothy of South Carolina in 1772, "to have any Interest." Franklin's loss of influence was also attributable to his disagreement over metropolitan western policy with Hillsborough, who adamantly and successfully opposed the schemes of Franklin and a group of associates, including many powerful members of the metropolitan political nation, to establish new settlements west of Pennsylvania under the aegis of the Vandalia Company.[56]

Another cause of Franklin's declining influence was Hillsborough's pointed neglect of colonial agents and his insistence upon relying for information about the colonies upon the royal and proprietary governors. Hillsborough was determined, Franklin wrote his Massachusetts correspondent James Bowdoin in January 1772, to pay "no Attention . . . to any Agent here whose Appointment" was "not ratified by the Governor's Assent." This policy meant that no agent who was disagreeable to either governors or ministers had much hope of accomplishing anything through official channels. Franklin lamented that colonial agents were not "treated with more respect," and he eventually concluded, as he told Hillsborough at the end of a sharp exchange in early 1771, that he had "not the least Conception that an Agent can *at present* be of any Use to any of the Colonies." For all these reasons, Franklin in 1771–72 was "on bad Terms" not only "with Lord Hillsborough, but with the *Ministry in general*" and found it increasingly "difficult . . . to get Business forward[ed] here, in which some Party Purpose is not to be served."[57]

In this discouraging situation, Franklin seems to have lapsed from

---

[55] Franklin to Cooper, Feb. 5, 1771, to Cushing, June 10, 1771, in *Franklin Papers* 18:25, 122–23; Franklin to Noble Wymberly Jones, Apr. 2, 1772, in *Franklin Writings* 5:390–91.

[56] Franklin to William Franklin, Apr. 20, 1771, in *Franklin Papers* 18:75; Franklin to Cushing, Jan. 13, 1772, to Peter Timothy, Nov. 2, 1772, in *Franklin Writings* 5:365, 447.

[57] Franklin, Interview with Hillsborough, Jan. 6, 1771, Franklin to Cooper, Feb. 5, 1771, to Cushing, Feb. 5, 1771, Strahan to William Franklin, Apr. 3, 1771, in *Franklin Papers* 18:15–16, 27–28, 65; Franklin to Bowdoin, Jan. 13, 1772, in *Franklin Writings* 5:359.

time to time into periods of at least minor depression. "His Temper," Strahan reported to Franklin's son William in April 1771, "is grown . . . very reserved, which adds [so] greatly to his *natural Inactivity*, that there is no getting him to take part in *anything*." A trip to Ireland and Scotland during the late fall and winter of 1771–72 buoyed his spirits. He was particularly encouraged to find the Anglo-Irish "to be friends of America," and his ego was tickled by the attentions he received from the "principal Patriots," who pointedly stretched the meaning of the term *English Parliaments* to include "American Assemblies" so that Franklin could be admitted to the floor of the Irish House of Commons under a "standing Rule to admit Members of the English Parliament to sit . . . in the House among the Members" instead of in the gallery.[58]

More and more during these years, however, Franklin was seized by "a violent longing for home," for the "repose" and good order of his own Philadelphia, the relative virtue of its citizenry, and the appreciation he could expect from them and from many other friends in America; for as his political credit in Britain had suffered, his stock in the colonies had climbed. Yet, he had not by any means lost his deep and abiding love for Britain. He was still, he reflected, widely respected by his associates among the intelligentsia, and he was encouraged by reports that George III himself had "lately been heard to speak of me with great regard." "I have indeed so many good kind friends here," he wrote his son in January 1772, "that I could spend the Remainder of my Life among them with great Pleasure, if it were not for my American connections, & the indelible Affection I retain for that dear Country, from which I have so long been an Exile."[59]

The dismissal of Hillsborough as colonial secretary in the summer of 1773 and his replacement by Lord Dartmouth, an avowed friend to the colonies, steps which Franklin liked to think he had had some role in bringing about, still again encouraged Franklin to hope for the eventual achievement "of a better Understanding between the two Countries." Thus, he decided for the time being to stay in Britain to see if he could "improve a little, for the general Advantage of our Country, the favourable Appearances arising from the Change of our American Minister, and the good Light I am told I stand in with the Successor. If I be instrumental in [putting] Things in a good train, with a prospect of their [being] on

[58] See Franklin to Jane Mecom, Apr. 7, 1769, Strahan to William Franklin, Apr. 3, 1771, in *Franklin Papers* 16:120, 18:65; Franklin to Cushing, Jan. 13, 1772, in *Franklin Writings* 5:367.

[59] Franklin to William Franklin, Jan. 30, Aug. 29, 1772, in *Franklin Writings* 5:382, 414.

a better Footing than they have had for some Years past," he wrote Galloway early in 1773, "I shall think a little additional Time well spent."[60]

A man of a political persuasion almost identical to that of Franklin, Dartmouth was clearly in favor of letting "all Contention subside, and by degrees suffer[ing] Matters to return to the old Channels," and Franklin detected that, although "some of the great" still regarded the colonists "with a jealous Eye" and others were "angry with us," the "Majority of the Nation rather wish us well, and have no desire to infringe our Liberties" but seemed to be convinced "that we have been ill used, and that a break with us would be ruinous to this country." At last, Britain appeared to be awakening to a true sense of its own self-interest:

> The Dissenters are all for us, and many of the Merchants and Manufacturers. There seems to be, even among the Country Gentlemen, a general Sense of our growing Importance, a Disapprobation of the harsh Measures with which we have been treated, and a Wish that some Means may be found of perfect Reconciliation. A few Members of Parliament in both houses, and perhaps some [besides Dartmouth] in high Office, have in a Degree the same Ideas; but none of these seem willing as yet to be active in our favour, lest Adversaries should take Advantage, and charge it upon them as . . . Betraying the Interests of this Nation.[61]

Franklin was confident, however, that if a war broke out with France and Spain, as had been frequently rumored from 1770 on and was particularly feared in 1773, "Every Step would . . . be taken to conciliate our Friendship, our Grievances would be redress'd, and our Claims allow'd." Even without war, Franklin hoped as late as the fall of 1773 that before a new election the ministry would move decisively to "consider . . . composing all differences with America" and readmitting the colonists "to all the Privileges of Englishmen" so that the American question could not be used against the government in the election.[62]

As yet, Franklin had no doubts "of the Advantages of a strict Union between the Mother Country and the Colonies," but he was less and less

---

[60] Franklin to Galloway, Jan. 6, Apr. 6, 1773, ibid., 6:6, 33; Franklin to Cushing, Dec. 24, 1770, *Franklin Papers* 17:308.

[61] Franklin to Cushing, May 6, 9, Nov. 9, 1773, to Cooper, Nov. 7, 1773, in *Franklin Writings* 6:48, 78–79, 93, 147.

[62] Franklin to Galloway, Apr. 6, 1773, to Cooper, Nov. 7, 1773, to William Franklin, Aug. 17, 19, 1772, Oct. 6, 1773, ibid., 5:410–11, 414, 6:33, 148.

sure how such a union might be obtained. He still believed in the utility of his old strategy of mutual restraint and continued to call for "the Exercise of prudent Moderation on" Britain's "part, mix'd with a little Kindness; and . . . a decent Behaviour on ours, excusing where we can excuse from a Consideration of Circumstances, and bearing a little with the Infirmities of her Government, as we would with those of an aged Parent." But he was also now willing to consider the possibility that a little well-directed militancy on the part of the colonists might be useful. Thus, he suggested to Thomas Cushing in May 1773 that it might "be best and fairest for the Colonies, in a general Congress now in Peace to be assembled, or by means of the Correspondence lately proposed, after a full and solemn Assertion and Declaration of their Rights, to engage firmly with each other, that they will never grant Aids to the Crown in any General War, till those Rights are recogniz'd by the King and both Houses of Parliament; communicating at the same time to the Crown this their Resolution."[63]

Whatever strategy was used to obtain it, a union, Franklin was now more thoroughly convinced than ever, would be genuinely advantageous to the colonies only if it might "be obtain'd and preserv'd on equitable Terms." "In every fair Connection," he wrote Cushing,

> each Party should find its own Interest. Britain will find hers in our joining with her in every War she makes, to the greater Annoyance and Terror of her Enemies; in our Employment of her Manufactures, and Enriching of her Merchants by our Commerce; and her Government will feel some additional Strengthening of its Hands by the Disposition of our profitable Posts and Places. On our side, we have to expect the Protection she can afford us, and the Advantages of a common Umpire in our Disputes, thereby preventing Wars we might otherwise have with each other; so that we can without Interruption go on with our Improvements, and increase our Numbers. We ask no more of her, and she should not think of forcing more from us.[64]

A union based upon such mutually understood benefits, Franklin thought, would make the "Connexion . . . as strong, perhaps stronger than ever." To hasten this happy prospect, Franklin wrote and published anonymously in the fall of 1773 two of his most famous and artful satires. In an *Edict of the King of Prussia* and *Rules by Which a Great Empire*

---

[63] Franklin to Cushing, May 9, 1773, ibid., 6:77–78.
[64] Ibid.

May Be Reduced to a Small One, both of which "stated . . . in out-of-way forms, as most likely to take the general Attention," he ridiculed with great effect the shortsighted, inequitable, and wrongheaded "conduct of this country towards the colonies" and thereby sought to push the metropolitan political nation ever further along the road toward a policy of conciliation.[65]

As had happened in 1766–67, however, Franklin's hopes for accommodation were quickly dashed by events in America, especially in Massachusetts Bay, where, during a debate with Hutchinson in January 1773, the House of Representatives emphatically denied that Parliament had any authority over the colonies whatever. Such an open and unqualified challenge to parliamentary authority, published in full in London, made it exceedingly difficult for Dartmouth to pursue his intention of leaving "things between us on the old Footing, the [basic] Points [in dispute being] undiscuss'd." But it was the Boston Tea Party in mid-December 1773 that set in motion the chain of events that quickly led to the irreparable breach Franklin had so long feared. "The Clamour against" Boston for that "Proceeding," Franklin reported in early 1774, was "high and general." Exactly how intense the feelings ran, Franklin discovered at first hand during his painful public humiliation at the Cockpit in late January. That experience left him "at a loss to know how peace and union are to be maintained or restored between the different parts of the empire," when "even the mere pipe which" conveyed "petitions and complaints of grievances" was so obviously "odious to government."[66]

Yet, not even his severe chastisement destroyed his hopes for accommodation. In the belief that it was "never too late to mend," he urged his Massachusetts constituents to make a "speedy Reparation" to the East India Company for the destroyed tea, in the hope that such action might forestall "compulsive Measures" by the metropolitan government.

---

[65] Franklin to Jane Mecom, July 7, 1773, to William Franklin, Oct. 6, 1773, ibid., 6:93, 145; Franklin, "An Infallible Method," in *Franklin's Letters to the Press,* 233. The two satires are conveniently reprinted in *The Political Thought of Benjamin Franklin,* ed. Ralph Ketcham (Indianapolis, 1965), 254–69.

[66] Franklin, "On Civil War," Aug. 26, 1768, in *Franklin Papers* 15:191–93; Franklin to Cushing, Dec. 2, 1772, May 6, 1773, Feb. 2, 1774, to William Franklin, Sept. 1, 1773, in *Franklin Writings* 5:448–51, 6:48–51, 117, 179; Franklin to Cushing, Feb. 15, 1774, in Ketcham, *Political Thought of Franklin,* 277.

Throughout the winter and early spring of 1774, he continued to lobby hard against the Coercive Acts passed by Parliament in the spring. In anonymous letters to the press, he reiterated his earlier warnings of the folly of resorting to force. "The Flame of Liberty in North America," he insisted in elaborating on an old theme, could never "be extinguished" by acts of "Cruelty and Oppression and revenge." Measures animated by such passions could "only serve as Oil to increase the Fire. A great Country of hardy Peasants is not to be subdued. In the Grave which we dig for the Inhabitants of Boston, Confidence and Friendship shall expire, Commerce and Peace shall rest together."[67]

Even after the Coercive Acts had passed, Franklin continued to hope for a change in metropolitan policy and a peaceful reconciliation. "The Coolness, Temper, & Firmness of the American Proceedings; the Unanimity of all the Colonies, in the same Sentiments of their Rights, & of the Injustice offered to Boston; and the Patience with which those Injuries are at Present borne, without the least Appearance of Submission," he wrote in September 1774, "have a good deal surprized and disappointed our Enemies." He predicted that a "Non Consumption Agreement[,] . . . general[ly], and . . . firmly adhered to," would ruin the ministry and bring to power the colonists' friends, who, with the backing of a virtuous king whose eyes had been opened by the folly of his former ministers, might then be expected to produce "a great Constitutional Charter to be confirmed by King, Lords, & Commons, whereby our Liberties shall be recognized and established, as the . . . sure Foundation of that Union so necessary for our Common welfare."[68]

By early 1775, however, it had become abundantly clear that British opinion would not run so strongly in favor of the colonies as to deter the administration from its settled determination to enforce the Coercive Acts by military means if necessary. Parliament took "little notice" of the many petitions "from all Trading Ports, and manufacturing Towns, concern'd in the American Commerce, setting forth the Loss & Ruin they are likely to suffer by the Stop put to that Commerce & praying that lenient Measures may be adopted for restoring it." At the same time, the House of Lords treated a bill prepared by Lord Chatham (with Franklin's help) "with as much contempt as they could have shown to a Ballad

[67] Franklin to Cushing, Feb. 2, 1774, to Cooper, Feb. 25, 1774, in *Franklin Writings* 6:179, 204; Franklin, "'Tis Never too Late to Mend," Sept. 14, 1773, "On the Boston Port Act," Apr. 2, 1774, "On Humbling Rebellious Vassals," May 21, 1774, in *Franklin's Letters to the Press*, 235, 257, 263.

[68] Franklin to Cushing, Sept. 3, 1774, in *Franklin Writings* 6:238–39.

offered by a drunken Porter." Far from intervening on behalf of gentle measures, George III emerged as one of the leaders in the demand for severe ones. The administration, Franklin observed dolefully in February 1775, seemed "determin'd on reducing the Colonies by Force to a solemn Acknowledgement of the Power claimed by Parliament of mak[ing] Laws to bind the Colonies in all Cases whatsoever." Britain, it now appeared, had become an "old Bloodthirsty Bully" intent upon making "Beasts of Burthen of" its *own children.*[69]

Despite so much abundant evidence of the direction in which "matters" were "driving," Franklin, as late as February 25, 1775, still clung to the hope that if the colonies "continue[d] firm and united, and resolutely persist[ed] in the non-consumption agreement," the "redoubled clamour of the trading, manufacturing, and Whig interests" in Britain would "infallibly overthrow all the enemies of America, and produce an acknowledgement of her rights and satisfaction for her injuries."[70]

Whether such an acknowledgment was worth having, whether a continuing connection with Britain would be beneficial to the colonies, Franklin was no longer so sure. "When I consider the extream Corruption prevalent among all Orders of Men in this rotten old State, and the glorious publick Virtue so predominant in our rising Country, I cannot but apprehend more Mischief than Benefit from a closer Union," Franklin confided to Galloway in late February 1775:

> I fear they will drag us after them in all the plundering Wars, which their desperate Circumstances, Injustice, and Rapacity, may prompt them to undertake; and their wide-wasting Prodigality and Profusion is a Gulph that will swallow up every Aid we may distress ourselves to afford them.
>
> Here Numberless and needless Places, enormous Salaries, Pensions, Perquisites, Bribes, groundless Quarrels, foolish Expeditions, false Accounts or no Accounts, Contracts and Jobbs, devour all Revenue, and produce continual Necessity to the Midst of natural Plenty.

---

[69] Franklin to Cushing, Jan. 28, 1775, to Thomson, Feb. 5, 1775, to Samuel Tucker and others, Feb. 4, 1775, Franklin, "The Intended Speech . . . ," Nov. 29, 1779, ibid., 6:299–308; Franklin, "Imaginary Speech . . . ," Feb. 7, 1775, in *Franklin's Letters to the Press*, 282; "A Dialogue between Britain, France, Spain, Holland, Saxony, and America," 1775, in Ketcham, *Political Thought of Franklin*, 284.

[70] Franklin, "Account of Massachusetts Petition," Apr. 25, 1774, "The Question Discussed," Nov. 19, 1774, in *Franklin's Letters to the Press*, 244, 271; Franklin to Bowdoin, Feb. 15, 1774, in *Franklin Writings* 6:309–10.

> I apprehend, therefore, that to unite us intimately will only be to cor-
> rupt and poison us also. It seems like Mezentius's coupling and bind-
> ing together the dead and the living.

Still, Franklin remained willing to "try any thing, and bear any thing that can be borne with Safety to our just Liberties, rather than engage in a War with such near relations, unless compelled to it by dire Neces-sity in our own Defence."[71]

Retaining only the slimmest hopes for reconciliation and—having been branded by "the ministerial people" as "the Cause of all the Misun-derstanding"—fearing for his own safety should war accidentally break out in Massachusetts, Franklin decided early in the spring of 1775, after more than a decade in Britain, to return to America. There was, in any case, no longer any place in metropolitan politics for the cautious and moderate approach of a public-spirited Trimmer like Franklin. The esca-lating conflict of the previous year had rendered such an approach irrele-vant. Arriving in America in early May, Franklin discovered "that prop-ositions" for "accommodation were not much relished" there either. The outbreak of hostilities at Lexington and Concord on April 19 had "so exasperated" "all minds" that it was only "with difficulty" that the Conti-nental Congress was persuaded to send "another humble petition to the crown" to give Britain "one Opportunity more, of recovering our Affections and retaining the Connection." Only "great Wisdom on your Side [of] the Water," he wrote his friend John Sargeant, M. P. for Sea-ford, in June 1775, could now "prevent a total separation."[72]

Because he no longer had any illusions that Britain might have "sense enough to embrace" the opportunity, he concluded that it had lost the colonies forever. Certainly, force could not retain them. The futility of military measures had already been demonstrated in just one campaign. "At the expence of three millions," he wrote Joseph Priestley in October 1775, Britain had "killed one hundred and fifty Yankees this campaign, which is twenty thousand pounds a head; and at Bunker's Hill she gained a mile of Ground, half of which she lost again by our taking post on Ploughed Hill. During the same time sixty thousand children have been born in America. From these *data* any . . . mathematical head will

---

[71] Franklin to Galloway, Feb. 25, 1775, to Thomson, Mar. 13, 1775, in *Franklin Writ-ings* 6:311–17.

[72] Franklin to Cushing, Jan. 5, 1774, to Galloway, Oct. 12, 1774, to Sargeant, June 27, 1775, to Priestley, July 7, 1775, to "A Friend in England," Oct. 3, 1775, ibid., 6:173, 254, 408, 430–31.

easily calculate the time and expense necessary to kill us all, and conquer our whole territory."[73]

As Franklin had predicted, Britain did not embrace the last opportunity for a reconciliation offered by Congress. Instead, "every ship from Britain" brought "some intelligence of new measures that tend[ed] more and more to exasperate." By October 1775, Franklin had decided that a "separation . . . will be inevitable." Confident in the glorious future of America, he did not shrink from such a development. His own allegiances were clear; he had no difficulty in choosing between America and Britain. "You are a Member of Parliament, and one of that Majority which doomed my Country to Destruction," he wrote Strahan, a friend of thirty years' standing, in July 1775: "You have begun to burn our Towns, and murder our People. Look upon your Hands! they are stained with the Blood of your Relations! You and I were long Friends: You are now my Enemy, and I am Yours."[74]

As this moving declaration of enmity so strongly suggested, however, Franklin could not relinquish his attachment to Britain without regrets. Animated by a vision of a "greater Britain" that would include—on equitable terms—America as well as the home islands, he had labored too long on behalf of union and accommodation not to feel disappointment and bitterness. "'Tis a million of pities," he wrote an English friend late in 1775, that "so fair a plan as we have hitherto been engaged in, for increasing strength and empire with *public felicity,* should be destroyed by the mangling hands of a few blundering ministers" who had managed in little more than a decade to alienate the overwhelming affections of the colonists for Britain and to replace them with total "enmity, hatred and detestation."[75]

The failure of the British Empire in 1776 might have been interpreted by Franklin as a personal failure attributable to his inability, though in a strategic position for doing so, to persuade men in power in Britain of the error of their approach. As he very well understood, however, the failure was not his. He had correctly assessed the situation from the beginning, and the validity of his assessment had been confirmed by devel-

---

[73] Franklin to Priestley, July 7, Oct. 3, 1775, ibid., 6:408, 430.

[74] Franklin to Strahan, July 5, 1775, to "A Friend in England," Oct. 3, 1775, ibid., 6:407, 430–31.

[75] Franklin to "A Friend in England," Oct. 3, 1775, ibid., 6:431.

opments he himself had lived long enough to see: by the alienation of colonial affections through the misguided measures of the metropolitan government, the failure of British arms to subdue the colonies by force, and the successful creation of the American republic.

Rather, as Franklin also understood, perhaps as well as any of his contemporaries, that failure was in large part traceable to the "groundless jealousies," ideological rigidities, and boundless pride that prevented the metropolitan political nation from comprehending either the cogency or the force of what it was being told by people like himself: that Americans were loyal to Britain, that their loyalty was deeply rooted in affection, and that that loyalty could best be preserved by a cautious and generous approach that eschewed debate over fundamental ideological divergences in pursuit of the larger and ultimately far more important objective of preserving the empire intact and harmonious.

In many ways unsuspected by the Lords of the Privy Council on the day of Franklin's humiliation at the Cockpit in January 1774, Franklin was indeed a surrogate for the vast majority of American colonists. Their growing estrangement from Britain between 1763 and 1774 was reflected in his. The relinquishment of his attachment to Britain had been for him, as it was for them, a long and painful process that he would have much preferred to avoid. They shared his deep veneration for Britain, his dismay at the treatment they received at the hands of the metropolitan government after 1763, his insistence upon equity as the foundation for a harmonious empire, and his lingering reluctance to break the ancient bonds of allegiance that had bound Britain and the colonies together for more than 150 years. What Franklin's experience suggests, then, about the Revolution he had worked so hard to prevent is that, like Franklin's own decision for independence, it is to be explained primarily as the result of the "alienation of . . . affections" he had so often predicted would follow from the posture of jealousy and hostility assumed by the metropolitan government toward the colonies during the crucial years before 1776.

This chapter was written in the fall of 1975 and presented as a lecture at the Royal Society of Arts in London on November 12, 1975. It is here reprinted with permission and minor changes from *Journal of the Royal Society for the Arts* (now the *RSA Journal*), 124 (1976): 52–73.

Twelve

Paine, America, and the "Modernization" of Political Consciousness

T HE FULL SIGNIFICANCE of the achievement of Thomas Paine has
perhaps never been thoroughly explained. His public career falls
into two neatly divisible phases: the American, lasting from 1774 to 1787,
and the European, stretching from 1787 to 1802. Few scholars concerned
with his American career have been much interested in his European,
while those studying his European activities have rarely demonstrated
much sensitivity to the bearing of his American experiences upon them.[1]
Numerous biographies have traced his life with varying degrees of detachment.[2] But biography, focusing as it does upon the discrete details
of an individual's life, has rarely been a satisfactory vehicle for exploring
the wider impact of that life. Paine's larger significance can perhaps be
understood only in terms of his relationship to one of the most important
transformations in modern history, a transformation that, to borrow a
set of conceptions from the social sciences, may most accurately be referred to as the *modernization* of political consciousness.

This transformation was characterized by basic changes "in ways of
perceiving, expressing, and valuing" within the political realm, changes
that were every bit as fundamental and as far-reaching as those produced in the religious sphere by the reformations of the sixteenth and

---

[1] The major exception is Eric Foner's recent *Tom Paine and Revolutionary America* (New
York, 1976), the best book thus far written on Paine.

[2] The best of these are David Freeman Hawke, *Paine* (New York, 1975); Audrey William-
son, *Thomas Paine: His Life, Work, and Times* (New York, 1974); and Alfred Owen Al-
dridge, *Man of Reason: The Life of Thomas Paine* (Philadelphia, 1959).

seventeenth centuries. The result was a wholly new political mentality for participants at every level of the political process, a mentality not only receptive to but eager for change, oriented toward the present and future rather than the past, confident of the efficacy of human reason to shape that present and future, and committed to the revolutionary beliefs that membership in the political nation should be based on universalistic rather than prescriptive criteria and that social and political advancement should be based on achievement rather than ascription.[3]

This transformation was accompanied by—and played a key role in bringing about—two crucial developments: the mobilization of large segments of society theretofore politically inert, and the desacralization of the traditional political order. As the title implies, the two principal, if highly speculative, contentions of this essay are that Paine played a central role in the initial phases of this transformation during the last decades of the eighteenth century and that the social and political facts of America, as Paine encountered them during his American career, were crucial in determining the shape and content of his special contribution to that transformation.

Paine was already thirty-seven when he arrived in Philadelphia on November 30, 1774. Although we know only the broad outlines of his life up to that time, he could scarcely have been described as a success: for more than two decades he had drifted from one livelihood to another without leaving much of a mark. Up to that time, he tells us, he had never "published a syllable in England." Encouraged by Benjamin Franklin, who found him *"a worthy, ingenious"* fellow, Paine had made the voyage to Philadelphia in the hope of getting yet another start in the world. His "particular design was to establish an academy on the plan [on which] they are conducted in and about London." Instead, he early became involved in editing and writing for the *Pennsylvania Magazine,* a job that finally brought him to the discovery, as he later remarked, of

---

[3] For a systematic discussion of the modernizing process, see Alex Inkeles and David H. Smith, *Becoming Modern: Individual Change in Six Developing Countries* (London, 1974), 15–17, 289–91. The term *modern* does not for me connote something better. It is here used as a convenient label for a set of structures and attitudes that began to achieve prominence in the early modern European and American worlds and have subsequently characterized much in the course of human development.

the "one kind of life I am fit for, and that is a thinking one, and, of course, a writing one." Like so many immigrants before and after, Paine found in America his true vocation. It was as an author, as "a *farmer of thoughts*," that he would satisfy a boundless passion for fame.[4] Although he soon abandoned all plans to open an academy, he persisted in his design to become a teacher. But he took for his pupils not a class full of adolescent Philadelphia boys but the whole of the emerging American political nation.

His success as a pedagogue with his new pupils was virtually instantaneous. Knowing from a friend, a former subpreceptor of George II, "the true character of the present King from his childhood upwards, and, you may naturally suppose, of the present ministry," Paine perceived that Americans "were all wrong, by an ill-placed confidence" in the king, who, no less than the ministry, Paine was persuaded, was bent upon "a total conquest" of the colonies. No doubt at the urging of friends, Paine "determined . . . to write the pamphlet [*Common*] *Sense.*" Published on January 10, 1776, just a few days more than thirteen months after his arrival in America, *Common Sense* was an uncompromising brief against monarchy and for American independence. More important, it enjoyed a literally unprecedented reception, at least in the Anglophone world. The "number of copies printed and sold in America," Paine wrote in 1779, "was not short of 150,000—and is the greatest sale that any performance ever had since the use of letters,—exclusive of the great run it had in England and Ireland." There were seventeen printings in London alone in 1776; French editions were published in 1776 in both Paris and Rotterdam, and German editions were published in Philadelphia in 1776 and in Lemgo in 1777.[5] So important in early 1776 was *Common Sense* in persuading strategic segments of the American political community that independence was a desirable and possible objective that on the basis of that achievement alone Paine could justifiably, as he wrote the Pennsylvania financier Robert Morris in February 1782, take "honest pride" in

---

[4] Written in 1772, Paine's "The Case for the Officers of the Excise" had been printed for the House of Commons but not published. The only known Paine writing before his arrival in America, it was not issued to the public until 1793. Paine, "American Crisis," Paine to Henry Laurens, Spring 1778, Jan. 14, Sept. 14, 1779, in *The Complete Writings of Thomas Paine*, ed. Philip S. Foner, 2 vols. (New York, 1945), 1:72, 2:8–9, 1143, 1161, 1178.

[5] Paine to Laurens, Jan. 14, 1779, ibid., 2:1161–63; Richard Gimbel, *Thomas Paine: A Bibliographical Check List of* Common Sense (New Haven, 1956), 57, 124.

"thinking and ranking myself among the founders of a new Independent World."[6]

But Paine was destined for an even larger role in an even grander theater. With publication—first in London, then in Paris, the United States, and most of the publishing centers of Europe—of part 1 of *The Rights of Man* in February 1791 and part 2 twelve months later, this "man of freedom," as his French translator said, undertook to explain "to the whole world with the same success as in America . . . the theory of the practice of the Rights of Man." Sales soon outstripped those of *Common Sense.* As Paine reported a decade later, *The Rights of Man* "had the greatest run of any work ever published in the English language. The number of copies circulated in England, Scotland, and Ireland, besides translations into foreign languages, was between four and five hundred thousand." From very unpromising beginnings extending through his first thirty-seven years and "with all the inconvenience of early life against" him, Paine had thus succeeded both in contributing "to raise a new empire in the world, founded on a new system of government," and in achieving, as he put it, "an eminence in political literature, the most difficult of all lines to succeed and excel in, which aristocracy, with all its aids, has not been able to reach or to rival." No other man, he liked to think, had *"contributed [so much] to the liberty of both worlds,"* in Europe as well as in America.[7]

Paine's phenomenal literary success, his ability "usefully and successfully [to] attract the public attention," fascinated contemporaries and has never ceased to intrigue scholars. It was a phenomenon that interested Paine himself, and he offered a number of plausible, if partial, explanations. His "disinterestedness," he thought, his publicly exhibited and carefully nurtured reputation as a man who was "determined to follow [his] . . . genius, and not [his] . . . fortune," a person who never attempted to make money from his public writings and had neither "profit, place [n]or power" in view, "compelled respect" among the reading and listening public. He also thought that the deep popular resonances he evoked were attributable to the power of his arguments, the simplicity of his style, and his faith in the capacity of the populace for political understanding. Men, he assured Lafayette in the dedication of part 2 of

---

[6] Paine to Morris, Feb. 20, 1782, in *Complete Writings of Paine* 2:1207.

[7] Translator's Preface to *Rights of Man,* Paine, *Rights of Man* and "To the Citizens of the United States," 1805, Paine to John Hall, Nov. 25, 1791, ibid., 1:346, 405–6, 2:910, 920, 1322.

The Rights of Man, could "always understand their true interest, provided it be presented clearly to their understanding, and . . . in a manner [calculated] not to create suspicion by any thing like self-design, nor offend by assuming too much."[8]

Modern historians have offered other, complementary explanations. Bernard Bailyn has emphasized Paine's ability to articulate and give concrete expression to the accumulated social rage of the late eighteenth-century world, while Eric Foner has stressed Paine's social affinity with the "mass audience" to whom he spoke so effectively. Whatever the explanation, there can be no doubt, as Foner has remarked, that "for Paine, the medium was of one piece with the message."[9] A crucial figure in the decisive late eighteenth-century shift from a primarily oral-aural culture to a mainly typographic one, Paine was the herald of the linear rationality of the emerging typographically literate society who could manipulate the new typographic medium in such a way as to communicate powerfully with those segments of society still attuned to the modes of intellectual exchange from the older oral-aural world.[10]

But it is important to emphasize that with Paine the medium was emphatically not the whole of the message. Why so many people on both sides of the Atlantic found the irreverence, iconoclasm, and rage that infused his writings so congenial and why they were so receptive to the particular sociopolitical vision he offered are questions that cannot be answered without close attention to the content—as well as to the form—of his writings.

Most fundamentally, perhaps, the corpus of Paine's political works constitutes a massive attack upon all the primary institutions and beliefs that had traditionally sustained the old European political and social order. His first concern was to strip the veil of sanctity from tradition, to expose the absurdities in what people had formerly revered, and thereby to wean them "from those narrow prejudices and partialities [they] . . . had imbibed" from the repressive cultures in which they had been raised. His initial task was to persuade people that rationally formed opinion, rather than prejudice, was the proper basis for individ-

---

[8] Paine, *Rights of Man*, "Address to the People of Pennsylvania," Dec. 1778, and "Six Letters to Rhode Island," Jan. 1783, Paine to George Washington, July 21, 1791, ibid., 1:347, 405–6, 2:279, 366, 1319.

[9] Bernard Bailyn, "Common Sense," in *Fundamental Testaments of the American Revolution* (Washington, D. C., 1973), 7–22; Foner, *Tom Paine*, 79–87.

[10] See Walter J. Ong, *The Presence of the Word* (New Haven, 1967), 22–87.

ual political action. "No man is prejudiced in favor of a thing, knowing it to be wrong," Paine wrote in *The Rights of Man:* "He is attached to it on the belief of its being right; and when he sees it is not so, the prejudice will be gone. We have but a defective idea what prejudice is. It might be said that until men think for themselves the whole is prejudice, and *not opinion;* for that only is opinion which is the result of reason and reflection."[11]

Thus, before Paine could obtain an effective hearing for his case in behalf of American independence in *Common Sense,* he had first to destroy some of the most integral components of the colonial belief system: that the connection with Britain was essential to the prosperity and safety of the colonies, that the British constitution was the most perfect political contrivance in the history of man, and that monarchy was both a legitimate institution and an essential component of that constitution. He had to persuade the colonists that their extraordinary prosperity under the aegis of Britain did not mean that they might not have done even better had they been on their own; that separation from Britain and neutrality in European wars might mean more, not less, safety; that the British was "a rotten constitution of government," the "base remains of two ancient tyrannies [monarchy and aristocracy], compounded with some new Republican materials"; and that monarchy, which gave one person *"a power which the people are afraid to trust, and [are] always obliged to trust,"* was unworthy of the attachment of any man and, along with aristocracy, incompatible with a truly free constitution. Hereditary succession, said Paine, was only a "superstitious tale conveniently [trumped up] and timed, Mohamet-like, to cram [monarchy] . . . down the throats of the vulgar" by obscuring the base beginnings of "the present race of Kings," whose "paltry rascally original" could have been "nothing better than the principal ruffian of some restless gang; whose savage manners or pre-eminence in subtilty obtained him the title of chief among plunderers; and who by increasing in power and extending his depradations, overawed the quiet and defenseless to purchase their safety by frequent contributions." So "exceedingly ridiculous" were monarchy and hereditary succession, said Paine, that only the mentally "weak" could possibly continue their attachment to them once their folly had been exposed.[12]

---

[11] Paine, *Common Sense, Rights of Man,* and "Emancipation of Slaves," 1779, in *Complete Writings of Paine* 1:7, 353, 2:22.

[12] Paine, *Common Sense,* ibid., 1:7–9, 13–14.

This equation of a continuing commitment to the old system with weakness and passivity was one of Paine's most effective rhetorical devices. It was high time, he later declared in *The Rights of Man*, for people to become "rational, and not be governed like animals for the pleasure of their riders." Americans, he had told the readers of the *Pennsylvania Magazine* in 1775, had to learn to "disdain" a connection with Britain that systematically "degrade[d] them to an equality with a war horse, or an elephant," and deprived them of "the liberty of thinking for themselves." "Man," said Paine, "ought to have pride or shame enough to blush at being thus imposed upon, and when he feels his proper character, he will." For only by "divest[ing] himself of prejudice and prepossession, and suffer[ing] his reason and his feelings to determine for themselves," he declared in *Common Sense*, could a man rouse himself out of the "fatal and unmanly slumbers" into which he had permitted himself to sink through centuries of neglecting to permit his rational faculties free play and once again "put on . . . the true character of a man." And only when enough men so behaved, only when a sufficient number reclaimed their manhood by conquering prejudice with reason, could America acquire "spirit enough to become her own master."[13] Paine thus inextricably linked American independence and manhood with reason, and continued dependence upon Britain and servility with prejudice, thereby virtually assuring a largely favorable response to his attack on the old system among a people so obsessed with their manhood (and the personal independence thought to be essential to that manhood) as were white male Americans.[14]

Never an admirer of Paine, John Adams once remarked that Paine was "a better Hand at pulling down than building."[15] But this judgment, so often reiterated by later scholars, seriously misreads the character of Paine's achievement. For Paine not only had to destroy those cherished misconceptions that caused so many Americans to "think better of the European world than it deserves"; he also had to teach Americans "the manly doctrine of reverencing themselves." For them simply to learn to treat "those imaginary beings called kings and lords, and all the fraudulent trumpery of court" with the contempt they deserved was not

---

[13] Paine, *Common Sense*, "American Crisis," *Rights of Man*, and "Dialogue between General Wolfe and General Gage," 1775, ibid., 1:17–18, 22–23, 121, 421, 2:49.

[14] In this connection, see Jack P. Greene, *All Men Are Created Equal: Some Reflections on the Character of the American Revolution* (Oxford, 1976).

[15] As quoted by Winthrop D. Jordan, "Familial Politics: Thomas Paine and the Killing of the King, 1776," *Journal of American History* 60 (1973): 298.

enough.[16] Americans had also to realize that so many of the features of American society for which they had traditionally been so apologetic— its simplicity, its newness, its rusticity, its innocence, its very size—were not deficiencies but advantages.[17]

"The infant state of the colonies, as it is called," wrote Paine, "so far from being against, is an argument in favor of independence." "Youth is the seed-time of good habits as well in nations as in individuals," he argued, pointing out that history revealed "that the bravest achievements were always accomplished in the non-age of a nation" and that a "vast variety of interests, occasioned by an increase of trade and population" might subsequently make it more "difficult, if not impossible, to form the continent into one government." The simplicity, rusticity, and innocence of America were virtues. The highly differentiated society of England only meant that there were a few overwhelmingly rich and a very large "class of poor and wretched people," while its "exceedingly complex" government caused "the nation [to] . . . suffer for years together without being able to discover in which part the fault lies." "The more simple anything is," Paine declared, "the less liable it is to be disordered, and the easier repaired when disordered." Nor were the disadvantages of size anywhere near comparable to the benefits. The vastness of their country, Paine contended, merely made it easier for Americans to "forget the narrow limits of three hundred and sixty miles (the extent of England)" and, "triumph[ing] in the generosity of . . . sentiment" that was the natural result of living in such an "extensive quarter of the globe," to "surmount the force of local prejudices."[18]

The vision Paine held out to Americans, moreover, not only gave them a new sense of worth but a place of the first importance in the unfolding course of human history. Discovered just before the Reformation as "if the Almighty graciously meant to open a sanctuary to the persecuted in future years," America had subsequently served as "the asylum for the persecuted lovers of civil and religious liberty from *every part* of Europe." But it was now destined for an even greater role. "Every spot of the old world is overrun with oppression," Paine wrote in a famous passage in

---

[16] Paine, *Common Sense,* "American Crisis," and Paine, "To Mr. Secretary Dundas," June 6, 1792, in *Complete Writings of Paine* 1:21, 59, 2:452.

[17] See Jack P. Greene, "Search for Identity: An Interpretation of the Meaning of Selected Patterns of Social Response in Eighteenth-Century America," *Journal of Social History* 3 (1970): 189–220.

[18] Paine, *Common Sense,* Paine to Dundas, 1792, in *Complete Writings of Paine* 1:6–7, 19, 36, 2:451.

Common Sense: "Freedom hath been hunted round the globe. Asia and Africa have long expelled her. Europe regards her like a stranger, and England hath given her warning to depart." "Had it not been for America," he would later write in *The American Crisis*, "there had been no such thing as freedom left throughout the whole universe."[19]

America's role was not just to be the last remaining asylum of liberty but, Paine wrote in 1776, to become "the theater where human nature will *soon* receive its greatest military, civil, and literary honors." "The cause of America," he said in *Common Sense*, "is in a great measure the cause of all mankind." A "people who" had "virtue enough to defend themselves against the most powerful nation in the world should [not] want wisdom to contrive a perfect and free form of government." Americans had "a blank sheet to write upon." It was "as if [they] . . . were the *first men* that *thought.*" They had it in their "power to begin the world over again. A situation, similar to the present, hath not happened since the days of Noah until now." "The birthday of a new world," he predicted, "is at hand, and a race of men, perhaps as numerous as all Europe contains," might "receive their portion of freedom" and form an ever-burgeoning stream of liberty that might ultimately wash the stains of tyranny from the world. "Not a place upon earth might be so happy as America," and in America's happiness lay the salvation, perhaps the last chance for the salvation, of the world.[20]

For America, Paine's was a powerful, self-legitimating, and exhilarating vision, a veritable "land-flood," wrote an anonymous contributor to the *Connecticut Gazette*, "that sweeps all before it. We were blind, but on reading these enlightening works the scales have fallen from our eyes; even deep-rooted prejudices take to themselves wings and flee away. . . . The doctrine of Independence hath been in times past, greatly disgustful; we abhorred the principle—it is now become our delightful theme, and commands our purest affections." Moreover, "as the independence of America became contemplated and understood," Paine subsequently wrote in his *Letter to the Abbé Raynal*, "the local advantages of it to the immediate actors, and the numerous benefits it promised mankind, appeared to be every day increasing; and we saw not a temporary good for the present race only, but a continued good to all posterity."[21]

---

[19] Paine, *Common Sense* and "American Crisis," ibid., 1:19, 21, 30–31, 123.

[20] Paine, *Common Sense*, "American Crisis," "The Forester's Letters," 1776, and "A Dialogue," 1776, ibid., 1:3, 45, 54, 2:82–83, 90–93.

[21] *Connecticut Gazette*, Mar. 22, 1776, as quoted by Jordan, "Familial Politics," 295; Paine, *Letter to the Abbé Raynal*, 1782, in *Complete Writings of Paine* 2:238.

During the two decades following publication of *Common Sense*, Paine transformed this vision into a grand and totally new conception of the sociopolitical order that was as resonant in the Old World as his original vision had been in America. In a series of occasional writings, the culmination of which was *The Rights of Man*, Paine proceeded to do for the Old World what he had previously done for the New: reverse the "underlying presumptions" and shift "the established perspectives to the point where the whole received paradigm within which" the traditional order had been conceived "came into question."[22]

Building upon the premise that "time, and change of circumstances and opinions, have the same progressive effect in rendering modes of government obsolete, as they have upon customs and manners," Paine constructed his new paradigm upon a whole series of sharp antitheses between what he referred to as "the old and new systems of government." "Government on the old system," said Paine,

> is an assumption of power, for the aggrandizement of itself; on the new, a delegation of power, for the common benefit of society. The former supports itself by keeping up a system of war; the latter promotes a system of peace, as the true means of enriching a nation. The one encourages national prejudices; the other promotes universal commerce. The one measures its prosperity, by the quantity of revenue it extorts; the other proves its excellence, by the small quantity of taxes it requires.[23]

The differences between these two systems were absolute and irreconcilable. They were based, said Paine, "on the two distinct and opposite bases of Reason and Ignorance." "There are two ways of governing mankind," Paine wrote in *A Serious Address to the People of Pennsylvania* in 1778. "First, By keeping them ignorant. Secondly, By making them wise. The former was and is the custom of the old world. The latter of the new." "The more ignorant any country," in fact, "the better it [was] . . . fitted for" the old system of government. That system, Paine contended in the mid-1790s in *Agrarian Justice*, supported "itself by abject civilization, in which debasement of the human mind, and wretchedness in the

---

[22] Bailyn, "Common Sense," 15.

[23] Paine, *Rights of Man*, in *Complete Writings of Paine* 1:343–44, 363–64.

mass of the people, are the chief criteria. Such governments consider man merely as an animal; that the exercise of intellectual faculty is not his privilege; *that, he has nothing to do with the laws but to obey them."* "All the forms of government . . . in the old world" thus depended "upon breaking the spirit of the people by poverty" and maintaining them in a state of "superstitious awe" and "enslaving reverence" as people who lived under those governments grew so "familiar to their absurdities" as to become "reconciled to them." *"Hereditary government over a people"* was thus *"a species of slavery,"* "a farrago of imposition and absurdity" that could only be "cram[med] . . . down the throat[s] of" those who were not sufficiently wise to "be *rationally* governed." Who could thus be in any way surprised "at the abject state of the human mind in monarchical countries" in which prejudice, that "spider of the mind," could find such a perfect "fitness of reception"?[24]

The old system of government had thus "crushed mankind" and deserved only the contempt, the "immovable hatred," of all "as being too debasing to the dignity of man." Its principal institutions were fit subjects only for ridicule. "The whole character [of monarchy] was . . . absurd and useless": "it first excludes a man from the means of information, yet empowers him to act in cases where the highest judgment is required." The whole "monarchical system" was "a system of mental levelling" that indiscriminately admitted "every species of character to the same authority" by putting "Vice and virtue, ignorance and wisdom, in short, every quality, good or bad . . . on the same level" and permitting kings to "succeed each other, not as rationals, but as animals." Moreover, the "idolatrous honors . . . expected to be paid to [a king] . . . under the name of a crowned head," the "kneeling to kiss a man's hand, wrapt up in flannels with the gout, and calling a boy of one and twenty the father of his people"—these were all "debasing absurdities" that should not be tolerated by rational men.[25]

Nor were the aristocracy and the church, the remaining two pillars of the old system, any more conducive to the benefit of mankind. Aristocracy was a "waxwork order," the "disgrace of" which "would be lessened if it could be considered only as childish imbecility." Its members were

---

[24] Paine, *Rights of Man, Agrarian Justice,* 1795–96, *Letter to the Abbé Raynal,* "Serious Address to the People of Pennsylvania," and *Letter to the Addressers,* 1792, ibid., 1:338–39, 364–66, 390, 620–21, 2:242, 289–90, 484.

[25] Paine, *Common Sense,* "American Crisis," *Rights of Man,* "Serious Address to the People of Pennsylvania," and "Letter to the Abbé Sieyès," ibid., 1:8–16, 51, 56, 72, 364–66, 2:289–90, 520.

mere "drones, a seraglio of males, who neither collect the honey nor form the hive, but exist only for lazy enjoyment." "We pardon foppery because of its insignificance," wrote Paine in his *Dissertation on First Principles* in 1795, "and on the same ground we might pardon the foppery of titles. But the origin of aristocracy was worse than foppery. It was robbery. The first aristocrats in all countries were brigands. Those of later times, sycophants."[26] Similarly, the church was simply another instrument of oppression that drained off a large share of the fruits of honest industry to support its ostentation and unwieldy establishment and sought to fetter the minds of men by its quest for religious orthodoxy. "Persecution," said Paine in *The Rights of Man*, "is always the strongly masked feature of all law-religions, or religions established by law."[27]

The old system was thus not only ridiculous but in all ways pernicious to the interests and debilitating to the spirits of the men who lived under it. Even the inclusion of a representative element in "the unnatural compounded system of the English Government" did not mitigate its ill effects. "The moving power of" that system, Paine declared, was "of necessity, corruption." However much in need of electoral reform, the British House of Commons still gave "exercise to a greater portion of reason than is convenient to the hereditary part." But those parts had easily resolved this problem simply by "buy[ing] the reason up." The crown had so much money and so many offices and monopolistic privileges at its disposal that it could easily convert the representative body into a mere "cipher" and its members into an unthinking herd of "*sinecure placemen and pensioners,*" the slavish clients of administration. Together these clients and the aristocracy used their resources to extend this system of clientage down to the bottom of the political nation until the whole of the ruling class, those "bears of the country," had become nothing more than "the spaniels of the government." Thus did a vast, unwieldy, expensive, and unnecessary system of privilege and patronage engross most of the resources of the country at the expense of the honest industry of the broad body of the people. There were thus "two distinct classes of men in the nation, those who pay taxes, and those who receive and live upon the taxes."[28]

Such an unreasonable system, founded as it was on an unjust distribu-

---

[26] Paine, *Rights of Man, Dissertation on First Principles of Government,* 1795, ibid., 1:289, 330–31, 412, 2:412.

[27] Paine, *Rights of Man,* ibid., 1:293.

[28] Paine, *Rights of Man,* "Serious Address to the People of Pennsylvania," and *Letter to the Addressers,* Paine to Onslow Craney, June 21, 1792, ibid., 1:281, 330–31, 338–39, 394–95, 2:293–94, 300–301, 463, 478, 482–83.

tion of rewards without regard to merit or industry and a patent and indefensible "inequality of rights," could only persist because the people who lived under it "had . . . resigned the prerogative of thinking" and "stood torpidly by" while advocates for the old system brazenly and against all "reason and common interest" defended it on "the mere score of antiquity." By thus "putting time in the place of principle," by "preaching up the doctrine of precedents" and "associating those precedents with a superstitious reverence for ancient things, as monks show relics and call them holy," such people were merely seeking to disguise the defects and injustices of the old system and to keep the people in the "universal languor" that had long gripped the "mass of the nation" in all the societies of the Old World. But "government by precedent, without any regard to the principle of the precedent," declared Paine, was a form of "political popery" and "one of the vilest systems that" could "be set up." It was either designed to keep men "in a state of ignorance, or . . . a practical confession that wisdom degenerates in governments as governments increase in age, and can only hobble along by the stilts and crutches of precedents."[29]

The whole of the old system was "founded on principles and opinions, the very reverse of what they ought to be," and it could be maintained only by thus "blinding the understanding of man, and making him believe that government is some wonderful mysterious thing." It demonstrated an "obedience to ignorance," and, Paine remarked in *The Rights of Man*, "when once the mind can bring itself to pay this indiscriminate reverence, it descends below the stature of mental manhood." In Europe, as in America, Paine's first task had been to demystify the old order, to expose its "absurdities," to shake "the fabric" and "to break the chains of political superstition, and [thereby to] raise degraded man to his proper rank" as a full man by persuading him of two fundamental truths Paine and all earlier immigrants had discovered in America: first, "that government was not that complicated thing, enshrined in mystery, which Church and State, to play into each other's hands, had represented," and second, that the capacity for political understanding of almost every man was such that he could be treated, as Paine sought to treat all his readers, *"as a man and not as a child."*[30]

[29] Paine, *Common Sense, Rights of Man, Letter to the Addressers*, "Answer to Four Questions," 1792, *Dissertation on First Principles*, and *Prospects on the Rubicon*, 1787, ibid., 1:3, 386, 446–47, 2:470, 483, 536, 573, 577–78, 623.
[30] Paine, *Rights of Man*, "Reflections on Titles," 1775, "Serious Address to the People of Pennsylvania," *Letter to the Addressers*, "To the People of England," 1804, and "To the

But Paine could not be "satisfied with the simple detection of error or imposition" in Europe any more than he had been in America. What Paine held out to Europeans was the vision of a freer—and less demeaning—life through "the progressive increase of political knowledge." "Notwithstanding the mystery with which the science of government has been enveloped, for the purpose of enslaving, plundering and imposing upon mankind," Paine assured his readers in 1795, "it is of all things the least mysterious and the most easy to be understood. The meanest capacity cannot be at a loss, if it begins its inquiries at the right point." Those who would free themselves from the influence of ancient prejudices and act "in a style superior to the little politics of narrow thinking" would quickly find that by taking "nature, reason, and experience" for their guides they could "elevate the science of government to a height of perfection of which we now have no conception" and contrive a form of government that would be "best calculated to secure the end for which a nation is at the expense of supporting it," that is, the public good, which Paine defined as the ability of "every man . . . to pursue his occupation, and enjoy the fruits of his labors, and the produce of his property, in peace and safety, and with the least possible expense."[31]

The best form to achieve this end, Paine himself was absolutely persuaded, was the representative. Men would smile, said Paine, at the suggestion that literature and the sciences be made hereditary. "As the republic of letters brings forward the best literary productions, by giving genius a fair and universal chance; so the representative system of government is calculated to produce the wisest laws, by collecting wisdom where it can be found." Once men had become aware of the many benefits of representative government, they would discover, Paine contended, that "all men are republicans by nature, and royalists only by fashion." For republican government actually had "more *true grandeur* in it than a kingly one." "On the part of the public," Paine pointed out, "it is more consistent with freemen to appoint their rulers than to have them born; and on the part of those who preside, it is far nobler to be a ruler by the choice of the people, than a king by the chance of birth." Representative

---

Citizens of the United States," 1802–3, ibid., 1:375, 386, 368, 2:33, 289–90, 471, 488, 676, 928.

[31] Paine, *Rights of Man*, "Rules of the Society for Political Inquiries," 1787, *Letter to the Abbé Raynal*, "Candid and Critical Remarks," 1777, *Letter to the Addressers*, "Answers to Four Questions," and *Dissertation on First Principles*, ibid., 1:367–70, 388, 2:41–42, 245, 274, 471, 487, 496, 531, 571.

governments were, moreover, necessarily more responsive and more sensitive to the newly discovered political truth that government "is not a trade which any man or body of men has a right to set up and exercise for his own emolument, but is altogether a trust."[32]

To provide "a rule for the conduct of [this] . . . government" a people needed a constitution, not, like the so-called English constitution (which was, in Paine's view, only a government and not a constitution), one that had been accidentally and mysteriously derived but one that had been freely established and would guarantee the natural rights of its citizens and the supremacy of the rule of law. A viable representative government also had to be based upon a wide franchise that included all independent adult males, an absolute equality of rights, and a total prohibition of monopolies so that "every man would be free [both to participate in government and] to follow any occupation by which he can procure an honest livelihood, and in any place, town, or city, throughout the nation." "*Representative government*," declared Paine, "*is freedom*," and "the floor of Freedom" had to be "as level as water."[33] Liberty, Paine thought, should always take precedence over "the defence of property," but there was no real danger to property from an equality of rights and a broad franchise. Freedom, he had learned in America, quieted, rather than promoted, contention. The free and "unceasing circulation of interest" and ideas in a broadly participatory society would, Paine predicted, invigorate "the whole mass of civilized man" so that "all property [would be] . . . safe under their protection."[34]

Paine's call for the people of the Old World to recognize "no majesty but that of the people, no government except that of its own representatives, and no sovereignty except that of the laws" was a call for them "to recast," in Eric Foner's words, the "government in the Old World on the model of the New." "It was the American principle of government," Paine assured George Washington in 1796, "that I was endeavouring to spread in Europe." The Old World would be regenerated "by the principles of the new," which Paine vowed "in the most undismayed manner

---

[32] Paine, *Rights of Man* and "The Forester's Letters," 1776, ibid., 1:367–68, 371, 379, 2:79–80.

[33] Paine, *Common Sense, Rights of Man, Letter to the Abbé Raynal*, "Serious Address to the People of Pennsylvania," and *Dissertation on First Principles*, ibid., 1:29, 281, 387, 390, 413–14, 2:259, 282–89, 579–80.

[34] Paine, *Rights of Man*, "Thoughts on Defensive War," 1775, "The Forester's Letters," *Letter to the Abbé Raynal*, "Serious Address to the People of Pennsylvania," and "Address to the People of France," Sept. 25, 1792, ibid., 1:359, 2:54, 87, 245, 250, 262, 286, 538.

to publish . . . on the house-tops, for the good of others."[35] Far from concealing "the hideous figure of anarchy, or the gloomy monster of tyranny" under "the fair name of liberty," as so many people had initially feared, the American Revolution, Paine thought, had "contributed more to enlighten the world, and diffuse a spirit of freedom and liberality among mankind, than any human event . . . that ever preceded it." Alone among all countries, America did not need to "be ashamed to tell her birth, nor to relate the stages by which she rose to empire." The American Revolution had marked the very "morning of reason" that had opened "a new system of extended civilization." It had given reason and liberty, said Paine, "*a place to stand upon.*" "So deeply rooted were all the governments of the old world, and so effectively had the tyranny and the antiquity of habit established itself over the mind, that no beginning could be made in Asia, Africa, or Europe, to reform the political condition of man," Paine declared in *The Rights of Man.* "Freedom had been hunted round the globe; reason was considered as rebellion; and the slavery of fear had made men afraid to think."[36]

By giving mankind "a revolution in the principles and practise of governments," America had thus become "the Parent of the . . . world." It would "be in magnitude" what "Athens was [only] in miniature[:] . . . the one was the wonder of the ancient world; the other is becoming the admiration and model of the present." The American "system of government," Paine told his European audience, was "free from corruption, and now administered over an extent of territory ten times as large as England, *for less expense than the pensions alone in England amount to;* and under which more freedom is enjoyed, and a more happy state of society is preserved, and a more general prosperity is promoted, than under any other system of government now existing in the world." "There the poor are not oppressed, the rich are not privileged. Industry is not mortified by the splendid extravagance of a court rioting at its expense. Their taxes are few, because their government is just; and as there is nothing to render them wretched, there is nothing to engender riots and tumults." That this utopian condition could be achieved by man in America was a standing example for the rest of mankind. A flame

---

[35] Foner, *Tom Paine,* 217; Paine, "To the Sheriff of the County of Sussex," 1792, "Address to the People of France," "Letter to George Washington," 1796, and "To the Citizens of the United States," Paine to Condorcet et al., June 1791, in *Complete Writings of Paine* 2:464–65, 538–39, 697, 707, 912, 1315.

[36] Paine, "American Crisis," *Rights of Man,* and *Letter to the Abbé Raynal,* in *Complete Writings of Paine* 1:230–32, 353–54, 396–97, 239–40, 256.

kindled by "a small spark . . . in America," Paine predicted, would wind "its progress from nation to nation" until man had acquired "a knowledge of his rights by attending justly to . . . [his] interests, and" had discovered "in the event that the strength and powers of despotism" consisted "wholly in the fear of resisting it, and that in order" for man "*to be free, it is sufficient that he wills it.*" Paine invited his readers to become free by becoming men.[37]

Where precisely Paine derived this vision of a new "modern" political world can perhaps never be accurately ascertained. Little is known about his beliefs before his coming to America. That he had already read sufficiently widely to appreciate the impact of commerce and science upon traditional ways of life and thought seems overwhelmingly probable.[38] Throughout his maturity, moreover, he had always lived so close to the line between independence and dependence that he could scarcely have failed to gain a sharp appreciation of the "trying and necessitous circumstances" of poverty and to be sensitive to the many injustices of a society in which "a small Part," as his friend Benjamin Franklin wrote of Scotland and Ireland in 1772, were "Landlords, great Noblemen, and Gentlemen, extreamly opulent, living in the highest Affluence and Magnificence," while the "Bulk of the People [were] tenants [or other dependents], extreamly poor, living in the most sordid Wretchedness, in dirty Hovels of Mud and Straw . . . cloathed only in Rags," and "abject in Spirit."[39] Whatever experiences and knowledge Paine brought with him to America—and, as he later wrote Nathanael Greene, "it was in a great measure owing to my bringing a knowledge of England with me to America that I was enabled [in *Common Sense*] to enter deeper into politics, and with more success, than other people"[40]—remaining evidence

[37] Paine, *Rights of Man*, "To Mr. Secretary Dundas," June 6, 1792, and "To the Sheriff of Sussex," Paine to Thomas Jefferson, Jan. 1, 1805, ibid., 1:353–54, 360–61, 371–72, 398, 2:449, 464–65, 1454.

[38] See Paine, *Letter to the Abbé Raynal*, ibid., 2:241–42.

[39] Paine, "The Case of the Officers of the Excise," 1772, Paine's only known piece of political writing before his emigration to America, ibid., 8–9, 11; Benjamin Franklin to Joshua Babcock, Jan. 13, 1772, in *The Writings of Benjamin Franklin*, ed. Albert Henry Smyth, 10 vols., (New York, 1905–7), 5:361–63.

[40] Paine to Greene, Sept. 9, 1780, in *Complete Writings of Paine* 2:1189.

strongly suggests that America provided him with the inspiration for and gave shape to his model of the modern world.

The traditional emphasis in Paine scholarship has been upon his impact on America, and one scholar has argued with force that Paine was so addicted to the heady wine of reason that his knowledge was rarely enriched by "observation of actual . . . facts."[41] But a powerful case can, I think, be made that what Paine did for America, America had already done for Paine; that Paine's subsequent conception of what political society should be like was in very large measure shaped not merely, as Eric Foner has suggested, by the "rapid social and political changes American society underwent in the Revolutionary era" but by the radical character of American society itself—before, as well as after, the Revolution.[42]

If, as Paine remarked in *The American Crisis*, "it was the cause of America that made" him "an author," America itself struck him with enormous force, unlocking the accumulated rage of thirty-seven years and sharpening and raising to an explicit level his own perceptions of and discontents with the evils of the Old World. "Paine, and other writers upon American politics, met with such amazing success," the Vermont cleric and historian Samuel Williams declared in 1794, "not because they taught the people principles, which they did not before understand; but because they placed the principles which they had learned of them, in a very clear and striking light, on a most critical and important occasion." Paine, Williams insisted, had learned his "principles from the state of society in America." Nor did Paine ever write anything that contradicted Williams's judgment. On the contrary, he always insisted that America, as he later wrote George Washington, had been "constantly in my mind in all the publications I afterwards made" and, as he suggested in his *Letter to Abbé Raynal*, that he had only gotten "a just idea of" America and appreciated its fullest implications for the subsequent transformation of the Old World "by coming to it."[43]

What struck Paine so forcefully about America was its almost total

---

[41] Cecelia M. Kenyon, "Where Paine Went Wrong," *American Political Science Review* 45 (1951): 1087.

[42] Foner, *Tom Paine*, xvii. Foner argues, in sharp contrast to the argument presented here, that most of Paine's "ideas were fixed by the time he arrived in America," tracing them to such "formative influences" as his father's Quakerism, his service as a government excise officer, his poverty, his acquaintance with the ideas of Newtonian science, and the ideas of radical British dissenting Whigs. Ibid., 3–17.

[43] Paine, "American Crisis," *Letter to the Abbé Raynal*, and "Letter to George Washington," July 30, 1796, in *Complete Writings of Paine* 1:235, 2:250, 694; Samuel Williams, *The Natural and Civil History of Vermont*, 2 vols. (Walpole, N. H., 1794), 1:371–72.

dissimilarity from the Old World. "The case and circumstances of America," he wrote, "present themselves as in the beginning of the world" before it had been engrossed and corrupted by the monopolizers of power and resources. As Winthrop Jordan has remarked, Paine identified the state of nature and "the beginnings of human society and government with the early settlement of America." "Those who are conversant with Europe," he wrote just a few months after his arrival in America, "would be tempted to believe that even the air of the Atlantic disagrees with the constitution of foreign vices; if they survive the voyage, they either expire on their arrival, or linger away in an incurable consumption. There is a happy something in the climate of America, which disarms them of all their power both of infection and attraction." What that something was was space and opportunity. No "country in the world," it seemed to Paine, had "so many openings to happiness as" America. "The vastness of its extent, the variety of its climate, the fertility of its soil, the yet unexplored treasures of its bowels, the multitude of its rivers, lakes, bays, inlets and other conveniences of navigation"— all made America "one of the richest subjects of cultivation ever presented to any people upon earth." "The scene" presented "to the eye of a spectator" had "something in it which generates and encourages great ideas. Nature appears to him in magnitude. The mighty object he beholds, acts upon his mind by enlarging it, and he partakes of the greatness he contemplates." "While men remained in Europe as subjects of some hereditary potentate [and in an unjust and evil society] they had ideas conformable to that condition," Paine wrote, "but when they arrived in America they found themselves in possession of a new character . . . and, like converts to a new religion, . . . became inspired with new principles."[44]

The result was that the "spring, the progress, the object, the consequences, nay, the men, their habits of thinking, and all the circumstances of the country" diverged sharply from those of the Old World. "Mutual prejudices" were "worn off, a humane and philosophical spirit . . . cherished, and youth . . . stimulated to a laudable diligence and emulation in the pursuit of wisdom." Political consciousness was awakened and reshaped. "Elevated above their former rank," immigrants to America soon learned to consider "government and public affairs as part of their

---

[44] Paine, *Rights of Man*, "An Act for Incorporating the American Philosophical Society," 1780, "Six Letters to Rhode Island," "To the People of England," and "The Magazine in America," Jan. 24, 1775, in *Complete Writings of Paine* 1:353–54, 375–76, 2:39, 346–47, 676, 1110; Jordan, "Familial Politics," 296.

own concern," "the theory of government" became "well known by almost every farmer in America," and there was "no such thing . . . as
power of any kind, independent of the people" and "no other race of men
. . . but the people." The differences between Europe and America were
thus the differences between a world with a numerous "class of poor and
wretched people" and one without, between a world "wrapt up in the
most absurd species of slavery, and the other possessing and enjoying all
their natural and civil rights."[45]

If Paine's vision of the modern world was fundamentally American,
the Revolution in America provided him with a powerful example of
how that vision might be achieved in the Old World. For the American
Revolution, Paine believed, had created the possibility of a vast political
awakening of a magnitude unparalleled in the history of the world and
not even dreamed of before that event. "As the mind closed itself toward
England" in America, Paine told his European audience, "it opened itself toward the world." Old prejudices "underwent . . . a mental examination" until "every corner of the mind" had been "swept of its cobwebs,
poison and dust," and "a mass of sense long lying in a dormant state"
had been activated. Relieved of the "shackles" of their former prejudices,
Americans thenceforth enjoyed "a freedom of mind" that was appropriate to the freedom of circumstance they had so long possessed. This
new freedom not only enabled them to make the first "improvement[s]
. . . in . . . principle and . . . practise" in "the science of government"
since antiquity but provoked a revolution in the "style and manner of
thinking . . . more extraordinary than the political revolution of the
country." With the Revolution, Americans came to "see with other eyes;
. . . hear with other ears; and think with other thoughts than those formerly used." So sweeping was the revolution in consciousness that
Americans "really [became] another people" and could never "again go
back to ignorance and prejudice." "If I ask a man in America if he wants
a king," Paine wrote in the early 1790s, "he retorts, and asks me if I take
him for an idiot." "The mind once enlightened," Paine believed, could
not "again become dark": "once the veil begins to rend, it admits not
of repair."[46]

---

[45] Paine, "Act Incorporating Am. Phil. Soc.," *Letter to the Abbé Raynal*, "Six Letters to
Rhode Island," "To Mr. Secretary Dundas," and "To the People of England," in *Complete
Writings of Paine* 2:39, 220–21, 258, 336–37, 344, 451–52, 676.

[46] Paine, *Rights of Man, Letter to the Abbé Raynal, Letter to the Addressers*, and *Dissertation on First Principles*, Paine to Thomas Jefferson, Sept. 18, 1789, ibid., 1:320, 326,
368, 2:243–44, 481, 571, 580, 1296.

The American Revolution had thus "thrown a beam of light over the world, which reaches *into* man" in ways that could never be reversed. It was the first bud in a political spring that, sooner or later, would necessarily be followed by a "political summer" with "a general revolution in governments" all over Europe. Once ignorance and superstition had been banished, once political consciousness had been awakened and extended and men began "to feel their consequences by their usefulness, and their right[s] as members of society," it would "no longer [be] possible to govern them as before." The only question was whether revolution would be violent, as it would become in France, or whether it would be as "passive, rational and costless" as it had been in America.[47]

In his tireless advocacy of using the experience of the New World to transform the Old, Paine became the self-appointed instructor in the "American system of government" to the rest of the world. As Arthur Sheps has shown, America had already become "the cynosure of radical eyes" in Britain well "before the influence of Paine could have been [widely] felt" following publication of *The Rights of Man* in the 1790s. "Under the impact of the example of the American republic," Sheps argues persuasively, the political ideas of British radicals underwent "a kind of paradigm revolution" in which "common words [and concepts] like the constitution, republicanism, the representative basis of government, and the sovereignty of the people . . . began to take on new or expanded meanings." The primary contribution of Paine, Sheps contends, came during the 1790s. By setting America up as a model of social as well as political reform, Paine helped to give British radicalism an entirely new dimension by stimulating its adherents to a hitherto missing "concern with the social benefits of political reform."[48]

If, however, British radicals had indeed already taken "America as a standard of reform" before Paine had achieved his major impact in Britain, he may still have been a "pivotal figure" in the "readjustment" of political ideas that occurred in Europe in the wake of the American Revolution. For no one else was either so persistent or so prolific in spelling out for Europeans the relevance of the American experience for the Old World; and no one else came close to achieving such widespread popularity. Once the French Revolution had opened up "the prospect . . . of extending the principles of liberty . . . through the greater part of Eu-

---

[47] Paine, *Rights of Man* and *Dissertation on First Principles,* ibid., 1:320, 447, 450, 454, 2:580.

[48] Arthur Sheps, "The American Revolution and the Transformation of English Republicanism," *Historical Reflections* 2 (1974): 4–28.

rope," Paine devoted himself compulsively to the task of teaching Europeans the political and social lessons he had learned in America, and he did not return to America until, having previously been harried out of Britain, he had become persuaded that the French would never "understand any thing at all of the principles of free government."[49]

However unsuccessful Paine had been in persuading the French to adopt the true "American" principles of free government, he had spearheaded—if he had not been the central figure in bringing about—a far more fundamental and sweeping revolution in political consciousness, a revolution that redrew the cognitive map and relocated the central—the underlying and previously virtually unchallenged—mental correlates of the traditional political world. In Paine's hands, much that had been thought to be right and good in that world became pernicious, while much that had been thought to be pernicious became right and good. Words themselves acquired new connotations, as he gave favorable meaning to hitherto essentially perjorative terms such as *innovation, novel, newfangled,* and *modern.*[50]

Paine helped even to transform the meaning of the word *revolution* itself. As J. H. Elliott has argued, the men of early modern Europe who might be classified as proponents of revolution were "obsessed with *renovation,*" with "the desire to return to old customs and priviledges, and to an old order of society." The contribution of Paine, with the circumstances of America constantly before him, was to redefine revolution as a phenomenon that looked to the future rather than to the past, stressed the need to "establish a new social order" rather than to "return to a golden age," and emphasized innovation rather than renovation. It was "in vain to look for precedents [for the American Revolution] among the revolutions of former ages," Paine told the abbé Raynal. "What were formerly called revolutions, were little more than a change of persons,

---

[49] Ibid.; Paine to George Jacques Danton, May 6, 1793, in *Complete Writings of Paine* 2:1395; Foner, *Tom Paine,* 253. See also Joyce Appleby, "America as a Model for the Radical French Reformers of 1789," *William and Mary Quarterly,* 3d ser., 28 (1971): 267–86, which shows that fascination with the American example in France also antedated publication of the *Rights of Man* by fifteen years and was deliberately distorted by *americanistes* to serve their own political objectives during their battles with the admirers of the English constitution.

[50] Foner makes the point in regard to Paine's use of such words as *republic, democracy,* and *revolution* (*Tom Paine,* xv, 217). But Paine's contributions in this area went far deeper. See Paine, *Rights of Man,* "A Dialogue between . . . Montgomery . . . and an American Delegate," 1776, *Letter to the Abbé Raynal,* and "Serious Address to the People of Pennsylvania," in *Complete Writings of Paine* 1:453, 2:91, 257, 281.

or an alternation in local circumstances," he wrote in *The Rights of Man;* they had all "been worked within the atmosphere of a court" or a small group within the ruling class "and never on the great floor of a nation. The parties were always of the class of courtiers; and whatever was their rage for reformation, they carefully preserved the fraud of that profession." Extending "only to a change of persons and measures, but not of principles," such revolutions "rose and fell like things of course, and had nothing in their existence or their fate that could influence beyond the spot that had produced them."[51]

But the revolution of the late eighteenth century, "revolving from West to East . . . by a stronger impulse than the government of the sword revolved from East to West," interested "not [a few] particular individuals, but [whole] nations, in its progress." It promised to bring "a new era to the human race," in "which every thing may be looked for," an era built upon a total reversal "of the natural order of things" and a new and constantly extending political consciousness committed to "a system of [political] principles as universal as truth and the existence of man, and combining moral and political happiness and national prosperity."[52]

With its emphasis on a political society based upon universal principles, choosing leaders on the basis of merit, and composed of informed, highly autonomous, cognitively flexible, and participatory citizens, each of whom had a pronounced sense of both personal worth and a belief in the efficacy of the individual in the drive to improve the condition of mankind, the new political consciousness stimulated by Paine was essentially modern.[53] That the world could be changed for the better and man liberated from the tyranny of his ancient prejudices was Paine's primary message to the world, and the model that gave shape—and credibility—to that message was America. Inspired by the openness, the basic modernity, of American society and impressed by the liberating and energizing character of its Revolution, Paine helped to give Americans an appreciation of their own social virtues, inner worth, and what he thought was their superiority over the Old World. In the process, he laid the founda-

---

[51] J. H. Elliott, "Revolution and Continuity in Early Modern Europe," *Past and Present,* no. 49 (1969): 43–44, 52–56; Paine, *Letter to the Abbé Raynal* and *Rights of Man,* in *Complete Writings of Paine* 1:341, 356, 360–61, 2:220.

[52] Paine, *Rights of Man,* in *Complete Writings of Paine* 1:342, 344, 356.

[53] Inkeles and Smith, *Becoming Modern,* 16, 19–25, 290. For another, somewhat different analysis of the specific aspects of Paine's thought that made him modern, see Foner, *Tom Paine,* xix–xx.

tions for his subsequent contributions to a powerful new vision of political society that was the product not merely of pure reason but of reason operating on—and generalizing from—experience, the American experience.

Eliciting strong resonances in the Old World, this vision quickly replaced, even in Britain where it was most effectively resisted, traditional conceptions of political society, and, for better or worse, has subsequently given—and still gives—structure to and dominates perceptions of much of the contemporary political world. Paine first achieved fame by rescuing the Americans from what he thought, having seen America at first hand, was a false and debilitating reverence for the traditional and metropolitan world. But he wound up helping to rescue not just Americans but the whole world. In a fundamental sense, we are today all Paine's children. Not the British defeat at Yorktown, but Paine, and the new American conception of political society that he did so much to popularize in Europe, turned the world upside down.

The earliest draft of this chapter was written for delivery as one of the Biennial Thomas Paine Lectures sponsored by the Thomas Paine Society on March 16, 1976, at the University of East Anglia, Norwich, England. It was also given as the evening address at the 45th Annual Meeting of the Pennsylvania Historical Association, at Cedar Crest College in Allentown, Pennsylvania, October 21, 1976, and at the Polish Academy of Science, Warsaw, Poland, April 1, 1977. It is here reprinted with permission and minor changes from *Political Science Quarterly* 93 (1978): 73–92.

THIRTEEN

Philip Mazzei:
Cultural Broker in America and Europe in the Age of Enlightenment and Revolution

W HEN IN THE LATE 1760s Grand Duke Leopold of Tuscany asked his subject Philip Mazzei to secure two Franklin stoves for him in London, he initiated a chain of happenings that significantly altered Mazzei's thitherto quiet and largely private life. Born into a modest Tuscan family in 1730, Mazzei studied medicine in Florence and spent three years as a doctor in Smyrna before he took up residence in early 1756 in London, where he achieved some modest prosperity as an importer of Italian products. Characteristically, Mazzei acted on the grand duke's request by going directly to Franklin himself, who not only helped Mazzei find an artisan who could produce his stoves but also introduced him to a number of other Americans then resident in London, among them Thomas Adams, a member of a prominent Virginia mercantile family. A developing friendship between Mazzei and Adams yielded a scheme to bring Mazzei to Virginia in an attempt to produce Mediterranean commodities, particularly wine, olives, and silk, an enterprise that had long engaged the fancies of that colony's enterprising elite.

Migrating to Virginia in the fall of 1773 with several Italian farmers, Mazzei subsequently secured the patronage and became well acquainted with many of the leading Virginians of the day. The roster of his acquaintances was virtually a *Who's Who* of Revolutionary Virginia. It included Thomas Jefferson, Peyton Randolph, Richard Bland, George Wythe, Robert Carter Nicholas, George Mason, George Washington, Archibald Cary, James Madison, and James Monroe. Settling next to Jefferson at Monticello, he not only managed to establish a successful vineyard but also became a strong partisan of the colonial cause in the unfolding controversy with Britain. In 1779, the Virginia state government sent him to Europe as its official envoy in an effort to secure financial assistance. Primarily because he destroyed his credentials when the ship on which he had taken his passage was captured by a British privateer, this mission proved abortive, and he returned to Virginia in the fall of 1783 to find his vineyard in ruins and to experience disappointment in his efforts to secure a post as representative of the United States in Europe.

For the next several years, Mazzei resided in France, where he continued in his private capacity as a citizen of the United States, as he had done throughout his unsuccessful mission for Virginia, to champion the cause of America in Europe. Produced to counter what Mazzei regarded as the extensive misinformation published on the United States by such popular writers as the abbés Mably and Raynal, his *Researches on the United States*, issued in French in Paris early in 1788, was received by French reviewers as the most accurate and comprehensive work on America published in France up to that time.[1] In 1792, events of the French Revolution drove him to Poland, where he served for a time as adviser to King Stanislas. Returning in the late 1790s to Italy, he subsequently resided in Pisa, wrote his *Memoirs*, and died in 1816 at the age of eighty-six.

One of the most interesting aspects about Mazzei's engagement with America is the evidence it provides about the role of the cultural broker in the increasingly interconnected world of the last half of the eighteenth century. By the term *cultural broker*, I mean to refer to those people who cross cultural boundaries and make a deliberate effort within their new host culture to diffuse knowledge about the culture whence they come. Such people can also send or, in cases where they recross cultural boundaries, actually carry information about the new culture they have encountered back to their old culture or on to yet another culture. If they frequently travel back and forth across cultural frontiers, they may perform this function repeatedly. In the early modern world, merchants, ship captains, sailors, travelers, immigrants, students, soldiers, and public and diplomatic officials were some of the categories of people who regularly filled the role of cultural broker.[2]

---

[1] Howard Marraro, ed., "Philip Mazzei, Virginia's Agent in Europe: The Story of His Mission as Related in His Own Dispatches and Other Documents," *Bulletin of the New York Public Library* 38 (1934): 163; Philip Mazzei, *Researches on the United States*, trans. Constance D. Sherman (Charlottesville, Va., 1976), xv–xvi.

[2] A penetrating discussion of the role of the cultural broker is Greg Dening, *Islands and Beaches: Discourses on a Silent Land, Marquesas, 1774–1880* (Melbourne, 1980).

During the late eighteenth century, the careers of the American Benjamin Franklin and the Englishman Thomas Paine offer two prominent examples of people who played especially significant roles as cultural brokers: Franklin as the advocate of America in Britain before Independence and the exemplar of republican America in France thereafter, and Paine as the demystifier of Britain in the colonies in 1776 and the proselyter for American republicanism in Britain and France in the 1780s. By virtue of his intimate knowledge of the culture from which he came, each was able to supply vital information that significantly affected his host culture's perceptions of that culture from which he had just come and thereby exerted a significant—in Paine's case perhaps even a profound—influence upon contemporary events and developments.[3]

This chapter represents a preliminary attempt to look at the career of Philip Mazzei, between his migration to Virginia in 1773 and the publication of his *Researches on the United States* in 1788, in terms of his role as a cultural broker. It focuses on two subjects: first, what he brought from Europe to America, and second and at greater length, what he took from America to Europe. The chapter makes no claim that Mazzei exerted an influence comparable in importance to that exercised by Franklin and Paine or even by Lafayette, Jefferson, or John Adams. But it does aspire to illuminate his particular contribution as cultural broker to late eighteenth-century European understandings of the new American republic. To that end, it makes no effort to assess the Tuscan or European intellectual influences upon Mazzei and devotes little attention to his influence on American thought. Rather, it focuses mostly upon the influence of Mazzei's perceptions of American society upon his principal work, *Researches on the United States.*

What made Mazzei valuable to Virginians, what made them willing to subscribe nearly £2,000 for his scheme to produce wine, olives, and silk in Virginia, was his Tuscan background and his presumed expertise in Mediterranean agriculture. How extensive and detailed that expertise was at the time Mazzei first began to entertain the idea of migrating to Virginia is not clear. Never had he functioned as an agricultural manager

[3] See in this connection Jack P. Greene, "The Alienation of Benjamin Franklin—British American," *Journal of the Royal Society for the Arts* 124 (1976): 52–73 [chap. 11 above], and "Paine, America, and the 'Modernization' of Political Consciousness," *Political Science Quarterly* 93 (1978): 73–92 [chap. 12 above].

or estate owner in Tuscany. But he did have the entrepreneurial skills to recruit people who had the necessary expertise, to organize their transport with the necessary equipment to Virginia, and to supervise their activities once they were there.

Moreover, he and his entourage supplied Virginians with a variety of unfamiliar "products" from Mediterranean or, more specifically, Tuscan culture. They brought new farm implements from Tuscany—"spades, bill hooks, sickles for flax, and others"—that, in Mazzei's words, were "unknown in America and even in England." They brought new techniques of clearing land and cultivation; new animals, in particular, Italian and Maltese asses for the express purpose of obtaining sturdier mules; and many new products, including vine cuttings and the seeds for several grains grown in Italy. For these gifts, Mazzei received much acclaim. Archibald Cary praised him for the many "fine things I had brought over, which they had not known of until then," and Benjamin Franklin congratulated him for his "laudable and meritorious endeavours to introduce new products." Mazzei himself took special pride in the fact that the fifty-day maize that he had brought from Tuscany was referred to in Virginia as "Mazzei's corn." Indeed, he noted delightedly in his *Memoirs*, in Virginia "my name is applied to all the products I was the first to introduce and to whatever I taught the people to do or brought to their knowledge."[4]

But Mazzei thought that the most important information he brought from the eastern side of the Atlantic to his new hosts in Virginia was not about the agriculture of the Mediterranean but about the political culture of England. Offended by the xenophobia of the English "and the insolent way in which" they "express[ed] themselves about other nations," Mazzei during the crisis over independence in 1773–76 systematically endeavored in newspaper essays and discussions to undermine "the prejudices of those [many] people [in Virginia] who were [still] accustomed to look upon England as a model of perfection" by pointing out "the essential defects" of the English constitution and showing "how fallacious the bases of public liberty were in England." When at a dinner gathering at Williamsburg, the capital, the treasurer of the colony, Robert Carter Nicholas, a noted advocate of moderation, expressed the fear that if the quarrel with Britain went too far it might result in the loss "of the Constitution," Mazzei replied, to the delight of many of his dinner companions, including Richard Bland, the colony's leading antiquary,

---

[4] *Memoirs of the Life and Pereginations of the Florentine Philip Mazzei 1730–1816*, trans. Howard Marraro (New York, 1942), 176–203.

and George Mason, later the author of the Virginia Declaration of Rights: "Mr. Treasurer, had I such [a] Constitution, I would think myself in consumption."[5]

"Ever since childhood," Mazzei told Virginians, "you have heard that" the English constitution "was the best possible type of government; you could see that it was such, in comparison with the other governments of Europe; you . . . have read English authors who proved that it is far better than that of the Roman republic; finally, never dreaming of having to change it, you lacked the incentive to examine it in detail." According to Mazzei, Peyton Randolph, speaker of the Virginia House of Burgesses and later president of the First Continental Congress, "applauded my task of enlightening the people, saying that I could not have picked a more appropriate time, and begging me not to tire of the job." Jefferson himself, Mazzei reported, "was amazed at the defects of the English form of government which I pointed out to him, saying that they had not [before] even occurred to him" and lauding Mazzei "for the valuable information he has given me about England."[6]

Mazzei's reputation as an authority on England caused his opinions "to be so highly regarded" that, he recorded proudly in his *Memoirs*, people "came to consult me from all parts of the country, which covered an area of about 150 square miles." They came, according to Mazzei, seeking "light on the true state of our affairs, explaining that since I was educated and they were not [and since I had lived in England and they had not], it was only right that I should inform them, just as they were in duty bound to tell their neighbours what they learned from me."[7]

Whether Mazzei actually did exercise such a powerful influence in the political education of Virginians at such a critical juncture in their history, whether his role in helping to open the eyes of Virginians to the defects of the English political system and to cast aside their old prejudices in favor of England and the English constitution was as critical as he liked to believe, is now impossible to assess. But the significant fact about his interpretation of his role in Virginia during the Revolution is his understanding of his strategic position as the possessor of knowledge crucial to Virginians in that situation and his social utility as a disseminator of that knowledge, an understanding that, if Mazzei may be believed, was shared by many important personages in the local Virginia

---

[5] Ibid., 204–5.

[6] Ibid., 204–6, 213.

[7] Ibid., 213.

establishment who were eager both to learn from him and to encourage him to employ his expertise for the "enlightenment" of the general public.

If Mazzei's role as a cultural broker in America is tantalizingly vague, his function in a similar guise in Europe in the 1780s can be explored much more fully. Even before he returned to Europe as agent for Virginia in 1780, he had translated a copy of the Declaration of Independence into Italian and sent it to the grand duke of Tuscany. During his agency in Paris in the early 1780s, he was a zealous advocate of the American cause. Intending to counteract the intensive disinformation campaign carried on by the British ministry and its literary apologists and to provide "a clear idea of the state of affairs in the United States," he wrote a number of pieces for the newspapers and had them "translated into several languages."[8] But far and away the most impressive expression of his zeal for "the asylum of liberty," as he referred to the United States, was his *Researches on the United States.*[9]

Divided into four parts and comprising more than four hundred pages, this substantial volume developed out of Mazzei's growing exasperation with "European prejudices about our governments and the present state of the [American] union," especially the charges of "pretended disorder, [and] the pretended anarchy of the United States" that had issued from the English press and had been given credence by the abbé Mably's *Observations on the Government and Laws of the United States,* which had been published in Amsterdam in 1784 and, in Mazzei's opinion, was a thoroughly irresponsible and uninformed work that had "contributed in large measure to consecrating the innumerable phantasies circulating throughout the continent to the discredit of the United States." But Mazzei conceived of the *Researches* not merely as a work of refutation but as a "complete and impartial description of that interesting country," a "precise and accurate account of the situation in the thirteen United States, especially with regard to their governments," that would enable the European reader "to consider these states intelligently."[10]

[8] Ibid., 218, 240–41.

[9] Mazzei to Thomas Jefferson, Oct. 26, 1785, in *The Papers of Thomas Jefferson,* ed. Julian P. Boyd et al., 24 vols. to date (Princeton, N. J., 1950–), 8:8, 677.

[10] *Researches,* 1–2, 4–5; *Memoirs,* 295–96.

Howard Marraro, the leading American student of Mazzei, has condemned the *Researches* as "superficial, badly planned, and poorly constructed" and charged that it betrays its "polemic intent and hasty execution, and, on the whole," has "slight historical importance." Mazzei, in Marraro's judgment, was simply "not the type of man who could discuss the grave questions of his time with any real penetration, nor was he capable of extensive research, thoughtful analysis, or accurate interpretation."[11] But this harsh judgment seems to be seriously misleading. From Mazzei's correspondence, it is clear that, however much time he took in the actual composition, he had been thinking about and collecting material with which to refute Mably and other writers for at least three years before he actually published the *Researches.* Similarly, although he apologized for his inability to do any research in the United States, his footnotes and references reveal extensive knowledge of both English and American political writings, of many of the leading American scientific and historical works, and of the contemporary descriptive literature on the United States.[12]

Moreover, so far from being polemical, the content of the volume, notwithstanding its powerful underlying partiality for America, reveals a scrupulous, perhaps even an overriding concern for critical accuracy and, in the quality of its observations on the contemporary state of American society and the several American polities, genuine understanding and penetration. "If you wish to understand the inhabitants of a country," Mazzei exhorted his readers in an observation modern intellectual historians might very well take to heart, "you should study their behavior without relying on the complaints of the dissatisfied or the falsehoods of the gazeteers." And it is precisely the quality of his observations upon and his explications of that behavior, some of which anticipate many of the most powerful themes in modern American cultural commentary and historiography, that recommended Mazzei's *Researches* to his contemporary readers in Europe and established his credentials as one of the more profound and accurate interpreters, for late eighteenth-century European audiences, of the new United States and the revolutionary society out of which it grew.[13]

Because Mazzei's credentials and achievements as a cultural broker depend so heavily upon the *Researches* and the capacity it reveals to con-

---

[11] *Memoirs,* xiii.

[12] See, for example, *Researches,* 26, 30, 37, 44, 194, 209, 251, 333–34.

[13] Ibid., xv-xvi, 314; *Memoirs,* xiii.

vey the impressions that this adopted "Citizen of Virginia" had obtained as a result of his fifteen-year association with America, the remainder of this chapter will focus upon that work and the picture of American political and social life it presents. If that picture seems to be heavily skewed toward Virginia, the one place in America of which Mazzei had extensive personal experience, it is well to remember that for the first fifty years of the American republic Virginia was not merely the largest, most populous, and most politically visible of the several new American states but also was at the very center of the emerging American culture.

The picture of America Mazzei presented emphasized what was most striking to most contemporary European visitors: the absence of legal social divisions and the vigorous commitment to personal liberty and political egalitarianism among the free population. In an extensive discussion of the early history of the colonies, Mazzei traced these features of American society in part to the character and goals of the early settlers, some of whom were mere "fortune seekers," but most of whom, lured by the promise of cheap land and envisioning America "as a sanctuary for liberty," left "England to seek the liberty and happiness they despaired of enjoying in their homeland." "Travelling at their own expense" and thinking "solely of liberty," these "simple adventurers" purchased land from the Amerindians, whom they mostly treated "with justice and consideration," established their own local representative institutions in each colony, and proceeded to build prosperous societies under the protective aegis of the English crown.[14]

But it was not only the orientation and experiences of the early settlers but also the physical circumstances and economic and political conditions in which they found themselves that, in Mazzei's view, contributed to the fortunate state of colonial American society. Liberty seemed almost endemic to the continent. "History does not describe any people which has ever preserved so much individual freedom in its social fabric," Mazzei wrote of the aboriginal inhabitants, and the same seemed to be true of the European settlers and their creole descendants. The "abundance of land and its low price" both continued to draw large numbers of immigrants and encouraged a high rate of natural population growth; it also enabled the inhabitants to build "a praiseworthy economy" with a relatively high standard of living that permitted virtually all free fami-

---

[14] *Researches,* 5, 10–11, 55–57, 117, 214.

lies to enjoy considerable prosperity and that enabled every "hardwork-ing man" to "obtain enough money to enjoy every privilege" available in the society. Nor did there seem to be any limits to the potential expan-sion of this economic competence to more and more people. "The terri-tory of the United States is vast," Mazzei reported, and "the cultivated portion very small," so that even the most populated state "could easily triple its population without finding it a burden."[15]

These socioeconomic conditions, said Mazzei, in echoing Crèvecoeur and anticipating Tocqueville, produced a society in which "the distinc-tion between classes was much smaller than it has been and still is in other countries" and in which the inhabitants, as the first article of Maz-zei's friend George Mason's Virginia Declaration of Rights underlined, were chiefly concerned with the individual "Enjoyment of Liberty, with the Means of acquiring and possessing Property, and pursuing and ob-taining Happiness and Safety." The profoundly individualistic and pri-vate priorities expressed in this phrase produced what Benjamin Frank-lin, in a short tract reproduced in full by Mazzei in the *Researches,* called "a general happy mediocrity" in which those with "a decided taste for agriculture, hunting, and solitude" could be supremely happy; hus-bandmen, mechanics, and other useful and productive members of soci-ety were "in honor"; and the laws provided sufficient protection that people had "no need of the patronage of great men, and everyone" could "enjoy securely the profits of his own industry."[16]

Having learned from the Georgia experiment that, in Mazzei's words, public "assistance does not make men happy," Americans, he contended, expected little from government, and the public realm was both too small and of insufficient scope to seduce men from their overwhelming preference "to look after their own business." A "spirit of economy" gov-erned "public expenses in America," civil offices and employments were "few," and even the most prominent public "leaders prefer[red] the simple pleasures of home to any kind of [public] position." "For an American," Mazzei observed, "to rest and enjoy domestic life . . . is the greatest bliss." "Not to attend to one's business, and to increase the public expen-ditures unnecessarily," were, in the eyes of Americans, equally condem-nable.[17]

This preference for the serenity of their "quiet Countryhouses" and

[15] Ibid., 58, 118–19, 122n, 220, 280, 348.

[16] Ibid., 74, 125, 326–27, 332.

[17] Ibid., 55, 113, 125, 169, 326; *Memoirs,* 223.

the simple pleasures of "rural life" did not mean that "distinguished men" in America did not attend to public affairs willingly and responsibly. It did mean, at least in ordinary times, that the American people were "very docile" and showed "the utmost confidence in those to whom they [had] confide[d] the conduct of their affairs," not, as in Europe, because they were so timid that they sought the favor and "protection" of the wealthy individuals whom they normally entrusted with public life, but because, as "satisfied citizens," they saw little need to interest themselves in politics except when times were "critical" and the "public welfare" was "more important than any other consideration." However, in "a free state" such as America, in which "sovereignty" was "in the hands of the whole [free] population," public leaders always had to be sensitive to public opinion. If in all societies, as Mazzei emphasized, opinion was "always more powerful than laws," in a free polity like the United States no government could "endure if the great majority of . . . citizens [were] . . . dissatisfied." As "representatives of a free people," he told his European readers, American leaders could never "force public opinion." They could only "hope to direct or reform" it "by setting an example of intelligence and prudence."[18]

By stressing the basic docility of the American public, Mazzei intended to illustrate the fundamental orderliness of American life. A society in which the inhabitants were consumed by the pursuit of their own domestic pleasures had no time for tumult. Indeed, along with the "basic affection" they "felt for their ancestral country," this strong desire for a peaceful life, according to Mazzei, had been the primary reason why, despite their awareness that "they and their ancestors had lost many of their rights" as a result of many oppressive actions by crown and Parliament during the century from 1660 to 1760, they neither considered trying to recover those rights nor examined their relationship with Britain critically until after 1763, when the British ministry, realizing that the colonies "were rapidly increasing in strength and vigor" and "taking their good nature for cowardice," proceeded to tighten "the bonds until they broke."[19]

Nor did the "gentle, calm nature of the American people" forsake

---

[18] Mazzei to Mr. Lomax, Apr. 5, 1785, in Richard Cecil Garlick, Jr., *Philip Mazzei, Friend of Jefferson: His Life and Letters* (Baltimore, 1933), 81; George Washington to Mazzei, July 1, 1779, in *The Writings of George Washington*, ed. John C. Fitzpatrick, 39 vols. (Washington, D.C., 1931–40), 15:348; *Researches*, 68, 81, 94, 113, 130, 137, 180, 196, 314, 337–39; *Memoirs*, 213–14.

[19] *Researches*, 58–59, 63, 81.

them with the Revolution. Throughout the trying years surrounding the decision for independence, Mazzei asserted, they "were guided less by enthusiasm than by intelligent patriotism," and they "never lost sight of the obedience owed to civil authority." Through "Congress, the assemblies, conventions, committees," and other ad hoc political institutions, they succeeded in making "all the inhabitants responsible for what was done during this kind of interregnum" and thereby fashioned "expedient[s] which, without destroying the suspended government, would maintain law and order." Although some people suggested that "the moderation which prevailed was due, at least partly, to circumstances," specifically, to the tendency of "a common peril" to bring "men together and" incline "them to sacrifice their private desires to a common weal," Mazzei thought that the "American people['s] high veneration for law and order" was just as important, an interpretation he supported by emphasizing the fact that Shays' Rebellion in Massachusetts in 1786–87 was the only uprising during the eleven years following Independence.[20]

Although Shays' Rebellion seemed to provide evidence for the charge of anarchy that Europeans leveled against republican America, Mazzei treated it as the exception which proved his point that "in no country" was "more public tranquility enjoyed than on our continent." "What is this in comparison to rebellions in England, such as Lord Gordon's riot, and recent troubles in Glasgow?" he asked. "Where else would you find companies of volunteers running to defend the government? This uprising, which has been laughed at in Europe, is one of the most convincing proofs that to keep good order, you need [merely] to entrust the task to the nation." The American experience during the Revolution made clear, he contended, that as long as "everyone can obtain satisfaction for his wrongs, public tranquility will be assured." "A country where equal rights prevail," he declared, "will uphold a government believed to be good. As there are no unjust social distinctions, national dissensions cannot have deep roots, and when happiness and safety depend on good order, everyone will be interested in preserving it."[21]

Mazzei thus traced the absence in America of those "popular disorders, which occur in other countries," not just to the American preference for order but also to the egalitarian character of American life. A passionate advocate of equality, a militant foe of aristocracy, and a powerful exponent of merit as the only basis for public preferment, Mazzei had initially ventured to America because he had been assured by Franklin

[20] Ibid., 65, 69n, 70, 80–81, 137, 266, 305, 384.
[21] Ibid., 165, 297, 299, 385, 402.

and others that it contained "no aristocracy, that the eyes of the people were not dazzled by the splendor of the throne, that the head of every family could cast a vote in . . . elections and could be elected to office, that the colonies had their own municipal laws, and that they had adopted only those English laws that fitted their needs," and in his *Researches* he rejoiced in the facts that the "Revolution had arrived before the English ministers thought we were worthy of their titles and decorations" and that "Pride had kept them from injecting us with the aristocratic poison."[22]

As a result, the American states "did not have to combat the distinction of rank," which, in Mazzei's opinion, was "the most terrible obstacle that can be opposed to the establishment of a free and just government." In the United States, he announced, no citizen could have "any power unless it" had "been given to him by his peers," and, although property requirements prevented some inhabitants from voting and serving in public office, "the path" to those privileges was "open, and not a single state" had "an aristocratic class." Mably had criticized the provisions of some state constitutions that permitted nontaxpaying adult sons of real property owners to enjoy the franchise and had predicted that such provisions would eventually lead to the establishment of a hereditary nobility. But Mazzei seized upon this suggestion as a vivid example of Mably's ignorance, pointing out that if the prediction came true, then this American "noble class" would "include about half the inhabitants (when the country is well-populated)" and "would number approximately seven-eighths of the present [free] population." Until land became scarce, Mazzei insisted, "the distinction still accorded in some states to landowners" and their families was "not one to make us fear the establishment of an aristocracy." Nor, Mazzei declared, did the "diversity of interests which some pretend will cause us trouble need [to] be feared in our governments, where the titles of doctor, lawyer, merchant, or laborer do not proclaim any class difference" and birth conveyed "neither nobility nor dishonor."[23]

In his advocacy of equality, Mazzei was careful not to confuse "equal rights with equal wealth." "Equal rights," he wrote in giving expression to a widespread American belief, "are just and easy to maintain when they have been well established; equal wealth is neither practical nor desirable." Arguing that the notion, set forth in various state declarations of rights and the Declaration of Independence, that all men were

[22] Ibid., 80, 125, 146; *Memoirs,* 173, 178.

[23] *Researches,* 80, 122, 140, 172, 316.

born equally free and independent was "the foundation of American liberty" and contained "all the principles necessary to preserve it," Mazzei contended that access to the franchise and public office should be denied only to criminals and "recipients of public welfare who" did "not contribute to the expenses of the state" and that artisans, stevedores, workmen, and others who "earn[ed] their daily bread more easily [in America] than elsewhere . . . love[d] their country [and were just as entitled to its privileges] as a wealthy real estate owner."[24]

Notwithstanding existing restrictions on the franchise and officeholding, however, Mazzei pointed out that there was "not a single one of the thirteen states where these rights" were "not more liberal than they have ever been in any other republic," while real property was "so easily acquired in America" that every able-bodied man could expect to acquire full civil rights. Never before, he wrote, had there "been a republic where the whole population exerted so much influence on government and where everyone could aspire to honors and wealth."[25]

The egalitarian nature of the American republic was also the primary reason why, according to Mazzei, antiquity contained so few lessons for Americans. Like many other exponents of Enlightenment principles, Mazzei was no friend to the blind veneration of either the authority of philosophers or the "knowledge of antiquity," the latter of which he compared to the evils "that spring from privileges, prerogatives, and other vicious institutions (which are often based on ignorance)." In his view, the contemporary world was in every way superior to that of the ancients. "When you think of the useful discoveries made by science," he remarked, "you realize [that] we have emerged from the shadow and that the light is brighter every day," and, although he did not deny that the modern world was "still a long way from the degree of science and contentment to which we can aspire," he insisted both that "the inhabitants of the polite world" were "far happier than ever before" and that it was absurd, as Mably had done, "to write glowingly about ancient civilizations" because "it makes us envy periods far less fortunate than our own." In Mazzei's opinion, "a real friend to mankind would exhort his fellow creatures to think about the advantages we enjoy today."[26]

For Mazzei, the American republic was the particular case that proved his point about the superiority of the present over the past. As a result

---

[24] Ibid., 83–85, 173.

[25] Ibid., 85, 125.

[26] Ibid., 131, 133, 167, 306.

of the new social and political order they were building, mysteries that "were so useful to the superstitious Romans," he declared, "would be considered childish by Americans." More to the point, perhaps, the Roman republic had problems "caused by conditions that have never existed in America," where the absence of a social order based on rank made the situation "altogether different." An "intelligent nation," like the United States, he declared, could not "be compared to a multitude shrouded in ignorance and superstition and dominated by oracles." "Among its senses," Mazzei remarked, the American people have "one called common sense" that made them skeptical about any authority not based on reason and confirmed by practice. Although they had less leisure and wealth than the intelligentsia in Europe, Americans, Mazzei reported, were already "fairly well educated" before the Revolution, and, as a result of the intensive debates about public affairs during the Revolution, debates in which every citizen had "a right to express an opinion," they had both increased their capacity "to reason" on public affairs and "made astonishing progress in their ability to discuss these matters." Hence, although Americans could admire the Roman example and "respected" philosophers as much "as elsewhere," they refused "to be dazzled" by the authority of either.[27]

Growing intellectual and political sophistication arising out of their deeply ingrained skepticism about authority and their newfound interest in public affairs was only one indication that the American Revolution was changing the American people for the better. Previously, the inhabitants of the colonies had been "free, . . . interested in [the] public welfare and, on the whole, well informed about the rights of man and the principles of free government." Having been taught by long experience that it was "impossible to govern without representation" and living in a society in which there were no hereditary social ranks, Americans realized that they "were in a much better position than other nations (if we can believe history) when they were establishing their governments." Because the "Revolution was not produced by domestic factions but by the necessity to cast off a foreign yoke," Mazzei wrote, Americans had "no need to overthrow a system of [internal] government or to change [their political] principles." Hence, they were able to incorporate "the good points of the English constitution" into their new polities while avoiding "its worst faults." As a consequence, Mazzei proudly proclaimed, they had provided themselves "with a model government and with laws whose wisdom and equity put to shame even the most enlightened nations." "Be-

[27] Ibid., 122, 125–26, 131–32, 178, 298, 305.

fore the American Revolution," he contended, "a truly rational republic never existed." Even "the least perfect" government in the United States appeared to him to be "closer to the principles of liberty than any ancient or modern republic."[28]

Like Paine, Mazzei delighted in spelling out for Europeans the leading principles of republican government as that genre had been redefined by Americans. These included popular sovereignty, written constitutions consisting of brief and clear expressions of "Fundamental principles," representative government with wide access to the suffrage and public office, equality of political rights among citizens, governments limited in power and scope, short terms of office and low salaries for public officials, separation of powers within government, low taxes, provisions for the extension of equal political status to new states, and separation of church and state, the last of which Mazzei thought was one of the most important advances of the Revolution as well as an area that still required considerable further extension in most of the states.[29]

Nor were political rights and church-state relations the only areas in which Mazzei thought the American polity could be improved. If the American republic had some "areas where we have ensured a solid basis of liberty," he acknowledged in the early pages of the *Researches*, "elsewhere . . . we have failed to guarantee it." Whatever deficiencies remained could not, however, be laid at the door of the founders, whose "intentions," Mazzei insisted in trying to counter the implications of Mably and Raynal, "were completely honorable." Rather, those deficiencies resulted from the lingering and powerful authority of "old prejudices, several of which were supported by famous [European] writers." Thus, "although reason [usually] triumphed theoretically" during the crucial early years of the establishment of republican government, "it was often forced to yield to prejudice." Neither had the experiment been undertaken in the best of conditions. "If you think of the stormy period when our governments were established and realize how the founders of our country were prejudiced from childhood and that we have scarcely had time to attend to our own business since peace was restored," Mazzei explained to his readers, "you will conclude that it would be astonishing if no reforms were necessary."[30]

If Mazzei was thus not an uncritical panegyrist and if he also conceded

---

[28] Ibid., 3, 78, 174–75.

[29] Ibid., 61n, 78, 89, 93, 112, 144, 156–58, 163, 166, 230, 300, 304–5, 385.

[30] Ibid., 3, 128, 166, 197.

"that the return of peace [might have] cooled the enthusiasm necessary to put our new edifice on a solid base," he also pointed out that "Calm [was] . . . as essential to complete our task as ardor and courage were necessary to begin it." What encouraged him to be particularly sanguine about the prospects for reform was the fact that many of the state governments were continuing to refine their polities. Hopeful that they would persist in "adopt[ing] what they think best until they reach the highest possible degree of perfection," Mazzei looked forward to the time "when the [American] constitution[s]" would be "formulated on a permanent basis."[31]

For Americans to achieve that goal, Mazzei was persuaded that, as was mentioned earlier, they had to extend the principles of political and religious equality considerably. He was no friend to special privilege or discrimination in the realm of either the secular or the sacred. He also thought that the Union and the national government "need[ed] to be strengthened." If he expressed some serious reservations about the new Constitution of 1787 in a last-minute supplement to the *Researches*, he was optimistic about the future of the national union. The facts that all the states shared the same political principles and that the Union "had been founded not only on sound politics but," according to Mazzei, also "on a fraternal affection of the citizens of each state for those of the others" seemed to him to override both the ancient jealousies among the colonies that had been so palpably manifest during the colonial period and the emerging sectional differences arising out of the great disparity between the numbers of slaves in the five southern states and those in the rest of the Union.[32]

A more immediate problem, one that had helped to lend credibility to European charges that the United States was degenerating into anarchy, was the uncertain economic and financial condition of the new republic. Having been, according to Mazzei, systematically drained of all liquid currency by the "commercial monopoly exercised by Great Britain" and with "no means of sending to market the produce" they had raised, the colonists had found themselves throughout the War for Independence without money to buy arms and ammunition. As a consequence, they had had to issue large quantities of paper money that had depreciated rapidly, a development that Mazzei himself regarded as merely the "fair" price each person had to pay for national independence. Compounded by significant losses during nine years of war, including the "Interruption

---

[31] Ibid., 77, 87, 316.

[32] Ibid., 277, 285, 299, 394–95, 398.

of employment . . . , [and the] destruction of houses, cattle, and agricultural equipment," the enormous accumulating war debt, Mazzei explained, was "enough to impoverish any country"; and he did not deny that, as late as 1787–88, the states were "only beginning to emerge from chaos, . . . [that] no state [had yet] . . . developed a good financial system," or that in some states, such as Massachusetts during Shays' Rebellion, taxes had been onerous and sometimes impossible to collect.[33]

Yet, Mazzei was persuaded that the country's debt was "small in comparison to [its] . . . resources" and that, along with the losses sustained during the war, it would quickly be overcome. As he pointed out, since the return of peace "both population and the value of land" had been "increasing daily" and the "Ordinary expenses of the various governments" in peacetime were "trivial." Thus, notwithstanding the fact that the burden of taxation in most states remained light in comparison to those in England or most European polities, they were already "sufficient" in more affluent states such as Virginia "to pay [the] ordinary expenses of running the government and [the annual] interest on the state debt."[34]

But far and away the most serious problem confronting the republic in Mazzei's view was the persistence of racial slavery. "Men who love justice and humanity," he wrote, would be "naturally surprised to learn that although the principles embodied in the new state governments proclaim[ed] liberty and equality, slavery still" existed "in the United States," and he conceded that the institution as it functioned in the five southern states was "the worst, the most humiliating, and the most difficult evil to correct," that "a great many" American whites yet "regard[ed] these unfortunates as a very inferior race," and that owning slaves made "people unhappy." But he contended that Americans wanted to give slaves "their liberty as soon as possible" and that only the dangers of suddenly altering the status of such a numerous and ill-prepared group had prevented Virginians from doing so in 1776.[35]

Having lived so long in Virginia, a state with one of the largest slave populations, Mazzei was well attuned, even sympathetic, to the many "excellent reasons for postponing the liberation of [such a] large number of slaves." But, directing his comments to his fellow Americans, he argued that those who were persuaded that blacks could "never possess the

---

[33] Ibid., 307, 310, 313–14, 316–17.

[34] Ibid., 312, 314.

[35] Ibid., 122–23, 332, 345; *Memoirs*, 221–22.

attributes of free citizens" had unfairly judged blacks "by what they see, instead of imagining what they would be had they been reared by free parents and breathed the air of liberty from childhood." Suggesting that "if white men became slaves," they and their descendants "after several generations . . . would be what Negroes are today," he endorsed Lafayette's plea to the Virginia legislature to "seize every opportunity in its power to promote the rights that all men without exception have to liberty." In the meantime, Mazzei denied that there was any "excuse for importing more" slaves, as the Carolinas and Georgia were then doing, and suggested that until emancipation could be carried out, most American slaveholders would treat their slaves "as kindly as" they could.[36]

Mazzei realized, however, that all of these remaining problems, including especially the abolition of slavery, required a degree of public spiritedness and self-sacrifice that, as he acknowledged in his more cautious moments, the profoundly privately oriented societies of the United States might never be able to achieve. Although Mazzei believed that Americans were an honorable people and that there was "a moral difference" between America and Europe in the sense that "our customs are not so corrupt as those in Europe," he denied that Americans flattered themselves by thinking "that we are perfect," a state that, he reminded his readers in ridiculing some observations of Mably, had "never been and never can be." Mazzei admitted "that since the revolutionary period [in America the] public welfare" had very "often taken precedence over everything else" and subscribed to the assertion in the Virginia Declaration of Rights that no free government could be maintained "but by a firm Adherence to Justice, Moderation, Temperance, Frugality, and Virtue." But he was under no illusions that Americans would continue to sublimate the pursuit of self, the cultivation of domestic happiness that had been so long their central animating concern, to the difficult and culturally uncongenial tasks of infusing a concern for civic virtue into the American polities or in a sustained assault upon those continuing problems that were either inconsistent with or actually inimical to the new republican polities they were trying to create. Mazzei asked his European readers to consider "that such self-sacrifice" was extremely "rare save in critical times." In America, no less than other regions of the globe, he declared, "Passions rule[d] the human heart, and the strongest always" prevailed.[37]

---

[36] *Researches*, 122–23, 344, 346.

[37] Ibid., 76, 125, 128.

By no means one of those spartan republicans who were suspicious of commercial activity and believed that self-denial was essential for the establishment of viable republics in America, Mazzei, like his friends Jefferson and Madison, understood that commerce was central to the already highly capitalistic and self-oriented societies of America. Although he recognized that "the extent and fertility of the soil" and low density of population deterred most of the people from going into trade and greatly inhibited the development of domestic manufacturing, he also believed that no modern commercial society like the United States could or should try to "draw everything possible from" its own "soil and industry" and that it was also desirable "to make worthwhile exchanges." Accordingly, Mazzei advocated seeking new markets and the free exchange of goods among countries, and he admonished Americans "never [to] believe that to preserve liberty, you must proscribe everything which makes men more civilized."[38]

With Franklin and Crèvecoeur, among many others, Mazzei was thus an early exponent of the concept of American exceptionalism. If, as he wrote Jefferon in June 1780, the "rapid & Surprising progress in Europe" of "notions of Equality among mankind" were "chiefly owing to our Glorious cause" in America, his primary message to Europeans about America was that the American republics were different from anything encompassed within their experience. What made them different was the extensive space and opportunity they provided for their free inhabitants; the industry and incitement to industry, activity, and schemes of improvement produced by that space and opportunity; the absence of aristocracy and a society organized into legally established ranks; the broad popular base of government; the political enlightenment of the citizenry; the citizenry's intense preoccupation with the pursuit of domestic happiness; and the laudably small scope of the public realm. In polities with such characteristics, the lessons of both the European past and the European present simply could not be applied in any meaningful way. European republics, both those of antiquity and those of more modern times, had all been attempted in societies that, in Mazzei's words, "were divided into classes which were constantly bickering. Equal rights did not

---

[38] Ibid., 118–19, 138, 179, 284, 322, 329, 377.

exist, and revolutions served to favor the ambition of an individual or a small group" and "never represented the wishes of a whole population."[39]

If, in America, no less than in Europe, men were "eager to be distinguished and respected," it was peculiarly fortunate, Mazzei believed, that the "yearning" for "public esteem" in America "guided [people] toward activity and virtue," occasionally and for short periods in the civic realm but more often and more intensely and more intimately in the private realm, which even more fortunately provided free people with a vast field for the active pursuit of private happiness. Indeed, so extensive was that field and so few social barriers did it contain that in America what Mazzei called the "national prosperity" could be defined largely in terms of the private welfare of its free inhabitants, as little more than the capacity for all those inhabitants to enjoy "an abundance of all the necessities of life . . . and a few luxuries."[40]

That no contemporary European society was—in any of these ways— anywhere nearly so fortunately situated as the American states was the implicit insight offered to Europeans by Mazzei, whose status as a cultural broker and whose explication of the American sociopolitical order, like those of that other highly visible European interpreter of the American republic, Thomas Paine, were enhanced and given authority by his long residence in America. For those inspired by Paine's promotion of the American republics as models for the modern political world, Mazzei's message could only have been profoundly disquieting. For if Americans had been able to go as far as they had in the achievement of stable and just republican polities largely because of the peculiar character of their inhabitants and the fortunate physical and social circumstances in which they found themselves, then their experience may have been as irrelevant and uninstructive for Europeans as, according to Mazzei, the experience of ancient and contemporary Europe was for them.

This chapter was written for presentation in an abbreviated version on November 29, 1986, at a symposium on "Pensiero Politico Toscano e Pensiero Politico-Institutionale Americano alle origini della Costituzione del 1787," held by the Instituto di Studi Nordamericani in Florence, Italy, on November 29, 1986. It is here reprinted with permission and minor changes from Anna Maria Martellone and Elisabetta Vezzosi, eds., *Fra Toscana e Stati Uniti: Il discorso politico nell'eta della Costituzione Americana* (Firenze: Leo S. Olachki Editore, 1989), 89–110.

---

[39] Mazzei to Jefferson, May 19, 1780, in Marraro, "Philip Mazzei, Virginia's Agent in Europe," 274; *Researches*, 174.

[40] *Researches*, 376.

FOURTEEN

The Intellectual Reconstruction of Virginia in the Age of Jefferson

FOR HISTORIANS, Thomas Jefferson's relationship to his native Virginia has always been problematic. While they have acknowledged the deep affection that underlay his frequent references to himself as "a Virginian" and to Virginia as "my own country"[1] and his pride in Virginia's many contributions to the American Revolution and its subsequent "enlightened" achievements, they have also emphasized the profound reservations implicit in his program for the social and political improvement of Virginia during the Revolution and his unflattering portraits of Virginia's old colonial regime during his later years,[2] reservations that seem to be thoroughly confirmed and made explicit by his many criticisms of Virginia society in his *Notes on the State of Virginia*. This chapter seeks to reexamine Jefferson's relationship to Virginia through an analysis of the broad intellectual reconstruction of Virginia that occurred during his lifetime and his role in that reconstruction.

The primary premise underlying the analysis that follows is that every corporate entity is constructed both behaviorally and intellectually. It is behaviorally constructed by the recurrent actions of those who compose it. It is intellectually constructed in the sense that those who undertake

---

[1] See, for instance, Thomas Jefferson to d'Anmours, Nov. 30, 1780, to James Monroe, Oct. 5, 1781, in *The Papers of Thomas Jefferson*, ed. Julian P. Boyd et al., 24 vols. to date (Princeton, N.J., 1950–), 4:166, 6: 127.

[2] See Jefferson to William Wirt, Aug. 5, 1815, Jefferson, "Autobiography," 1821, in *The Writings of Thomas Jefferson*, ed. A. A. Lipscomb and A. E. Bergh, 20 vols. (Washington, D.C., 1903), 15:336–37, 1:54.

the daunting task of trying to render it comprehensible, both to those who belong to it and those who do not, do so by identifying and defining those common features of behavior and belief, of collective and individual experience, that give it personality or character and provide it with intellectual coherence. A secondary underlying premise is that the identities of such entities change in response to shifting temporal circumstances.[3]

From its very beginning, Virginia had been an enigma for those who sought to understand and identify it. From the early seventeenth century through the lifetime of Jefferson, commentator after commentator—residents and nonresidents; writers of promotional tracts, descriptions, travel accounts, and histories; correspondents and diarists—pondered how a country rendered so fine by nature had turned out to be in so many ways a profound cultural disappointment. "The most general true Character of *Virginia*," said Henry Hartwell, James Blair, and Edward Chilton in their assessment of the state of Virginia at the close of the seventeenth century, was that it was at once "the best" and "the worst Country in the World." "As to all the Natural Advantages of a Country," these authors wrote, "it is one of the best, but as to the Improved Ones, one of the worst of all the *English* Plantations in *America*."[4] In rendering this judgment, these writers were merely expanding upon a point made several decades earlier by observers such as John Hammond and Sir William Berkeley.[5] Robert Beverley's 1705 *History of Virginia* revolved around an elaborate exploration of this palpable and evidently intractable puzzle.[6]

Expanding wealth and population permitted the generation that came to maturity during the first quarter of the eighteenth century to develop a society that was in many respects far more improved and civil than Virginians of earlier generations could possibly have predicted on the basis of the colony's record during its first century. Still lacking the social

---

[3] This problem is discussed at greater length in Jack P. Greene, *Imperatives, Behaviors, and Identities: Essays in Early American Cultural History* (Charlottesville, Va., 1992), 13–16, 113–14.

[4] Henry Hartwell, James Blair, and Edward Chilton, *The Present State of Virginia, and the College*, ed. Hunter Dickinson Farish (Williamsburg, Va., 1940), 3.

[5] John Hammond, *Leah and Rachel, or, The Two Fruitful Sisters, Virginia and Maryland* (London, 1656), in Clayton Colman Hall, ed., *Narratives of Early Maryland, 1633–1684* (New York, 1910); Sir William Berkeley, *A Discourse and View of Virginia* (London, 1663).

[6] Robert Beverley, *The History and Present State of Virginia*, ed. Louis B. Wright (Chapel Hill, N.C., 1947).

and cultural density of metropolitan Britain, Virginia could nonetheless plausibly be depicted by writers such as Hugh Jones, in his *Present State of Virginia*, as an example of that simple, tranquil, and uncorrupted rural society so frequently idealized in Georgian Britain, a place whose sociable inhabitants could scarcely avoid being contented and virtuous and, with care and diligence, might also become prosperous, independent, and polite.[7] Indeed, the worry of some members of this generation was that free Virginians were sacrificing their English ancestors' traditional devotion to liberty to their growing politesse and moderation. Thus, in his *History of the First Discovery and Settlement of Virginia*, published in 1747, William Stith sought to recall his countrymen to a proper dedication to this aspect of their English inheritance by emphasizing their predecessors' contributions to the establishment of liberty in English America during the first generation of the colony's history.[8]

But the behavior of many members of the generation that came to maturity in the 1740s and 1750s seemed—to both Virginians and visitors—to present a formidable challenge to the emerging conception of Virginia as an Anglophone arcadia. Indeed, that behavior strongly suggested that the indolence, extravagance, and dissipation, as well as the degrading dependence that those three vices brought in their train, might soon become the most pronounced features of the Virginians' identity as a people. During the third quarter of the eighteenth century, at the very moment when people of the generation of Thomas Jefferson were reaching adulthood and Virginia was transforming itself from a colonial to an independent political society, the questions of whether Virginians would be a virtuous or a vicious, a polite or an abandoned people were still very much in doubt. The late colonial period was a critical time for Virginians as they sought to comprehend what kind of society they had created and what kind of people they had become.

During the American Revolution and the early national period, Virginia's experience operated to amplify and redefine these conceptions of the new state and its free white inhabitants. This process of intellectual reconstruction may be studied through an analysis of the principal texts that reflected and in turn helped to define contemporary understanding of Virginia and Virginians.

Three of these works were of special importance. First published in

---

[7] Hugh Jones, *The Present State of Virginia*, ed. Richard L. Morton (Chapel Hill, N.C., 1956).

[8] William Stith, *The History of the First Discovery and Settlement of Virginia* (Williamsburg, Va., 1747). See also Thad W. Tate, "William Stith and the Virginia Tradition,"

London in 1787, Thomas Jefferson's *Notes on the State of Virginia* was the most ambitious work of description produced on Virginia since Hugh Jones published his book over sixty years earlier.[9] A four-volume *History of Virginia*, the longest and most comprehensive history of the colony produced up to that time, was mostly written by John Daly Burk, an Irish immigrant and follower of Jefferson who took up the subject under Jefferson's tutelage. Burk published the first three volumes in Richmond in 1804–5. After he was killed in a duel in 1808, Skelton Jones and Louis Girardin, two of Jefferson's other clients, completed the last volume, which was not published until 1816. This work covered the history of Virginia from the beginning of the colony to the end of the War for Independence in 1781.[10] In much briefer form, Edmund Randolph's *History of Virginia* also treated the period from Jamestown through the Revolution. Scion of an old Virginia family and a relative of Jefferson's, Randolph had himself played a prominent role in the Revolution and had served with Jefferson in Washington's cabinet as the first attorney general of the United States. Randolph was gathering material for his history as early as the 1780s but probably did not write it until the years just before his death in 1813. The volume remained in manuscript until the 1930s and was not published in full until 1970.[11]

In addition to Jefferson, Burk, and Randolph, a variety of other observers produced analyses of the new state between 1775 and 1815. Except for the dissenter John Leland's "Description of Virginia," published in 1790,[12] the jurist St. George Tucker's *A Letter to the Rev. Jedidiah Morse* and *A Dissertation on Slavery, with a Proposal for the Gradual Abolition of It, in the State of Virginia*, issued respectively in 1795 and 1796,[13]

in Lawrence H. Leder, ed., *The Colonial Legacy: Historians of Nature and Man's Nature* (New York, 1973), 121–45.

[9] Thomas Jefferson, *Notes on the State of Virginia*, ed. William Peden (Chapel Hill, N.C., 1955).

[10] John Daly Burk, *History of Virginia*, 4 vols. (Richmond, 1804–16). On Burk, see Michael Kraus, *The Writing of American History* (Norman, Okla., 1953), 80–81, and Joseph I. Shulim, "John Daly Burk: Irish Revolutionist and American Patriot," American Philosophical Society, *Transactions*, n.s., 54 (1964), pt 6: 5–60.

[11] Edmund Randolph, *History of Virginia*, ed. Arthur H. Shaffer (Charlottesville, Va., 1970), xvii, xxxvii–xxxix, 3.

[12] John Leland, "The Virginia Chronicle," in *The Writings of John Leland*, ed. L. F. Greene (New York, 1969), 92–124.

[13] St. George Tucker, *A Letter to the Rev. Jedidiah Morse* (Richmond, 1795), and *A Dissertation on Slavery, with a Proposal for the Gradual Abolition of It, in the State of Virginia* (Philadelphia, 1796).

and John Marshall's *Life of George Washington,* the first volume of which was published in 1805 and contained a brief history of Virginia down through the middle of the eighteenth century,[14] these were all written by outsiders from continental Europe, Britain, or other parts of North America.[15]

Some of Virginia's many outside observers during the Jeffersonian era praised the character and style of life of at least some members of the prominent gentry class and expressed an appreciation for the political capacities exhibited by many of the state's leaders during the Revolution. But most were sharply critical of both the state and its inhabitants. Together, they limned an overwhelmingly negative picture. Complaining about the slovenly character of Virginia's rural landscape, agriculture, and housing, these writers decried its lack of urban development, economic enterprise, and investment of either time or money in religion and education, and its continuing commitment to chattel slavery. Denouncing the pride, selfishness, indolence, carelessness, extravagance, dissipation, and penchant for violence on the part of its white male inhabitants, they argued that Virginia lagged far behind its bustling, more developed, and, many thought, far more enterprising, accomplished, and civilized neighbors to the north.

In the well-developed tradition of self-criticism displayed by Robert Beverley and many other earlier Virginians, analysts of the Revolutionary and early national eras contributed to reinforce this highly unflattering reputation, and this observation applies with special force to Jefferson. No inhabitant at any time during the period considered in this

---

[14] John Marshall, *Life of George Washington,* 4 vols. (Philadelphia, 1805–7), 1: esp. 50–77, 188–94, 314.

[15] These included new general histories of Britain's early colonizing efforts in America by George Chalmers and Dr. William Robertson as well as an abundance of travelers' accounts: for the late 1770s, by Benjamin West, a New England lawyer, Ebenezar Hazard, a New York bookseller, Elkanah Watson, a Rhode Island merchant, J. F. D. Smyth, a British doctor, August Wilhelm Du Roi, a German officer; for the 1780s, Baron von Closen, an officer in the French army, Thomas Anburey, a British officer, the Marquis de Chastellux, Johann David Schöpf, Rev. Thomas Coke, the English dissenting minister, Noah Webster, a New England scholar, James Joyce, an Irish immigrant, Robert Hunter, Jr., a British merchant, and J. P. Brissot de Warville, a French savant; and, for the 1790s, William Loughton Smith, a prominent South Carolinian, Médéric Moreau de Saint-Méry, a French refugee, the duke de La Rochefoucauld-Liancourt, another French emigré, Benjamin Henry Latrobe, an architect, and Isaac Weld, another Irish immigrant. Finally, Samuel Miller's brief survey of eighteenth-century intellectual developments in 1803 and the geographies of Jedidiah Morse and William Guthrie contained descriptions of the state and its people.

chapter provided a more powerful social and cultural critique of the state than did Jefferson in his *Notes on the State of Virginia,* first published in the early 1780s.

As, in this work, he evaluated Virginia by the standards of the cosmopolitan Western tradition with which he often sought to identify, Jefferson, like Beverley in his *History* eighty years earlier, found much to deplore. Implicitly contrasting the "enterprising temper of the Pennsylvanians" with the "indolence" of his countrymen, Jefferson in the *Notes* decried the "indifferent state" of Virginia agriculture, the "infinite wretchedness" produced by its heavy economic reliance on tobacco culture, the dilatoriness of Virginians in undertaking desirable public works such as the improvement of inland navigation, and the state's failure to develop major urban centers. Lamenting the absence of any system of public education, he complained about the ugliness and temporary character of most Virginia private housing and outbuildings, the paucity and indifferent architectural quality of its public buildings, and the scarcity of competent tradesmen, and he chided his countrymen for continuing to live in a formal condition of "religious slavery" with a state-established church.[16]

Writing the *Notes* while he was still licking his wounds from his inglorious governorship of 1779–81, Jefferson was particularly hard on Virginia's republican state constitution. Worrying whether Virginians after the war might disregard "their rights in the sole faculty of making money," he condemned the mutability of a constitution that had been adopted by no greater authority than an act of the legislature without recourse to the people and cited, among its several "capital defects," its failure to extend the franchise to all those who paid taxes and fought for the state, to provide for an equality of representation among the several political units of the state according to the size of their free populations, and to achieve a genuine separation of powers among the several branches of government so as to prevent the concentration of power in the hands of the legislature.[17]

In contrast to Beverley or any other earlier Virginian interpreter, however, Jefferson reserved his most stringent criticism for the institution of chattel slavery. The sudden rise of antislavery sentiment throughout the enlightened world after 1750 powerfully called attention to what Ed-

[16] Jefferson, *Notes,* 85, 108, 125, 135, 146–49, 152–54, 158–59, 166; Jefferson, *Notes,* in *The Writings of Thomas Jefferson,* ed. Paul Leicester Ford, 10 vols. (New York, 1892–99), 3:100.

[17] Jefferson, *Notes,* 118–29, 161.

mund Randolph would later refer to as the great "pollutions and cruel-ties of slavery."[18] Not just Jefferson and Randolph but St. George Tucker, John Daly Burk, and many other contemporary Virginia inter-preters agreed with outside observers that slavery was a "blot in our country," a "great political and moral evil" that was "more portentous and afflicting" than any other imaginable.[19]

Together, these Virginia writers took pains to point out the many ways by which slavery had "stained" the country. By requiring Africans to undergo the most "degrading submissions," it forced them into an "un-natural debasement" that reduced them almost "to the condition of brutes." "Among the blessings which the Almighty hath showered down on these states, there is a large portion of the bitterest draught that ever flowed from the cup of affliction," declared Tucker. "Whilst America hath been the land of promise to Europeans, and their descendants, it hath been the vale of death to millions of the wretched sons of Africa. The genial light of liberty, which hath shone with unrivalled lustre on the former, hath yielded no comfort to the latter."[20]

But the liberty to have slaves, several Virginians conceded to their critics, had by no means been an unmixed blessing for whites. On the one hand, it had enabled the wealthy to cultivate a lifestyle of ease and gentility and helped to nourish among all free whites that "habitual arro-gance and assumption of superiority" that had in turn given rise to the "quick and acute sense of the rights of freemen" that Virginians had so amply exhibited during the American Revolution. The association of slavery with passivity, both Randolph and Tucker suggested, contrib-uted to make men exceptionally jealous of their liberty and proud of the conditions—specifically, their capacity for independent and self-directed activity and their white skins—that distinguished them from the depen-dent and passive servile black population all around them. In a slave society such as Virginia, even the poorest of the free whites thus had some basis for a sense of worth.[21]

But that sense of worth had to be tenaciously preserved. For any free white man not to make an active defense against even the slightest chal-lenge to his capacity for action and self-control was to behave like a slave and thus to forfeit both self-esteem and respect of peers. For white Vir-

---

[18] Randolph, *History,* 202.

[19] Jefferson, *Notes,* 87; Burk, *History* 1:211.

[20] Randolph, *History,* 202; Jefferson, *Notes,* 162; Chalmers, *Political Annals,* 49; Tucker, *Dissertation,* 9.

[21] Tucker, *Dissertation,* 77; Randolph, *History,* 193.

ginians, these writers suggested, fear of passivity thus underlay both
their praiseworthy devotion to personal independence and an unattrac-
tive and inflammatory pride that expressed itself in what outsiders had
long perceived as a hypersensitivity to insult and a too eager readiness
to defend their honor—and thereby demonstrate their capacity for activity—by fighting and dueling.

Nor were such pride and the indolence arising from the identification
of work with slavery the only ways in which slavery was "baneful to
virtue" among whites. Indeed, declared Jefferson in a famous passage in
his *Notes on the State of Virginia*, the whole relationship between masters
and slaves was little more than "a perpetual exercise of the most boister-
ous passions, the most unremitting despotism." By nursing and educat-
ing white children in the "daily exercise . . . [of] tyranny," he contended,
slavery destroyed not just the industry and civility but the very "morals
of the people." Finally, for Virginia as a whole, slavery introduced into a
society of free people a discordant and dangerous element that gave rise
to severe apprehensions among whites that "so large a number of oppressed individuals" among them might "one day be roused to an attempt to shake off their chains." [22]

To stress only the critical dimensions of Jefferson's *Notes* is, however,
highly misleading. It is important to recognize that Jefferson, no less
than Beverley and other earlier Virginia interpreters, intended for his
criticisms to provide the foundations for reform. As Jefferson wrote his
friend Chastellux in September 1785, well before arranging for publication of the *Notes*, he regarded it as "good" for a people to have "the vices
of their character . . . pointed out to them [so] that they may amend
them; for a malady of either body or mind once known is half cured,"
and his subsequent efforts to get his volume into the hands of "all the
young men of Virginia" who were then, as students of the restructured
College of William and Mary, in "preparation for public life" demonstrated his deep conviction that Virginians were capable of undertaking
and achieving fundamental reform. [23]

Again like Beverley in his 1705 *History*, Jefferson, in the *Notes*,
affirmed not only a commitment to the cosmopolitan tradition of the
Enlightenment but also a profound respect for the provincial traditions
of Virginia. In no sense was he one of those people who had "contempt

---

[22] Randolph, *History*, 193; Jefferson, *Notes*, 162–63; Tucker, *Dissertation*, 41.

[23] Jefferson to Chastellux, Sept. 2, 1785, to Richard Price, Aug. 7, 1785, in *Jefferson Papers* 8:467–69, 356–57.

for the simplicity of his own country." Indeed, in its totality, the *Notes* provides not a negative but an affectionate and highly positive reading of Virginia's experience and promise. Modern analysts of the *Notes* have rarely failed to recognize the profound appreciation Jefferson revealed for the sublimity of Virginia nature, the richness and extent of the state's natural resources, its astonishing capacity to produce a wide range of agricultural and mineral products and to sustain a burgeoning population, and its enormous potential for economic development through navigational and other public improvements.[24]

A close reading of the *Notes* also reveals that it celebrated not just the promise but the achievements of Virginia and Virginians. Jefferson's impatience with the rate and extent of Virginia's development should be set against his quiet emphasis upon its extraordinary population growth, the progress it had already made in exploiting its iron and coal deposits, and the virtual absence of poverty among its native free white population. His lamentations about the evils of tobacco culture need to be considered alongside his appreciation of the diversity of Virginia agriculture and of the openness to agricultural innovation revealed by the rapid strides the state's farmers were already making in the cultivation of wheat and the breeding of Arabian horses. His remarks about the absence of towns should be juxtaposed to his well-known approbation of Virginia's continuing "attachment to agriculture" and his characterization of the "discreet farmers" who dominated Virginia society—those "worthy" men who, though "not rich," were "easy in" their "circumstances"—as "the most virtuous independent citizens" for republics. His complaints about the absence of public education were to some extent mitigated by his pride in the recent modernization and secularization of the curriculum at his alma mater, the College of William and Mary. His denunciation of the Virginia religious establishment might well be put in the context of his insistence upon the "moderation" of the Anglicans and his faith that the "people of this country" never "would suffer an execution for heresy, or a three years imprisonment for not comprehending the mysteries of the trinity." Even Jefferson's condemnation of the inhumanity among whites produced by slavery was counteracted by his suggestion that the proliferation of the black population was the result of "mild treatment." Further, Jefferson sought to emphasize the underlying moderation of the Virginia social system by his denial that whites had ever

---

[24] Jefferson to John Banister, Jr., Oct. 15, 1785, ibid., 636; Jefferson, *Notes*, 1–3, 13, 19, 24–25, 29–30, 45–46, 82–84, 169.

taken lands from the Indians by conquest and his assertion that from early on they had been careful to reserve lands for those Indians who chose to stay within the bounds of white settlement.[25]

Perhaps most important, Jefferson's litany of criticisms against Virginia's new state constitution must be balanced against his profound appreciation for the virtues of the traditional political culture of Virginia. Praising that culture for the public-spiritedness of local magistrates, he lauded the commitment to "temperate liberty" on the part of the citizenry as epitomized by the lenient treatment of Tories and general obedience to laws during the Revolution, and the state's low taxes and small bureaucracy. Further, in the *Notes,* Jefferson emphasized Virginia's long tradition of self-government and its leaders' unswerving dedication to the preservation of their constituents' "most essential rights." That dedication, he noted, had repeatedly been made manifest in a series of actions stretching from their refusal to accede to the authority of the English republican regime in 1651 until representatives of that regime had acknowledged those rights, through their inauguration of opposition to the Stamp Act in 1764, and the "frequent assertions of the public rights" that filled Virginia legislative journals thereafter. Although the adoption of the legal reforms that he and two colleagues, George Wythe and Edmund Pendleton, had undertaken after Independence to purge the legal code of all laws "inconsistent with republicanism" had been delayed by the war, Jefferson also expressed little doubt that these reforms would be implemented with the "restoration of peace."[26]

In the *Notes,* Jefferson not only displayed a profound veneration for Virginia but also provided the essential foundations for and made a significant contribution to its intellectual reconstruction during the following quarter century. Between 1780 and 1815, Virginia analysts, including especially Tucker, Burk, and Randolph, built on the optimistic portrait Jefferson presented to create a new and highly positive sense of corporate identity for Virginia and Virginians. Stressing the "conspicuous patriotism" and "great-mindedness" Virginians had so amply displayed during the American Revolution, these analysts seized upon Virginia's experi-

[25] Jefferson, *Notes,* 29–31, 45–46, 82–84, 87, 95–96, 133, 141–42, 151, 158, 161, 164–65, 168–69, 175; Jefferson to C. W. F. Dumas, Oct. 4, 1785, in *Jefferson Papers* 8:582.

[26] Jefferson, *Notes,* 85, 113–17, 130, 137, 155, 172–73, 177–78.

ence during the Revolution to help Virginians recast their conception of their past and enhance their sense of collective self-worth.[27]

The Virginians' interpretation of their own behavior during the Revolutionary years strongly reinforced their corporate self-esteem. As the "most ancient American possession" of Britain and as the "most extensive, richest and most commanding colony in America," Virginia, they proudly declaimed in elaborating a point made by Jefferson in the *Notes,* had naturally assumed the leadership of the opposition to Britain—and, to its credit, without "any parade or assumption of superiority." From the very "beginning of the disturbances," from the Stamp Act crisis in 1765 onward, Virginia, said Randolph, had "produced public agents suitable to every crisis and service." Such heroic figures as Patrick Henry, Richard Bland, Peyton Randolph, Thomas Jefferson, George Washington, Richard Henry Lee, Edmund Pendleton, George Wythe, and George Mason had "stepped forth willingly" in behalf of the American cause. Virginians had been "the first to offer assistance to the Bostonians" in 1774 following the Coercive Acts "and the first also to set on foot a considerable body of troops"; and when in the 1780s the new Union had seemed on the verge of collapse, they again took "a leading, active, and influential part in bringing about the . . . grand revolution in our Federal Government."[28]

Such "generous attention . . . to the general interest of all the colonies, so distant from the selfish policy but too apt to influence rival states, produced every where" during the Revolution, John Daly Burk happily reported, "a sentiment of tender respect and just admiration." To Virginia "was every where allowed the honourable praise of having originated every capital measure since the commencement of the disputes, and having supported them all with a constancy and wisdom nowise inferior to the ardour with which they had been adopted." No state, suggested Tucker, had contributed a higher "quota of men of eminence on the political theatre of the United States."[29]

Nor did outsiders dispute these claims. Virginia, noted the French traveler the duke de La Rochefoucauld-Liancourt, in repeating a com-

---

[27] Burk, *History* 3:373; Johann David Schöpf, *Travels in the Confederation,* trans. Alfred J. Morrison, 2 vols. (Philadelphia, 1911), 2:92.

[28] Burk, *History* 3:373; Randolph, *History,* 178, 251; marquis de Chastellux, *Travels in North America in the Years 1780, 1781, and 1782,* trans. Harold C. Rice, Jr., 2 vols. (Chapel Hill, N.C., 1963), 2:435; Jedidiah Morse, *The American Geography,* 2d ed. (London, 1792), 400.

[29] Burk, *History* 3:373; Tucker, *Letter to Morse,* 15.

mon observation, "was one of the first [colonies] to take a part in the
revolution [against Britain]: and no one of the states made more vigorous
efforts, expended greater sums, or displayed more signal energy, to accomplish that happy object." Virginia, wrote the geographer William
Guthrie, also "had the honour of leading the way to" the "most important reform in the [national] government" in 1785–87. "Some of the
most illustrious characters that America can boast, either of those who
now guide her councils, or of those who live but on the records of history," he pointed out in the mid-1790s, "derive[d] their birth from this
state." Virginia, even the New England critic Jedidiah Morse acknowledged in 1791, had indeed "produced some of the most distinguished and
influential men that have been active in effecting the two late grand and
important revolutions in America. Her political and military character
will rank among the first in the page of history." Thus reinforced by
outside opinion, Virginia's local interpreters could plausibly conclude
that the Revolution had finally provided an appropriate occasion for the
full flowering of the true Virginia "genius."[30]

From the perspective of Virginia's actions during the Revolution, indeed, it had become abundantly clear that Virginians had always been
"a jealous and high spirited people," and, taking a cue from Jefferson in
the *Notes*, both Burk and Randolph searched Virginia's past for earlier
instances of their resistance to attacks upon their liberty and for evidence that an absolute revulsion against all forms of "tractable" behavior
had ever marked the Virginia character. In ways that were perfectly
compatible with the interpretation Jefferson offered in the *Notes*, these
writers completely reinterpreted Virginia's earlier history in the service
of the new corporate identity they were constructing.[31]

If the "noble and spirited resistance" to Cromwell's forces in 1651 that
Jefferson had pointed to in the *Notes* constituted, for him, an ample,
"honorable and lasting record of the spirit . . . of Virginians," both Burk
and Randolph found many others. "As far as they depended on constitutions and conventions," wrote Burk, the Virginians' liberties were
"scanty and precarious" throughout the colonial period,

> but as they were practically enjoyed, they were ample and substantial:
> and they were principally indebted for them to their own spirit and

---

[30] Duke de La Rochefoucauld-Liancourt, *Travels through the United States of North
America*, 2 vols. (London, 1799), 1:53; William Guthrie, *A New System of Modern Geography* (Philadelphia, 1794–95), 500, 506; Morse, *American Geography*, 387.

[31] Burk, *History* 2:226, 299.

intelligence. Not all their obsequiousness to sir William Berkeley; not even their unfeigned respect and affection for his person and government, induced the slightest concession of their privileges. And when, at length, the sense of colonial grievances, added to the pressure of parliamentary restrictions dissolved the charm, which bound them for so long a time to this extraordinary man, they displayed in their resistance [in Bacon's Rebellion] the same ardent and determined spirit by which they had ever been distinguished.[32]

Rooted in their situation as independent rural landholders, that spirit, Virginia's post-Revolutionary interpreters declared, had given Virginians "an honester and more manly pride" and encouraged them in "free, unprejudiced modes of thinking." "In point of abilities of manly spirit," they suggested, no one excelled "the real Virginian planter," who, to his enormous credit, ever disdained "any abridgement of personal independence." There had never been, perhaps, these post-Revolutionary writers agreed, "a community so high spirited and independent as that of Virginia." The absence of "the style, and splendor" of Europe or even of the growing cities of the North was thus far more than "amply compensated [for] by the simple manners" and the virtuous and "independent spirit"—the "native spirit"—of Virginians.[33]

"From the first moments of" its "existence," post-Revolutionary writers argued in direct contradiction to those of the previous generation, "the conduct of Virginia," as Burk asserted, was thus "exactly the opposite" from the "unjust," if "universally received opinion . . . that Virginia was distinguished for her invariable loyalty, and her submissive and tractable temper, during the greater part of her colonial existence," "her yielding policy" contrasting sharply "with the sturdy patriotism of New-England." Neither Burk nor Randolph denied that Virginia began under the auspices of a charter in which "a mass of despotism" darkened "the scene." But they argued that the establishment of a representative assembly in 1619, as the historian Stith had affirmed a generation earlier, had "put the colonists once more under the protection of the laws of England" and provided them with the means to protect themselves against "such invasions of liberty as they had been taught to dread from

[32] Ibid., 2:11, 91, xxxi.

[33] Ibid., 1:5, 2:83, 226; *The Virginia Journals of Benjamin Henry Latrobe 1795–98*, ed. Edward C. Carter II et al., 2 vols. (New Haven, 1977), 2:304; Randolph, *History*, 153, 178; Fred Shelley, ed., "The Journal of Ebenezar Hazard in Virginia, 1777," *Virginia Magazine of History and Biography* 62 (1954): 414.

their own experience and from the small though sturdy advances toward sound principles which English theory had even then made."[34]

Throughout Virginia's first century, these writers insisted, Virginians had stood up on behalf of liberty. When in 1624 the Virginia Company, composed of many of the "most conspicuous asserters of liberty in parliament," fell victim to "that power in the constitution which had long menaced with annihilation, the privileges of parliament, and the rights of the people," Burk wrote, the Virginians' "noble and spirited resistance" managed to save colonial representative government from the early Stuarts' "native propensity to tyranny." Thereafter, Virginians had repeatedly demonstrated themselves to be "animated . . . by the ardor of liberty," exhibiting a "daring and determined resistance" to governors such as Harvey and Howard, who behaved like petty tyrants.[35]

Burk actually rewrote some of the central episodes in seventeenth-century Virginia history to demonstrate that, contrary to the assertions of earlier historians, Virginians had never wavered in their commitment to liberty. Although he admitted that "a spirit of complaisance and accommodation was reciprocated between the different branches [of the legislature] during the greater part of sir Wm. Berkeley's administration," he insisted that "religious zeal alone," more specifically, hostility to the religious zeal of the puritans, was "the principal cause of" the Virginians' "supposed attachment to the king" during the English Civil War. "Their political attachments," said Burk, "were obviously on the other side; and in the career of liberty and resistance, they had even anticipated and outstripped the parliament. They had the same pointed regard for their rights and privileges, as this illustrious body; they resisted with equal ardor, and for a long time with greater success, the encroachments and insolence of the crown. Their cause was palpably the same."[36]

To suggest that Virginians "would have sacrificed any thing so essential, so precious in their estimation, as their rights, or the principles of freedom to" the "mere influence of sir William Berkeley," as had been so often asserted by previous historians, was, for Burk, patently absurd and could not "be collected from any part of their history." Clearly, "nothing but the infatuation or phrenzy of [religious] superstition" could

---

[34] Burk, *History* 1:203, 2:233; Randolph, *History*, 19, 87.

[35] Burk, *History* 1:207, 231, 294, 2:11, 33, 292.

[36] Ibid., 2:75–76, iv.

account for their not immediately rushing to the banners of Parliament and the Commonwealth. So "mild and liberal, and even popular" was "the government of the English commonwealth . . . in Virginia" that its overthrow in 1659–60, even before the Restoration in England, Burk was persuaded, had to have been "the work of a mob" and not reflective of the true wishes of the people at large.[37]

Also in the hands of Burk, Bacon's Rebellion was for the first time incorporated into the story of the Virginia struggle for liberty. Set off by a disagreement over Indian policy, as earlier writers had argued, that uprising was, in Burk's view, also the result of "that crisis in the political malady when all ranks and classes" were "equally affected with . . . public grievances and oppressions [under Berkeley], and impatiently longed for an occasion, by one great and violent effort, to burst their chains and assert their independence."[38]

For Burk, Bacon became a heroic figure, a man of "a sanguine temper, a bold and dauntless courage, great promptness and decision of character, added to a presence of mind that rarely deserted him." Bacon's great "ardor and enthusiasm of liberty," said Burk, impelled him to come to the aid of a people whose liberties were "in danger" from an oppressive political regime. In sharp contrast to Berkeley, who, when he regained control of the colony, "was daily executing men by mock trials," Bacon was "never reproached with shedding a single drop of innocent blood, save what was unavoidably spilt in the heat and hurry of battle."[39]

Burk transformed Bacon and the "intrepid" Robert Beverley, father of the historian—whose "noble ardor and constancy in opposing the encroachments on the liberties of his country" by Berkeley's successors, Culpeper and Howard, deserved a lasting "monument"—into suitable precursors to the famous defenders of liberty in Virginia during the Revolution. The exploits of these local heroes constituted a standing reminder that champions in the cause of liberty had never been wanting in Virginia. Received "by the people at large with every demonstration of unfeigned joy and exultation," the Glorious Revolution of 1688 had rendered "the principle of resistance to arbitrary power," as represented by

---

[37] Ibid., 2:76, 120. Contemporary examples of the traditional interpretation of Virginia's behavior during the Civil War and Interregnum may be found in Dr. William Robertson, *The History of America*, 2 vols. (Albany, 1822), 2:325–27, and George Chalmers, *An Introduction to the History of the Revolt of the American Colonies*, 2 vols. (Boston, 1845), 1:75.

[38] Burk, *History* 2:192.

[39] Ibid., 2:193–94.

men like Bacon and Beverley, "popular and even fashionable," albeit Burk lamented that the "entire essence" of that Revolution had not been "universally imparted" into the colony.[40]

If Burk rewrote the history of seventeenth-century Virginia to stress the Virginians' continuous devotion to liberty, he also emphasized, with Randolph, the extent to which that devotion had usually been tempered by a prudence, a moderation, an equanimity that appeared to be an integral component of the Virginia identity. It was "the happiness of Virginia character," wrote Randolph, "hardly ever to push to extremity any theory [or spirit] which by practical relations may not be accommodated." Agreed Burk, "The conduct of the colonists was invariably marked by great order and moderation."[41]

These historians found little difficulty in illustrating this point. Thus, Burk wrote, in the uncertain days between the revocation of the charter of the Virginia Company and the establishment of royal government, "habits of rational submission and decent manners" proved to have been "so confirmed . . . that the ordinary operations of government, and the settled regulations of laws and commerce, were carried on unembarrassed by riot, and unstained by excesses." Similarly, Randolph noted, during the Interregnum and Restoration, Virginians scrupulously avoided both the "fanaticism and hypocrisy of Cromwell" and the "licentiousness of the second Charles," and he cited this same "principle of accommodation" to explain Virginia's acceptance of the metropolitan monopoly of its trade and many other similar "claims of usurpation" by the home government that eventually "grew . . . into a metropolitan right[,] upon a mere reluctance to quarrel with the mother country."[42]

Within the colony, these writers affirmed, "a spirit of mildness" also pervaded social relations. The Virginia aversion to excess was particularly reflected in the "mildness of church government." Anglicanism was established by law, but, a few zealots excepted, its essential spirit, as even Jefferson agreed, had very early, like all other aspects of life in Virginia, "subsided into moderation." "Virginia soil," the Baptist John Le-

---

[40] Ibid., 2:298, 307, 333. Both Randolph and John Marshall challenged Burk's effort "to metamorphose" Bacon's Rebellion "into one of those daring efforts which gross misrule sometimes suggests, if it may not strictly vindicate." Reaffirming the traditional interpretation as recently reiterated by both George Chalmers and Dr. William Robertson, they insisted that Berkeley was guilty of no "palpable or . . . clearly meditated" tyranny (Randolph, *History*, 153, 202; Marshall, *Washington* 1:188–93).

[41] Randolph, *History*, 157; Burk, *History* 2:10.

[42] Burk, *History* 2:10; Randolph, *History*, 116–17, 153.

land confirmed, had "never been stained with vital blood for conscience sake." Virginia, said Randolph, had received from the parent state "an original stamina, perhaps . . . something phlegmatic in her temper, which inclined her to regulated liberty by saving her from those ebullitions which teem with violence and subordination." That "original stamina," he was persuaded, had given Virginia "manners . . . a polish which without enfeebling courage" had moderated, even in the early decades of the colony's existence, "that ferocity which suspicion sometimes ascribes to the rough inhabitants of a newly cultivated desert." Happily for Virginians, they had repeatedly proven themselves to be "equally aloof from the frenzy of reform and the abjections of vassalage."[43]

Bacon's Rebellion was the single exception to the temperate character of Virginia public life after the Restoration, and the Glorious Revolution further encouraged this spirit of moderation by producing "a profound calm" in the colony. For the next seventy years, as Burk wrote, "the interior concerns of the colony were conducted with moderation, and blessed with content and tranquility." As George Chalmers had affirmed in the 1780s, from the early 1720s on, "the love of order, the obedience to law, and the peacefulness of the province of Virginia [had] offered a striking contrast to the tumult, the refractoriness, and [the] anarchy of its . . . neighbors." Beginning with Edward Nott in 1705, Burk noted, royal lieutenant governors in the colony were "model[s] of virtue and excellence." Such "liberal conduct" and "mild" government proceeding from such an "apparent regard to justice and equity" on the part of the home government so intensified the deep loyalty Virginians had traditionally manifested for the mother country that they, said Burk, "looked back with a mingled pride and admiration on the land of their ancestors" as "the seat of arts, the sanctuary of liberty, terror of tyrants, like the Roman senate, the hope, the refuge, the consolation of the distressed." Having from early in their history been intent upon adhering "to those excellent and refined customs of their native land, as nearly as the capacity of the country would admit," Virginians were so proud of their connection with Britain, said Randolph, that "every political sentiment, every fashion in Virginia appeared to be imperfect unless it bore a resemblance to some precedent in England."[44]

Virginia interpreters also took pride in contrasting their "own loyalty

---

[43] Randolph, *History*, 147, 153, 158, 247; Burk, *History* 2:xxxi; Jefferson, *Notes*, 158; Leland, "Virginia Chronicle," 107.

[44] Burk, *History* 2:328, 330, 334, 3:280–81; Chalmers, *Introduction* 1:101, 2:198; Randolph, *History*, 176.

with the turbulent spirit" of the New England colonists, and, they thought, the colony's common effort with the crown to defend its western territories against the French and Indians during the Seven Years' War "still further cemented the bonds of nativity and attachment." But this "almost idolatrous deference to the mother country," these strong "ties of affection" and deep loyalty, were, Randolph stressed, "debased by no servile compliance." Rather, they were accompanied by that "patriotic watchfulness" that had always been so conspicuous in the Virginia character. Although that watchfulness never degenerated "into the mere petulance of complaint," Virginians, as Lieutenant Governor Robert Dinwiddie discovered when he tried to levy a fee upon land patents without authorization of the legislature in 1753–54, knew "when to complain with truth and how to complain with dignity." Among such "watchful patriots," asserted Randolph, there was obviously "an elevation of character" that would render them "incapable of being seduced by the artifices" of any set of men.[45]

This strong attachment to Britain and the powerful drive toward anglicization that accompanied it were further strengthened, as Randolph phrased it, by a confident consciousness that Virginia had, perhaps, "more nearly approached the British model . . . of excellence" than any other American colony, a development that had been made possible by the extraordinary growth of the colony during the first six decades of the eighteenth century. Neither Burk nor Randolph challenged the assessment of George Chalmers that Virginia, "notwithstanding every possible natural advantage," had "remained for ages poor, inconsiderable, and feeble." But they noted that the "assurance[s] of freedom and security" provided by the Glorious Revolution had "introduced the concomitant blessings of industry and peace" while the "patient industry of the English character" thereafter had finally given "a direction to those natural benefits" that all earlier commentators had praised in the Virginia environment. From 1700 on, they observed, the "Virginians augmented their numbers, their commerce, their wealth, and their power . . . beyond the example of other colonies." By 1750, this populous and prosperous society of independent landowners with no beggarly poor had, in terms of tobacco exports alone, become of greater commercial consequence to Britain "than all the other continental settlements" in combination.[46]

[45] Burk, *History* 3:122, 281; Randolph, *History,* 160–61, 163, 176, 248.

[46] Randolph, *History,* 146, 177; George Chalmers, *Political Annals of the Present United Colonies, from Their Settlement to the Peace of 1763* (London, 1780), 70; Burk, *History* 1:203; Chalmers, *Introduction* 2:70–71.

Economic success, Burk proudly reported, had been accompanied even by some cultural advances, although he admitted that Virginia's "present high reputation in the arts" dated only from the era of the Revolution. Throughout the seventeenth century, that "dark age in Virginia['s history]," the colony had been "stationary, if not retrograde in her taste and acquirements," producing, said Burk, "not a remnant . . . of any moral disquisition, of the investigation of any problem; in any science," "no ode, no sonnet" to shine "even for a moment, thro' the gloom." With most of its inhabitants "actuated chiefly by the love of gain" and few who "could boast of any considerable acquirements or taste in literature," with no printing press and few educational institutions, it was scarcely surprising, in Samuel Miller's words, that Virginians in those early days "paid little attention to literary institutions" and slowly sank into a kind of creolean degeneracy.[47]

In the early eighteenth century, however, Virginia, its interpreters contended, at last began to exhibit some "instances of honourable literary enterprize," principally in the histories of Beverley and Stith. The latter, Burk insisted, was "little, if any thing inferior in execution to lord Clarendon's history of the civil disputes in England." During the same period, the college improved considerably, largely through the appointment as professors of "men of erudition" from abroad, and a newspaper was established in Williamsburg in 1736, an event that finally roused "the genius of the country" out of "its long and death-like sleep" and provided a foundation for the subsequent flowering of the literary talents of Richard Bland, Jefferson, and others during the 1760s and after.[48]

But it was in the field of politics that Virginia's development in this period was most impressive. Under the long tutelage of Speaker John Robinson, who held office for thirty years before his death in 1766, the House of Burgesses, Randolph explained, became a model of "decorum," equal in every way to the British House of Commons under his contemporary the great Onslow and drawing out of "a constellation of eminent lawyers and scholars" a group of brilliant and patriotic political leaders.[49]

As the German traveler Johann David Schoepf would later observe, the "impulse to political affairs" was the one thing, other than the prospect of pleasure and money, that could rouse Virginians from their customary "inactivity." "There is probably no College in the United States,"

---

[47] Burk, *History* 3:333–35; Samuel Miller, *A Brief Retrospect of the Eighteenth Century*, 2 vols. (New York, 1803), 2:334–35.

[48] Miller, *Brief Retrospect* 2:361; Burk, *History* 3:399–400.

[49] Randolph, *History*, 173, 179.

Samuel Miller observed in 1803, in "which political science is studied
with so much ardour, and in which it is considered so pre-eminently a
favourite subject" as at the College of William and Mary. Such a deep
fascination with politics, as well as the "perpetual political or legal discussions" of the sort visitors repeatedly encountered in Revolutionary
Virginia, had clearly produced "an assemblage" of men whose political
acumen admirably equipped them to assume the leadership of the opposition to Britain beginning in the 1760s and to demonstrate beyond any
possibility of contradiction that from "a political view [Virginia was] inferior to no other colony." [50]

The spirited exertions of these brilliant political leaders, Virginia's
post-Revolutionary apologists never tired of pointing out, won for Virginia the "exalted opinion" of the other colonies before and during the
Revolution: the Virginians' "courage, intelligence and patriotism" made
them and their colony objects of "grateful panegyric" and willing "defer-
ences" throughout America. Through the whole of the long struggle with
Britain, they had exhibited a "steady adherence to the maxims of their
ancestors" and in particular to what Jefferson referred to in the *Notes* as
that "temperate liberty" for which, Virginians liked to think, they had
always been famous. They were always both firm and "cool and deliberate" in their protests. During the Stamp Act crisis, their "spirited behaviour," which had had such "a wonderful effect in animating and confirming the zeal of the other colonies," had been accompanied by "no riots or
popular excesses" to stain "the reputation of Virginia," and at no later
point did they fail to keep "public dissentions within limits of moderation." [51]

Nor, both Burk and Randolph insisted, were Virginians in haste to
abandon efforts at reconciliation. Even after the Stamp Act, they continued to regard "England as a model of all that was great and venerable"
and for the better part of the next decade remained "a people, devoted
indeed to liberty, and ready to seal their attachment with their blood;
but at the same time loyal, just, humane, disposed to affection, and won
even by trifling kindness[es]" such as those displayed by Governor Norborne Berkeley, Baron de Botetourt, during the late 1760s. Only after
British attacks on Massachusetts in the spring of 1775 had "changed the

---

[50] Schöpf, *Travels* 2:92; Miller, *Brief Retrospect* 2:504; Latrobe, *Journals* 2:304, 341; Randolph, *History*, 161.

[51] Burk, *History* 3:299, 310, 331, 347; Randolph, *History*, 177, 238, 248; Jefferson,
Notes, 85.

figure of Great Britain from an unrelenting parent into that of a merciless enemy, whose malice was the more severe, as her affection had been the more earnestly courted," only after, in Jefferson's words, "no alternative was presented but resistance, or unconditional submission," were Virginian affections for Britain finally and irrevocably alienated. So deep had the loyalty of the colony run, that independence, as Randolph averred, could only have been "imposed upon us by the misdeeds of the British government."[52]

Moreover, the Virginia commitment to "temperate liberty" had continued to serve Virginia well throughout the Revolution. Notwithstanding the "relaxation of law" during the transitional period from royal government to independence in 1775 and 1776, noted Randolph, "order was maintained, and licentiousness discouraged by general morality" all over the colony, which "glide[d] from monarchy into self-government, without a convulsion or a single clog to its wheels from its novelty or from disaffection" and with remarkable unanimity among its inhabitants. There were few Tories, and the Virginia government treated them with such leniency that, as Jefferson announced, there was not "a single execution for treason" in the state during seven years of war. "From the experience of nearly sixty years in public life," Edmund Pendleton, one of the foremost lawyers and judges in Virginia, wrote in 1798, "I have been taught to . . . respect this my native country for the decent, peaceable, and orderly behavior of its inhabitants." Even in the midst of revolution, he noted, justice had been "duly and diligently administered—the laws obeyed—and constituted authorities respected, and we have lived in the happy intercourse of private harmony and good will."[53]

The Revolution may have generated some modest social reforms in Virginia, including the abolition of the slave trade, primogeniture, and entail and the disestablishment of the Anglican church. Moreover, the fragility of liberty was revealed by two separate efforts, one in December 1776 and the other in June 1781, to invest, in Jefferson's words, "a *dictator* . . . with every power legislative, executive and judiciary, civil and military, of life and of death, over our persons and over our properties." But the traditional moderation of the Virginia character, its post-Revolutionary analysts emphasized, always preserved the new state

---

[52] Randolph, *History*, 166, 227, 234; Burk, *History* 3:361–62; Jefferson, *Notes*, 117.

[53] Jefferson, *Notes*, 85, 155; Randolph, *History*, 199, 227; Edmund Pendleton to Citizens of Caroline County, Nov. 1798, in *The Letters and Papers of Edmund Pendleton, 1734–1803*, ed. David J. Mays, 2 vols. (Charlottesville, Va., 1967), 2:650.

from rash changes in the political fabric that might, in a less prudent polity, have resulted from a too easy application of what Randolph referred to as "the pruning knife of reformation."[54]

The unanimity, moderation, generosity, patriotism, and political expertise that Virginians demonstrated at every stage of the Revolution seemed to be a standing proof of the appropriateness of the state's claim, so vividly symbolized in the new state seal devised in mid-1776, that virtue was indeed, as Randolph put it, "the genius of the Commonwealth." There was obviously no truth in the "evil" insinuations, spread by the enemies of Virginia, that the "revolution was coveted only by those whose desperate fortunes might be disencumbered by an abolition of debt" to British merchants. Quite the contrary, most of the leaders, Randolph argued, "had at stake fortunes which were affluent or competent and families which were dear to them," and to suppose that they would "have jeopardized" either "of these blessings . . . upon a political speculation in which their souls were not deeply engaged" was absurd. Nothing but the purest motives of patriotism and devotion to the preservation of the temperate liberty and independence of Virginia, he observed, could possibly have accounted for their behavior.[55]

For these Virginia interpreters, the one deeply disturbing flaw in the positive image they constructed for Virginia out of the state's Revolutionary experience was slavery. Although they emphatically did not try to justify that institution, they found much to say to explain its rise and perpetuation. The initial settlers, they explained, had neither brought slavery with them nor deliberately sought to introduce it into Virginia. Rather, the institution arrived by chance in 1619 when a storm drove a Dutch ship loaded with slaves into the Chesapeake Bay. Just as "considerations of profit" had earlier induced English merchants, inhabitants of "the freest nation, at that time in the world, to embark in so nefarious a traffic, as that of the human race," so also had similar motives prevented early Virginians, "most of whom" had come to America because of "the allurement of amassing gold without toil," from resisting the temptation to purchase such productive sources of labor.[56]

[54] Jefferson, *Notes*, 126; Randolph, *History*, 255.

[55] Randolph, *History*, 195, 208–9, 276; Burk, *History* 3:373.

[56] Tucker, *Dissertation*, 15; Randolph, *History*, 96.

No less motivated by economic considerations than Virginians, New Englanders, Tucker took pains to point out, had similarly begun to acquire slaves within five to ten years after their arrival in the New World. In contrast to the situation in New England, however, natural conditions "contributed extremely" to the proliferation of slavery in Virginia. The "violent heats of the summer," the "overwhelming indolence of white men" in such temperatures, and the "infatuation" of Virginians with tobacco as the surest way to satisfy their "eagerness for present gain" eventually combined to rivet the institution on the heart of Virginia. At the same time, the colony's climate proved to be "so congenial to the African constitution" as to cause blacks to multiply rapidly.[57]

By the early eighteenth century, as the Scottish historian Dr. William Robertson remarked, slavery had come to be seen, in Britain and Virginia, as "essential to the existence of the colony." Thus, with a few slave purchases in the colony's earliest years, Tucker lamented, "had our forefathers sown the seeds of an evil, which, like a leprosy, hath descended upon their posterity with accumulated rancour, visiting the sins of the fathers upon succeeding generations" as slavery slowly but steadily "diffuse[d] itself in a variety of destructive shapes."[58]

Nevertheless, as Burk pointed out, Virginians derived much "honor" from the fact that they did not "pretend to justify" slavery. Rather, as Tucker endeavored to show at length, the Virginia legislature as early as 1669 had manifested a "disposition to check its progress," a disposition that gained strength over the following century. Had it not "been uniformly opposed" by British authorities, he contended, it would no doubt have resulted in the prohibition of further slave imports well before the American Revolution. "A system uniformly persisted in for nearly a whole century, and finally carried into effect" soon after Virginia had declared its independence, he was persuaded, throughly evinced "the sincerity of that disposition which the legislators had shewn during so long a period, to put a check to the growing evil." More important in terms of their own self-esteem in a world in which slavery was more and more becoming an object of widespread condemnation, the legislature's persistence, Tucker was convinced, provided white Virginians with a "clear . . . vindication . . . from the opprobrium, but too lavishly bestowed upon" them, of "fostering slavery" at the same time as they boasted "a sacred regard to . . . liberty."[59]

---

[57] Tucker, *Dissertation*, 13–14; Randolph, *History*, 71, 96; Robertson, *History* 2:310.

[58] Robertson, *History* 2:310–11; Tucker, *Dissertation*, 13; Randolph, *History*, 96.

[59] Burk, *History* 1:212; Tucker, *Dissertation*, 41, 46–48.

"A very large proportion of" white Virginians thus both considered slavery "an evil of the most serious and afflicting nature" and professed "an entire willingness to apply a remedy, whenever it shall appear safe or practicable." "Is it not our duty to embrace the first moment of constitutional health and vigour," asked Tucker, "to effectuate so desirable an object, and to remove from us a stigma, with which our enemies will never fail to upbraid us, nor our consciences to reproach us?"[60]

But no Virginia analyst believed that the immediate prospects for abolition were very bright. Both Jefferson and Tucker, its most ardent proponents, took pains to explain to their readers the many extraordinarily powerful "obstacles" that stood in the way of such a measure. Especially from the perspective of the "recent history of the French West Indies" in the early 1790s, it appeared obvious that any sudden abolition would bring economic ruin to white slave owners, misery to blacks, and destruction to the state, as ex-slaves, like the rebels of St. Dominigue, would licentiously combine into ungovernable "hordes of vagabonds, robbers and murderers."[61]

Nor was gradual abolition without severe difficulties. Though Jefferson hoped that elimination of the slave trade would retard the spread of slavery "while the minds of our citizens" were being "ripened for a complete emancipation of human nature" within the state, he was concerned, along with Tucker and Burk, about the effects of such an eventuality upon Virginia society. Differences in skin color, culture, and intellectual ability, all of these writers feared, would prevent blacks from ever achieving full civic competence or being satisfactorily incorporated into the polity as a whole. If that turned out to be the case, if it was "true, as Mr. Jefferson seems to suppose, that the Africans are really an inferior race of mankind," Tucker worried, "sound policy" strongly advised against admitting them into free society either immediately or "at any future period," lest such a step "eventually depreciate the whole national character."[62]

In the face of such a dilemma, Virginians could only take solace in their belief that they were "with few exceptions . . . humane and liberal masters" and that Virginia slavery was comparatively benign. They did not deny that Virginia's early laws systematically degraded slaves "below the rank of human beings" and provided for a form of slavery "so malig-

---

[60] Tucker, *Dissertation*, 11, 67; Burk, *History* 1:212.

[61] Tucker, *Dissertation*, 79, 81, 86.

[62] Jefferson, *Notes*, 87; Tucker, *Dissertation*, 89.

nant" that it did not "leave to its wretched victims the least vestige of any civil right, and even" divested "them of all their natural rights." But they did contend that the harshness of the law did "not proceed from a[ny] sanguinary temper in the people of Virginia, but from those political considerations indispensably necessary, where[ver] slavery prevails to any extent" and that the "rigours of slavery in this country were [n]ever as great" as the laws seemed to suggest. Indeed, Tucker argued, the legislature had significantly ameliorated slave laws, beginning with the "dawn of humanity" in 1769. Since the Revolution, he asserted, "Our police respecting this unhappy class of people" had been "not only less rigorous than formerly, but perhaps milder than in any other country where there are so many slaves, or so large a proportion of them, in respect to the free inhabitants."[63]

Notwithstanding the "misfortune" of slavery, then, Virginia's analysts during the post-Revolutionary era had finally constructed for Virginia and Virginians a credible positive—and, in many respects, satisfying— sense of corporate identity. In view of the political contributions of Virginians during the "new and more splendid aera" represented by the Revolution, the many other cultural and character deficiencies that had long worried earlier generations of Virginia interpreters no longer seemed quite so urgent. Unlike Burk and Randolph, earlier Virginians had, after all, as Randolph said, written "before the country could be said to have been explored in its political concerns with much accuracy, and," even more important, "before the era of Virginia luster" during the Revolution.[64]

To outsiders, however, Virginians still appeared, as the English traveler J. F. D. Smyth put it in the early 1780s, to be "a strange combination of incongruous contradictory qualities, and principles directly opposite; the best and the worst, the most valuable and the most worthless, elegant accomplishments and savage brutality, being in many of them most unaccountably blended." Indeed, for outsiders, such incongruities seemed to define the character of Virginia and Virginians.[65]

Deservedly known for their hospitality, politeness, and sociability, Virginians, visitor after visitor claimed, were among the most inactive and indolent people in the world. Inordinately fond of elegance, they permitted their houses to fall into disrepair and their agricultural lands

---

[63] Burk, *History* 1:212; Tucker, *Dissertation*, 51–52, 54, 67.

[64] Tucker, *Dissertation*, 67; Burk, *History* 3:167; Randolph, *History*, 5.

[65] J. F. D. Smyth, *A Tour of the United States of America*, 2 vols. (London, 1784), 1:67.

to be slovenly worked. With a reputation for being good mates and tender parents, they frequently gave themselves over to jealousy and improvidence. Though "a taste for reading" was "more prevalent among the gentlemen of the first class than in any other part of America," "no state" seemed to be "so entirely destitute of all means of public education" or exhibited such widespread ignorance among the "common people." With many "men of public spirit and extensive information, occupied with the welfare of the country and desirous of effecting it," Virginia had one of the "most imperfect" constitutions in the United States, and a growing number of its able men were forsaking public service in pursuit of more lucrative careers in private life. Having, "since the revolution, produced more men of distinguished talents than, perhaps, any other state of the Union," Virginia was filled with people who seemed to have fallen into total dissipation. "Equally distinguished for their valour and love of liberty" during the Revolution, the latter of which visitors found was "yet trembling alive among all classes of the [free] people," Virginians had not yet by any means sufficiently imbibed modern "sentiments of philanthropy" to be able to commit themselves to the emancipation of their slaves. Indeed, for people who had come from nonslave societies, the contrast between the Virginians' love of liberty and their "maintenance of slavery" seemed especially incongruous, "speeches on liberty and independence sound[ing] rather strangely from the lips of masters of slaves."[66]

At least in part because of the negative elements in these contradictory pairs of characteristics, visitors throughout the generation following the Revolution suggested, in reiterating what had been a nearly continuous theme among Virginia's interpreters from the colony's first settlement, the state still fell considerably short of its potential. Despite the "influence which it is supposed to have over the Union," Rochefoucauld-Liancourt observed in 1799 after constructing a careful balance sheet of Virginia's desirable and undesirable features, its population was still too low, its agriculture too backward, its commerce and manufactures too undeveloped, its wealth too little and too unevenly distributed, and its leading inhabitants a little too complacent in their "pride of family" and too "contempt[ous] of the commercial spirit" to make it plausible for any impartial observer "to praise with any degree of justice the power of the state of Virginia."[67]

Rochefoucauld-Liancourt did not dispute that the state had been "un-

[66] Rochefoucauld-Liancourt, *Travels* 2:112, 115, 117–18.

[67] Ibid., 2:111, 115; Chalmers, *Political Annals*, 69.

doubtedly invited by nature to become the most powerful, or one of the most powerful, [members] of the Union." He even conceded that its "time of improvement may be near." But he insisted that that time had "not yet come" and could not be expected until its inhabitants' "manners [had been] . . . corrected, industry encouraged, and the bounties of nature turned to advantage."[68]

Virginians were by no means impervious to negative reports by outside observers, as attested by Tucker's indignant defense of Williamsburg against Jedidiah Morse's "wanton aspersions" in his *American Universal Geography*. In response, they developed a series of apologies in which they claimed that many of the reputed flaws in the Virginia character could be dismissed as unworthy English inheritances, while others could be excused as in some respects beneficial.[69]

Carried out in behalf of virtue, as well as liberty, the Revolution could scarcely have failed to refocus the attention of Virginians upon the adverse effects of their notorious tendency to bring "ruin upon themselves by their extravagance" and addiction to a "spirit of gaming." But such extravagance, Randolph explained, was the product of the Virginians' habit of sinking "too often . . . into . . . English vices," one of the most pronounced of which was "ostentatious hospitality." Similarly, the "fatal propensity to gaming," which, as Randolph granted, had "been often lamented . . . as breaking forth in Virginia in ways destructive to morals and estates," had been rendered especially "fashionable" in the decades just before the Revolution by the example of Francis Fauquier, a popular British governor, who, though he had many fine qualities, was an inveterate gamester whose bad habits were copied by many of "the most distinguished landholders" in the colony.[70]

Though Randolph liked to think that during the Revolution both extravagance and gambling had been largely confined to the "most worthless part of society," he had to admit that they had not yet "been extirpated." In any case, such behavior could be excused as the "natural offspring" of that laudable spirit of hospitality and liberality that had always "marked the character of Virginians." As Virginia had become more affluent during the middle years of the eighteenth century, the old "unaffected hospitality" of Virginians, Burk and Randolph suggested, had slowly—and unwittingly—slipped into an "ostentatious hospitality"

---

[68] Rochefoucauld-Liancourt, *Travels* 2:115–16.

[69] Tucker, *Letter to Morse*, 12.

[70] Randolph, *History*, 61, 147, 279; Burk, *History* 3:334.

characterized by extravagant display and the indulgence of "passions
. . . to profusion and excess." "Amongst a class proverbial for their hospitality, their politeness and fondness of expence," the habit of spending
lavishly and the "rage of playing deep, reckless of time, health, or
money," they argued, had, once Fauquier had lent legitimacy to such
behavior, quickly "spread like a contagion."[71]

Nor, they contended, was the situation with regard to education quite
so lamentable as visitors and other outsiders suggested. Virginia had
many private primary and secondary schools, and, in addition to the
several new private colleges noted by outsiders, the College of William
and Mary, Virginia apologists claimed, was slowly regaining the eminence it had begun to achieve in the decades just before Independence.
The Revolution had deprived the college of three-fourths of its revenues
and, through the dispersion of its faculty, left it wholly disorganized.
But by the 1790s, William and Mary had two faculty members and fifty
to sixty boys in the grammar school and six professors and forty to fifty
students in the college, a number that was "considerably greater" than
at any time before the Revolution. It taught mathematics, classics, four
modern languages, moral philosophy, and chemistry.[72]

Most students reportedly were attracted to natural philosophy or law,
the two subjects in which the college took special pride. "Almost constantly growing in the number of its votaries, and in the degree of attention it has received," the former, which was "much more comprehensive
than is usual in most colleges," had been developed by the president of
the college, Bishop James Madison, and the latter successively by
George Wythe, state chancellor of Virginia, and St. George Tucker, both
of whom during their tenures as professor of law annually gave a celebrated course of lectures on the principles of law, civil government, and
the constitutions of Virginia and the United States. A sharp rise in the
number of students reading natural philosophy instead of law suggested,
at least to Tucker, that science was "beginn[ing] to be more generally
cultivated among the citizens at large." Having already produced a
higher proportion of national political leaders than could possibly have
been expected for such a small institution, as well as many "men of high
professional character in law, physic, and divinity," the college, its defenders claimed, was "so far from being in a declining state" that its prospects were becoming infinitely "more favorable."[73]

---

[71] Randolph, *History,* 147, 193, 279–80; Burk, *History,* 2:226, 3:334, 402.

[72] Tucker, *Letter to Morse,* 14–15.

[73] Miller, *Brief Retrospect* 2:337, 377–78; Tucker, *Letter to Morse,* 14–15.

If their claims to respectability in education were patently weak, Virginians now began to argue with far more conviction that their "fixed and unconquerable repugnance" to living in towns and their deep attachment to agriculture were not, as most earlier writers and many contemporary visitors had argued, a liability but an asset. Expanding on themes earlier writers such as Robert Beverley and William Byrd of Westover had only tentatively advanced, Jefferson, Burk, and Randolph agreed that, as Randolph put it, "men who are occupied by labor in the country are more exempt from the vices prevailing in towns." "Those who labour in the earth are the chosen people of God, if ever he had a chosen people, whose breasts he has made his peculiar deposit for substantial and genuine virtue," wrote Jefferson in a much-quoted comment: "It is the focus in which he keeps alive that sacred fire, which otherwise might escape from the face of the earth. Corruption of morals in the mass of cultivators is a phaenomenon of which no age nor nation had furnished an example." People in towns depended "for their subsistence . . . on the casualties and caprice of customers," and the abject dependence that was necessarily so rife in urban areas, Jefferson insisted, begat "subservience and venality," suffocated "the germ of virtue," and prepared "fit tools for the designs of ambition" and unfit materials for the preservation of "a republic in vigour." That the rural character of Virginia and the commitment of its inhabitants to agriculture were the primary sources of that "high sense of personal independence" that had been so laudably and universally revealed in Virginia behavior during the Revolution seemed obvious.[74]

For Virginia's own analysts, the glorious contributions of the state and its inhabitants to the Revolution and the new American nation thus seemed thoroughly to overshadow any deficiencies in their own character and society. From the perspective of 1790 or 1815, the story of their country seemed, in Randolph's words, to have been one of a gradual rise to greatness, as it progressed "from infancy and a wilderness, through various fortunes, into wealth, a character, and an influence which largely contributed to the establishment of American independence and to the formation of that most illustrious among civil acts, the Constitution of the United States of America."[75]

"Being the earliest among the British settlements in North America, having been soon withdrawn from the humiliation of proprietary dependence to the dignity of a government immediately under the crown, ad-

---

[74] Burk, *History* 2:126–27, 3:404; Randolph, *History*, 197, 257; Jefferson, *Notes*, 109, 164–65, 175; Rochefoucauld-Liancourt, *Travels* 1:502.

[75] Randolph, *History*, 3.

vancing rapidly into wealth from her extensive territory and the luxuriant production of her staple commodities," and with "the sons of the most opulent families trained by education and habits acquired in England," Virginia, even before the Revolution, explained Randolph, had acquired a pride that "had so long a topic of discourse in the other colonies that it had almost grown into a proverb."[76]

But it was not primarily the circumstances that underlay that growing pride, or the unease that pride disguised, but "the public spirit and intelligence of her citizens" during the Revolution that gave Virginia such a "conspicuous" place as "the elder branch of a confederacy." Virginia, its protagonists insisted, had taken the lead in throwing down "the gauntlet to kings" and had become "the asylum of oppressed humanity; the faithful guardian and depositary of public spirit." These actions, they announced, amply confirmed their image of Virginia as a commonwealth of virtue whose independent, patriotic, but prudent sons were ever watchful of public liberty and ever ready to defend it with manly, courageous, and wise exertions. With such glorious accomplishments behind them, who could possibly gainsay the proud boasts overheard by Schoepf in 1783 that Virginia was "superior to the other American states" and that no other American could possibly "count himself the equal" of the polished, the virtuous, and the genuinely "noble Virginian"?[77]

By providing, in the *Notes* and elsewhere, the positive reading of Virginia's past and future and by sponsoring or endorsing much of the literature in which other post-Revolutionary analysts rewrote the history of Virginia and constructed a positive sense of collective self for Virginia and Virginians, Jefferson both participated in and made a major contribution to that undertaking. In so doing, he revealed that his famous and cultivated cosmopolitanism always coexisted symbiotically with deep loyalties to the local and provincial peculiarities that gave Virginia its distinctive shape—including even slavery. No matter how urgent his pleas, in the *Notes* and elsewhere, for the reformation of many aspects of Virginia society, his relationship to his native state was ever defined by an abiding Virginia patriotism.

The first draft of this chapter was discussed on October 15, 1992, at a seminar at the Jefferson Legacies Conference held in Charlottesville, Virginia, October 14–19, 1992. It is here reprinted with permission from Peter S. Onuf, ed., *Jeffersonian Legacies* (Charlottesville: University Press of Virginia, 1993), 225–53.

[76] Ibid., 177.

[77] Burk, *History* 1:i.

—FIFTEEN—

The Limits of the
American Revolution

Invariably, revolutions raise as many problems as they resolve. The American Revolution is no exception to this pattern. Initially undertaken to secure for British Americans guarantees of local autonomy and individual rights equivalent to those enjoyed by Englishmen in the home islands, it quickly became in 1775–76 a struggle for political independence. But the transition from dependent colonies to independent states, from monarchy to republic, from membership in an extended empire in which the several members were connected only through the center to participation in a single federal nation, brought a wholly new and unforeseen set of problems that were not resolved by the formal achievement of independence in 1783. To an important degree, these problems and the ways they were—or were not—confronted and resolved defined the character of the American Revolution and expressed the basic underlying predisposition of the new American society that emerged out of the Revolution and the new American nation it helped to create.

Historians of the American Revolution have long been interested in defining the nature of that event. Indeed, why they occur and what they are are the two classic questions upon which studies of all revolutions have traditionally focused. Notwithstanding the efforts earlier in this century of J. Franklin Jameson, Evarts B. Greene, and others to put the Revolution in a larger social framework, however, most of the work on the character of the Revolution has, until relatively recently, focused very largely upon the public sphere, upon such questions as federal-state relations; the movement for a stronger national government; and the effect of competing economic interests, state and sectional rivalries, and prevailing patterns of social relations upon public life at both the state and national levels.[1]

Only during the mid-1960s did students of the Revolution begin to take a broader approach to this subject. The impetus for this approach came from two complementary directions. One was a deepening concern with the perceptual world within which the Revolution occurred. This concern derived directly out of the important studies of Revolutionary political ideology by Bernard Bailyn and Gordon S. Wood. Like most earlier historians, Bailyn and Wood focused almost entirely upon the public realm. But their work stimulated a new and fuller appreciation of the ways in which ideas spilled over from politics to other areas of American life to challenge and, in some cases, even to force a reconception of some of the basic underlying assumptions about the nature of the existing social order in Anglophone North America.[2]

To an important degree, Bailyn and Wood built their analyses upon J. G. A. Pocock's early essays on the character and importance of civic humanism in early modern British political culture. Published in the mid-1970s, Pocock's *The Machiavellian Moment,* which traced in detail the movement of the civic humanist or classical republican tradition from Renaissance Florence through the political world of early modern England and argued for its centrality to Revolutionary and early national American political and social life, provided still further stimulus to the growing concern with the ideological dimensions of the early American republic.[3]

By suggesting how the emerging ideology of American republicanism ramified so widely throughout American public life, these works helped to shift the attention of Revolutionary historians to the intellectual and cultural realms. Using the contemporary linguistic and conceptual worlds depicted by Bailyn, Wood, and Pocock as a point of departure, a large number of younger scholars began, especially in the mid-1970s, not only to reexamine traditional questions but also to look at aspects of

---

[1] J. Franklin Jameson, *The American Revolution Considered as a Social Movement* (Princeton, N. J., 1926); Evarts B. Greene, *The Revolutionary Generation, 1763–1790* (New York, 1943).

[2] Bernard Bailyn, *The Ideological Origins of the American Revolution* (Cambridge, Mass., 1967); Gordon S. Wood, *The Creation of the American Republic, 1776–1787* (Chapel Hill, N.C., 1969).

[3] J. G. A. Pocock, *The Machiavellian Moment: Florentine Political Thought and the Atlantic Republican Tradition* (Princeton, N.J., 1975). Pocock's early essays upon which Bailyn and Wood drew are collected in his *Politics, Language, and Time* (New York, 1971).

the American Revolutionary experience that had not previously been systematically studied. Together, this literature has resulted in what one commentator has referred to as a "republican synthesis" of the American Revolutionary experience.[4]

Although this new republican paradigm has by no means commanded universal acceptance as the appropriate framework for analyzing the Revolution, it has been enormously influential. Indeed, as several critics have pointed out, it has no doubt produced an exaggerated emphasis upon the ideological dimensions of the Revolution. But it has also helped to stimulate several scholars to begin once again to take a new look at the many substantive socioeconomic issues, problems, conditions, behaviors, and developments that shaped American public life during the Revolutionary era.

A second significant source for the renewal and expansion of interest in the character of the Revolution has been the powerful movement toward the construction of a more inclusive history. Over the past two decades, a sweeping revolution in historical studies has taken historians out of the halls of government and into the busy and variegated scenes of private activity that have traditionally comprised the essence of American life. This movement has produced a new concern with analyzing the social impact of war; the nature of political dissent; the experiences of nondominant groups such as Amerindians, African Americans, and women; the character of family and community relations; and the history of religion and other symbolic cultural systems. With specific regard to the Revolution, this movement has generated an intensifying interest in exploring the ways in which the Revolution affected contemporary conditions in these and other areas of American life.

This new work has identified a number of problems that the Revolution and the adoption of republicanism posed for Americans. Some were relatively short-term and arose directly out of the conclusion of the war. These include the problems of demobilization and how a society skeptical about standing armies and reluctant to pay for more than a token military force could defend itself,[5] and how the victorious American polities

---

[4] Much of this new work in the ideological realm is summarized in Robert E. Shalhope, "Republicanism and Early American Historiography," *William and Mary Quarterly*, 3d ser., 39 (1982): 334–56.

[5] See E. Wayne Carp, "The Problem of National Defense in the Early American Republic," in Jack P. Greene, ed., *The American Revolution: Its Character and Limits* (New York, 1987), and *To Starve the Army at Pleasure: Continental Army Administration and American Political Culture, 1775–1783* (Chapel Hill, N.C., 1984); Charles Royster, *A*

were to deal with loyalists and other disaffected groups who, having thrown in their lot with the losing side and being unwilling to emigrate, had to be reintegrated into their local societies.[6]

Other essentially political problems did not demand immediate attention but were of continuing concern to contemporary leaders: how to achieve a viable federal union;[7] how to organize a new republican political world that would not violate traditional and still cherished conceptions of the sociopolitical order;[8] how to secure economic independence and diplomatic respect for the new republic;[9] how to organize the process of territorial expansion and then to incorporate the new polities that resulted from that process into the United States;[10] and how the lives of Amerindians would be affected by American independence.[11]

Still other problems arose out of the implications of the Revolution for the new American society it was helping to create. What did republican ideology mean for dependent groups such as slaves and women?[12] How

---

Revolutionary People at War: The Continental Army and American Character, 1775–1783 (Chapel Hill, N.C., 1979).

[6] See Robert M. Calhoon, "The Reintegration of the Loyalists and the Disaffected," in Greene, *American Revolution*, 51–74, and *The Loyalists in Revolutionary America* (New York, 1973); James H. Kettner, *The Development of American Citizenship, 1608–1870* (Chapel Hill, N.C., 1978).

[7] See Jack N. Rakove, "From One Agenda to Another: The Condition of American Federalism, 1783–1787," in Greene, *American Revolution*, 80–103, and *The Beginnings of National Politics: An Interpretive History of the Continental Congress* (New York, 1979).

[8] See Lance Banning, "The Problem of Power: Parties, Aristocracy, and Democracy in Revolutionary Thought," in Greene, *American Revolution*, 104–23, and *The Jeffersonian Persuasion: Evolution of a Party Ideology* (Ithaca, N. Y., 1978).

[9] See Drew R. McCoy, "An Unfinished Revolution: The Quest for Economic Independence in the Early Republic," in Greene, *American Revolution*, 131–48, and *The Elusive Republic: Political Economy in Jeffersonian America* (Chapel Hill, N.C., 1980); Jonathan R. Dull, "Two Republics in a Hostile World: The United States and the Netherlands in the 1780s," in Greene, *American Revolution*, 149–63.

[10] Peter S. Onuf, "Settlers, Settlements, and New States," in Greene, *American Revolution*, 171–96, and *The Origins of the Federal Republic: Jurisdictional Controversies in the United States, 1775–1787* (Philadelphia, 1983).

[11] James H. Merrell, "Declarations of Independence: Indian-White Relations in the New Nation," in Greene, *American Revolution*, 197–223.

[12] Sylvia R. Frey, "Liberty, Equality, and Slavery: The Paradox of the American Revolution," in Greene, *American Revolution*, 230–52, and *Water from the Rock: Black Resistance in a Revolutionary Age* (Princeton, N.J., 1991); Elaine F. Crane, "Dependence in the Era of Independence: The Role of Women in a Republican Society," in Greene, *American Revolution*, 253–75; Linda Kerber, *Women of the Republic: Intellect and Ideology in Revo-*

could Americans develop a new individual and corporate identity that would be commensurate with the values of the new American republic? By developing a new system of education appropriate for a republican citizenry?[13] By fashioning a national past?[14] By defining and depicting in a new and specifically American literature the salient features of the emerging American national culture?[15] How did Revolutionary ideology affect American attitudes about church and state and the more general problem of religious freedom?[16]

Further problems involved short-term economic conditions such as management of the Revolutionary debt and the creation of adequate banking facilities and a stable currency system; social reform issues involving such questions as capital punishment, penal reform, poor relief, imprisonment for debt, prostitution, indentured servitude, and the care of illness and insanity; and revision and simplification of the legal system. Finally, some scholars have tried, thus far with limited success, to link directly to the Revolution some broader social developments such as the shift in craft industries from an independent artisanal to a wage labor system, which does seem to have been in its early stages during the last decades of the eighteenth century, and the alleged transition from a more subsistence-oriented to a more commerce-oriented agriculture, which, in all but the most stagnant areas of British North America, seems to have occurred a long time before the Revolution.

Taken together, this new work strongly suggests that the possibilities for change during and after the American Revolution were drastically

lutionary America (Chapel Hill, N.C., 1980); Mary Beth Norton, *Liberty's Daughters: The Revolutionary Experience of American Women, 1750—1800* (Boston, 1980).

[13] Melvin Yazawa, "Creating a Republican Citizenry," in Greene, *American Revolution,* 282–308, and *From Colonies to Commonwealth: Familial Ideology and the Beginnings of the American Republic* (Baltimore, 1985).

[14] Lester H. Cohen, "Creating a Usable Future: The Revolutionary Historians and the National Past," in Greene, *American Revolution,* 309–30, and *The Revolutionary Histories: Contemporary Narratives of the American Revolution* (Ithaca, N.Y., 1980).

[15] Jay Fliegelman, "Familial Politics, Seduction, and the Novel: The Anxious Agenda of an American Literary Culture," in Greene, *American Revolution,* 331–54, and *Prodigals and Pilgrims: The American Revolution against Patriarchal Authority, 1750—1800* (New York, 1982); Catherine L. Albanese, "Whither the Sons (and Daughters)? Republican Nature and the Quest for the Ideal," in Greene, *American Revolution,* 362–87.

[16] Nathan O. Hatch, "In Pursuit of Religious Freedom: Church, State, and People in the New Republic," in Greene, *American Revolution,* 388–406, and *The Sacred Cause of Liberty: Republican Thought and the Millennium in Revolutionary New England* (New Haven, 1977); Catherine L. Albanese, *Sons of the Fathers: The Civil Religion of the American Revolution* (Philadelphia, 1976).

circumscribed by the character and orientation of the society in which it occurred. In the years following the war, political leaders enjoyed only limited success in resolving the various problems confronting American society in ways that were compatible with the goals they had articulated before and during the war. By the end of the 1780s, the loyalists had been largely reintegrated into American society with surprisingly little retribution, Congress had established a western policy that would permit the orderly expansion of settlement and the extension of republican society and government into new areas, and the Federal Constitution of 1787 had established an ambiguous but, at least in the short run, viable division of authority between the states and the national government.

In most other areas, however, the record was much less impressive. As the War of 1812 would so amply demonstrate, the nation had not by then managed to resolve the problem of how to achieve an effective defense force in a society that was rarely threatened by external attack and therefore regarded money devoted to maintain a permanent military force as a waste of valuable resources. Tensions among exponents of competing ideologies about the nature and goals of the American polity had, by the 1790s, produced deep party divisions and a vigorous competition for power of a kind traditionally regarded as a harbinger of the collapse of popular governments. Commanding very little diplomatic respect from the major European powers, the United States continued in a state of galling economic dependence upon Britain. Efforts of the national government to implement a policy of justice and assimilation toward the Indians were nullified by the behavior of states and individuals.

Although a few states had adopted measures leading to the abolition of chattel slavery, that blatant anomaly in republican America was still the condition of the overwhelming majority of black people. The status of women had improved almost not at all. Nor did the vision of a self-sacrificing, public-spirited society held out by republican enthusiasts in the immediate wake of Independence any longer seem to be attainable. Despite the efforts of historians, belles-lettrists, and other opinion leaders to define and inculcate a sense of republican national self-consciousness among the broader American public, individual Americans showed, in one arena after another, that they had neither the will, nor the commitment, nor the interest required to sustain the selfless patriotism and devotion to the public good that so many Revolutionary leaders in 1776 had thought necessary for the successful functioning of a republic. While elite figures continued to celebrate simplicity and public-spiritedness, ordinary Americans showed themselves far more interested in accumulating material goods and promoting the immediate welfare of themselves and their families. Nor were they sufficiently concerned with changing their priorities and the predominant patterns of behavior that derived from those priorities to be willing to spend the money necessary to implement the educational schemes for inculcating republican virtue in the young proposed by Benjamin Rush and others. More and more, even, religion appeared to be becoming a source of discord rather than stability, as people seemed to be more intent on following their own personal dispositions than on the larger interests of society.

Perhaps the most important general questions raised by these findings are why, at the conclusion of the War for Independence, the American Revolution, especially as its goals had been defined by political and other opinion leaders in 1775–76 and after, remained incomplete and why, several decades later, the new "American" political society spawned by the Revolution had yet to meet those goals. These questions are susceptible to a variety of answers on several different levels of analysis. On one level, it is valid to say that the exigencies of war prevented American leaders at both the national and state levels from addressing all but the most pressing problems between 1776 and 1783. On a more general level, it is equally correct that no revolution or other large-scale political movement has ever achieved all of the aspirations of its proponents and that the American Revolution was no exception.

If these answers are true, they are also truistic. Surely, a more interesting and revealing approach lies in the analysis of the particular pattern of successes and failures exhibited by the Revolution, not simply during the war but in its aftermath over the next quarter century. Such an approach can be used to define the specific limits of the revolutionary impulse—what might be called the social boundaries of potential political action—within the American Revolution. Perhaps no other single subject is more revealing of the nature of a revolution than the identification of its political and social limits.

What the specific pattern of failures and successes in the American Revolution reveals, I would suggest, is that the new United States was composed of a group of societies without much capacity for—or interest in—collective public action. From the earliest days of settlement of the English-American colonies, the pursuit of individual happiness had been the primary shaping social value. No other imperative was so important in determining the character of early American society or in forming early American culture. As so much of the new social history has revealed, moreover, for the overwhelming majority of Americans, the pursuit of happiness had always resided in the private, rather than in the public, realm. Except for the orthodox Puritan colonies of Massachusetts Bay and Connecticut, where, at least during the first generation or two of settlement, the corporate impulse was strong and the public sphere relatively large, every society in colonial British America, including New England after about 1700, exhibited a basically private orientation, a powerful underlying predisposition among the members of its free population to preoccupy themselves with the pursuit of personal and family independence and the social improvements that would guarantee and enhance their individual economic and social achievements, enrich their lives, and give them a sense of personal self-worth.

For all but a few Americans, the pursuit of happiness did not involve the pursuit of public office or even the active occupation of a public— that is, a political—space. There was simply too much scope for the pursuit of individual and family goals in the private sphere for most people to be much interested in having a public space. Although the intensity of civic responsibility differed from place to place and time to time during the colonial era, the primary concerns of most independent Americans were private rather than public. Their allegiances were to themselves and their families rather than to the larger social entities to which they belonged. To quote one observer, they were mostly "too engaged in their respective occupations for the enticements" of public life.[17]

They or their ancestors had, in any case, left Britain or Europe not only to escape want and to gain independence but also, as contemporaries were fond of pointing out, to get away from excessive public intrusions into their private lives, intrusions in the form of high taxes, rapacious civil and religious establishments, obligations to military or naval service, and war. The most popular cultural image invoked by early Americans was the biblical image of the industrious husbandman who sat contentedly, safely, and without want under the shade of his own vine and fig tree, presiding over—and luxuriating in—the development of his family and estate.

This new emphasis upon the private orientation of early American society has at least implicitly raised the question of how it affected public life, public institutions, and the collective goals of national life as they were defined by leaders before, during, and after the American Revolution. Throughout the colonial period, the private orientation of American society had meant that in most places and at most times the public realm had been small. With only a tiny bureaucracy and no police, a localized judicial system that rarely met more than fifteen to thirty days

---

[17] Duke de La Rochefoucauld-Liancourt, *Travels through the United States of North America*, 2 vols. (London, 1799), 1:679.

in any given year, and legislatures that in peacetime were rarely in session for more than a month in any given year, government was small, intermittent, and inexpensive. Except during wartime, taxes were low, and the only public activities that engaged most men were infrequent militia or jury service and somewhat more frequent participation in vital public works such as building and repairing bridges and roads. With little coercive power—and very little presence—government in America was consensual and depended for its energy upon the force of community opinion, which was, in practice, if not yet in theory, little more than the sum of individual opinions.

Government in early America was thus most importantly a device, in the traditional sense, for maintaining orderly relations among people and protecting them from their own and others' human frailties. Even more significantly, it was an agency for the protection of one's individual property in land, goods, and person, one's property in person including the right of striving, of pursuing (as well as protecting) one's interests, of seeking to alter one's place on the scale of economic well-being and social status. While they wanted enough government to secure peace and to maintain a just and open civil order, most Americans were usually, to quote one contemporary, in favor of just "so much government as will do justice, protect property, and defend the country."[18]

The critical point about the implicit conception of political society that underlay this pattern of governance is that it assigned to political society no more authority over the individual, and to the individual no more obligation to political society, than was absolutely necessary to make sure that all free individuals had approximately the same scope for private activity. Political society was thus regulative, as it was in the traditional societies of Europe. But it was also facilitative in at least two senses. First, it acted to "enlarge" the scope of opportunity in the private realm by overseeing and stimulating those public improvements that would provide people with an ever-larger field for the pursuit of happiness, for the realization of their individual potentials. Second, it encouraged individuals to pursue their own goals without forcing them to be much concerned with the social well-being of the community as a whole.

The American Revolution represented a radical challenge to these enduring and already quite ancient arrangements and to the traditional preference for devoting energy to the pursuit of activities in the private sphere. To be sure, as Gordon Wood and David Ammerman have shown,

---

[18] Samuel Williams, *The Natural and Civil History of Vermont*, 2 vols. (Walpole, N. H., 1794), 2:358, 424.

the challenge presented by the Coercive Acts and the initial stages of their military enforcement in 1774–76 produced a contagion of "self-sacrifice and patriotism" that was surprisingly extensive, if by no means universal. This contagion seems even to have stimulated, among the very large proportion of the population that was swept up in it, a powerful and remarkably widely shared sense of public-spiritedness and willingness to subordinate private interests to public demands.[19]

But this early flush of enthusiastic national patriotism proved impossible to sustain among a population whose most basic drives were individual rather than collective, private rather than public. Wanting most of all to be left alone, they quickly found themselves confronted with many new and burdensome public intrusions into their private lives. The demands of war both raised taxes and significantly increased the range of public demands upon individuals in the form of military service, supply levies, and demands for declarations of allegiance. At the same time, the imperatives of the new republicanism and the absence of a strong controlling central power encouraged the state governments to involve themselves in a variety of new activities. The result was a dramatic growth of government, especially at the state level, an enlargement of the public realm that represented a massive—and thitherto unprecedented—intrusion of the public into the private realm. Never before in the history of British America had the public realm made such heavy demands upon the citizenry.

At the conclusion of the War for Independence, people expected a return to the old order, a restoration of the old system whereby, in the vast majority of areas, the private realm took precedence over the public. Once the objectives that had mobilized the polity had been secured, the people's concern with public affairs invariably took a back seat to their pursuit of their own welfares as individuals. As Jack Rakove has remarked, "After eight long years of war and economic dislocation, Americans were [simply] too exhausted to do much more than put their own affairs, too long neglected, in order."[20]

Like George Washington, they had throughout the war looked forward to their return to those domestic and private pursuits that had traditionally engaged most of their attentions, and the energy with which they threw themselves into those pursuits in the immediate postwar years was evident in the rapid recovery of the United States from

[19] Wood, *Creation of the American Republic,* 413–25; David Ammerman, *In the Common Cause: American Response to the Coercive Acts of 1774* (Charlottesville, Va., 1974), 89–101.

[20] Rakove, "From One Agenda to Another," 81.

many of the effects of the war. "It is wonderful," Washington wrote to a French correspondent less than three years after the war, "to see how soon the ravages of war are repaired. Houses are rebuilt, fields enclosed, stocks of cattle which were destroyed are replaced, and many a desolated territory assumes again the cheerful appearance of cultivation. In many places the vestiges of conflagration and ruin are hardly to be traced. The arts of peace, such as clearing rivers, building bridges, and establishing conveniences for travelling &c. are assiduously promoted."[21]

As Washington's remark suggests, ordinary free white Americans showed by their behavior that they did not necessarily regard the Revolution as incomplete simply because it had failed to realize the expansive aspirations of some of its leaders. Rather, as Gordon Wood has noted, "most ordinary people were ebulliently confident of the success of the Revolution and the promise of America."[22] But they defined that promise almost entirely in terms of their ability to pursue their own goals as individuals. The predominant tendencies in a society with such a profoundly private orientation were centrifugal, not centripetal. Without powerful countervailing pressures, public goals simply could not be sustained unless they promised to enhance the capacity of individuals to pursue their own and their families' private welfares.

The extent to which this private orientation of early American society and this lack of interest in enlarging the public sphere both set limits upon the political potentialities of the American Revolution and continued to shape American public life during the post-Revolutionary era is nowhere better revealed than by the new nation's pattern of successes and failures in coping with the many problems it faced in the wake of the Revolution. Leaders simply could not implement any goals that were incompatible with the basically private and highly individualistic predisposition of the society over which they presided. Whatever was compatible with or facilitative of that predisposition was handled with reasonable success; whatever was not was neglected. Thus, Americans were too busy cultivating their own private interests to bother with the sustained persecution of loyalists. They endorsed the national government's western policy because it offered individual settlers both favorable opportunities to acquire land and a high degree of local political autonomy. They threw their support behind the new federal government after 1788 be-

[21] Washington to Chevalier de La Luzerne, Aug. 1, 1786, in *Writings of George Washington*, ed. John C. Fitzpatrick, 39 vols. (Washington, D.C., 1931–40), 28:500–501.

[22] Gordon S. Wood, "Illusions and Disillusions in the American Revolution," in Greene, *American Revolution*, 360–61.

cause it seemed to promise to diminish the intrusive power assumed by the state governments during the Revolution, to provide more effective assistance against those Indians who blocked the path of expansion, and to enable the nation to command more respect abroad so that it might secure the commercial advantages so necessary to the successful pursuit of their individual interests.

On the other hand, any problems whose solutions seemed to require large public expenditures and significantly higher taxes without holding out much promise of immediately contributing to the pursuit of profits and happiness by private individuals were either not systematically addressed or not energetically pursued. These included establishing a viable defense force, fulfilling promises to Indians, abolishing chattel slavery, elevating the status of women, improving education, or enlarging the public sphere. At the same time, Americans failed to prevent—and ultimately even accepted—the emergence of political parties and endorsed the principle that government should be neutral in matters of individual religious conviction because those developments seemed to be a logical expression of the self-interested and individualistic society in which they lived.

This pattern of dealing with the problems raised by and during the Revolution only serves to underline the fact that American society during the Revolutionary era was one whose members were overwhelmingly preoccupied with the cultivation of their own individual goals in the private realm and had little interest in devoting sustained energy or committing major resources to activities in the public sphere. As many scholars have suggested, American society in the late eighteenth century was still, to a considerable degree, trapped within the conceptual universe of classical republicanism. But the way that society dealt—and did not deal—with public problems also powerfully argues that the imperatives of classical republicanism had relatively little impact on the behavior of many of its members. Rather, in virtually every area, that behavior served to ensure that, no less than the colonial societies established by their ancestors in the previous century, Americans of the Revolutionary era would build their republic not on self-denial and the cultivation of civic virtue in the public realm but on the avid pursuit of self and family concerns in the private sphere.

This chapter was initially written as the introduction to the book of essays in which it first appeared. It was given as a lecture at the Institute of African Studies, University of Ghana, Accra, January 20, 1987. Reshaped for this volume, it is here reprinted with permission from Jack P. Greene, ed., *The American Revolution: Its Character and Limits* (New York: New York University Press, 1987), 1–13.

—SIXTEEN—

The American Revolution and Modern Revolutions

T HIS CHAPTER is a preliminary exploration of the relationship between the American Revolution and the development of the modern revolutionary tradition over the past two hundred years. More specifically, it asks the question of whether the American Revolution has
made any difference to the history of the modern world. That question
is, of course, rhetorical. No event of the magnitude of the American Revolution can fail to make a difference. The questions are: differences to
what and to whom? The Revolution obviously made a difference to all
those who took some active role in it, and it has certainly made a difference to the several hundred scholars—and their families—who have
spent their lives studying it.

With regard to the larger entities immediately involved, however, its
effects are less clear. The loss of the American continental colonies was
hardly the national disaster for Britain that the many proponents of coercive measures during the three decades before the Revolution had predicted and that nearly everybody within the British political nation—
Josiah Tucker and Adam Smith obviously excepted—had expected. For
reasons Smith elaborated in detail in *The Wealth of Nations,* published
in the same year as the Declaration of Independence, economic domination, as we all now understand so well, did not require political control:
Britain continued to derive vast profits from the American trade for
much of the next century, and Britain did not, as one of many prophets
of doom had suggested in the mid-1760s, immediately "dwindle and decline every day in . . . trade, whilst [the former colonists] . . . thrive and
prosper exceedingly" so that Britons ran "away as fast as they" could

"from this country to that, and Old England" became "a poor, deserted, deplorable kingdom" of no more consequence in the world than it had been under the Tudors—before it had acquired colonies—or than those equally small but colonyless countries of the Baltic—Denmark and Sweden—were then at the time of the Revolution.[1]

Within Britain, the Revolution began the process by which political radicalism was discredited among those powerful new entrepreneurial classes for whom it had seemed to exercise a growing appeal before the 1770s, but in this process it was the French, not the American, Revolution that was decisive.[2] With regard to other peripheral areas of the late eighteenth-century British Empire, the American Revolution helped to stir successful demands for greater home rule among the Anglo-Irish.[3] But it only operated to weaken similar feelings among the settler populations in the more distant colonies that remained under British hegemony after 1783. The extreme economic and military dependence of both the Caribbean and Canadian colonies upon Britain, so vividly underlined for local leaders by their total incapacity to follow the example of the rebellious colonies during the Revolution, contributed to the creation of a psychology of passive dependence that would continue for the foreseeable future.[4]

Nor can it be contended that the Revolution has made as much difference as American historians have conventionally suggested to the later history of the area now encompassed by the United States. The significance of the Revolution as an occasion—and a continuing source—for the corporate cultural and political self-definition of the American people should not be discounted. Given the subsequent history of Canada, Australia, and New Zealand, however, there is no reason to suppose that a continued connection with Britain would have much retarded or greatly altered subsequent patterns of territorial, demographic, and eco-

---

[1] "John Ploughshare," from the *London Chronicle*, Feb. 20, 1766, in Edmund S. Morgan, ed., *Prologue to Revolution: Sources and Documents on the Stamp Act Crisis, 1764—1766* (Chapel Hill, N.C., 1959), 103.

[2] See J. H. Plumb, "British Attitudes to the American Revolution," in Plumb, *In the Light of History* (Boston, 1972), 70–87.

[3] David Noel Doyle, *Ireland, Irishmen, and Revolutionary America, 1760—1820* (Dublin, 1981).

[4] See Jack P. Greene, "Changing Identity in the British Caribbean: Barbados as a Case Study," in Nicholas Canny and Anthony Pagden, eds., *Colonial Identity in the Atlantic World, 1500—1800* (Princeton, N.J., 1987), 213–66; T. R. Clayton, "Sophistry, Security, and Socio-Political Structures in the American Revolution; or, Why Jamaica Did Not Rebel," *Historical Journal* 29 (1986): 319–44.

nomic growth or have prevented the development of either a liberal society or a federal, democratic, republican, and independent state of enormous power on the world stage. Indeed, it can even be argued that, by
prematurely cutting the colonies off from Britain and the passionate and
powerful antislavery forces that developed in that country after 1785,
the Revolution may well have helped to perpetuate the institution of
black chattel slavery in the American republic for an additional thirty to
fifty years and thereby have been directly responsible for the bloody Civil
War that was fought over that issue.

But it is not primarily from the parochial perspective of the Anglo-
American world that the impact and meaning of the American Revolution ought to be considered. For that Revolution had an immediate—
and ramifying—importance that extended well beyond the narrow confines of the Anglo-American diaspora. The most extensive and learned
analysis of the changing impact of the Revolution over the past two centuries remains Richard B. Morris's study of *The Emerging Nations and
the American Revolution* (New York, 1970). In this work, Morris traces
the "contagious" influence of the Revolution upon contemporaries to the
fact that it "offered the world the first example of a successful secession
of colonies from empire, of the overthrow of a monarch, and of the formulation of states and nation on principles of constitutionalism and federalism."[5]

In a strict sense, however, none of these claims for first place is mer-
ited. The Revolution was not the first successful modern war for colonial
self-determination. As American Revolutionaries widely recognized, the
Netherlands Revolt had preceded it in that category by nearly two centuries. Nor was it the first overthrow of a monarch by local magnates.
The Glorious Revolution of 1688–89 in England was a modern example
of a familiar phenomenon in the European past. Nor was it the first
republican revolution. The Dutch again furnish a modern precedent,
and the English Revolution of the 1640s and 1650s was a prior, if ultimately unsuccessful, experiment in republican government. And it was
not the first modern model of the creation of a federal state based upon
principles of constitutionalism: still again the Dutch provide a precedent.

---

[5] Richard B. Morris, *The Emerging Nations and the American Revolution* (New York,
1970), 78.

What gave the American Revolution such widespread appeal and what both distinguished it from all previous modern political revolutions and linked it to all subsequent ones was its association with the idea of progress, with the belief that it was possible for men deliberately to re-mold human institutions in such a way as to create a freer, more just, better, and perhaps even materially more comfortable world.[6] As explicitly enunciated and seemingly epitomized by the new American republic and the social conditions which that republic expressed, this belief gave the American Revolution an intellectual and emotional force that stretched far beyond that of any earlier revolution in the modern world and enabled it, in Morris's words, to inaugurate "the Age of Revolutions that has still not come to an end."[7] The American Revolution, not the earlier Dutch Wars for Independence or the English Revolution, put human liberty upon the agenda of fundamental concerns of the modern world beginning first in America and Europe but ultimately stretching over the entire globe. "In the stricted sense," wrote Lord Acton, "the history of liberty dated from 1776, for never till then had men sought liberty knowing what they sought."[8]

No group has appreciated the unique contribution of the Revolution in this regard more fully than did its leaders themselves. The American Revolution, said James Madison, the principal architect of its principal achievement, the Federal Constitution of 1787, "has no parallel in the annals of human society."[9] "The progress of society," rhapsodized John Adams, "will be accelerated by centuries by this revolution. . . . Light spreads from the dayspring in the west, and may soon it shine more and more until the perfect day."[10] America, agreed Madison's friend George Turberville, "may rejoice, and plume" itself "in the idea of having made the Rent in the great curtain that withheld the light from human na-

---

[6] John Dunn, *Modern Revolutions: An Introduction to the Analysis of a Modern Phenomenon* (Cambridge, Eng., 1972), 5; J. H. Elliott, "Revolution and Continuity in Early Modern Europe," *Past and Present*, no. 42 (1969): 43–56; Jack P. Greene, "Paine, America, and the 'Modernization' of Political Consciousness," *Political Science Quarterly* 93 (1978): 73–92 [chap. 12 above].

[7] Morris, *Emerging Nations*, x.

[8] As quoted by Martin Diamond, "The Revolution of Sober Expectations," in *America's Continuing Revolution: An Act of Conservation* (Washington, D.C., 1975), 34.

[9] Madison, *Federalist No. 14*, in Benjamin F. Wright, ed., *The Federalist* (Cambridge, Mass., 1961), 154.

[10] John Adams to Abigail Adams, Dec. 18, 1781, in *Familiar Letters of John Adams and His Wife Abigail Adams during the Revolution* (Boston, 1876), 403.

ture—by her exertions she has let the day and the Rights of Man become legible and intelligible to a Shakled World."[11] "America's purpose," declared the South Carolinian Dr. David Ramsay, the most perceptive contemporary historian of the Revolution, "is to prove the virtues of republicanism, to assert the Rights of Man, and to make society better."[12] Henceforth, America's founding fathers hoped, America would serve as a beacon of freedom for the rest of mankind. "The flames kindled on the 4th of July 1776," Thomas Jefferson later assured John Adams, "have spread over too much of the globe to be extinguished by the feeble engines of despotism."[13]

Nor was this confident expectation that the Revolution would "advance the liberation of mankind" limited to Americans. Throughout the middle decades of the eighteenth century, the extraordinary freedom of the white settlers in the American colonies had been a source of anxiety for British colonial officials. For a considerable segment of the British public, however, for many of those outside the establishment, American freedom was a rare plant to be encouraged rather than to be carefully pruned. Those who exhibited such sentiments included members of that "purposeful, expanding" middle-class community who "were ready for a new world, freer from tradition, closer to the rational principles upon which they modelled their industry and commerce," and stood outside the prevailing "system of oligarchy and patronage which created not only injustice but also practical obstacles to their industrial and commercial activities." Many contemporary social critics in Britain, ranging from the independent country gentry on the right to the dissenting radical republicans on the left, shared this favorable estimation of America. When they railed against the corrosive effects within Britain of increasing luxury in society and corruption in politics, they sometimes pointed to the American colonies as the only remaining seat of virtue in the British world.[14]

Thus, one Yorkshire gentleman in the 1760s counseled his son to "follow the course of the sun to that country [—America—] where Freedom

---

[11] George de Turberville to James Madison, Jan. 28, 1793, as quoted by Morris, *Emerging Nations*, 39.

[12] Ramsay, as quoted by Don Higginbotham, "The Relevance of the American Revolution," *Anglican Theological Review*, Supplementary Ser., no. 1 (1973): 32.

[13] Jefferson to Adams, Sept. 12, 1821, in *The Adams-Jefferson Letters*, ed. Lester J. Cappon, 2 vols. (Chapel Hill, N.C., 1959), 2:575.

[14] Michael Zuckerman, "The Irrelevant Revolution: 1776 and Since," *American Quarterly* 30 (1978): 241; Plumb, "British Attitudes to the American Revolution," 76–78.

has already fixed her standard and is erecting her throne." America, another Englishman said in August 1767, would "be an asylum to those Englishmen who have spirit and virtue enough to leave their country, when it submits to domestic or foreign tyranny," an event which, as another observer declared in an opinion widely shared by his contemporaries, appeared to be "at no great distance." Some Englishmen even hoped that the colonies would become "free and independent" so that, safely separated from the corruption of the parent society, they could better "serve as a retreat to . . . Free men."[15]

Although the Revolution offended the patriotic sensibilities of many of the former celebrants of America who temporarily turned against the republican monster that had reared its ugly head on the other side of the Atlantic, some radical British political thinkers hailed American independence as both an appropriate expression of the freedom with which the colonies had so long been identified and a "revolution in favour of universal liberty." By "disseminating just sentiments of the rights of mankind, and the nature of legitimate government; by exciting a spirit of resistance to tyranny . . . ; and by occasioning the establishment in *America* of forms of government more equitable and more liberal than any that the world has yet known," the Revolution, the radical English thinker Dr. Richard Price declared in 1784, had opened up "a new prospect in human affairs" and begun "a new era in the history of mankind," perhaps, "next to the introduction of Christianity among mankind," the "most important step in the progressive course of human improvement."[16]

Men such as Price in Britain looked to the new United States as "the seat of liberty, science and virtue . . . from whence there is reason to hope those sacred blessings will spread, till they have become universal, and the time arrives when kings and priests shall have no more power to oppress, and that ignominious slavery which has hitherto debased the world is exterminated," when, he quoted Montesquieu, "the members of a civil community" would be *"confederates,* not subjects; and their rulers, servants, not masters," and "all legitimate government" would consist "in the dominion of equal laws made with the common consent; that

[15] Plumb, "British Attitudes to the American Revolution," 73–74.

[16] Richard Price, *Observations on the Importance of the American Revolution* (London, 1784), in Jack P. Greene, ed., *Colonies to Nation, 1763–1789: A Documentary History of the American Revolution* (New York, 1975), 423–25.

is, in the dominion of men over *themselves;* and not in the dominion of communities over communities, or of any men over [any] other men."[17]

Similarly extravagant predictions issued forth from all over continental Europe, especially from France, where the administration, improvidently it soon turned out, intervened on the colonies' behalf. "All Europe is on our Side of the question, as far as applause and good Wishes can carry them," Benjamin Franklin wrote from his ambassadorship in Paris in 1777:

> Those who live under arbitrary Power do nevertheless approve of Liberty, and they wish for it; they almost despair of recovering it in Europe; and they read the Translations of our separate Colony Constitutions with *Rapture;* and there are Numbers everywhere, who talk of Removing to America, with their Families and Fortunes, as soon as Peace and our Independence shall be established, that 'tis generally believed we shall have a prodigious Addition of Strength, Wealth, and Arts. . . . Hence 'tis a Common Observation here, that our Cause is the *Cause of all Mankind,* and that we are fighting for their Liberty in defending our own. "'Tis a glorious task assign'd us by Providence; which has, I trust, given us Spirit and Virtue equal to it, and will at last crown it with success."[18]

The Revolution, Thomas Jefferson, Franklin's successor in Paris, wrote a few years later, has "awakened the thinking part of this nation from the sleep of despotism in which they were sunk."[19]

Along with the successful establishment of wholly new polities based on the rule of law and involving extensive participation by the people at large, the universalistic pronouncements of the Revolution gave Europeans a sense "that they lived in a rare era of momentous change," a time of new beginnings in which an enlightened world would, with America showing the way, enjoy vastly more political freedom and civil justice than at any time in modern history. In R. R. Palmer's words, the American Revolution "added a new content to the conception of progress. It gave a whole new dimension to ideas of liberty and equality made familiar by the Enlightenment. . . . It dethroned England, and set up

---

[17] Ibid.

[18] Franklin to Samuel Cooper, May 1, 1777, in *The Writings of Benjamin Franklin,* ed. Albert H. Smyth, 10 vols. (New York, 1905–7), 7:56.

[19] Jefferson, as quoted by Morris, *Emerging Nations,* 38–39.

America, as a model for those seeking a better world."[20] "Nothing has excited more admiration in the world," crowed James Madison, "than the manner in which free governments have been established in America, for it was the *first* instance, from the creation of the world—that free inhabitants have been seen deliberating on a form of government, and selecting such of their citizens as possess their confidence, to determine upon and give effect to it."[21]

Englishmen and Europeans alike found special inspiration in the social character as well as in the political achievements of the new United States. The absence of hereditary privilege, restrictive institutions, and fettering traditions; the relative equality of the free segments of society; the fierce jealousy of individual liberty that seemed to be so deeply engraved upon the American character—all seemed to be integral components of a model to be emulated by the rest of the world.[22]

If, as the Polish historian Jerzy Topolski has noted, the role of the American Revolution in triggering "revolutionary consciousness in Europe [in the 1770s and 1780s] was immense," if its ideas immediately became "dynamic elements in stimulating liberal-aristocratic movements in Europe toward revolutionary action,"[23] its preeminence as an exemplar of revolution was short-lived. Within two years after the adoption of the Federal Constitution in 1787–88, the American Revolution had to share the spotlight with the more violent, cataclysmic, far-reaching, beguiling, and romantic French Revolution that it had helped to inspire.

What happened over the next century is a familiar story to all students of the history of revolutions in the modern world: the French, not

---

[20] R. R. Palmer, *The Age of Democratic Revolutions: A Political History of Europe and America, 1760–1800,* vol. 1, *The Challenge* (Princeton, N.J., 1959), 239, 282.

[21] Madison, as quoted by Higginbotham, "Relevance of the American Revolution," 30.

[22] See Arthur Sheps, "The American Revolution and the Transformation of English Republicanism," *Historical Reflections* 2 (1975): 4–28; Joyce Appleby, "America as a Model for the Radical French Reformers of 1789," *William and Mary Quarterly,* 3d ser., 28 (1971): 267–86.

[23] Jerzy Topolski, "Revolutionary Consciousness in America and Europe from the Mid-Eighteenth Century as a Methodological and Historical Problem," in Jaroslaw Pelenski, ed., *The American and European Revolutions, 1776–1848: Sociopolitical and Ideological Aspects* (Iowa City, Iowa, 1980), 91.

the American, Revolution became the model for most subsequent revolutionaries. The American Revolution continued to have some appeal
for peoples who found themselves under the domination of other
peoples. During the nineteenth century, leaders first of the Hispanic-
American and Greek wars for independence and then of the separatist
movements in Ireland and within the Ottoman and Austro-Hungarian
empires all drew inspiration—and encouragement—from the example of
the First New Nation. As Louis Kossuth, the protagonist of Hungarian
autonomy assumed in 1852 while on a tour of the United States seeking
American support, America's mission was to serve as "the cornerstone of
Liberty" for all the subject peoples of the world.[24]

But in the twentieth century, the American Revolution increasingly
lost its appeal even for subject peoples involved in similar movements
for self-determination. In proclaiming their independence, many of the
new states in Africa and Asia drew directly upon the universalistic rhetoric of the American Declaration of Independence. Still other new nations
found some features of the Federal Constitution, especially the federal
system it embodies, of relevance in working out constitutional political
systems for themselves. But despite the many manifest similarities between the American experience and their own, most leaders of most
twentieth-century colonial movements for independence—the Chinese
Republican and Irish revolutions early in the century being two notable
exceptions—like most twentieth-century revolutionaries do not seem to
have drawn much explicit guidance from the American Revolution.

The result has been, as the political philosopher Hannah Arendt has
put it in her uncompromising brief for the primacy of human liberty
within the world's political councils, that "revolutionary political
thought in the nineteenth and twentieth centuries has proceeded as
though there never had occurred a revolution in the New World and
as though there never had been any American notions and experiences
in the realm of politics and government worth thinking about."[25] No
wonder, then, that the American Revolution is not even mentioned once
in the most thoughtful and penetrating recent study in English of the
structure and theory of *Modern Revolutions.*[26] The American Revolution
with its great political achievements culminating in a constitution that

---

[24] Kossuth, as quoted by Morris, *Emerging Nations*, x.

[25] Hannah Arendt, *On Revolutions* (New York, 1963), 218.

[26] Dunn, *Modern Revolutions.*

has survived for nearly two hundred years may indeed have had an electrifying and far-reaching impact upon contemporaries. In Arnold Toynbee's words, the "world revolution" of this century may even be said to have been "American-born." But the judgment of a considerable and strategic segment of informed political opinion seems to have been that its half-life as a model for political revolutions was exceedingly short. It may indeed mark the beginning of the modern history of revolutions, but its continuing relevance is insufficient to endow it with more than antiquarian interest for the contemporary public world. The answer to the question about whether the American Revolution made any difference then might be: some difference, for a brief period, a very long time ago.[27]

But if all of this is so, if the American Revolution with its overriding concern for constitutionalism has indeed had little relevance for the last 170 of the past 200 years, and let us concede for the moment that this judgment is correct, then it is at least an interesting academic exercise—and because I am an academic I hope I will be indulged in engaging in an academic exercise—to raise two further questions: why it has had so little relevance and whether its past and continuing neglect is desirable.

Part of the answer to the question of why the American Revolution has seemed increasingly irrelevant lies in the very character of the event itself: its concerns and preoccupations were overwhelmingly political. Like the French Revolution, at least in its initial stages, the American Revolution saw "political problems as the central problems of the revolution and economic demands and [social] unrest as [largely peripheral] . . . distractions." But the French Revolution was "the last great revolution to see political problems" as primary. The advent of industrialism "made the structure of society and economy into the subject matter of revolution" in at least three ways. First, it created enormous resentment against the social and economic restraints of traditional society among the articulate and powerful entrepreneurial classes, resentment that could be—and was—channeled into opposition to the existing holders of power. Second, it produced, in the new industrial cities, concentrated social misery of an intensity and continuance without precedence in traditional rural society—and focused attention upon it. The congregation of large numbers of workers in cities and their incorporation into the "process of capitalist production" created for the first time "a politically

---

[27] Arnold J. Toynbee, *The Continuing Effect of the American Revolution* (Williamsburg, Va., 1961), 11.

educated mass—and a mass educated [quite as much] by its own situation [as] . . . by the grace of middle-class intellectuals."[28] Third, industrialization not only led to an exponential increase in the extent and depth of exploitation of larger and larger sections of the globe by the few new industrial states, including the United States—indeed, it was the competition among such states for raw materials and markets that constituted the primary impetus behind the revival of "imperialism" during the latter half of the nineteenth century after much of the previously colonized world had been decolonized during the previous century—but it ultimately created an enormous and seemingly ever-widening gap between economic and social conditions in the imperial, "modern," and developed nations and the colonial, traditional, and undeveloped societies under their hegemony.

By the 1870s for men in developed countries grappling with the social inequalities and other problems of industrialization and by the 1930s and 1940s for people struggling not merely for independence but for social and economic modernization sufficient to close the gap between their own and more developed countries, the political achievements of the American Revolution seemed to have little relevance. In the words of the radical Russian populist Peter Lavrov as early as 1873, these "rising 'social question[s]' had '*buried* the political creations of the [American] revolutionary period.'"[29]

After the middle of the nineteenth century, all political revolutions would ultimately have to involve themselves with the social question and with problems of economic, social, political, and even religious and cultural modernization. As the political scientist Barrington Moore has pointed out, through the abolition of chattel slavery, that blatant anomaly in republican and egalitarian America, even the American Civil War was a revolution of modernization. In the twentieth century, all major revolutions from the large-scale Communist revolutions in Russia and China through the nonsocialist revolutions in Mexico and Turkey during the early decades of the century and post-World War II anticolonial revolutions such as those in Indonesia, Vietnam, and Algeria have all been or have become in large measure revolutions of modernization. Even the fascist revolutions in Italy, Germany, and Spain during the 1920s and 1930s were revolutions of modernization to the rather large extent that they were expressive of entrepreneurial, middle-class, and proletarian

---

[28] Dunn, *Modern Revolutions*, 7.

[29] Morris, *Emerging Nations*, 106.

resentment against the last vestiges of traditional social and political authority.[30]

An understanding of the intimate relationship between political revolution and modernization over the last century and a half brings us closer, I think, to a comprehension of why the American Revolution has not provided a model for most later revolutions. The American Revolution has recently been referred to as the first revolution of modernization. But such a characterization is fundamentally misleading. Unlike the French Revolution, which had a social problem but failed, despite the ambiguous urgings of the sansculottes, to deal with it in any very sweeping or effective way, the American Revolution did not have a serious social problem, at least within the confines of the free population.

We have become accustomed to thinking of a modernized society as exhibiting several primary characteristics: first, more rational and less traditional patterns of social, economic, and political relations and institutional structures and, second, values that put high premiums upon individual autonomy, self-fulfillment, and pursuit of self-interest and emphasize economic returns, accumulation, achievement rather than ascription, and universalistic criteria for membership in the polity and society.[31]

If these characteristics constitute an adequate index to modernity, then, despite the efforts of its many organizers and leaders, the several societies in early modern British North America had been modern from the very beginning. The American Revolution thus took place not in a society in need of modernization but in one that was already highly modernized, perhaps the first and certainly up to that time the most

---

[30] See Dunn, *Modern Revolutions;* Barrington Moore, *Social Origins of Dictatorship and Democracy* (Boston, 1966).

[31] E. A. Wrigley, "The Process of Modernization and the Industrial Revolution in England," *Journal of Interdisciplinary History* 3 (1972–73): 225–39. A systematic discussion of the modernizing process may be found in Alex Inkeles and David H. Smith, *Becoming Modern: Individual Change in Six Developing Countries* (London, 1974), 15–17, 289–91. For a critique of the use of modernization theory by historians of the American Revolution, see Kenneth A. Lockridge, "The American Revolution, Modernization, and Man: A Critique," in Richard Maxwell Brown and Don E. Fehrenbacher, eds., *Tradition, Conflict, and Modernization: Perspectives on the American Revolution* (New York, 1977), 103–19.

completely modernized society, and the Federal Constitution was a modern instrument, an expression of the modern society that produced it.

The very circumstances of life in the colonies had dictated that this would be so. As William Knox, British undersecretary of state for the colonies and formerly a royal official in Georgia, pointed out during the Revolution, conditions in the colonies had never been congenial to the complete re-creation of the traditional society of the Old World. The absence of a proper religious hierarchy, the easy availability of land and the consequently wide diffusion of real property, the relatively undifferentiated social system in which there were no legally sanctioned distinctions of rank and degree and men could obtain influence with the public only "by following the humor or disposition of the People," and the relatively low social requirements for office—all of these conditions had combined to prevent the development of those feelings "of subordination that property, ancestry or dignity of station . . . naturally . . . excited" in traditional society and "excluded all ideas of . . . dependence."[32]

The result, as the great French social theorist Alexis de Tocqueville later pointed out, was that "the aristocratic element" had "been feeble from its birth" and the traditional patterns of family and corporate authority that lay at the heart of the patronage societies of the Old World had never managed to achieve any vigor in the New. When the early settlers sought to "establish a gradation of ranks" in the colonies, wrote Tocqueville, they soon found "that the soil of America was opposed to a territorial aristocracy." From early on, then, he observed, the British colonies had witnessed "the growth, not of the *aristocratic* liberty of their mother country, but of that freedom of the middle and lower orders of which the history of the world had as yet no complete example."[33]

Jean de Crèvecoeur, the French mapmaker who came with the French army to America during the Seven Years' War and subsequently settled as a farmer in New York, had earlier written expansively in a similar vein in his famous *Letters from an American Farmer* in 1782. The European coming to British North America for the first time, said Crèvecoeur, was confronted with "a *modern* society . . . different from what he had hitherto seen. It is not composed, as in Europe, of great lords who possess everything, and a herd of people who have nothing. Here are no aristocratical families, no courts, no kings, no bishops, no ecclesiastical

[32] Jack P. Greene, ed., "William Knox's Explanation for the American Revolution," *William and Mary Quarterly*, 3d ser., 30 (1973): 299–300.

[33] Alexis de Tocqueville, *Democracy in America*, ed. Phillips Bradley (New York, 1964), 30–31, 55.

dominion, no invisible power giving to a few a very visible one." Instead, he found "a people of cultivators" with but few towns scattered among them, "a pleasing uniformity of decent . . . habitations," and a lexicon that was "but short in words of dignity, and names of honour."[34] As Tocqueville appreciated, even the great plantation owners of the southern colonies, were not "altogether aristocratic, as that term is understood in Europe," because "they possessed no privileges; and the cultivation of their estates being carried on by slaves, they had no tenants depending on them, and consequently no patronage."[35]

From very early on, then, British America exhibited in its "social state an extraordinary phenomenon. [Free] Men there" were "seen on a greater equality . . . than in any other country of the world, or in any age of which history has preserved the remembrance."[36] America, as Karl Marx appreciated in seconding Tocqueville and Crèvecoeur, possessed no "feudal alp" to serve as an insurmountable social barrier to the aspirations of its free inhabitants.[37]

Not only were the British colonies free from most of the traditional barriers that had so long fettered society in the Old World, but they also enjoyed remarkable political freedom and more independence from metropolitan authority than did the colonies of any other contemporary European power. As Adam Smith put it with some slight exaggeration, "In every thing, except their foreign trade, the liberty of the English colonists to manage their own affairs their own way is complete. It is in every respect equal to that of their fellow citizens at home, and is secured in the same manner, by an assembly of the representatives of the people."[38] Along with the relatively egalitarian social and economic order in the colonies, this extensive political autonomy and the laxity of metropolitan control that lay behind it also contributed to the emergence of social polities that, as one contemporary observer remarked, were deeply "tinctured with republicanism" and by contemporary standards extraordinarily inclusive.[39]

In combination with an extremely favorable land/man ratio which

---

[34] J. Hector St. John de Crèvecoeur, *Letters from an American Farmer* (New York, 1957), 35–36.

[35] Tocqueville, *Democracy in America*, 49.

[36] Ibid., 55.

[37] Diamond, "The Revolution of Sober Expectations," 36.

[38] Adam Smith, *An Inquiry into the Nature and Causes of the Wealth of Nations*, 2 vols. (Oxford, 1972), 1:585–86.

[39] Greene, "William Knox's Explanation," 299.

provided an extraordinary amount of elbowroom and a bountiful food supply, this remarkable social and political freedom exercised a profound effect upon the formation of the American character. From the very first days of settlement, the challenges and opportunities of the American environment had put a high value upon initiative and self-control. Wilderness conditions and later the lack of many of the traditional restraints and supportive social institutions that the colonists had had in England had early forced men to rely heavily upon their own resources and had nourished a jealous regard for personal autonomy, in the contemporary vernacular, for independence. The weakness and simplicity of traditional social and political institutions in the colonies, Lord Acton noted, stimulated "the habit of local independence, self-reliance, and self-government."[40]

Physical and social circumstances in America, in other words, had forced the inhabitants, as Crèvecoeur said, "to become men." In Europe, he observed, they "were as so many useless plants, wanting vegetative mould, and refreshing showers; they withered, and were mowed down by want, hunger, and war: but" in America, "by the power of transplantation, like all other plants, they have taken root and flourished! Formerly they were not numbered in any civil list of their country, except those of the poor; here they rank as citizens." "From [the] involuntary idleness, servile dependence, penury, and useless labour" they had known in the Old World, they passed in America "to toils of a very different nature" and were "rewarded by ample subsistence."

As Crèvecoeur penetratingly noted, this "great metamorphosis" had "a double effect": first, it encouraged men to forget "that mechanism of subordination, that servility of disposition which poverty had taught" them in Europe. Second, it greatly enlarged their aspirations and prompted them to form "schemes of future prosperity," to attempt to educate their children better than they had been educated themselves, and, with their enlarged ambitions ever before them, to develop "an ardour for labour" they had never before felt. The possibility of acquiring substance and status thus turned men from passive dependence to active independence.[41] In the hands of such men, as Tocqueville later exclaimed, "political principles, laws, and human institutions" came to seem "malleable, capable of being shaped and combined at will"; old social barriers and restrictive beliefs lost their ancient mystery and awe; "a course almost

---

[40] Lord Acton, "Colonies," in *Essays in the History of Liberty: Selected Writings of Lord Acton*, ed. J. Rufus Fears (Indianapolis, 1985), 183.

[41] Crèvecoeur, *Letters from an American Farmer*, 38, 40, 56.

without limits, a field without horizon," were revealed; and "the human
spirit" rushed "forward and" traversed "them in every direction."[42]

But colonial society was not only a modern society; it was also a reasonably highly developed one by the standards of the day. This was especially true in the political realm. During the century before the American
Revolution and especially through the middle decades of the eighteenth
century, most of the colonies had experienced a major development of
political resources that contributed to a significant increase in the capabilities of colonial political systems. By the 1770s and 1780s, they had
coherent, effective, acknowledged, and authoritative political elites with
considerable social and economic power, extensive political experience,
confidence in their capacity to govern, and—what was crucially distinguishing between them and their European counterparts—broad public
support. Second, they had viable governing institutions at both the local
and provincial levels and a vigorous tradition of internal self-
government. Third, their political systems were probably more inclusive
and more responsible than any in the world at that time, and they were
capable of permitting the resolution of conflict, absorbing new and diverse groups, and providing political stability in periods of rapid demographic, economic, and territorial expansion.[43]

Nor was colonial development limited to the political sphere. During
the eighteenth century, the colonies experienced a dramatic enlargement
of internal and external trade, travel, and migration; an increasing availability of knowledge through a broad spectrum of educational, cultural,
social, economic, and religious institutions; the development of more
efficient means and networks of communication within and among the
colonies and between the colonies and the outside world; and the emergence of relatively large numbers of people with the technical skills requisite for the successful functioning of an autonomous society. Well before the Revolution, these developments had helped to liberate the
colonists from their earlier isolation and rusticity; to give them the po-

---

[42] Tocqueville, *Democracy in America*, 56.

[43] See Jack P. Greene, "The Growth of Political Stability: An Interpretation of Political
Development in the Anglo-American Colonies, 1660–1760," in John Parker and Carol
Urness, eds., *The American Revolution: A Heritage of Change* (Minneapolis, 1975), 26–52.

tential for cooperation, for overcoming the inherent localism and traditional disunity they had stubbornly manifested throughout most of their existence; and to provide them with the technical wherewithal necessary for the creation of a stable new nation.[44]

Finally, the tremendous increase in the size and wealth of the colonies—in terms of numbers of people and the amount of productive land, labor, and skills—during the eighteenth century provided the colonies with the economic capacity to function effectively in the contemporary world economic system and put them on a level that was still behind—but not that far behind—the most developed European economies of the time.

Unlike practically all subsequent revolutions, then, the American Revolution took place in a society that was already extraordinarily modern; unlike most later colonial wars for self-determination, it also happened in a society that was remarkably well developed. Thus the Americans, in contrast to "the French, Russian, or Chinese revolutionists," did "not have to build their new order on the ruins of an old one."[45] The American Revolution placed itself firmly and unequivocally on the side of those who opposed hereditary privilege and "embodied" political and social authority and favored greater political equality and social and economic opportunity, but, for the free population, these were not goals to be achieved but conditions to be maintained. Because American nationalism was a result rather than a cause of the Revolution, moreover, there was little need even to reject those aspects of the British inheritance that had previously served colonial societies well.

From the perspective of most modern revolutions, then, the "outstanding thing about the American effort of 1776," as Louis Hartz remarked forty years ago, "was . . . not the freedom to which it led, but the established feudal structure it did not have to destroy." Living in the "freest society in the world" in 1776 and taking for granted the continued "reality of the atomistic social freedom" they had long enjoyed, American Revolutionaries did not have to destroy an ancien régime. The relics of feudalism that were abolished during the Revolution were precisely that—relics with no necessary social function—and the success and,

---

[44] See Jack P. Greene, "An Uneasy Connection: An Analysis of the Preconditions of the American Revolution," in Stephen G. Kurtz and James H. Hutson, eds., *Essays on the American Revolution* (Chapel Hill, N.C., 1973), 39–41.

[45] Leo Marx, "The American Revolution and the American Landscape," in *America's Continuing Revolution*, 258.

from a modern perspective, relatively conservative character of the Revolution were in many ways, as Hartz insisted, directly attributable to the "social goals *it did not need to achieve.*"[46]

Why the experience of a country that had long traditions of self-government, a stable political system, tested institutions, a set of shared and integrative values that were deeply rooted in physical and social circumstances, no great social inequality and little residual poverty among its free population, seemingly boundless and immediately and easily exploitable resources, a private space available for all of its free inhabitants, and a comparatively short gap between its own economy and those of its most advanced European nations—why the experience of such a country should seem uninstructive, even irrelevant, to most modern revolutionaries is obvious. But if this reading of the American Revolutionary experience helps us to understand why it has not been seized upon as a model for subsequent revolutions, it does not necessarily suggest that that neglect has been beneficial or that it is desirable.

In its twentieth-century form, one analyst has recently noted, "revolution is not authoritarian in manner, as Engels proclaimed, and liberating in effect. It is authoritarian in manner and authoritarian in effect. It does not come as Marx saw it, as a decisive summit of the development of civilization, the coming of real equality to a society which . . . no longer" suffers "from real political problems and thus can be organized without needing to be hierarchical. Rather it comes in countries which have heard that material civilization is possible, but which feel that their leaders are failing to bring it about. It comes as a transfer of authority to those who set themselves to solve the extraordinarily acute problem of how to bring it about and to those who have the moral nerve . . . to subordinate *all* other ends to this single end."[47] In the process, as Hannah Arendt long ago pointed out, concern for human liberty and political freedom, a concern that was central to the American Revolution, not only has been subordinated to the difficult tasks of modernizing and promoting the material development of revolutionary societies but also in many cases has been virtually eliminated as a matter of revolutionary concern.[48]

---

[46] Louis Hartz, *The Liberal Tradition in America* (New York, 1955), 35, 47, 50, 62.

[47] Dunn, *Modern Revolutions*, 22–23.

[48] Arendt, *On Revolution.*

No wonder then that the "twentieth century has been the great century of revolution" as "far as sheer destructive power" and "capacity for upheaval" have been concerned but far less impressive, and much more ambiguous, "as far as sheer creativity" —what John Dunn in his book *Modern Revolutions* calls "the general enhancement of human freedom"—has been concerned.[49] From my point of view, however, it is lamentable that so few modern revolutions have managed to preserve much concern for the preservation and extension of human liberty. But it is equally true, I think, that both the American Revolution and the revolutionary society it both expressed and perpetuated constitute the single most notable exception to that bleak judgment. For the American Revolution not only resulted in the Federal Constitution, the principal device through which Americans were able to "establish and maintain the sovereignty of the people."[50] It also gave birth to a set of ideological commitments that permitted—more accurately, demanded—the subsequent expansion of the category *people* to the widest possible definition.

For, despite the universalistic pronouncements of the Declaration of Independence and the apparent inclusiveness of the phrase "We the People" in the Constitution, the American Revolution was a limited revolution that really fully applied, immediately, only to adult white independent men. Because such a large proportion of the American population fell into that category, the American Revolution seemed to contemporaries to be far more egalitarian and inclusive than it actually was. But whole groups of people—slaves, servants, propertyless workers, women, minors, free people of African and Amerindian descent, and even, in some places, non-Christians—were systematically excluded from the suffrage and the public space that the suffrage guaranteed.

Nevertheless, the Revolution enunciated a body of principles to which the excluded could later appeal in their quest for incorporation as full members of the American polity, while the Constitution created a set of political arrangements within which they would be able to achieve success. For each generation, the phrase "all men are created equal" from the Declaration of Independence has served as a compelling and omnipresent reminder of what was left to be achieved in order to fulfill the commitment imposed upon them by the Revolution, and much of the American experience from the adoption of the Constitution to the present can be viewed as a continuing movement toward an expanding conception of citizenship, of who should be included in the political category

---

[49] Dunn, *Modern Revolutions*, 2, 11–12.

[50] Tocqueville, *Democracy in America*, 56.

people. The United States has always been a nation of change. In the political realm, that change traditionally has been largely, if at times very slowly and with many deviations along the way, in the direction of the expansion of civil rights and civil liberty.[51]

It is the historic role—and, if it is to remain true to its revolutionary heritage and achieve for the American Revolution the enduring importance to which its leaders aspired, the obligation—of the United States through its conduct—abroad as well as at home—to epitomize and to stand for that militant dedication to human liberty that, during the late eighteenth century, gave rise to our present form of constitutional governance and thereby made such a powerful contribution to that "enhancement of freedom" that most subsequent revolutionary and nonrevolutionary societies have neglected.

For if Hannah Arendt is right, if the social question can only be—and will only be—solved by technology, a task to which the United States and other developed nations ought to make a major contribution;[52] if, as it now appears, the sociologist Robert Nesbit is wrong in his pessimistic judgment that the "congealed despotisms" of so many postrevolutionary states "have made [further] revolution all but impossible";[53] and if the United States can remain not just—or even necessarily—a society rich in material resources and destructive power but also, and much more importantly, the seat of liberty and virtue the founding fathers projected—if all three of these propositions turn out to be true, then we may find that Karl Marx had the revolutionary process backwards and that, the social question having been resolved by technology, "the objective of liberty," in Toynbee's phrase, "may then come to the fore as the next item on the majority agenda."[54] Instead of libertarian revolutions being the prelude to socialist revolutions, socialist revolutions will turn out to have been but a stage in the progress to libertarian revolutions as more and more of the world comes to exhibit that "mature and thoughtful taste for freedom" that Tocqueville found among the free population of the United States during the early nineteenth century and that was so appropriately institutionalized in the Federal Constitution of 1787.[55] Only

---

[51] See Jack P. Greene, *All Men Are Created Equal: Some Reflections on the Character of the American Revolution* (Oxford, 1976).

[52] Arendt, *On Revolution,* 53–110.

[53] Robert A. Nisbet, "The Social Impact of the Revolution," in *America's Continuing Revolution,* 95.

[54] Toynbee, *Continuing Effect of the American Revolution,* 19.

[55] Tocqueville, *Democracy in America,* 73.

in such a utopian situation would it be possible to claim that the American Revolution had made as much difference as its leaders and contemporary admirers predicted it would.

Entitled "The Relevance of the American Revolution," the earliest draft of this chapter was written for presentation on September 13, 1975, as the plenary lecture at the NAMESA Conference on American Studies, held at Pahlavi University in Shiraz, Iran, September 13–16, 1975, one of five regional bicentennial conferences held in 1975–76 by NAMESA. Revised under the title "The American Revolution: Has It Made Any Difference?" it was presented at the American Studies Students' Seminar at Castle Retreat, in Wels, Austria, March 18, 1976; at the American Center, Nicosia, Cyprus, April 29, 1976; at a symposium on the American Revolution at St. Olaf College, Northfield, Minnesota, September 27–28, 1976; at the English Institute, University of Trondheim, Norway, October 5, 1976; at the Bicentennial Forum sponsored by the Norwegian-American Foundation and the University of Oslo, Norway, October 8, 1976; at the American Institute, University of Oslo, Norway, October 11, 1976; at the English Institute of the University of Strasbourg, France, March 16, 1977; at the History Department, University of Leiden, The Netherlands, March 21, 1977; in the Department of History at the University of Sarajevo, Yugoslavia, March 30, 1977; at the North American Section of the Institute of History, University of Warsaw, Poland, April 1, 1977; as the annual Society of the Cincinnati Lecture at the Virginia Polytechnic Institute and State University, Blacksburg, February 13, 1978; as the Annual Phi Beta Kappa Lecture, Duke University, Durham, North Carolina, April 4, 1978; at the Department of History, University of South Carolina, Columbia, February 23, 1979; at the Department of History, Ben Gurion University, Beersheva, Israel, June 11, 1979; at the American Cultural Center, Jerusalem, Israel, June 19, 1979; and as the Ervin Frederick Kalb Lecture at Rice University, Houston, Texas, September 19, 1979. Revised and adapted under the title "The American Revolution and Modern Revolutions," the chapter was offered at a conference, "Celebrating the Treaty of Paris," sponsored by the Maryland Humanities Council, Baltimore, December 2, 1983; at the United States Information Service Center, St. George's, Grenada, West Indies, April 7, 1984; at the Administrators' and Supervisors' Meeting, The Garrett County Board of Education, Oakland, Maryland, April 17, 1984; at the University of Georgia Program at Oxford, Oriel College, Oxford, England, August 8, 1986; at the Colloquium on "France and the United States: The Era of the Constitutions, 1787–1789," sponsored by the Franco-American Educational and Cultural Exchange Commission, Paris, France, October 21, 1986; at the Department of English, University of Toulouse-Le Merail, France, December 11, 1986; at the Department of English, University of Franche Comte, Besançon, France, December 17, 1986; at the Historians' Conference of the German American Studies Association, Hamburg, Germany, January 2, 1987; as the Martin Luther King Day Lecture, at the Martin Luther King Library, Accra, Ghana, on January 19, 1987; at the Accra Kiwanis Club, Accra, January 22, 1987; at the North Carolina Department of Cultural Resources, Raleigh, February 9, 1987; at the Tenth Annual Irvine Seminar on Social History and Theory, University of California, Irvine, March 21, 1987; as the Annual Phi Alpha Theta Lecture at North Carolina State University, Raleigh, April 14, 1987; at the Faculty of Law, Waseda University, Tokyo, Japan, July 4, 1987; at the Faculty of Law, Hokkaido University, Sapporo, Japan, July 24, 1987; in the University Lecture Series, Washington and Lee University, Lexington, Virginia, November 4, 1987; in the Humanities Honors Program, William Paterson College, Wayne, New Jersey, March 30, 1988; as the Martin Luther King Day Lecture, American Cultural Center, Yaounde, Cameroon, on January 21, 1991; at the University Center-Buea, Cameroon, January 24, 1991; at the Fort Jesus Society, Mombasa, Kenya, January 28, 1991; at the Kenya-U.S. Studies Association Meeting, Nairobi, January 30, 1991; at Kenyatta University, Nairobi, January 31, 1991; and at the National Taiwan University, Taipei, Republic of China, March 5, 1992. It was first published in an expanded form in Ghana in *Amannee,* February 1, 1987, i–ix, and then in Daniel Hasse-Dubosc and Genevieve Ramos Acker, eds., *Le temps des constitutions, 1787–1795* (Paris, 1988), 1–10, from which it is here reprinted with permission and minor corrections. A short version appeared in *Amerikastudien 33* (1988): 242–49.

INDEX

Virginia (*cont.*)
ture, 316; character of, 169,
172, 239, 330–31, 333, 341–
42, 344, 346, 349, 353–54,
355; charter, 188, 341, 344;
commercial value to England,
346; compared to other colonies, 141–46, 330, 333, 345–
46, 348; constitution, 334,
354; contributions to Seven
Years' War, 5; criticized by
Virginians, 333; cultural development of, 347; Declaration of Rights, 164, 235, 239,
313, 317, 326; economic development of, 346; education in,
354, 356; English culture idealized in, 331, 346, 348–49;
evaluated by outsiders, 333,
353–54; House of Burgesses,
168, 175, 178, 182, 190, 201,
235, 313, 347; identity
shaped, 331; leadership in,
211–12, 223, 237–38, 243–46,
339–40, 348, 358 (*see also* Robinson, John); legal reforms in,
338; as loyal to England, 341,
345–46; moderation in, 184,
229–30, 344–46, 348–50; motives for revolution in, 350;
patriotism in, 350; political
acumen in, 348, 350; political
culture in, 172–74, 179, 338;
political development of, 169,
203, 347–48; politics compared with English model,
347; rural society advocated
in, 357; seal of, 164–66; social
reforms in, 349; vices in, 176,
355; virtue in, 173, 193, 198,
244, 350; war debt, 54, 182,
325. *See also* Slavery
Virginia Company, 342

Virtue: in America, 22, 124, 358;
civic, place in American politics, 165, 172, 326; as goal of
Revolution, 65, 114, 355, 370

Waller, Benjamin, 170, 210
Walpole, Sir Robert, 178, 227,
228, 229; administration, 4,
167
War debt, Revolutionary, in
America, 324–25
Washington, George, 192, 209,
210, 234, 235, 239, 242, 245,
299, 302, 309, 339, 368–69
Wayles, John, 205
Wealth, 330–31, 387
Wedderburne, Alexander, 247,
248, 249
West Indies, 67, 143
Westmoreland Association, 190
Whateley, Thomas, 247
Whiggism, 38, 39, 160, 281, 353
White, Alexander, 178
Wilkes, John, 38, 61, 219, 265, 272
Williams, Samuel, 147, 302
Wilson, James, 90, 135
Witherspoon, John, 128, 129, 152,
153, 156, 160
Wolcott, Oliver, 138
Women, 361, 364
Wood, Gordon S., 99, 110, 112–13,
116, 136, 161, 162, 360, 367,
369
Wrigley, E. A., 118
Wythe, George, 170, 182, 183, 185,
210, 245, 309, 338, 339, 356

Xenophon, 249

Yeomanry in America, 125–26

Zubly, Johan Joachim, 82–83